# All Our Families
## New Policies for a New Century

*A Report of the Berkeley Family Forum*

SECOND EDITION

*Edited by*

Mary Ann Mason
Arlene Skolnick
Stephen D. Sugarman

*New York   Oxford*
OXFORD UNIVERSITY PRESS
*2003*

Oxford University Press

Oxford   New York
Auckland   Bangkok   Buenos Aires   Cape Town   Chennai
Dar es Salaam   Delhi   Hong Kong   Istanbul   Karachi   Kolkata
Kuala Lumpur   Madrid   Melbourne   Mexico City   Mumbai
Nairobi   São Paulo   Shanghai   Taipei   Tokyo   Toronto

Published by Oxford University Press, Inc.
198 Madison Avenue, New York, New York 10016
http://www.oup-usa.org

Oxford is a registered trademark of Oxford University Press

**Library of Congress Cataloging-in-Publication Data**

All our families : new policies for a new century : a report of the Berkeley family forum /
edited by Mary Ann Mason, Arlene Skolnick, Stephen D. Sugarman.—Expanded and
updated 2nd ed.
      p. cm.
    Includes index.
    ISBN 0-19-514881-9
    1. Family—United States.   2. Family policy—United States.   3. Stepfamilies—United
States.   4. Adoptive parents—United States.   5. Single parents—United States.   6. Gay
parents—United States.   7. Social change—United States.   8. United States—Social policy.
    I. Mason, Mary Ann.   II. Skolnick, Arlene, 1933–   III. Sugarman, Stephen D.

HQ536 .A537 2003
306.85′0973—dc21                                                                    2002074980

Printing number  9 8 7 6 5 4 3 2 1

Printed in the United States of America
on acid-free paper

# Contents

# Preface to the Second Edition

- At this moment, most American children live in a two-parent household (even if, for many, one parent is a stepparent or perhaps the lesbian partner of their mother, or their biological parents with whom they live are unmarried to each other).
- Divorce rates are down (even if they are much higher than they were in the 1960s).
- Teenage pregnancy rates were higher in the 1950s than they are today (even if a much higher proportion of teen mothers then were married).
- It is the out-of-wedlock birth rate of whites (not blacks) that more recently was on the upswing (even if a much higher proportion of black children are born to single mothers). Indeed, according to the 2000 census, two-parent families are on the rise among African-Americans and Latinos.
- The welfare rolls are shrinking (even if the United States continues to have a child poverty rate that is significantly higher than that of just about every other Western industrialized nation).

These few, perhaps jarring, "facts" show that an assessment of the state of the American family is necessarily a complex matter. They also make clear that very different pictures may be painted depending upon which facts are emphasized.

At a minimum, it needs to be clearly said that to equate "the family" with a stable, married couple and their biological children is decidedly misleading and has been so for quite some time. Single-parent families were a serious social concern at the time of the first White House Conference on Children, in 1909, (when single mothers were mainly widows). Parental kidnapping of their own children is not a new phenomenon, but a longstanding one (although its social meaning has changed). Substantial rates of adoption by "strangers" go back to the 1800s (when older inner city children were taken on by rural farm families, as much for the value of their labor as for their welcome addition to the family ranks). Significant rates of spousal battering and desertion existed long before divorce was a common event.

The socially "desirable" family structure is also a matter of great controversy. Especially today, sheer economics usually means that having two adults in the home is better than one. But surely not always. In some cases "staying together for the sake of the kids" is only a recipe for childhood misery. It all depends on how the adults behave, and the sad reality is that not all parents behave well. Is it enough to bemoan the fact? Many people (quite often liberals) believe that society should step in on behalf of the children, to assist both when the parents misbehave and when the child and one parent need to escape from the second parent. However, other people (especially certain outspoken conservatives) seem willing to allow children to suffer out of a fear that popular forms of social assistance only encourage more misbehavior by parents. There is also controversy about what is bad conduct. Is it really irresponsible to have a child if you are not certain that you can provide financially for its needs? If so, most parents throughout the world and throughout history have been irresponsible. If not, should the rest of us help out those families who wind up in need? Again, some worry about the consequences of what others see as the obviously right and generous response.

Right now all sorts of issues like these surrounding "the American family" are hotly contested, and these controversies have prompted us to write this book. In the early nineties, about the time the national debate on "family values" began, the editors of the book realized that among our own faculty at the University of California at Berkeley are many distinguished scholars in various fields who are studying the family. We established a series of monthly seminars aimed at drawing this group together. Our goal has been to elicit a wide range of perspectives and scholarly findings from several disciplines, and to work together at creating policy solutions to difficult issues relating to the family. Our discussions have reflected the complexity of modern families, including proposals for making divorce harder, the new reproductive technologies, role of race in foster care and adoption placements, welfare reform, the recognition of domestic partnerships, and European family policies.

Following two years of these seminars, a core group of faculty participants concluded that it was time to put ideas on paper, and this book project was born. We decided that each chapter would focus on a single family configuration or issue, for example, the teen parent family, and would be drafted by a single scholar. Yet each chapter would also receive close attention from other members of our author team, which includes faculty from psychology, social welfare, law, history, sociology, public health, and public policy. In a series of all-day conferences, the author team reviewed drafts of each chapter, seeking mutual understanding and, where possible, consensus on the interpretation of data and direction for policy reform. In short, unlike typical "collections," this book is very much a group project.

In its coverage, our book is different from other books on the family. First, no other work we know about explores the family as broadly as we do, or from so many disciplines. Second, we have not simply described the issues, we have also provided specific policy initiatives for each type of family issue. Third, and perhaps most important, we bring together a team of scholars who have already been meeting and talking with each other in an intimate setting for several years. The ideas presented here have been truly cross-fertilized by a number of disciplines.

The family has become perhaps *the* domestic political issue of the new century. We hope that our book provides the information and insight to help straighten out the often confused ongoing debate.

We would like to thank the Earl Warren Legal Institute at the University of California at Berkeley for its support of this project.

This expanded and updated second edition contains two new chapters, and each chapter from the first edition has been revised to take into account new developments and new data that have arisen since the initial publication.

# Authors

**Richard P. Barth** is Frank A. Daniels Distinguished Professor, School of Social Work, University of North Carolina at Chapel Hill.

**Carolyn Pape Cowan** is Adjunct Professor of Psychology, University of California, Berkeley.

**Philip Cowan** is Professor of Psychology, University of California, Berkeley.

**Ira Mark Ellman** is Willard H. Pedrick Distinguished Research Scholar and Professor of Law, Arizona State University and Visiting Fellow, Earl Warren Legal Institute, University of California, Berkeley.

**Paula S. Fass** is Preston Hotchkis Professor of United States History, University of California, Berkeley.

**Neil Gilbert** is Milton & Gertrude Chernin Professor of Social Welfare, University of California, Berkeley.

**Sylvia Guendelman** is Associate Professor of Public Health, University of California, Berkeley.

**Mary Ann Mason** is Dean of the Graduate Division and Professor of Social Welfare, University of California, Berkeley.

**Jane Mauldon** is Associate Professor of Public Policy, University of California, Berkeley.

**Arlene Skolnick** is Visiting Scholar, Sociology Department, New York University.

**Judith Stacey** is Streisand Professor of Contemporary Gender Studies and Professor of Sociology, University of Southern California.

**Stephen D. Sugarman** is Agnes Roddy Robb Professor of Law, University of California, Berkeley.

**Judith Wallerstein** is Founder of the Judith Wallerstein Center for the Family in Transition, Corte Madera, California, and Senior Lecturer Emerita, School of Social Welfare, University of California, Berkeley.

# 1

# Introduction

## Mary Ann Mason, Arlene Skolnick, and Stephen D. Sugarman

Teen pregnancy. Single mothers. Divorce. Child abuse and neglect. Most of us could add other items to the litany of problems said to be afflicting the American family. Indeed, at the beginning of the twenty-first century, worry over the family has become a national obsession. Each day, the media serve up new stories and statistics documenting that marriage is going the way of the horse and buggy, that we are becoming a nation without fathers, and that, as a result, children are suffering and society is falling apart. The breakdown of the family is taken for granted as a simple social fact. The only question is who or what is to blame and how can we restore the family to the way we imagine it used to be.

The authors of this book think that something is seriously wrong with this approach to the American family. To be sure, family life has changed over the past few decades—in America and in every other Western society. We do not mean to minimize the stresses and troubles that beset all too many families—indeed, this book focuses on some of the most disturbing of them. But the facts about family life are far more complex than they seem. Indeed, to speak of "the family" often obscures more than it reveals. Families today do come in many varieties—two-parent, single-parent, stepfamilies, gay and lesbian families, foster families, and so on. More important, different families, located at different points in the American social structure, face different problems and pose different policy challenges.

In thinking about the family, a historical perspective can be revealing. Anxiety about the family is nothing new. Every generation of Americans, including the first European settlers to reach our shores, thought it was witnessing the decline of the institution. A major reason for this is that social change has been a constant in American life, and, as a result, families have constantly had to adapt to new realities.

Changes in family life are almost always regarded for the worse, at least initially. Thus the current debate starts from the idealized American family of the 1950s—middle class, two biological parents, a breadwinner husband and homemaker wife, and two or three biological children—and assumes that any departure from that pattern is negative. Since most contemporary families do depart in one way or another from that pattern, most commonly because the wife and mother is in the paid workforce, the fifties norm implies by definition that the family is in decline or in trouble.

This way of looking at the family exaggerates the extent of change. For one thing, the great majority of Americans are still likely to marry at some point in their lifetime. For another thing, even in the fifties very many families differed from *Ozzie and Harriet*. Worse, and paradoxically, insistence on single-mindedly contrasting today's families with a nostalgic view of the past leads us away from focusing on the actual problems experienced by the majority of families in America now. Being divorced, remarried, or a single parent, or even being a gay or lesbian parent, does not imply an alternative value system, or no values at all. The important question to ask about American families, therefore, is not how much they conform to a particular image of the family, but rather how well do they function—what kind of love, care, and nurturance do they provide?

In this book we focus on families who are in the midst of raising children, because we believe that they are carrying out the most important family task, and, at the same time, are the most vulnerable and in need of policy attention. Despite the continued predominance of marriage as an adult experience, more than half of all children born this year will not be raised to adulthood with their two biological parents. Teen mothers are much more rarely married than before, and about a third of all children are now born outside of marriage. Couples who do marry often divorce, so that about 40 percent of those children born in a marriage will experience the breakup of that marriage. The high rates of divorce and out-of-wedlock birth mean that mothers are increasingly the head of the family—at least temporarily—and that family is all too likely to be reduced to a limited income that puts it below the poverty line. So, while many single-parent families fare well, many others need help.

Single parents often go on to marry again—about 70 percent of divorced mothers do so within six years—forming stepfamilies. Yet this second (or more) marriage is itself more likely to break up than the marriage of origin, funneling children once again into a single-parent family. Other family forms are evolving, including the new gay and lesbian families, and the not so new, but changing, foster families. All of these family forms are viewed by some as problematical for children and, in any event, offer challenges to successful child raising. Even families with two biological parents face new difficulties that may require help. More mothers now work outside the home than before, and many of today's families strain under the dual career life. Furthermore, an increasing number of these families are immigrant families, as America is in the midst of an immigration wave perhaps as great as that at the start of the twentieth century.

It is this complexity that has not been sufficiently grasped and responded to by policymakers. Both on the left and on the right, policymakers and advocates tend to have a very limited vision of this shifting portrait, and their solutions reflect this limitation. Put very generally, the conservative position is that, as a result of hedonistic individualism, we are letting our "family values" slip away, and what is needed now is nothing short of a moral rearmament on behalf of parental responsibility. From this movement come proposals to make divorce more difficult and to discourage strongly, or even punish, giving birth outside of marriage.

Liberals have crossed swords with conservative "family values" advocates for their insistence that responsible parenting comes in only one form—the idealized nuclear family. But that does not mean that most liberals either understand or embrace the complexity of today's family, or have firm ideas about how to help children. Moreover, there is among liberals today something of a crisis of confidence in the ability of government to solve many of our society's problems, especially those of the family.

Each chapter in this book examines a part of this complex, shifting phenomenon we call the American family. We identify the particular strains and strengths of each part, seeking not to be distracted by the stereotypes and fears that surround some of these new family forms. Our focus is on promoting the welfare of the children, not assigning blame to their parents or to the society at large. What we have to offer are analyses based on scientifically derived evidence and specific intervention proposals.

## Toward a More Child-Centered Family Policy

Let us begin with married couples and their children—the model accepted by many Americans as the ideal family form. However, as discussed in the chapters by Carolyn and Philip Cowan, Neil Gilbert, Richard Barth, and Sylvia Guendelman it would be a great mistake to assume that having children during marriage is by itself a recipe for successful child rearing, or that current public policy toward these families makes sense.

For one thing, the Cowans tell us, even among educated couples with good jobs, the transition to parenthood is very frequently highly stressful for the couple, and if early warning signs are not attended to, that stress can translate into both harm to the child (running the gamut from educational failure to physical abuse) and the breakdown of the marriage.

As the Cowans explain, while expectant parents have many prenatal, health-oriented services accessible to them, there is little assistance available to help new parents. They must deal on their own with the novel and changed relationships that arise when a child first comes into the home.

Our new family arrangements have made today's parents pioneers of sorts. Many young couples now live farther from their own parents than in the past, and in many more marriages both partners work before and expect to continue working after the child is born. Besides, today's young parents often do not have the knowledge or ready family guidance to make the transition to successful parenthood. The consequence is that a startlingly high proportion of new parents, as many as one in six, suffers serious depression or similar burdens.

In order to try to forestall these problems, the Cowans offer guidelines, based on research, that can often predict which couples are most vulnerable to these negative consequences of first-time parenting. Moreover, they describe newly developed couples-based interventions that could work to alleviate this stress and to prevent family rupture. Government promotion of these interventions would be a start toward making our family policy more child-centered.

Assuming that the couple gets through the stress of the first year or so of parenting, Neil Gilbert's chapter tells us they are likely to find that our major social insurance arrangements are not well suited to the lives they hope to lead. As Gilbert points out, if, as in the typical case, the father has remained in the workforce and the mother returns to her job after several months of unpaid leave, they will already be aware that they have paid for Social Security and unemployment benefits that didn't help cover the wages she lost during her maternity leave. And later, on retirement, she will be offered dependent spouse retirement benefits that she won't need because she will by then have earned her own Social Security pension.

In the meantime, the couple faces costly child care burdens with no prospect of assistance when they need it most. Unlike many European countries that socialize the cost of child minding from an early age, in the United States universal schooling begins only at kindergarten. Policy, Gilbert suggests, has not kept up with needs of the new two-parent working family.

How to revise child care and Social Security benefits are complicated questions, in part because not all couples follow the same path. For example, should our society simply extend public schooling down to, say, age two and make this day care optionally available for any family who wants to use it until the child is five? Or, as Gilbert suggests, should all couples with young children be given financial assistance to be used by them as they wish? This latter solution identifies itself with a pluralistic view of parental roles, allowing couples themselves to decide how to deal with child care needs—to use the money to purchase public or privately offered day care, or simply to replace some of the income lost to the family's budget when one of the spouses remains at home to care full time for the young child. Either way, a shift of public resources from Social Security to child care would be part of a more child-centered public policy.

Like two-earner couples generally, immigrant families are another special class of families in need of social support. More than a million immigrants a year entered the United States during the 1990s. In contrast to European immigrants of a century earlier, these newcomers were primarily from Latin America and Asia. As compared with the past, a higher proportion of immigrants is highly skilled and well educated. Moreover, in comparison with native borns, a greater share of immigrant families is comprised of a married couple with a working father and a mother who cares for the children. Yet many immigrants are uneducated and in need. Moreover, a distressing pattern exists among many immigrant households. Notwithstanding the embrace of America and early, if modest, successes by their parents, too many children of immigrants fail in school, go on to have substantial health problems as teens, and fare poorly in the job market.

As explained in Sylvia Guendelman's chapter, the United States has a complex (if controversial and changing) immigration policy. Yet it has nothing at all resembling an immigrant policy. That is, there is little sustained focus on how collective efforts can help achieve better results for immigrant children in the domains of health, education, and welfare. Of course, some immigrant children are doing splendidly. We see some of them as winners of national spelling bees, then in strong numbers in competitive academic high schools, and still later as students at elite universities. Many of these young people no doubt benefit from cohesive cultural enclaves in which they have grown up and which have helped to boost their psychological well-being, maintain their family unity, and shelter them from racism. But other immigrant communities are fractured, and acculturation there has often meant falling into gang membership, unwanted teen pregnancy, and the like. As Guendelman argues, an effective immigrant policy would seek to promote the health of immigrant families, and yet in recent years prominent legislative efforts aimed at immigrants have singled them out for harsher treatment at the hands of helping public agencies.

This discussion has so far primarily focused on married couples, but they, of course, are not the only ones having children. Indeed, as noted previously, in the past fifty years there has been a large increase in the proportion of children born outside of marriage. The common public perception of their mothers is that they are teenagers, but, in fact, most are not. Nonetheless, as related in the chapter by Jane Mauldon, unmarried teens do account for a significant share of births, and they are a matter of great public concern. For the small proportion of these women who are under the age of sixteen, there is little doubt that they should be discouraged from having babies so young—for their child's sake and for their own. Serious public efforts should be made to reduce those births, a fair number of which now arise because of predatory behavior by men who are considerably older than the girls. Nonetheless, as both Mauldon and Stephen Sugarman in his chapter argue, it is rather more promising to improve knowledge about and availability of contraceptive and abortion services than it would be to cut off welfare payments to these young teens or seek to solve the problem by trying to enforce rape and statutory rape laws against the fathers.

Older teen parents are a more complicated matter; eighteen and nineteen year olds are no longer minors and normally have finished high school (or whatever schooling they are going to complete) before getting pregnant. Sixteen and seventeen year olds who become pregnant often do have their schooling interrupted or truncated. Nevertheless, according to Mauldon, so many of these young mothers now face such bleak job and schooling prospects that it is by no means clear that they would fare better by delaying childbirth. Furthermore, she argues, it is not at all clear that a delay of merely a year or two makes a great difference to the babies, who are often at least partially raised by the young mothers' own mothers.

To be sure, many of these young women don't really wish to become pregnant, and, once again, more effective family planning services might help them avoid this condition. For most young mothers, however, Mauldon contends, in order to change their conduct we would need to make more dramatic and positive social change than is now being suggested in public policy debates. Mauldon maintains that instead of threatening pregnant high schoolers with poverty and disdain by the middle class, a more child-centered public policy would seek to improve the benefits of staying in school and trying to get into the job market.

Single mothers are not the only concern. As Ira Ellman's chapter explains, public policy has increasingly focused on biological fathers. The driving factors are a new scientific ability, through DNA teting, to identify positively who fathered a child and a new determination by society to obtain child support payments from such fathers. And yet these developments have generated a different problem. It turns out that a not insignificant number of children of married (or cohabiting) couples are biologically fathered by someone else, a fact that may remain unknown for some time to the husband (or partner) who assumes the role of the child's psychological parent.

In these cases of ambiguous paternity, Ellman shows how conflict can arise if the couple's relationship ends, say, in divorce. By proving he did not sire the child, should a psychological father be able to escape ongoing child support obligations if he wishes to? Or, by contrast, should he be able to insist on ongoing custodial or visitation rights with the child even if the child's mother can show that someone else is the biological dad? Should the answer to these questions turn on how long the psychological parenting relationship has lasted or whether the biological father comes back into the picture? Should it matter whether the psychological father has long known that he is not the child's biological father?

Ambiguous fatherhood issues arise in other contexts as well. What rights and duties should be assigned to a man who fathers a child in a "one night stand"? What about a man who is eager to maintain long-standing connections with his children, but whose former wife moves to a new location to form a relationship with another man?

Although childbearing by an unwed mother is one way to form a single-parent family, more children enter that state by way of divorce. While the divorce rate is now slightly down from its all-time high, it still stands well above what it was fifty years ago. Researchers agree that divorce is a stressful event for children. But there is less consensus about the long-term effects of parental divorce, or whether the ending of a failed marriage hurts a child more than its continuation would. Nevertheless, as Judy Wallerstein explains in her chapter, psychological problems of children with divorced parents can often continue into adulthood and impact negatively upon future family formation.

These outcomes have caused some conservatives to blame no-fault divorce and, as noted previously, to argue for policy changes that would make divorce much more difficult to obtain when minor children are involved. This, however, is probably a misguided idea, Sugarman argues. In the first place, the home lives of couples who divorce are very different before the divorce from the home lives of couples who do not divorce. Therefore, it is wrong to assume that merely deterring divorce would sharply improve the outcomes for children whose parents now divorce. Second, there is the practical reality that blocking divorce does not prevent couples from splitting up and may simply place a legal hurdle in the way of one of the spouses remarrying (and having subsequent children inside instead of outside of marriage).

Assuming that there will continue to be a considerable amount of marital breakup, Wallerstein insists that we need to be more child-centered in our approach to divorcing families. Past reforms such as mediation and joint custody arrangements may have been child oriented in their motivation, but in a large number of cases the remedies have been insufficiently attentive to the needs of the actual children involved. This is true as well for permanent visitation arrangements established when the child is young, which often become highly ill suited to the lives of many teens.

Rather than cookie-cutter solutions, Wallerstein argues that the legal and social services systems must be acutely attuned to the children most at risk from divorce—often those whose families are characterized by high conflict—and must arrange for these children to have substantial assistance from mental health professionals qualified to help them deal with their stresses. Just as we now provide too little psychologically oriented assistance to couples at the time of their child's birth (as noted earlier), so too, as part of a child-centered family policy, we need to make these sorts of interventions available to the child at the time of, and often following, divorce.

After divorce, the child and his or her custodial parent (still overwhelmingly the mother) typically suffer financial distress as well as psychological distress. However shared, the couple's former income rarely supports two households at the standard of living the family enjoyed when it was a single unit. Moreover, because noncustodial support orders are not large, the custodial parent and child are often left with too little of their former income to maintain a reasonable lifestyle, often slipping below the poverty line. Many custodial mothers seek on their own to improve their financial situation by entering the workforce. But this is often a very poor time for them to be able to boost their income without neglecting their child's other needs. To make matters worse, all too many noncustodial parents fail to pay the child support imposed on them. Indeed, the default rate is far greater for unwed fathers; for a significant portion of these fathers, there aren't even formal paternity determinations or child support orders in place. Noncustodial parents in general often lose interest in their biological children, focusing their attention and their money on their new lives, frequently including new children.

While nearly everyone agrees that more effective child support enforcement is desirable, according to Sugarman it is not clear that we have the policy tools to do much better than we do now. What is very different about the United States as compared with many other nations is that our collective financial assistance around the time of becoming a single-parent family is stingier. Until recently, funds were guaranteed only to prevent the single mother and her children from falling deep into poverty. Even then, welfare benefits rarely brought her family up to the poverty line. Now, even that federal guarantee has been eliminated by Congress.

Sugarman asserts that it is unfair and unwise for our society to be so miserly to children with an absent parent, especially when we are reasonably generous, by way of Social Security insurance, to children whose breadwinner parent has died. Hence, as part of a child-centered family policy, Sugarman recommends that Congress enact a child support assurance scheme for all children in single-parent families that parallels the Social Security benefit now provided only to children living in single-parent families owing to the death of a parent. Such a child support assurance plan could apply to the full range of children in single-parent families, including children of divorce and those born to unmarried mothers.

A different route to greater financial stability for single-parent families is marriage. For divorced custodial parents, this means remarriage. For unmarried birth mothers it most often means initial marriage. Although sometimes the marriage will be to the father of the child(ren), our focus here is on the creation of stepparent relationships. Indeed, as noted earlier, a majority of divorced single parents do later marry, although many of them subsequently divorce and at a higher rate than occurs among conventional couples. As the chapter by Mary Ann Mason puts it, at present residential stepparents (more than 80 percent of whom are stepfathers) tend to exist in a legal and policy limbo in terms of their relationship to their stepchildren. As Mason explains, if the stepparent and the child's custodial parent then divorce, the child has no claim for ongoing support from the stepparent—even if the residential stepparent has in fact been the child's sole source of support since infancy. Furthermore, at divorce the stepparent's rights to custody or visitation are cut off. This means that, under current policy, it would be extraordinary for the stepfather to win visitation rights with respect to his stepchildren even if he is their most important psychological parent. Instead, full child custody would go first to the mother and then to her former husband and/or to her biological kin. Indeed, if the child's biological mother dies, the stepparent would have no rights to the custody of the children.

If the stepparent dies during the marriage, Mason explains, the child will receive no automatic inheritance, nor will he or she have the right to bring a wrongful death action for money damages. The stepchild will usually qualify for Social Security benefits; but if the stepfather dies even days after a divorce from the child's mother, Social Security benefits will not be available.

For the stepparent to gain any rights and to have any obligations imposed on him, current policy dictates that he must adopt his stepchild. This, however, is impractical in many circumstances, and undesirable in others. Instead, Mason proposes a new, more child-centered solution by creating a policy category called the "de facto parent." As de facto parents, stepparents who primarily support their stepchildren would be granted legal duties and powers akin to adoptive parents, but without extinguishing the parental status of the noncustodial biological parent.

While stepparents may exist in a legal limbo, stepfamilies themselves are a familiar, ages-old variation on the family theme. The same cannot be said about gay and lesbian families. While for many people in American society, homosexuality is an abomination, and homosexual parenting and the homosexual family even worse, Judith Stacey makes clear in her chapter that the homosexual family is a growing phenomenon that seems very much here to stay. Indeed, with all the talk of "family values," it is ironic that stable, loving lesbian and gay couples are not entitled to the formal legal trappings of family open to heterosexual couples.

In 1996, in complete contrast to what Stacey recommends, Congress passed a law intended to allow states to refuse recognition to lesbian and gay marriage in the event that any state chooses to authorize such unions. Earlier in the history of gay and lesbian activism—in the 1970s especially—many in the homosexual community would have supported this antigay marriage sentiment because they opposed all marriage as an outmoded and oppressive institution. But now, especially in lesbian circles, nonradical middle-class women are taking up lifelong partners and are seeking both the social recognition and legal benefits that arise from formal marriage. Moreover, the few recent studies that have been conducted show that the outcomes for children in these families tend to be better than average.

Where children are involved, a fair number of the desired legal outcomes could be achieved if, as in the typical case, the nonbiological partner could adopt and become a coparent with the biological mother. But in many states this child-centered reform has been rejected, resulting, as Stacey argues, in frequent harm to children. For example, the child may not gain access to health insurance otherwise available from the job held by the nonbiological parent; the child may be denied death benefits if the nonbiological parent were to die; and the child may be denied desired and desirable contact with the nonbiological parent if the lesbian couple breaks up or the biological mother dies.

In the last few years, Vermont and then California have enacted comprehensive laws that, while not actually recognizing gay and lesbian marriage, give nearly all the legal benefits of marriage to registered domestic partners. Despite these reforms, there appears to be continuing fear among some people that the children raised by lesbians and gays will themselves all be homosexuals, although the research findings are very much to the contrary. Indeed, homosexual teens raised in heterosexual households are likely to be real beneficiaries of the legal acceptance of the idea of lesbian and gay marriage—since they would be better able to imagine a socially fitting future for themselves.

Sometimes marital disharmony is so severe that no stable arrangement for a child's custody can be worked out and one or both sides take the drastic step of "snatching" the child. As Paula Fass recounts in her chapter, parental kidnapping has gained more attention in recent years, even though it has a long history in the American family. In the past, however, parental kidnapping took place against a cultural backdrop in which the family was understood to be functioning well as an effective unit in socializing the next generation. Kidnapping by former spouses (or by separated spouses or by others on their behalf) was played up in the media as the behavior of eccentric dysfunctional celebrities. The kidnappers always claimed that they were acting in the child's best interest (although many were equally or more driven by selfish motivations). But, in any event, the family as an institution was never seen to be implicated.

Nowadays, parental kidnapping is depicted as a more commonplace event and has become symbolic of the pathology of the family. As explained by Fass, when mothers today steal their children and take them into hiding to prevent them from alleged risks of sexual or physical abuse by their fathers, this action is portrayed as one more indicator of the downfall of the American family and a reflection of its pathological quality. Twenty years ago, public policy toward parental kidnapping shifted—broadly criminalizing this behavior so as to deter unjustified, selfish parental acts and to force parents with genuine disputes to work out their differences in court rather than through self-help. But now many blame the courts for misguided custody awards that lead some allegedly desperate parents to take the law into their own hands.

Parental kidnapping involves only a modest portion of the alarmingly large number of American children subjected to serious abuse (both physical and sexual) or neglect. As Richard Barth explains, each year brings nearly three million formal reports of child abuse and more than a half million confirmed cases (plus many more instances that go unreported to, or undetected by, the badly understaffed child protective services agencies). Many of these abused and neglected children are living with both of their biological parents and are mistreated by one or both of them. Many others live with their mother and may be abused by her and/or a stepfather or their mother's boyfriend. In addition, some children are abused by more distant relations or unrelated people.

Thirty years ago, there was great concern that, by using an expansive notion of neglect, the courts and the child welfare system were taking children away from people who were better understood to be unconventional rather than bad parents. Moreover, once removed from their homes, these children all too often languished in foster care, frequently being moved from one foster family to another every couple of years, never establishing anything like permanent, new family ties. This arrangement brought calls to make removal more difficult, to work hard with the parents to allow the child to return home promptly, where that was a good idea, and to move speedily to terminate parental rights and have the child adopted where reunification was unwise.

Barth argues that, in practice, the child welfare system has now become too attached to the idea that abused and neglected children need to stay connected to their parents, or failing that, to their near relatives and their community. Under the banner of "family preservation," too many children who have been badly abused are kept at home or too quickly returned home only to be abused again. Or they are placed with grandparents or other kin who serve as foster parents but often do not provide an effective upbringing for the child.

Emphasis on parental rights is partly a result of the politics of race and class that, Barth maintains, has put the interests of adults ahead of those of individual children. A new approach proposed by Barth would be more child-centered and would take more seriously the child's developmental needs. These would include considering who will assure the child better schooling, including higher education, and who will continue to be a family for the child when he or she becomes an adult. This developmentally oriented policy would free more abused and neglected children for permanent adoption, and they would more likely be adopted by parents who live outside the child's old neighborhood and who are of a different race and financial standing as compared with the child's biological parents.

As shown in the chapter by Arlene Skolnick, a common theme that runs throughout much of this book is the past overreliance in both law and policy on blood ties over psychological ties. This emphasis is most vivid in battles over child custody that arise in a wide variety of contexts. The traditional rule has been that the biological connection triumphs in disputes, for example, between a custodial stepfather and a long absent biological father (say, after the death of the mother), between the lesbian "coparent" and the biological parent after they split up, between adopting parents and a biological parent (say, a father who claims he was given no notice of the birth), and between foster parents and a biological parent who has seemingly abandoned the child and now wants it back. Judges imposed this outcome even when the child had been long living with, and seemingly a healthy part of, the family of the loser in the dispute.

In reaction to this reliance on blood ties, many have urged a shift to a standard that looks to "the best interests of the child." This standard has also been especially attractive in conventional divorce custody disputes where contemporary notions of gender equality have made it unacceptable to continue the prior practice of automatically awarding the child to the mother. While, in principle, this is a child-centered move, applying the "best interests" concept in practice is fraught with difficulties. Does this mean the child goes to the adult whose lifestyle most matches the judge's (or the social worker's) private preferences? Does this mean the child goes to the wealthier claimant? If not, exactly how do you decide what is in the child's best interest?

Into this gap has emerged the notion of the "psychological parent," a term developed by a prominent legal-psychological team based upon their good judgment and some clinical practice. Their claim was that children ordinarily have one parent to whom they are psychologically most connected and that, in general, that parent should win these difficult child custody disputes. Yet, as Skolnick explains, however intuitively appealing, the "psychological parent" is not a well-established notion in the psychology research literature. The closest thing to it is "attachment" theory. According to this theory, healthy children can form secure attachments to a key adult figure and that security enables them to function effectively in their lives generally. If that attachment is severed, the child suffers a substantial psychological loss.

The evidence is clear that, starting in infancy, children form intense emotional bonds to those who provide ongoing love and care. Further, it is clear that a child's attachment depends on something other than merely spending time with the adult, as in the case of a nanny. There is also no doubt that removing a child from the home or separating the child from a primary attachment figure is an act of major psychological significance to the child, and one which may pose developmental risks.

Unfortunately, the cases that come before the legal system do not always present clear-cut choices. While attachment theory can point the legal system in the right direction—giving heavy weight to the child's emotional well-being, especially the existing ties between the child and the contending adults—we should not assume that there is an easy template for determining the "psychological parent" in application of the "best interests" test. This does not mean, in Skolnick's view, that we should return to clearer bloodline-based legal rules. Rather, we need more research and more collaboration between researchers and the legal system if we truly aim to resolve these custody disputes in the best interest of the child.

## Achieving Greater Security for Children

Child and family insecurity is an overriding theme that runs throughout this book. All of today's family forms and the family issues addressed here can lead to an insecure situation for the child. This insecurity may be psychological, physical, financial, or legal. The child may not always be aware of it; nonetheless, too much insecurity for the family or the child puts too many children at risk. As the chapters ahead demonstrate in detail, some children are insecure because they are abused or neglected; others because their family is living in poverty; still others because they or their parents are newcomers to America. Some experience their parents' transition to parenthood or divorce as too stressful; others find their connection to their new stepparent difficult, still others are uncertain about who to consider their real father. Some children suffer from the legal and social stigma attached to their mother's lesbian partner (their second mother). Other children are trapped in foster care, many of whom would probably be much better off had they been adopted. And a surprisingly large number have been snatched by one feuding parent from the other.

Family policy can help reduce a child's insecurity, but, we believe, too many of our existing policies actually promote insecurity, partly because current policy is too closely wedded to a biological conception of family, rather than relying on a conception based in the psychological, sociological, and cultural reality of contemporary American family life. Another part of the problem is that families are commonly expected to solve their own problems during those periods of greatest need.

Moreover, we believe, today's "family values" advocates aren't really helping. First of all, this debate casts family issues into unnecessarily extreme ideological conflicts. Second, there is an illusory quality to it: America has evolved away from the norm of the two-parent lifelong married couple in which the husband works in the paid labor force and the wife raises the children, and there is no reason to believe that we are going back.

We need, instead, to accept the reality that a large proportion of American children will experience one or more changes in their family structure during their growing up years, and we must refocus our policy attention on making those transitions more successful for parents and children. Granting recognition to evolving families and concentrating psychological, financial, and other services and resources around the transitional periods is a good place to start—and the place where most of the policy reforms proposed here are aimed. By embracing these new policies for our new families, our nation could move a long way toward assuring a more secure childhood for many more of our children.

# 2

# Single-Parent Families

## Stephen D. Sugarman

What do the former First Lady Jackie Kennedy, Princess Diana, the movie star Susan Sarandon, and the TV character Murphy Brown have in common? They all are, or at one time were, single mothers—unmarried women caring for their minor children. This chapter concerns public policy and the single-parent family, a family type dominated by single mothers.

Because these four women are fitting subjects for *Lifestyles of the Rich and Famous*, they are a far cry from what most people have in mind when the phrase "single mother" is used. Many picture, say, a nineteen-year-old high school dropout living on welfare in public housing. Hence, just mentioning these four prominent women vividly demonstrates the diversity of single mothers. These four also illustrate the major categories of single mothers—the widowed mother, the divorced or separated mother, and the single woman who bears her child outside of marriage. (Women in this last category are often misleadingly called "never married" even though approximately one-fourth of the women who are unmarried at the birth of their child had been married at an earlier time.[1])

One further distinction should also be made here. The usual picture of the single mother is of a woman living *alone* with her children—Jackie Kennedy, Princess Diana, and Murphy Brown. But those we call "cohabitants" are also single mothers as a legal matter, even though their children are living in two-adult households. Indeed, where the woman, like Susan Sarandon, is cohabiting with the father of her child (Tim Robbins), although the mother is single, from the child's perspective it is an intact family.

*14*

As with single mothers generally, these four prominent women arouse a wide range of feelings, from support to dismay, in the public at large. Jackie Kennedy surely gained the maximum empathy of our foursome when her husband was murdered in her presence. Even those women who are widowed in less horrifying ways have long been viewed as victims of cruel fate and strongly deserving of community compassion.

Not too long ago, having been divorced was by itself thought to disqualify those seeking public office or other positions of public prominence. That no longer holds, as Ronald Reagan's presidency made clear. As a result, once Prince Charles and Princess Diana split up, she probably appeared to most Americans as facing the challenging task confronting many divorced women of having to balance the pursuit of her career with raising children on her own. Yet, despite Diana's wealth and fame, her marital breakup brought to the fore our society's general uneasiness about how well children fare in these settings, as well as our uncertainty about the appropriate roles of divorced fathers as providers of both cash and care.

In Sweden today, Susan and Tim's family structure is commonplace. There, a very large number of men and women live together and have children together, but do not go through the formalities of marriage— or at least have not done so at the time their first child is born. Lately, in America as well, the cohabitation category, long ignored by the census, is rapidly growing. This is not to say that most Americans, unlike the Swedes, accept cohabitation as though it were marriage. Indeed, American public policy, as we will see, treats cohabitation very differently from marriage.

Perhaps because Murphy Brown is a fictional character, this has allowed those who are on the rampage against unmarried women who bear children to be candid about their feelings without having to be so openly nasty to a "real" person. Yet Murphy Brown is an awkward icon. To be sure, she flouted the conventional morality of an earlier era. She had sex outside of marriage and then decided to keep and raise her child once she discovered she had unintentionally become pregnant. Although many people in our society still rail against sex other than between married couples, sex outside of marriage has become such a widespread phenomenon that it is generally no longer a stigma. And while it would be easy to chastise Murphy Brown for carelessly getting pregnant, as Jane Mauldon's chapter explains, this also is so commonplace that it is barely remarkable any more. Indeed, Murphy Brown might have come in for more censure had she, as a single woman, deliberately become pregnant.

As for deciding to raise her child on her own, this *by itself* does not arouse great public outcry. After all, it is not as though widowed mothers who make that decision are castigated for choosing not to remarry. As for the unmarried birth mother, shotgun weddings are seen to be less promising than they once were; abortion, while still a right, is hardly thought to be a duty; and while giving a child up for adoption is often commendable, today this is seen primarily as the route for women who do not want to, or cannot afford to, take care of their children themselves.

In short, the strongest objection by those who have assailed Murphy Brown is that she is a bad role model—in particular, that she is a bad role model for *poor* women who, unlike her, cannot provide for their children on their own, but go ahead and have them anyway, planning to turn to the state for financial and other assistance. In many quarters those single mothers are doubly condemned. First, they are seen to be prying money out of the rest of us by trading on our natural sympathy for their innocent children; yet this is said to leave taxpayers both unhappy because they have less money to spend on their own children and with the distasteful feeling that society is condoning, even promoting, the initial irresponsible and self-indulgent behavior by these poor single mothers. Then, these low-income women are rebuked as high-frequency failures as parents—for example, when their children disproportionately drop out of, or are disruptive at, school or turn to criminal behavior. Of course, not everyone disapproves of Murphy Brown or even those poor women who choose to have children on their own knowing that they will have to turn to the state for assistance. Many people believe that every American woman (at least if she is emotionally fit) ought to be able to be a mother if she wants to be.

These various types of single mothers are significant because they raise different issues, and, in turn, they have yielded very different policy solutions and proposals for reform. But before we turn to policy questions, some general demographic information is presented that, among other things, shows single-parent families to differ significantly from some common myths about them. The policy discussion that follows begins with a historical overview that demonstrates how American policies have changed sharply in the past century. Next the focus shifts to the conflicting ideological outlooks on single-parent families reflected in the thinking of conservatives and liberals today. This clash of views is then applied to some current policy initiatives most importantly, the bipartisan reform of welfare that occurred during the Clinton presidency. The chapter concludes with a call to refocus public attention on the needs of the children in single-parent families.

## Single-Parent Family Demographics: Myths and Realities

### *Father-Headed Single-Parent Families*

In the first place, not all single-parent families are headed by women. In 1970, three-quarters of a million children living in single-parent families lived with their father (about 10 percent of such families); by 2000, more than two million children lived in father-headed single-parent families (an increase to approximately 15 percent).[2]

These families are not the subject of much policy attention, however. First, most of them are headed by divorced (or separated) men; a few are widowers. It is rare, however, that the father of a child born outside of marriage will gain physical control of that child, and this takes custodial fathers largely outside the most controversial category of single-parents. Furthermore, single fathers caring for their children tend to be financially self-supporting and therefore generally beyond the purview of welfare reformers. Finally, they tend to remarry fairly quickly and hence remain heads of single-parent families for only a short time. In fact, the main public policy controversy involving these men today concerns divorce custody law—in what circumstances should fathers be able to become heads of single-parent families in the first place? This topic is discussed in the chapter by Judith Wallerstein.

Noncustodial fathers are quite another matter—whether divorced from or never married to the mothers of their children. As we will see, they are the subject of a great deal of public attention and concern.

## Unmarried as Compared to Divorced and Widowed

Turning back to families headed by single mothers, one myth is that they are predominantly women who have never been married to the father of their child. Yet there are actually more divorced (and separated) single mothers. For example, in 2000, 55 percent of single mothers were divorced or separated, and another 4 percent were widowed.[3] Moreover, because of the predominance of widowed and divorced mothers, large numbers of women become single mothers, not at their child's birth, but later on in their child's life, often not until the child is a teenager. Hence, among the children in single-parent families, living one's entire childhood apart from one's father is by no means the norm.

## Cohabitants

Cohabitants with children in their household are a complicated category, and, in turn, they complicate the data.[4] As noted earlier, although the women in these families are decidedly single mothers in a legal sense, in many respects these couples resemble married couples. So, many of these households are better described as two-parent, not single-parent, families. Some demographers have recently suggested that "cohabitation operates primarily as a precursor or a transitional stage to marriage among whites, but more as an alternative form of marriage among blacks."[5]

In any case, these cohabiting households come in several varieties. One first thinks of two biological parents not married to each other but living with their child—as exemplified by Susan Saradon and Tim Robbins and the Swedish model. Cohabiting mothers in this situation still often show up in U.S. surveys as though they were never married mothers

living on their own, because survey instruments tend to categorize respondents only as married or single.

A second variety of cohabiting households includes a single mother
with her child who is now living with, but not married to, a man who is
*not* the child's father. These women are drawn out of the ranks of the
never married, the divorced, and the widowed; they, too, are frequently
counted in surveys as living on their own. Moreover, in this second category especially, it is often quite unclear to outsiders whether the man is
a de facto spouse and stepparent, a casual boyfriend, or something in between.

Yet a third category of cohabiting households contains a homosexual couple (more often two women) in which one of the partners is the
legal (usually biological) parent and the other is formally a stranger (although some lesbian couples of late have successfully become dual mothers through adoption). These families are discussed in the chapter by Judith Stacey.

## Working and Not

Although the myth is that single mothers (especially never-married welfare moms) spend their time lounging around the house, watching TV,
doing drugs, and/or entertaining men, this is a wild exaggeration. A large
proportion is in the paid labor force. Official data from 1999 show that
more than two-thirds of *all* women with children are in the labor force.
Married women's rates are about 62 percent where the youngest child is
under six and about 77 percent where the youngest child is six or more.
Within the ranks of single mothers, divorced women work *more* than
married women, whereas never-married women are less likely to *report*
working.[6]

Single mothers often feel compelled to work full time even when their
children are very young, although the official data again show a difference between divorced and never-married women. According to 1999
figures, of those women with a child under age six, 60 percent of divorced women and 41 percent of never-married women worked *full time*;
this was higher than the rate for married women, 39 percent of whom
were working full time.[7]

A decade ago, fewer than 10 percent of single mothers who were
receiving welfare officially acknowledged earning wages.[8] Research by
Kathryn Edin suggests that, in fact, a high proportion of them was actually employed at least part time.[9] They tended to work for cash in the
underground (and sometimes illegal) economy. According to Edin's findings, they did not typically do so to be able to buy drugs or booze, but
rather in order to keep their households from utter destitution or to avoid
having to live in intolerably dangerous public housing projects. They kept
this work a secret from the welfare authorities because if the authorities
knew they would so cut back those women's welfare benefits as to make

their wages from work nearly meaningless. Although these women would be viewed by the welfare system as "cheaters," they tended to remain living in fairly impoverished circumstances. As Edin puts it, they felt compelled to break the law by the skimpiness of the welfare benefits they received. As we will see later in this chapter, welfare reform of the 1990s has changed this picture somewhat.

## Poor and Nonpoor

Even with the receipt of government assistance, more than a quarter of family households headed by single mothers officially live below the poverty level (as compared with less than 5 percent of families headed by a married couple).[10] Although this is a distressingly high number, to the extent that the myth is that single mothers are poor and on welfare, the myth is false. A substantial share of single mothers provides a reasonable level of material goods for their children, and well more than half of all single mothers are not on welfare. In 1998, for example, about 30 percent of female-headed households with related children under age eighteen received means-tested cash assistance.[11]

Those who escape poverty for their families have tended to do so primarily through earnings and secondarily through child support and government benefits (or through a combination of these sources)—although typically not by receiving welfare. In 1998, *nonpoor* single mothers received about 81 percent of their income from earnings, 6 percent from child support and alimony, and 7 percent from Social Security, pensions, unemployment compensation and the like, but only 5 percent from welfare, food stamps, and housing assistance.[12] It is not surprising, then, that, in 1998, the poverty rate for single-parent families with children under age eighteen was 43 percent before the receipt of means-tested cash transfers and 37 percent after their receipt, a relatively modest reduction indeed.[13] A different, and often more promising, route out of poverty for single mothers and their children is through marriage and thereby into a new family structure. These stepfamilies are discussed in the chapter by Mary Ann Mason.

## White and Nonwhite

The myth is that single mothers primarily come from racial and ethnic minorities. While it is true that these groups are disproportionately represented given their share of the population, in fact, these days more single mothers are white than any other group. For example, in 1999, 40 percent of nonmarital births were to whites, 33 percent to blacks, and 25 percent to Hispanics.[14] On a cumulative basis, as of 2000 there were 6.2 million white, mother-headed family groups (including white Hispanics) as compared with three million black, mother-headed family groups (including black Hispanics)—even though 32 percent of all black family groups were headed by mothers and only 10 percent of all white family groups were headed by mothers.[15]

## Change over Time

The demography of single-parenting has changed a lot over the twentieth century. There are many more single parents today than there were several generations ago, both in absolute numbers and, more importantly, in terms of the percentage of all children (or all parents) affected.

In 1900, the typical single parent was a widow. Male deaths through industrial and railway accidents were very visible. By contrast, divorce was then scarce (although desertion was a problem). And becoming a single mother by becoming pregnant outside of marriage was not very common, especially because so many who got pregnant promptly married the father.[16] Now, especially since the 1960s, all that is changed. Divorce is more frequent. "Illegitimacy" and cohabitation are also more prevalent than in earlier periods. For example, of women born between 1940 and 1944, only 3 percent had lived with a partner of the opposite sex by age twenty-five; of those born between 1960 and 1964, 37 percent had done so.[17] Moreover, the stigma of bearing a child outside of marriage and/or what some still call "living in sin" is much reduced.

Nonetheless, along with these changing characteristics of the single-parent family has come a change in public empathy. Earlier there was very widespread compassion for single parents and their children when single parents were mainly widows and divorcees, especially in the pre-no-fault era, when divorce usually was triggered (formally at least) by the misbehavior of the husband. Today, at least in some quarters, single mothers are loathed—as those receiving welfare who have borne their children outside of marriage or who are suspected of bringing about the end of their marriages through their own selfishness. As of 1996, the last full year that AFDC ("welfare") was in effect, about 60 percent of those receiving welfare had children outside of marriage as compared with but a trivial share in the 1930s and less than 30 percent as late as 1969.[18]

## Changing Policies toward Single Parents

### Widows

In 1909, President Theodore Roosevelt convened a historic first White House Conference on Children, which identified the poverty of widowed mothers and their children as a central policy problem. Then, if states and localities provided any assistance at all, it was too often through the squalid conditions of the "poor house" into which single-parent families might move—something of a counterpart to today's shelters for homeless families. The poor house itself was the successor to an earlier system in which desperate mothers farmed their children out to others, in effect providing young servants to those people who took these semiorphaned children into their homes, farms, and businesses. Reflecting the outlook of the social work profession that was then just getting underway, the White House Conference pushed instead for the adoption of Mothers' Pensions plans. Soon enacted, at least on paper, in most of the states, this new approach envisaged cash payments to single (primarily widowed) mothers who were certified by social workers as capable of providing decent parenting in their own homes if they only had a little more money in their pockets.[19]

Mothers' Pensions, the precursor to Aid to Families with Dependent Children (AFDC), reflected both the psychological perspective that it was best for the children to be raised in their own homes and the sociological outlook that it was appropriate for the mothers to stay at home and raise them (perhaps taking in other families' laundry or sewing, but not leaving their children to join the regular paid labor force).[20] As we will see, this benign attitude toward the payment of public assistance to single parents, which was reinforced by the adoption of AFDC in 1935 at the urging of President Franklin D. Roosevelt and maintained at least through the 1960s, has substantially evaporated.

## Divorcees

Much earlier in the 1900s, while widows were pitied, marital breakup was broadly frowned upon. Nonetheless, it was increasingly acknowledged that some spouses acted in intolerable ways and should be censured by allowing their spouses to divorce them. Adultery, spousal abuse, and desertion were the main categories of unacceptable marital conduct, and most of it seemed to be engaged in by husbands. As the decades rolled by, however, the divorce law requirement of severe wrongdoing by one spouse and innocence on the part of the complaining spouse soon ill-fit the attitudes of many couples themselves. Especially starting after World War II, and accelerating in the 1960s, many more couples came to realize that their marriages had simply broken down and they both wanted out. Until divorce law changed to reflect this new outlook, couples were prompted to engage in fraudulent charades (often involving the husband pretending to engage in adultery) so as to satisfy domestic relations law judges.

No-fault divorce law first emerged in California in 1970 and was rapidly followed by other states.[21] As a practical matter, not only did this reform allow couples amicably to obtain a divorce without having either one of them adjudicated as the wrongdoer but also, in most states, it permitted any dissatisfied spouse to terminate the marriage unilaterally. Whether no-fault divorce actually caused an increase in the divorce rate or merely coincided with (indeed, grew out of) the spiraling demand for divorce is unclear.[22] What is clear, however, is that divorce rates today are enormously greater than they were before 1970, thereby contributing to the great increase in single parenting.[23] As we will see, that state of affairs, in turn, has recently generated something of a backlash movement, one that seeks to reintroduce legal barriers to divorce in families with minor children.

## *Illegitimacy*

Public policies toward illegitimacy (and, in turn, toward both abortion and teen pregnancy) have also changed significantly during the 1900s. At an earlier time, children born outside of marriage were pejoratively labeled "bastards" and denied inheritance and other rights connected to their fathers, although their biological fathers did generally have the legal duty to support them.[24] If a single woman became pregnant, a standard solution was to promptly marry the child's father, perhaps pretending that the pregnancy arose during marriage after all. Adoption was available to some, who would be encouraged to go away before their pregnancies began to "show," only to return childless afterwards as though nothing had happened. Pursuing an abortion instead then risked criminal punishment and subjected the woman to grave risks to her life and health.

Rather suddenly, a little more than two-thirds of the way through the twentieth century, policies in these areas turned around dramatically. For those who wanted it, abortion became legal. More important for our purposes, remaining unmarried and then keeping a child born out-of-wedlock became much more acceptable. For example, instead of expelling pregnant teens, schools adopted special programs for them. Fewer women gave up their newborns for adoption—for example, 19 percent of white, unmarried birth mothers did so in the 1960s, but only 3 percent did so in the 1980s.[25] The courts forced states to give many legal rights to illegitimates that had previously been enjoyed only by legitimates;[26] and many legislatures voluntarily expanded the inheritance rights and other entitlements of out-of-wedlock children. Soon, unmarried pregnant women far less often married the biological father during the course of the pregnancy—a drop of from 52 percent to 27 percent between 1960 and 1980.[27]

Women who had children outside of marriage were no longer casually labeled unsuitable mothers and, as noted previously, soon became the largest category of single mothers receiving welfare. In terms of public acceptability, something of a high-water mark may have been reached in the early 1970s with the conversion of welfare into a "right" by the federal courts, the elimination of welfare's "suitable home" requirement, and the end to one-year waiting periods for newcomers seeking welfare.[28] This ignited an explosion of the welfare rolls,[29] and for the first time in many states, African-American women gained reasonably secure access to benefits. At that time Republican President Richard Nixon proposed turning AFDC from a complex state-federal program into a uniform national scheme.

At the end of the century, however, a policy backlash emerged. Between 1967 and 1997, the proportion of African-American children born outside of marriage skyrocketed from around 25 percent to nearly 70 percent; and the rate for white children was viewed by some as poised for a similar trajectory—and in any case has grown from 8 percent thirty years ago to around 22 percent today.[30] Now, curbing illegitimacy, or at least unmarried teen pregnancy, seems to be near the top of many politicians' lists.

## Child Support

It has been long understood that fathers have a moral obligation to provide for the financial support of their minor children. In the absent parent context, this means paying "child support." For most of the twentieth century, however, a substantial proportion of men failed to pay the support they might have paid.[31] The default rate by divorced fathers has long been very high, and in out-of-wedlock births the father's paternity often was not even legally determined. (Stepfathers with no legal duties were frequently a more reliable source of support.)[32] Moreover, in many states, even if noncustodial fathers paid all they owed, this was judged to be a pittance when compared with the child's reasonable needs. Deceased fathers were no more reliable, frequently dying with estates of trivial value and without life insurance.

Through the 1930s, AFDC and its predecessors were the main public response to these failures—providing means-tested cash benefits to poor children (and their mothers) deprived of the support of a breadwinner. In 1939, however, special privileged treatment was afforded widows and their children. The Social Security system was expanded so that, upon the death of the working father, "survivor" benefits would be paid to the children and their caretaker mother based upon the father's past wages.[33] This, in effect, created publicly funded life insurance for most widows and their children, with the result that today hardly any widowed mothers find it necessary to apply for welfare.

No comparable "child support insurance" was provided, however, so that divorced and never-married poor mothers have had to continue to turn to the socially less favored means-tested welfare programs instead of Social Security. On behalf of these families, the effort, much enlarged since the mid-1970s, has been to increase the amount of child support an absent father owes and to beef up child support enforcement efforts.[34] Notwithstanding those reforms, it is still estimated that more than ten billion dollars of child support annually goes uncollected, and many custodial mothers are unable to collect any support for their children.[35]

## Cohabitation

It appears that American society generally is becoming more accepting of cohabitation, even if it remains frowned upon in many circles. (Clearly, same-sex cohabitation continues to be highly controversial.) So far as public policy is concerned, however, marriage still makes a significant difference. For example, when children are involved and the cohabitants split up, the woman who keeps the children (as is typically the case) continues to be disadvantaged as compared with the woman who had married. Although she is entitled to support for her child, only in very special circumstances can she gain financial support for herself from her former partner. So, too, upon the death of her partner who was the father of her children, while her children can claim Social Security benefits, she does not qualify for the caretaker Social Security benefits that a legal widow would have obtained.[36]

## Conflicting Conservative and Liberal Perspectives

The conservative critique of single-parent families has partly been a financial one. The typical rhetorical question has been: Why have taxpayers who work hard for their money had to turn it over to single mothers who are not being forced to work and, in many cases, should not have had their children in the first place? This complaint was focused on poor single parents claiming welfare—and more particularly on those mothers rather than the men who impregnate them.

A second aspect of the conservative critique, however, is cast more generally. It asserts that single parent families are inferior families. These claims tend to fly under the heading "Dan Quayle was right," a reference to the former vice president's much publicized attack on Murphy Brown.[37] This "family values" claim has stirred up a hornets' nest of controversy.[38]

The underlying theory starts with the notion that when there is no father around, the child loses the parenting benefits that the father would have provided; indeed, some argue that "fatherlessness" is an inherently pathological condition that inevitably leads to deep psychological wounds.[39] In any event, with the mother now overburdened by having to raise the child on her own, the quality of her parenting is also thought to erode. Children in these families are seen as deprived of proper role models—no working father who embodies and imposes something of the work ethic; instead, all too often, a mother who is permitted to remain a long-term dependent on the state. A further inference is that the child often loses community support because the single mother moves more frequently. In addition, when single parenting arises from a marital breakup, it is surmised that the child suffers from the conflict surrounding the dissolution.

Indeed, when simple correlations are made, being a child in a single-parent family is associated with worse outcomes than being a child in a two-parent family.[40] Moreover, not only are these outcomes worse for the child (such as lower educational attainment, being more likely to become a teen parent, being more likely to be unemployed), they are also worse for society (such as, more likely to be on welfare as an adult).[41]

In the face of this evidence, what has infuriated many conservatives is that several public policies could be construed as actually encouraging single parenting. These include easy access to divorce and to welfare and the coddling of pregnant school girls, as well as the fact that, by contrast, poor two-parent families generally have not qualified for welfare.

A grave problem with resting the conservative case on simple correlations, however, is that single-parent families are simply not a random sample of all families. Therefore, just because children in single-parent families are in certain respects comparatively worse off, that in no way proves that they are worse off *because* they are part of single-parent families.

For example, poorer married couples break up at a greater rate than do richer couples. Hence to compare children of divorced families with children of all still-married families is the wrong comparison. At the least we would want to compare them with a subset of poorer still-married families in order to try to get at how they might be doing had their parents remained married. But, then, of course, when we start thinking like that it is easy to appreciate that even among couples who are in the same economic situation, those who break up are not just like those who stay married. So to compare even these two sets may misleadingly suggest how children of the divorced would have fared had their parents not divorced. It is simple to imagine, for example, that were their parents to have stayed together, the children would have suffered from severe spousal conflict, from abuse (physical, sexual, or emotional), and so on. In other words, the actual children who are in single-parent families might have been worse off, or no better off, had their actual parents remained married— even if other children whose parents choose to stay married have real advantages.[42] In the same vein, even before they have children there are many differences, on average, between those women who go on to bear children outside of marriage and those who bear children when married; so, for example, perhaps children of married women with similarly low education, income, and work experience also have worse outcomes than the average child.

Sorting through all of this is a very difficult task. Nevertheless, a few years ago Sara McLanahan and Gary Sandefur[43] carried out some highly sophisticated statistical analysis designed to get at these more difficult questions. They concluded that, even after adjusting for initial differences in race, parents' education, family size, and residential location, there are indeed significantly worse outcomes for children in single-parent families of all sorts, as compared with those living with two biological parents. They also found that these outcome differences do not importantly vary as between single-parent families created by divorce and those created by a nonmarital birth (although outcomes are less bad for children of widows).

Notice that these comparisons do not yet take income differences into account. This is especially tricky to deal with because income differences exist among families before family disruption *and* income declines are caused by the creation of a single-parent family. McLanahan and Sandefur's analysis shows that about half of the lower outcome differences for children in single-parent families is accounted for by income differences, and that most of that is accounted for by the loss of income that occurs by becoming a single-parent family (and only a little because of preexisting income differences). Put differently, they find that the single most important factor accounting for the lower measured well-being of children in one-parent families is the loss of income suffered by the custodial parent upon becoming a single parent whether by divorce, death, or nonmarital birth. While this is clearly not the same thing as saying that single parents are worse parents, for their children it is nonetheless a negative outcome.

A second important factor in explaining worse outcomes for children, according to McLanahan and Sandefur, is what they call residential mobility. Children living in single-parent families tend to move around more (and especially at the time the single family is created) and this, on balance, also appears to be harmful to children. This is probably so because it means the loss of what McLanahan and Sandefur call "community capital"—the community friendship and support networks that come along with living for a long period in the same place. Again, although the women who, for reasons of economic necessity, have to move their children to a new home following divorce can hardly be termed bad parents merely for making the move, their children may nonetheless suffer as a consequence.

Finally, although they could not fully adjust, for example, for the greater predivorce conflict among couples who do divorce and those who do not, McLanahan and Sandefur conclude that a significant share of the remaining difference in children's outcomes is accounted for by differences more closely intertwined with family structure itself—for example, less contact with the biological father and less intense supervision by the (relatively more burdened) custodial mother in single-parent families as compared with two-biological-parent families. It is not at all clear, however, whether this factor leads to a little loss in children's well-being in a large number of single-parent families or a large loss in only a few of them. The latter is more consistent with the conventional liberal outlook that many single parents can do as good a job of child rearing, and some do a better job, than do couples.

Moreover, liberals tend to see the focus on nontraditional family structure as starting at altogether the wrong end of things. When they look out across American families today, they are foremost struck by the staggeringly high rate of child poverty (especially in single-parent families)—probably the highest child poverty rate of all industrialized nations[44] in a country that prides itself on being the most powerful and in many respects the richest in the world.

When liberals start to look for explanations for this appalling situation, they first fasten, not on changing family structure, but on joblessness and pervasive racism. Therefore, instead of faulting our current policies as responsible for promoting the breakdown of the traditional family, liberals see them as failing to address the actual needs of children and families and unfairly stigmatizing those victims who are not to blame for their circumstances. So, while conservatives might draw on McLanahan and Sandefur's findings to point to the desirability of men and women staying together for the sake of the kids, liberals are more likely to ask why more is not being done collectively to get more income into the hands of single-parent families. Given McLanahan and Sandefur's findings, more income could help reduce outcome differences for children not only directly but also indirectly by reducing the need for new single parents to move out of the neighborhood.

Furthermore, among many liberals, there is a celebration of diversity of family forms and hence a rejection of the conventional family structure (married couple, husband employed, wife at home) as the social ideal to which everyone should aspire. From this perspective, there is considerable long-term social benefit to be gained from dislodging what many see as the implicit patriarchy of the traditional nuclear family even if, during the transitional period, there might be some modest cost to children raised in the nonconventional manner (e.g., by single mothers or by lesbian couples). This outlook may also cause liberals to discount the significance of McLanahan and Sandefur's findings. For example, the 50 percent greater high school dropout rate they found for children in single-parent families as compared with children living with two biological parents may feel rather different when it is understood that we are talking about a 19 percent dropout rate as compared with a 13 percent rate. So while liberals are not likely to say that it is unimportant to have six more children graduate out of every one hundred who attend school, still when put this way they may conclude that the worse outcome for children in single-parent families is really rather modest.

The bottom line is, as explored in the following section, these very different outlooks on today's American families makes one expect that it would be extremely difficult for liberals and conservatives to reach any sort of genuine agreement on the direction of family policy toward children living with a single parent.

## Recent Policy Reforms and Current Initiatives

### Child Support

In the past few years, much policy reform has been directed toward getting noncustodial parents to put more money into the hands of single-parent families. Put more simply, the goal has been to force absent fathers (often termed "deadbeat dads") to transfer more of their income to their children and the children's mothers. One reason for these policy changes is that they are among the few solutions on which most liberals and conservatives can agree.

Congress has on several recent occasions prodded states to change their child support regimes in a number of ways. The size of the non-custodial parent's support obligation has been considerably increased in most states. At the same time, the calculation of the sum is now largely determined by formula, instead of being left to the discretion of a local judge in the course of adjudicating a divorce or paternity determination. On the collection side, most of the effort has been directed toward making the process routine, especially through the automatic withholding of support obligations from wages and the direct payment of such obligations over to the custodial parent (or to the welfare authorities if the mother is on welfare).

Nonetheless, child support enthusiasts are by no means satisfied. Although inflation of late has been very low, in the past even moderate inflation has quickly undermined the value of child support awards, necessitating difficult courtroom battles over modifications. Hence efforts are underway to establish a regime of automatic modification based upon changing costs of living. On another front, too many noncustodial fathers remain unidentified, at least formally. In response, some states have posted officials in hospital nurseries on the theory that when unmarried men come in to see their newborns they can be coaxed into admitting paternity on the spot.

An important part of the child support shortfall occurs in the welfare population. There, however, increased support collection generally will benefit the taxpayers, not children in single-parent families. This is because welfare recipients have had to assign their child support rights to the government and have been entitled to keep only fifty dollars a month from what is collected. This helps explain why fathers of children on welfare are not so eager to pay the child support as they might otherwise be. Indeed, a fair proportion of these absent fathers now secretly and informally pay support directly to the mothers of their children,[45] because, if the welfare department managed to capture those funds, the outcome would be the enrichment of the public fisc at the expense of poor children. While redirecting those funds from mothers to the welfare department would strike a blow against what now qualifies as fraud, the result would nonetheless be the further impoverishment of children.

Moreover, one has to be realistic about collecting increased child support from absent fathers. Many of them have new families and new children to support. While some people might find it irresponsible for them to have taken on these new obligations, the practical reality is that we are often talking about shifting money from one set of children to another. In other cases, the nonpaying father is unemployed. Should he be forced to find work, or be placed in a public service job, so that income could be siphoned off to satisfy his child support obligation? Some are urging this very solution.[46] Yet, what is to happen when the men fail to comply with their work obligations? Are we going to imprison thousands of these dads?[47]

In any event, child support policy largely strikes at the single-parent family issue after the fact—even though some men arguably might be deterred from fathering children or abandoning their families if they knew they faced substantial, and nearly certain, collection of child support obligations. Other current policy initiatives are more openly "prevention" oriented.

## Divorce Law

Among those who have concluded that it often would be better for the children for the parents to stay together, rather than split up, it is not surprising that no-fault divorce has become a target for reform. The picture these critics present is that some parents selfishly divorce even though they realize they are putting themselves ahead of their children and are likely to harm their children as a result—or else they blithely divorce unaware of the harm they will do to their children. The goal of the critics, they say, is to make divorce more difficult in hopes of helping the children.[48]

The problem, however, arises in deciding exactly how to change divorce law. The most sweeping proposal is simply to bar divorce entirely to those with minor children. This solution, however, carries costs that most people would find unacceptable. Suppose one spouse (stereotypically the father) is guilty of domestic violence against the children and/or the other spouse. It seems unimaginable today that, in such circumstances, we would insist that the victim spouse remain married. To be sure, the divorce ban advocates might concede that she would be entitled to a legal separation and/or a protective order keeping him away from the children. But, at that point, to continue to prevent divorce seems gratuitously nasty. Since keeping the parents together for the sake of the children has been abandoned in this case, the only real consequence of the bar would be to prevent the victim spouse from remarrying—and perhaps giving the children a stable new family relationship. So, too, suppose one spouse abandons the family. What good is possibly served by denying the other spouse a divorce and thereby keeping her from remarrying—especially if the alternative is for the abandoned spouse to live with, but not marry, her new love?

These examples make clear that a complete ban on divorce by those with minor children is unsound and unlikely to be adopted. They also demonstrate that even to enact a strong presumption against divorce with special exceptions will inevitably embroil the spouses and the courts in wrangles over individual fault, a prospect that makes most of those familiar with the operation of pre-no-fault divorce law shudder. After all, if you made an exception for physical abandonment, wouldn't you have to make an exception for emotional abandonment, especially if it were combined with extramarital love affairs? And if you made an exception for physical abuse, why not for emotional abuse?

This prospect has caused some of those who want to make divorce law tougher to retreat to the seemingly simple idea that only unilateral divorce would be banned. If one spouse objected, the other could not force a divorce on the one who wanted to remain married. These critics claim that American law seems to have jumped directly from fault-based divorce to unilateral divorce, when it might have stopped in between by allowing divorce only by mutual consent.[49]

Proponents argue that requiring both parents to agree will put an extra roadblock in front of indiscriminate sacrificing of the child's interest. They seem to have in mind the father who gets tired of marriage and family and selfishly wants out—perhaps because he has a new "girlfriend." But, if so, how useful is it really to give his wife a veto? If, as a result, he resentfully stays in the marriage, will this actually be good for the children? Alternatively, what is to prevent him from simply moving out without obtaining a divorce, perhaps taking up housekeeping with another woman? Again the rule really only means that he cannot remarry. Furthermore, this regime is already the law now in the State of New York, and yet we certainly don't hear no-fault divorce critics arguing that everything would be so much better if only the more liberal states tightened up their rules to match New York's.

A final restrictive approach would impose a substantial waiting period (say, two or more years) before one parent could obtain a unilateral divorce and/or insist on marriage counseling before filing for divorce. Although some have argued that either of these measures would benefit the children, here again there is reason to be skeptical. A long waiting period could cause people to file for divorce even more quickly than they now do, or, in any event, simply to treat the rule as a time-hurdle to remarriage. Offering willing parents marriage counseling is probably a good idea, and legislatures might consider making this a mandatory benefit in all health insurance plans (as part of the coverage of mental health services generally). But coerced counseling is likely to have a low payoff.

This analysis suggests that legal change intended to make divorce more difficult to obtain would largely be a symbolic matter and is not a very promising way actually to help children avoid harms that may come from divorce. Perhaps more promising, then, are incentive approaches designed to help cooperative parents who are at risk of divorce to stabilize their marriage. These could include financial support provided through the tax law. For example, in the late 1990s, Republicans pushed through a universal child tax credit of $500 a year, although many Democrats opposed this on the ground that it means spending too much money on families who do not need help. They would rather spend the money through an expansion of the Earned Income Tax Credit, which is better tailored to low-income families. Other reformers would prefer to direct the financial rewards to young families who are first-time home buyers. Yet other intervention strategies designed to help maintain marriages are educationally and psychologically oriented. Some of them are discussed in the chapter by Carolyn and Philip Cowan.

## *Unmarried Childbearing*

A different prevention strategy is to try to discourage women from becoming single unwed mothers at the outset. From the rhetoric one hears these days, this is widely understood to be a problem of "teenage pregnancy," and liberals and conservatives do seem united in their determination to reduce its incidence. However, as the chapter by Jane Mauldon shows, it is important to keep in mind that minors (girls under age eighteen) actually account for a rather small share of mothers of children born out-of-wedlock. To be sure, hardly anyone would argue that it is desirable for a young woman (or for her child) to give birth when she is under age sixteen (although births to females that young remain, statistically, rather unusual events). Moreover, recent research shows that a very significant share of young teen pregnancies involve men who are by no means "age peers" of the pregnant girls. It is not simply a case of two fifteen year olds "fooling around" and the girl carelessly getting pregnant; rather, all too often, the father is an adult male.[50] Hence for a large proportion of these very young women, we are, candidly, talking about sexual abuse prevention. Yet given the staggering amount of child and spousal abuse generally in our society, it is, alas, not surprising that we also are not very effective at preventing the abuse that causes a young teen to get pregnant.

Some have pushed for a return to statutory rape prosecutions—in which the girl's youth makes her legally incapable of giving consent to sexual relations. In the 1970s and 1980s most district attorneys seem to have abandoned bringing these cases. There has been a renewed hope since the mid-1990s that threatening the predators with the criminal law could discourage their reckless procreation. To that end, Florida, for example, passed tougher statutory rape laws for cases where there is a substantial gap in the ages of the parties, and Georgia passed stronger minimum prison sentences for statutory rape. It is easy to be enthusiastic about this idea if you do not have to worry about funding it, or if you imagine that the mere threat of prosecution would alter the men's conduct dramatically. But once we picture the result as putting large numbers of inappropriate fathers in prison, the idea becomes much less attractive.

Again, therefore, it might be more productive to deal with the problem through positive measures rather than with threats. If these young men faced better job prospects, they would also be better candidates to marry adult women closer to their own age. With these two more desirable outlets for displaying their masculinity, perhaps many fewer of them would be drawn to the idea of preying on underage girls to demonstrate their virility.

Nonetheless, many policymakers will despair at the prospect of effectively controlling the conduct of men and so will return their focus to young women. As Jane Mauldon's chapter emphasizes, one promising strategy is to provide young women with better access to sex education, contraception, and abortion. These ideas, however, begin to divide liberals and conservatives. Obviously, many conservatives find abortion (and sometimes contraception) immoral; and often they argue (even in the face of evidence to the contrary) that, in practice, this strategy will only increase premarital sex, something they also oppose on moral and/or pragmatic grounds. In any event, information alone is unlikely to affect the behavior of those young women who, however misguided, want to get pregnant to demonstrate their love for the guy—or for that matter the conduct of the guy who wants to give her a baby to prove he loves her.

One possible way to change young women's preferences is to bribe them not to get pregnant. Planned Parenthood, a private organization, has actually experimented with programs like this, and some say they work—not so much because of the financial reward given to teenage girls who do not get pregnant, but because of the peer pressures that arise from many teens being in the program together, say, through their school.[51] But widespread implementation of such a scheme would be a very tricky business. If you were not extremely careful about whom you bribed, you would end up spending most of the money on those who were not really at risk of pregnancy in the first place. Moreover, conservative ideology generally resists the idea paying people to do what conservatives believe they have the moral duty to do anyway.

If it is not easy to gain consensus in favor of public policies of these sorts, what about solutions that take a harsher stance against pregnant young teens? Schools could return to their prior practices of threatening to expel pregnant teens. Poor teenagers could be told that if they got pregnant, they would under no circumstances be given money to move out of their home (as welfare traditionally allowed them to do). The state could make clear that very young women who had babies would be deemed unfit parents and have their children taken away and adopted or, if necessary, raised in orphanages. If a package of these provisions worked completely to stop young teens from getting pregnant, it might be a popular solution. But that is an implausible outcome. Even a 50 percent reduction in the pregnancy rate would be heralded by most policy analysts as a dazzling success. The upshot, however, is that the social costs of imposing the penalties on those who would remain undeterred would be very high. The teen mothers would be much worse off than today—less educated, perhaps abused at home, and poorer—and the children they bear would, in turn, also suffer. Or else the public would face huge new expenses for foster and institutional care of children removed from their mothers. Maybe we could distract teens from sex by offering to them other enjoyable activities during those parts of the day when they otherwise tend to go unsupervised. But exactly what those distractions should be is not altogether clear, and anyway conservative antipathy toward new spending as well as conservative sneering at analogously motivated "midnight basketball" programs suggest that this approach is also unlikely to win bipartisan support.

## Welfare Reform

The traditional outlook from staunch liberals is that single parents should be entitled to the same recognition and largely the same treatment whether they became single parents through the death of their spouses, through divorce, or by having a child when unmarried.

Should that entitlement include an entitlement to cash so long as they have a child in their care? Although that had seemed to be the liberal view for many years, of late this commitment seems on the wane. Liberals (like conservatives) do seem generally pleased about increased efforts to get cash to single-parent families through the private child support system; and although almost no one talks about it, liberals (and conservatives) seem wholly pleased with Social Security's payment of cash to single widows with young children in their care (even though this benefit arguably deters widows from remarrying). Yet, during the Clinton presidency, Democrats joined with conservatives in calling for radical changes in our welfare system.

In the past, from the liberal side, the call for reform usually emphasized *increasing* cash benefit levels, reducing intrusion into the lives of single mothers who receive welfare, and ending the stigma (to the extent possible) attached to the program and its participants. But no longer. In the 1990s, Clinton and most Democratic national legislators began playing a new tune—although this lead to criticism that they had abandoned liberal principles.

The upshot was that 1996 yielded a strongly bipartisan welfare reform law that President Clinton signed. During the debates, both sides said that long-term dependency on welfare is a bad thing for poor women and their children. While it has been repeated so often that it sounds almost self-evident, this principle is actually a bit puzzling. After all, long-term dependency on child support or on Social Security does not attract the same criticism.

Perhaps the real point is that it is now widely thought to be unacceptable for able-bodied women to be supported by taxpayers while remaining out of the paid labor force for so long. Although this is a complete reversal of the underlying basis for the original Mothers' Pensions scheme, the role of mothers in our society generally has changed radically during the course of this century. And mothers receiving AFDC appeared from official records to be working a great deal less than other mothers.

One has to be very cautious in making comparisons here, however, to say nothing of what policy changes should follow from the comparison. For example, it is much easier for single mothers receiving child support or Social Security to combine that income with wages than it had been for AFDC recipients. Earnings just supplement child support, and for those widows on Social Security substantial part-time employment is possible before benefits are reduced. By contrast, as noted earlier, in AFDC most of one's wages had simply gone back to the government to reduce one's welfare check.

Without coercion, society might get many more single women voluntarily to enter the paid labor force if it were more advantageous to work. For example, if all regular jobs carried health insurance, and if the collective support we provide for public schools were extended to include preschools and day care for working parents, then not only would many of those single parents who always have worked be better off, but also many others would find work far more attractive. So, too, if the rules about combining welfare and wages were more like the rules for combining child support or Social Security and wages, more single mothers would probably choose to work at least part time. But all these reforms would also cost money at a time when all politicians, and especially conservatives, seem to be trying to reduce federal public spending.

It is also true that a significant share of women who have been receiving welfare are not able-bodied and available for work in the way that might be hoped. Some are mentally disabled, others have very low educational attainment and no work experience, still others are abusers of drugs and alcohol, and so on. This does not mean that most mothers who have been on welfare cannot work, but it does mean that if all welfare recipients were all cut free to seek work themselves, many would find it impossible to obtain jobs on their own.

What President Clinton's advisors discovered, therefore, is that if we are going to force single mothers to work, we are going to have to create a lot of jobs for them, often public service jobs. But any jobs strategy that true liberals are likely to endorse will involve much higher administrative costs, new child care costs, education and training costs, and substantial wage subsidies. That means lots more public spending than simply sending a monthly check to these mothers. But for conservatives, "ending welfare as we know it" was decidedly not meant to impose new financial burdens on the taxpayers. As a result, it looked as though it was not going to be easy to achieve a political consensus on getting most poor single mothers into the workforce.

Of course, simply cutting off all welfare would cause some women to take paid jobs (and make some welfare mothers now secretly working live on those wages and not the combination of earnings and welfare). But just as we saw with proposals for harsh treatment of teen parents, the anguish comes when we think about those who are not going to succeed in the private jobs market. As always, we need to be realistic, and not overly optimistic, about the behavioral responses we are likely to achieve through policy reforms.

To be sure, some of these women and their children could be taken care of by their extended families (frequently to the detriment of the other children in those families). Perhaps a few would be deterred from having children in the first place, and a few others would wind up holding their marriages together. Private charity could make up some of the remaining gap, but hardly all of it. But what about the rest?

In the face of these difficulties, the 1996 welfare reform law eliminated the federal entitlement to welfare and kicked the problem back to the states. Under the compromise, no longer would the federal government match state welfare spending according to a formula. Instead, the states were given great freedom to design their own welfare programs. To finance them, they have been awarded an annual lump sum (a so-called block grant) from Washington to which they must, at least during the early years, add some of their own money. In principle, under the new welfare policy few recipients are supposed to be allowed to remain on cash assistance for more than two years at a time or five years in a lifetime.

Through 2001, the 1996 welfare reform scheme (renamed TANF, for Temporary Assistance for Needy Families) was far more successful and far less harmful than its critics predicted.[52] First, by the start of 2000 the welfare caseload nationwide had, astoundingly, declined by more than 50 percent. This sharp decline, combined with the block grant federal funding, was a financial bonanza for many governors. Overall, states wound up with much more money to support each family remaining on welfare, and most have used that increased cash to provide income supplements, child care, job search, and other services to assist those families. Second, more single mothers report being employed, both among those who remain on TANF and among those low-wage earners who have left (or never entered) welfare altogether; and these mothers are reporting higher earnings than in the past. Third, as of 1999, child poverty rates nationwide declined back to 1979 levels. Fourth, at least some child outcome studies have shown improvements in the well-being of children of the poor, although other study results are much less promising, and in any case, it is difficult to connect such changes to welfare reform per se.

On the other hand, there are some disturbing trends as well. Many of those mothers who have left welfare do not seem to be employed, or only hold jobs temporarily, and in other cases wind up financially no better off than they were before welfare reform. Moreover, the proportion of families living at one-half the poverty level or below (i.e., "deep poverty") has alarmingly increased. Furthermore, by the end of 2001, only a few families on TANF were beginning to reach their lifetime 5-year limits on federal support, and it remains uncertain how well individual states will support single mothers and their children after many hit that limit. Finally, of course, the years between 1996 and 2000 were economic boom times, and many analysts are extremely fearful about how poor families will fare as the nation moves toward or into recession at the end of 2001.

Of course, no one wants American cities and towns to look like those third world places that are filled with children begging in the streets. While this seems a highly unlikely prospect in the short run, the longer run outcome is less clear. TANF comes up for reauthorization in 2002. Although there will be some sticky issues to work out, as of the end of 2001, it does not look as though this reauthorization will occasion further welfare reform as a high priority issue. But one should not blithely assume that there will be no welfare crisis later in the decade.

## Refocusing the Policy Perspective

When it comes to single-parent families, much of our current policy focus is on parents: whether they divorce, whether they pay child support, whether they have children outside of marriage, whether they work, and so on. Suppose instead that policy attention were aimed at the *children* in single-parent families. For example, as we have seen, if a child's breadwinner parent dies, the government ordinarily assures that child far better financial security than it does if that child's breadwinner parent is simply absent from the home: Social Security steps in to satisfy the deceased parent's obligation to have provided life insurance but not the absent parent's duty to provide child support.

Comparable treatment for the latter group implies some sort of publicly funded "child support insurance" scheme. Plans of this sort (including those that would expand Social Security in exactly this way) have in fact been proposed, most notably by Irwin Garfinkel, although so far at least they have not won widespread endorsement.[53] This sort of scheme could assure all children living in single-parent families of equal financial support—say, up to the poverty level. Or, like Social Security and private child support obligations, the benefits could be related to the absent parent's past wages. In either case, earnings by the custodial parent could supplement, rather than replace, the child support benefit.

Such a plan could be financed by general revenues or Social Security payroll taxes. But it might also be funded, at least in substantial part, by absent parents, thereby making the plan one that guarantees that a suitable level of child support will actually be provided and makes up the shortfall when the collection effort fails. Were this second approach adopted, not only should it dramatically reduce our sense of the cost of the plan but also it should offset any tendency that the plan might otherwise have to increase divorce.

It is important to emphasize that a plan like this would much improve the lot of many children who in the past have been dependent on welfare and large numbers of children with working-class and even middle-class mothers whose absent fathers now default on their child support obligations. It must be conceded, however, that in view of the direction of recent welfare reform, the prospects at present are not favorable for any new initiative to provide cash for children in single-parent families.

A different child-centered approach, therefore, is to try to provide all children with essential goods by means other than providing cash. Ought not all American youths live in decent housing, obtain a quality education, receive adequate food, have access to decent health care, and so on? This is not the place to detail the many alternative mechanisms by which these critical items might be delivered. What needs emphasizing, however, is that any program guaranteeing these sorts of things to all children would have vastly disproportionate benefits to children now living in single-parent families. Moreover, if we can keep the focus on the needy and innocent members of the next generation, perhaps we can escape ideological battles over the worthiness of these children's parents. This is perhaps a naive hope, but one that may be enhanced when the thing delivered to the child's family is other than money: witness the greater public and legislative popularity of the federal food stamps program and federal aid to elementary and secondary education as compared with the now-decimated federal welfare program.

The many policy reforms discussed here are unlikely to have large impacts on people like Jackie Kennedy, Princess Diana, Susan Sarandon, and Murphy Brown. But ordinary single mothers (and their children) who are in analogous situations have a great deal at stake.

## Notes

1. Dore Hollander, "Nonmarital Childbearing in the United States: A Government Report," *Family Planning Perspectives* 28(1):30, 1996.

2. U.S. Census Bureau, "America's Families and Living Arrangements" in *Current Population Reports* P20–537, at p. 7, 2001. (Herein "America's Families and Living Arrangements")

3. "America's Families and Living Arrangements," Table 4 at p. 8.

4. Larry L. Bumpass and R. Kelly Raley, "Redefining Single-Parent Families: Cohabitation and Changing Family Reality," *Demography* 32(1):97, 1995.

5. Wendy D. Manning and Pamela J. Smock, "Why Marry? Race and the Transition to Marriage among Cohabitors," *Demography* 32(4):509, 1995. See also Ronald R. Rindfuss and Audrey Vandenheuvel, "Cohabitation: A Precursor to Marriage or an Alternative to Being Single?" *Population and Development Review* 16:703, 1990.

6. Committee on Ways and Means, U.S. House of Representatives, Overview of Entitlement Programs, 2000 Green Book (hereafter 2000 Green Book). Table 9-2.

7. 2000 Green Book, Table 9-4.

8. In 1992, for example, just over 2 percent of single mothers on AFDC reported working full time and another 4 percent reported working part time. Another 12 percent were said to be seeking work. 1994 Green Book, Table 10-28.

9. More specifically, Edin found that about 15 percent were working full time (typically under another name) and many others were working part time. Kathryn Edin and Christopher Jencks, "Reforming Welfare," in Christopher Jencks, (ed.), *Rethinking Social Policy: Race, Poverty and the Underclass* (Cambridge: Harvard University Press, 1992), 204–235.

10. "Poverty in the U.S.," in *Current Population Reports* P60–210, 2000, vi. Table A. Available online at http://www.census.gov/prod/2000pubs/p60–210.pdf. (Herein "Poverty in the U.S.")

11. 2000 Green Book, Table G-30.

12. 2000 Green Book, Table G-30.

13. 2000 Green Book, Table H-21.

14. Centers for Disease Control and Prevents, "Nonmarital Childbearing in the United States, 1940–1999," in National Vital Statistics Reports, 48:16, at p. 6, 2000. Available online at http://www.cdc.gov/nchs/data/nvsr/nvsr48/nvs48_16.pdf. (Herein "Nonmarital Childbearing in the U.S.").

15. "America's Families and Living Arrangements," Table 4, at p. 8.

16. Mary Ann Mason, *Father's Property to Children's Rights* (New York: Columbia University Press, 1994), 11–16.

17. Hollander, "Nonmarital Childbearing," 30.

18. 2000 Green Book, section 7.

19. Winifred Bell, *Aid to Dependent Children* (New York: Columbia University Press, 1965).

20. Committee on Economic Security. Social Security in America, The Factual Background of the Social Security Act as Summarized from Staff Reports to the Committee on Economic Security, 1937.

21. Herma Hill Kay, "Beyond No-fault: New Directions in Divorce Reform," in Stephen Sugarman and Herma Hill Kay (eds.), *Divorce Reform at the Crossroads* (New Haven: Yale University Press, 1990), 6–36.

22. H. Elizabeth Peters, "Marriage and Divorce: Information Constraints and Private Contracting," *American Economic Review* 76:437, 1986; Gary S. Becker, *A Treatise on the Family* (Cambridge: Harvard University Press, 1981), 228–229.

23. Centers for Disease Control and Prevention, National Center for Health Statistics, "Monthly Vital Statistics Report," 44(4), 1995.

24. Ira Mark Ellman, Paul M. Kurtz, and Elizabeth S. Scott, *Family Law: Cases, Text, Problems*, 3rd ed. (Charlottesville: Michie Law Publishers, 1998), 1035–1142.

25. Hollander, "Nonmarital Childbearing," 31.

26. Levy v. Louisiana, 391 U.S. 68 (1968); Weber v. Aetna Cas. & Sur. Co., 406 U.S. 164 (1972).

27. Hollander, "Nonmarital Childbearing," 31.

28. Goldberg v. Kelly, 397 U.S. 254 (1970); King v. Smith, 392 U.S. 309 (1968); and Shapiro v. Thompson, 394 U.S. 618 (1969).

29. 1994 Green Book, Table 10-1.

30. "Nonmarital Childbearing in the U.S.," 5–6.

31. David L. Chambers, *Making Fathers Pay: The Enforcement of Child Support* (Chicago: University of Chicago Press, 1979).

32. For further discussion see the chapter by Mary Ann Mason.

33. Stephen D. Sugarman, "Children's Benefits in Social Security," *Cornell Law Review* 65:836–908, 1980.

34. 2000 Green Book, section 8.

35. 2000 Green Book, Table 8-7.

36. This rule was unsuccessfully challenged in Boles v. Califano, 443 U.S. 282 (1979).

37. Barbara Dafoe Whitehead, "Dan Quayle Was Right," *Atlantic Monthly* (April 1993). 47–84; David Popenoe, "The Controversial Truth: Two-Parent Families Are Better," *New York Times*, Dec. 26, 1992, 21.

38. Letters. "Dan Quayle Was Right," *Atlantic Monthly* (July 1993): 9–12; Arlene Skolnick and Stacey Rosencrantz, "The New Crusade for the Old Family," *American Prospect* 59(Summer 1994):65; Nancy Dowd, "Stigmatizing Single-Parents," *Harvard Women's Law Journal* 18(1995):19; Stephanie Coontz, "The American Family and the Nostalgia Trap," *Phi Delta Kappan* 76(7):K1, 1995.

39. David Blankenhorn, *Fatherless America: Confronting Our Most Urgent Social Problem* (New York: Basic Books, 1995).

40. Whitehead, "Dan Quayle Was Right."

41. Sara McLanahan, "The Consequences of Single Motherhood," *American Prospect* (Summer 1994):48–58.

42. Paul R. Amato and Alan Booth, "A Prospective Study of Divorce and Parent-Child Relationships," *Journal of Marriage and the Family* 58:356–365, 1996; Donna Ruane Morrison and Andrew J. Cherlin, "The Divorce Process and Young Children's Well-Being: A Prospective Analysis," *Journal of Marriage and the Family* 57:800 812, 1995; Paul R. Amato, "Children's Adjustment to Divorce: Theories, Hypotheses, and Empirical Support," *Journal of Marriage and the Family* 55:23–38, 1993.

43. Sara S. McLanahan and Gary Sandefur, *Growing Up with a Single Parent: What Helps, What Hurts* (Cambridge: Harvard University Press, 1994).

44. Timothy M. Smeeding, Michael O'Higgins, and Lee Rainwater (eds.), *Poverty, Inequality and Income Distribution in Comparative Perspective: The Luxembourg Income Study (LIS)* (Washington, DC: Urban Institute Press, 1990).

45. Edin and Jencks, "Reforming Welfare."

46. Michael Novak, et al., The New Consensus on Family and Welfare: A Community of Self-Reliance," American Enterprise Institute for Public Policy Research, Washington, DC, 1987. Paul Offner, "Welfare Dads," *New Republic* (Feb. 13, 1995):14.

47. David L. Chambers, "Fathers, the Welfare System, and the Virtues and Perils of Child-Support Enforcement," *Virginia Law Review* 81:2575–2605, 1995.

48. William Galston, "Divorce American Style," *The Public Interest* 124:12, 1996.

49. Mary Ann Glendon, *The Transformation of Family Law* (Chicago: University of Chicago Press, 1989).

50. Mireya Navarro, "Teen-Age Mothers Viewed as Abused Prey of Older Men," *New York Times*, May 19, 1996; Mike A. Males, *The Scapegoat Generation: America's War on Adolescents* (Monroe, ME: Common Courage Press, 1996), 45–76.

51. Nancy Kates, "Buying Time: The Dollar-a-Day Program." Case study prepared for use in the Kennedy School of Government, Harvard University, 1990.

52. The analysis that follows draw upon Ron Haskins, Isabel Sawhill, and Kent Weaver, "Welfare Reform," Policy Briefs No. 1 and 2, January 2001, the Brookings Institution. Available online at www.brookings.edu/wrb.

53. Irwin Garfinkel, *Assuring Child Support* (New York: Russell Sage Foundation, 1992); Stephen D. Sugarman, "Reforming Welfare through Social Security," *University of Michigan Journal of Law Reform* 26:817–851, 1993; Stephen D. Sugarman, "Financial Support of Children and the End of Welfare as We Know It," *Virginia Law Review* 81:2523–2573, 1995.

# 3

# Families Started by Teenagers

## Jane Mauldon

### Introduction

Families in the United States are more diverse than they have ever been, and almost every type of family has its proponents—with the exception of families started by teenagers. In twenty-first-century America, teenagers are not supposed to have children. "Adolescent parenthood"—the phrase only entered the lexicon of social problems in the early 1970s—is a problem almost by definition. Adolescents do not have the rights and responsibilities of adults; parenthood is quintessentially an adult role; ergo, adolescents should not be parents.

But many are. More than 900,000 teenagers become pregnant each year in the United States, and about half a million give birth. Some 12 percent of all births—and 19 percent of first births—are to teenagers.[1] President Clinton in his 1995 State of the Union address termed teen childbearing "our most serious social problem." Yet teenage childbearing (usually to married teens) was considerably more common in the 1950s and 1960s than now. The teen birthrate dropped markedly through the 1970s and early 1980s.[2] Although it rose sharply between 1986 and 1991, it has fallen since to (in 2000) 49 births per 1,000 teens.[3] This rate is even lower (slightly) than the previous low record set in 1986.

So if the current rate is low in historical terms and is declining, should teen childbearing still be considered a significant social problem? An affirmative answer might be suggested by the experiences of other developed English-speaking and western European nations, which have rates far lower than the United States. This chapter reviews the evidence for and against the view that teen childbearing is still a serious social problem in the United States. We also explore the successes and failures of policies intended to help teen parents and their children and policies to discourage teen childbearing.

Teen parenting appears problematic for many reasons, but chiefly because it is, from a middle-class perspective, premature. Adolescents, both male and female, are expected to be acquiring education and experience to prepare themselves to work at the highest level they are capable of. Teenage childbearing occasioned no public concern in the 1950s and early 1960s, partly because most of the young mothers at that time were married but also because wives were not expected to have jobs. Now, most wives and mothers are employed. Because early parenthood interferes with a young woman's acquisition of education and job-related skills, it seems to guarantee a lifetime of poverty and hardship for a teenage mother and her baby. Indeed, precisely because it seems incompatible with developing a middle-class career trajectory, adolescent childbearing is perceived by many as reflecting, and perpetuating across generations, the values of an "underclass" whose behavior is shaped by a "culture of poverty."[4]

Central to the perceived link between teenage motherhood and "underclass" behaviors is concern about *unwed* teenage births. Unlike the 1950s, the majority of young mothers today are unmarried. Only about one in five—20 percent—of teenage births are in wedlock. The younger the teenage mother, the less likely she is to be married. These statistics trouble many people. For one-third of adults, any sex outside marriage is immoral,[5] and for a larger number, unmarried teenage sex is inappropriate. Hillary Rodham Clinton probably spoke for many when she remarked, "My theory is, don't do it till you're twenty-one and then don't tell me about it."[6] As well as violating norms against premarital teenage sex, unmarried teenage parenthood seems to exclude the babies' fathers from the obligations of parenthood. Only 15 percent of never-married teenage mothers ever have a child support order against the father of their child, and even those who have orders typically receive only one-third of the amount originally awarded to them.[7] In short, very few of these fathers, on paper at least, are required to provide financial support for their children over the long term, and many of their children grow up in persistent, unremitting poverty.

Throughout her first twelve years of parenthood, the income of the typical adolescent mother averaged barely 40 percent of the median income of all families with children—just $18,850 annually in 2001 dollars.[8,9] About 20 percent of that income comes from welfare benefits. More than 60 percent of African-American teenage mothers, half of Latinas, and just over one-quarter of whites are still in poverty when they are in their late twenties.[10]

Given the low educational attainment of so many teen mothers, their poverty is not surprising. Only 30 percent of women who give birth before age eighteen earn a regular high school diploma and a further 27 percent earn a GED (the high school equivalency certificate, which is less valued in the labor market than a regular diploma),[11-13] compared to a high school completion rate of 87 percent among all young adults. The children of teen mothers have numerous problems, which is no surprise given that most grow up in persistent poverty.[14] By age thirty, women who gave birth before turning age eighteen have on average 2.5 children. Compared to children born to older mothers, these children are more likely to be born at low birth weight, less likely to be rated in "excellent" health by their parents, more likely to be abused or neglected, more likely to repeat a grade in school, and more likely to run away from home. As adolescents, they more often drop out of high school; daughters are more likely to become adolescent mothers themselves, and sons are more likely to be in trouble with the juvenile justice system and go to prison.[15]

Clearly, teenage mothers and their children need help, and their problems are costing the nation dearly. To many people, teenage motherhood, especially unmarried teenage motherhood, seems grossly irresponsible, the result of carelessness at best and outright selfishness at worst. Young mothers want the rewards of parenthood, so critics argue, before they are financially or emotionally able to handle its responsibilities. Most teenagers are too self-centered or irresponsible to properly care for a child. A young woman whose education is interrupted by motherhood may never get back on track to support herself and her children above the poverty line. All too often, critics say, the price of her early motherhood is paid by her children and by the taxpayer.

The view of teenage motherhood as a life gone badly awry seems indisputable—until we take a close look at the young mothers themselves, study their lives, and listen to their experiences. Then the picture becomes more complicated. To many of the young women who become mothers, early parenthood does not seem such a disaster. Most middle-class girls see that motherhood would dash their hopes for college, travel, jobs, boyfriends, and fun; they do not become parents, and if they become pregnant they usually have an abortion. But what is true for middle-class teenagers is not so for the poor—and more than 80 percent of teenage mothers are poor or low-income before they ever give birth.[16]

## A Portrait of a Teenage Mother-to-be

Jackie, sixteen, the second of four children, has just learned she is pregnant. She is bright and strong-willed—for several years she was placed in the "gifted and talented" classes in her school, until she had to leave because of her disruptive behavior. Jackie fights often with her mother, who is worried by her daughter's willfulness and tries to impose strict rules about where she goes and with whom. Jackie's mother has struggled against the odds to raise her children. Having dropped out of high school when she was pregnant, she later took her GED and some community college classes. The family was on welfare until Jackie was three, but since then her mother has worked continuously, mainly in retail jobs.

Over the last two years Jackie's behavior in school has become quite erratic. While she can be passionately enthusiastic and involved when leading the cheerleading squad and in her music and PE classes, she is more often disaffected and "difficult," sometimes cutting school and often talking and playing jokes in her classes. She wants attention and affection from her peers, a job, and independence. Now she is startled to find herself pregnant by her new twenty-year-old boyfriend.

Jackie does not long ponder what to do. She decides to say nothing about her pregnancy until she is far enough along that nobody will nag her to have an abortion, for she has always been adamantly opposed to abortion on principle. She figures that even if she has to drop out of high school, she will eventually get her GED. She has already given up on her earlier ambition of going to college, because her grades are not good enough for a scholarship and her mother could not afford to help her with fees and living expenses. And while she is anxious about telling her family she is pregnant and wonders how she will cope, she is also excited to imagine herself a mother.

Jackie is a real person (with a different name) who is typical of teenage mothers in several ways, chief among them that she did not deliberately intend to become pregnant. More than 80 percent of all teen pregnancies, and more than 90 percent of pregnancies to unmarried teens, are inadvertent.[17] While many of these unplanned pregnancies are aborted, many others are carried to term, sometimes because a young mother decides she wants the baby, sometimes because she is opposed to or frightened by abortion, and often because she does not acknowledge her pregnancy early enough for an abortion or does not have ready access to abortion services. Indeed, 73 percent of all births to teenagers (and about 86 percent of births to unmarried teenagers) are not planned babies: the mothers say they would have preferred to be pregnant later, or not at all. These teenagers failed to take steps to prevent pregnancy. If teenagers needed to plan ahead in order to become pregnant—if, for example, they had to take a pill to do so, instead of taking a pill to avoid pregnancy—there might be only about one-fifth as many unmarried teen births as there are now.

## Unplanned Pregnancy among Teenagers

Teenagers are relative novices in sexual matters and are still acquiring the intellectual and emotional skills to act "responsibly" in these matters—that is, in accord with their own long-term goals. Many become pregnant precisely because sex is still relatively unfamiliar to them and because it evokes powerful and conflicting desires. In a letter to the editor in the

*San Francisco Chronicle*, one woman writes, "I grew up . . . in a white middle-class family. Although . . . always a good student, . . . I became pregnant during my last year of high school. As far as I can determine there were no deep psychological reasons I became pregnant—simply that old adolescent bugaboo, denial—the "it-can't-happen-to-me" syndrome."[18]

The rest of this chapter focuses on the economic, educational, and environmental difficulties that many teenage mothers have experienced throughout their lives, difficulties that can make teenage childbearing look "rational," for some. But we must not forget that most teenage parents, even those from the harshest backgrounds, typically say they did not intend to become pregnant. Preventing *unplanned* pregnancies among teenagers would have several benefits apart from the obvious one of reducing births to women who are unprepared to be mothers. Births to young teens would be decreased proportionately more than births to older teens (only 22 percent of births to fifteen to seventeen year olds in 1988, compared to 32 percent of births to eighteen to nineteen year olds, were described as "planned").[19] The average well-being of the children who are born to teenage mothers would be better than it is now, since babies who are unwanted or even just mistimed tend to have worse health and more developmental problems than babies who are planned.[20]

## The Demography of Teenage Childbearing

In all, there were about 750,000 teenage women with children in 2000, comprising about 8 percent of teenage women aged fifteen to nineteen.[21] Of the 485,000 teens who gave birth in 1999, about two-thirds (64 percent) were eighteen or nineteen, one-third (33 percent) were fifteen to seventeen, while only 2 percent were aged under fifteen.[22]

Even though girls under age fifteen are a very small fraction of teenage mothers—only two or three junior high girls (aged twelve to fourteen) in a thousand give birth each year (although the numbers are rising)—this group rightfully attracts considerable media and policy attention. Many of them have been victims of rape and molestation. Among teenagers who started to have sex before age fifteen, 60 percent report having had sex involuntarily, and 43 percent report that they have had *only* involuntary sex.[23] Even among those who have not been abused, motherhood is associated with very serious problems. Still children themselves, these girls have difficulty functioning effectively as parents. Most have not yet acquired the logical and objective thinking needed to make good decisions for themselves and their children.[24] Poor health at birth is common among the infants of very young mothers, who frequently receive no prenatal care or delay it until the third trimester of pregnancy.[25] School failure is almost guaranteed for these mothers, who have not yet made the difficult transition into high school. And the chances that their first teenage birth will be followed by another is very great. Nearly one-fourth (22 percent) of teen births are second or higher-order births, usually to teenagers who had their first child in their adolescence. These families face exceptionally bleak prospects.

Teenage parenthood is a community phenomenon as well as an individual one, and efforts to understand or change it need to keep that perspective in mind. Research suggests that young people respond to the cues provided by their neighborhoods as well as to their family environments.[26,27] Some neighborhoods and communities (defined for statistical purposes as a shared zip code) have persistently high teenage childbearing rates, exceeding 150 births each year per thousand teenagers, while others have persistently low rates, fewer than ten births per year.[28] Thus, some children grow up seeing adolescents all around them having babies, while others do not know a single teenage mother.

Jackie herself knows many teenage mothers. Her family lived in a public housing project until Jackie was twelve, when her mother finally earned enough to move the family out. Jackie still has many friends there and visits often. To the casual observer, it looks as though most of the teenage girls living there are either pregnant or have children; in fact, about half do. From Jackie's perspective, being a mother is something that every woman will come to sooner or later, and becoming a mother at a young age has its advantages. The teen mothers that she knows have a lot of energy for their babies and seem to enjoy them. Jackie knows that she will be at least as good a mother as most of them are. After all, her own mother was a teenage parent too.

We can imagine two broad types of explanations for the highly localized variations in birth rates evident in the statistical data. One explanation is cultural. In the United States, with its history and present practices of racial, ethnic, and linguistic segregation,[29] culturally similar people often live close to each other. Women who live nearby might share a set of cultural norms about families, women's roles, marriage, and sex that would tend to lead to early childbearing.

The other explanation, described as "structural," focuses on how the local economic and social structures might influence birth rates. Adolescents living in a poor neighborhood may respond in similar ways to the limited educational and economic opportunities they encounter. The cultural and structural explanations can coexist—indeed, cultural practices and norms can be shaped by the economic and educational context.

Recent research has confirmed that neighborhood characteristics—specifically, the degree of racial segregation of a neighborhood and the extent of poverty—have a significant impact on the rate of childbearing among teens in that community.[30] Highly segregated and very poor neighborhoods are typically described by teens living in them to be violent, physically deteriorated, and characterized by criminality and social disorder (drug dealing, gangs, and gun violence.).[31] Black and Latino teens face these neighborhood problems far more frequently than white teens. Data from the 1990 Census show that three of every ten poor blacks (compared to one in ten poor whites) live in a "concentrated poverty neighborhood," meaning a census tract where at least 40 percent of their neighbors are also poor. Communities of such concentrated poverty have bad schools, high unemployment, and few opportunities for teens. Most adults are unemployed and undereducated, so cannot help young people with finding work or furthering their education. In such a neighborhood, young, low-income women, whether black or white, may be less vigilant in avoiding pregnancy, and are certainly less likely to find employed or educated young men to marry.[32]

Welfare is often suggested as a reason that a teenager might have a child. After all, welfare offers a young woman an income if she has a baby.[33] Many people are surprised to learn, therefore, that only about half of all teenage mothers are on welfare at any given time, and as many as 30 percent never receive any public assistance.[34,35] Moreover, there is no good evidence that the existence of welfare causes teenagers to have babies. In fact, historical trends contradict this notion: the increases in out-of-wedlock births since the mid-1970s and the rise in the teen birth rate in the late 1980s occurred while welfare benefits were falling. In a comprehensive review of recent literature on this topic, the economist Robert Moffitt concluded that the research "shows little relationship between illegitimacy or marriage and receipt of welfare benefits."[36]

It is tempting to claim, as many politicians do, that young mothers are imposing an unnecessary burden on the public purse: that if they only waited to have their first child, or were married when they did so, most of them would not need welfare. As we shall see, this is largely a false hope. Teen mothers use welfare because they are poor. Even if they waited until they were older to have their first child, they would still be poor; if they married, their husbands would still be poor. They need welfare because they are poor, not because they are young.

## Who Are the Fathers?

A word is in order at this point about the fathers of babies born to teenagers. Fewer teen boys become fathers than teen girls become mothers. One-third of the California birth certificates for teenage mothers reported a teenage father. Nationally, in 1988, twenty-two teenage males per one thousand fathered a child. Most of the fathers of babies born to teenage women are adults between the ages of eighteen and twenty-four (75 percent, according to California birth certificate data from 1990).[37] On average, they are two and a half years older than the young women, so typical young couples would be a mother of seventeen and her boyfriend of twenty, or a mother of nineteen and her boyfriend of twenty-one. Among young men, there is evidence that early fatherhood imposes developmental and economic burdens on them which can disrupt their maturing or their educational attainment.[38] Many find it hard to maintain relationships with their children even when they want to, if they are no longer intimate with the mother.

A significant minority of fathers are much older than the teen mothers of their children. About 17 percent of fathers in 1990 were reported as aged twenty-five or older,[39] and about one-fifth (19 percent) of teen mothers report that their partner is at least six years older than they are.[40] Older fathers pose different challenges for policy than do the younger men and boys who have children with teenage girls. They are no longer engaged in the transitions of adolescence, and many of them dropped out of school long ago. More important, their relationships with their children's mothers may be more exploitative than those of younger men. Certainly policymakers and the general public appear to think this is so.

Most fathers of children born to teen mothers live apart from their children (although a substantial number of them have regular contact at least while the children are young), so policymakers are now searching for ways to compel them to pay child support. However, any difficulties fathers may encounter in finding work that pays enough to support a child are rarely addressed. Jackie's boyfriend, like many of the fathers just discussed, is not a teenager but is still very young, and he has neither a high school diploma nor a job.

Partly as a way to strengthen fathers' ties to their children, some policymakers and researchers have proposed trying to increase marriages among teenagers.[41] However, given the instability of teenage marriages,[42] the realistic fear that a young mother might be less likely to complete high school if she marries,[43] and the low levels of education and work experience of many of the fathers, marriage may not be a solution to the problems of teenage mothers (even if public policy were able to encourage it). As one study concluded, "For a majority of young women, early marriage has proven to be a temporary and unsatisfactory solution to adolescent motherhood. The immediate benefit is far outweighed by the foreclosure of life options by lack of education and underemployability [arising from early marriage]."[44]

For a young woman like Jackie who does not expect to go to college, there may be no compelling incentives to avoid pregnancy or to abort a pregnancy once conceived, just as there are no compelling reasons to marry the father of her child. While becoming a teenage single parent was not what Jackie had planned for herself, neither is she particularly worried by the prospect—in fact, she is happy about it. Teenagers, even more than older parents-to-be, underestimate the demands of babies and the long-term challenges of parenthood. They simply do not anticipate the efforts they will have to make in the future to get an education, a job, or even a steady boyfriend, nor how much more difficult those tasks will be with a baby than without one. Nor do they think that their children would suffer by having a young mother. Rather, they look around them and see families started when the mother was a teenager and oth-

ers started by older women and, for the most part, do not see any no-
ticeable differences between those two types of families. In low-income
neighborhoods, raising children is difficult for all families.

## Why Have a Baby—Why Not?

Indeed, given the alternatives, teenage motherhood looks quite appealing.
It is a route into adulthood, one that permits a young mother to remain
in some respects dependent on her family and, often, the government.
This pseudo-adulthood offers the adolescent meaningful responsibilities
and status without requiring that she become completely independent and
without cutting her off from her support systems. Higher-income youth
who avoid teenage parenthood may encounter a similarly protected transition when they go to college, where they typically remain financially dependent on their parents and on the government through grants, loans,
and work-study jobs.

Perhaps even more powerfully attractive is the opportunity to create
a brand new relationship—with the baby—and to reshape existing relationships with kin, boyfriend, and peers.[45] Teenage participants in a focus group of low-income mothers offered interesting remarks on this aspect of parenthood. One said, "Babies are unconditional love, they will
always love you." Another noted, "My mom wanted the baby, she was
happy." A third woman in this group remarked, to general agreement
and laughter, that some teenagers pretend to be pregnant: "A lot of girls
want babies, they want to be grown up. They get some attention while
everybody thinks they're pregnant and they have the miscarriage [later]."
And several people reported that their boyfriends ". . . just want to be
having babies."[46] These various reasons are certainly relevant to Jackie.
While she may not be entirely conscious of her motives, having a baby is
one way to ground herself in a family of her own making. She vaguely
hopes it will improve her relationship with her mother, and she expects
it will gain her status among her peers.

Many teenage mothers are emotionally needy, the consequence of
abuse, neglect, or molestation. One in four girls (24 percent) who become sexually active before age seventeen report experiences of involuntary sex.[47] A study of welfare recipients in Washington State revealed that
among welfare mothers who gave birth before they were eighteen, half
had been sexually abused and 10 percent or more physically abused.[48,49]
In parenthood many are seeking a more nurturing and healing relationship than they had experienced as children. Parenthood sometimes even
protects a young mother from further sexual abuse.[50] It can certainly
counterbalance the stress of living in a disorganized, possibly violent,
neighborhood. A young mother seen by one researcher in the field decided to carry a pregnancy to term because she "felt her life could be
truncated by a bullet in the violent neighborhood in which she lived . . .
at least she would have left a child behind to carry on."[51]

Teenage childbearing is strongly related to previous failure in school—girls who have not succeeded in other aspects of their lives find in motherhood an opportunity to demonstrate mastery of important skills. One study found that teenage girls who scored in the bottom fifth in math and literacy skills were five times as likely as girls who scored in the top fifth to have a child in the two years after being tested.[52] Teenage mothers' poor basic academic skills are undoubtedly one reason why so many remain poor throughout their lives. Emmy Werner, a scholar who has studied the contexts that lead to success or failure for children growing up in poverty, found that a child who has acquired effective reading skills by the fourth grade is more likely to avoid poor outcomes, including premature childbearing, in early adulthood.[53]

A large fraction of teenage mothers, in fact, drop out of school before they ever become pregnant. One analysis of a nationally representative sample of 5305 adolescent girls found only 5 percent giving birth while still enrolled in school. In contrast, 12 percent dropped out and then gave birth—and almost all of these had dropped out before becoming pregnant.[54] Graduation and GED recipiency rates were quite high—at 61 percent—among the young women who gave birth while still enrolled in school, but were very low—at 29 percent—among those who had dropped out before giving birth. Teen mothers who quit school before becoming parents are among the most difficult to reach and to help with school-completion programs. Nevertheless, motherhood does prompt some to return to school or to persist in their classes with greater enthusiasm, despite past failures and the difficulties of combining education with child rearing. Academic programs serving young mothers offer many examples of resilient and determined participants earning diplomas and going on to community college or even four-year universities. The evaluation of one program cited the case of Mercedes, who "is happy that her children see that she is going to school 'so they know that life isn't just sitting on your butt collecting welfare,' " or Jodie, who "displayed considerable persistence in the face of limited academic proficiency (she read at only the 7.0-grade level when she entered [the program]). . . . She took 15 months to get her GED: After failing the test the first time, she grew discouraged and took a four-month leave of absence from the program, but when she rejoined, she did well and earned the certificate four months later, when she was eight months pregnant with her third child."[55]

## Poverty and Teenage Childbearing: Twinned Experiences

Teenage pregnancy has numerous intertwined roots and its consequences branch out in many directions, yet amidst the complexity, two elements appear over and over: poverty and lack of opportunity. Teens from low-income or poor families (who are 38 percent of all teens, but account for 83 percent of teen births) are nine times more likely than teens from higher-income families to have a child.[56] They are more likely to start having sex at a young age, less likely to use contraception successfully (or at all), and less likely to have abortions.

Factors that are associated with poverty, such as the education of a teen's parents, her own educational motivation and expectations, her prior success in school, and the kind of neighborhood she lives in, are important predictors for whether a teen becomes pregnant. One study found that teens from families of low socioeconomic status who are doing poorly in school and who do not expect to continue their educations have childbearing rates five to seven times higher than the rates observed among more advantaged or successful teenagers from the same ethnic background.[57] The researchers emphasized, however, that substantial numbers of teenagers from even the most disadvantaged backgrounds did not become mothers. The study suggested that certain so-called protective factors, such as the strictness, supportiveness, and attentiveness of the teen's parents and her own religious observance, shielded these young women from the impacts of their environments.

Poverty makes it difficult for families and communities to offer young people the type of adolescence that, since the early nineteen hundreds, has been idealized in American culture: that is, a sheltered period of limited independence but intensive education that launches young people into adulthood. Affluent communities can offer a range of supervised recreational activities and appropriate part-time jobs for adolescents. Most importantly, middle-class adolescence has, since the 1950s, lengthened to include several years of college education, accompanied by work-study and other ready-made job opportunities, often followed by traineeships or internships after that. With these years of education and work experimentation, about half of all adolescents delay their transitions to full-time employment into the early twenties and beyond.

The other half of our youth are less fortunate. About one teenager in eight drops out of high school (13 percent of all young people ages eighteen to twenty-four in 1993), and a further third (33 percent) do not enter college within a year of finishing high school. Most of these young people face bleak alternatives. The earnings of high school dropouts and of people who complete only high school are exceedingly low and have been falling for the past two decades.[58] Employers look askance at young job-seekers with little education. Neighborhoods with high dropout rates tend also to have few jobs to offer.

Ethnic differences in income and education, as well as differences in adolescent childbearing rates, suggest that African-American teenagers, Latina teenagers, and white teenagers all experience adolescence differently.[59] The poverty rates of African-American and Hispanic teens are more than double the poverty rates of whites: two-thirds (68 percent) of Hispanic teenagers aged fifteen to nineteen and nearly the same fraction (63 percent) of African-American teenagers, compared to 28 percent of white teenagers, were living in poor or low-income households in 1992. Many of these disadvantaged teenagers have spent their entire lives in the deepening poverty and weakened social safety net that many American families have faced since the mid-1970s. Poverty means restricted access to opportunities for young people, particularly educational opportunities. Ninety-one percent of white youth graduate from high school and 58 percent go on to college.[60] By contrast, 84 percent of African-Americans graduate but only 34 percent go on to college, and 66 percent of Hispanic youth graduate and 28 percent go on to college. (Hispanics received only 4 percent of all bachelors' and associate's degrees granted in 1992 although they made up 12 percent of young adults.) The reasons African-American and Latino youth fare so poorly in the educational arena include discouragement and failure in inner-city schools, lack of family resources to pay for college, no family tradition supporting college attendance, and language barriers.[61]

These dramatic contrasts in educational attainment are mirrored by variations in ethnic-specific birth rates. Latina teens had a birth rate of 93.6 births per thousand women aged 15–19 in 1998, followed closely by African-Americans (85.4 births per thousand). These rates are about double the rates for white non-Hispanic teens, at 45.4 births per thousand. Since 1990, the Latina teen birth rate has fallen by 7 percent, the African-American rate by 24 percent and the white rate by 10 percent.[62] Even so, there are more white teenage mothers (about 45 percent of the total) than there are African-American (26 percent), Latina (25 percent) or teen mothers of other races (4 percent).[63]

Living arrangements vary across racial and ethnic lines. An African-American teen mother is the most likely overall to be living with her own or another family (64 percent), but that is mainly because she is unlikely to be married (only 4 percent are). Her alternative is living with friends, with an unmarried partner, or alone with her child, and one-third (32 percent) of African-American teen mothers are in one of these situations. One in five (18 percent) white teen mothers and a similar fraction (19 percent) of Latina teen mothers are similarly living apart from either family or husband. Approximately 50 percent of white teenage mothers and 40 percent of Latina teenage mothers are married.[64]

Set the approximately 40 percent of African-American and Latina women who give birth before they reach age twenty beside the approximately 70 percent of African-American and Latino teens whose education stops at high school or earlier, and it appears that early parenthood may be a response to, not merely a cause of, low levels of high school completion and college attendance in many neighborhoods. Some young, low-income women may think that they will lose little if they have a child early, and often their environments and the circumstances of their lives seem to support this opinion. While by most people's standards few of the teenagers who become parents are well equipped to raise a child,[65] these women might not be in a much better position if they waited. These young women probably have greater claim on familial resources (however limited) if they are teenage parents than if they give birth in their twenties. They may also have greater claim on social resources, in the form of specialized education programs for teenage parents, health care, or counseling. The employment picture for them could also favor teenage childbearing: they probably cannot find good jobs as teenagers, but by the time the are in their mid-twenties, when employers might more inclined to hire them, they will have completed their childbearing and their children will be in school full time.[66] In short, they may believe that having a child early in life is no worse than, and may even be better than, waiting until they are in their twenties.

And an influential minority among researchers are inclined to agree with the young women who believe this about their lives.[67,68] Adolescent childbearing, these researchers argue, can be an adaptive strategy in conditions of poverty and restricted opportunities, existing as an "alternative life-course" for young women ("alternative," that is, to the traditional life-course of education, then marriage, then childbearing.)[69-71] Even if it is adaptive or functional for only a minority of adolescent mothers, this minority is important and must be attended to by policymakers. These young women become parents (even if their pregnancy was originally unplanned) because it is the best option they see for themselves. Accordingly, in the last section of this chapter I outline some ways that the transition to adulthood could be improved for those young men and women who currently see no great benefit for themselves in delaying childbearing.

## Should Teenage Mothers Wait to Give Birth?

A central concern among researchers into teenage childbearing is to assess how much the *teenagerhood* of these young mothers matters: is their youth the source of the problems that they encounter, or is it their familiy's poverty, or the neighborhoods they live in, or the schools they attend? To answer this question, we need to know what fraction of teenage parents are disadvantaged by having children "too early," and what fraction are not disadvantaged or even benefit. And what is it about starting childbearing young that is most disadvantageous? Does it disrupt a young woman's education, as the conventional wisdom asserts? Is it that young mothers are not good at mothering or not healthy enough to bear children? Or does the impact chiefly lie in the consequences for parents and children of having more children in total? And if there are young women who are not disadvantaged by teenage motherhood, who are they? Are they drawn from certain groups of teenage mothers—older adolescents, or adolescents in the inner city, or African-American teens? Over the past decade researchers have explored such questions by applying modern statistical techniques to the rich stores of data describing individuals and families in the United States.

An ambitious effort to assess the consequences of teenage childbearing was published in June 1996 as the report *Kids Having Kids: A Robin Hood Foundation Special Report on the Costs of Adolescent Childbearing.*

This report, based on specially commissioned research by sixteen respected social scientists, compared outcomes for women whose first birth occurred before they were eighteen to the same outcomes for later childbearers, that is, women whose first birth occurred when they were twenty or twenty-one. Early and late childbearers are different kinds of people, in terms of race, ethnicity, family background, and other characteristics, and these researchers used statistical techniques to adjust as far as possible for important background differences that could affect the mothers' and children's chances later in life. The goal was to assess the *net* effect of teenage childbearing, calculated after taking into account background characteristics (such as family poverty) associated with teenage parenthood, on such outcomes as the mothers' incomes, years of education, and welfare use, the number of children they bore, and their children's health, schooling, and experiences in the foster care and the criminal justice systems. These effects were then translated into "costs to society of teenage childbearing," costs that are borne by teenage parents themselves as well as by their families, by government, and by health-care and other institutions. The sum total of these "costs of teenage childbearing" was estimated as $9 billion annually.

Nine billion dollars is a large figure. However, because the researchers were not able to adjust very precisely for pre-existing background differences between younger and older mothers, some of the "costs" of teenage childbearing might be misattributed; that is, these families might in fact have "cost" society as much even if the mothers had been over age twenty at their first births. This suspicion becomes more plausible once we look at the sources of the "costs" that are attributed in the report to teenage childbearing. Most of these costs are not associated with impacts on mothers' behavior: only 15 percent of the estimated costs of teenage childbearing are associated with mothers' employment and earnings that are reduced by their early childbearing. Rather, the researchers observe that *fathers* of children born to teenagers are employed less and earn less than similarly educated men who father children by older women; indeed, their labor market productivity is lower by $4.3 billion over the first thirteen years of their children's lives. This lower productivity is treated as a cost of teenage childbearing, constituting about half of the total estimated cost. But is it plausible to assume, as the report implicitly does, that these men would work more if their girlfriends delayed their first birth until age twenty-one?

More important, the majority of the studies in the report did not make very close comparisons between early and later childbearers, because, unfortunately, the data available to the researchers did not contain the information necessary to adjust statistically for many of the background factors that we know are relevant to adult success. Combine this problem with the fact that the report failed to find very large social costs of teenage childbearing in the place that we usually expect to find them—labor market outcomes for mothers—and it seems that the report does not provide compelling evidence for its claim that teenage childbearing itself imposes large costs on society. The evidence is more compelling that poverty, school failure, and disadvantage among adolescents impose large costs on society, both in the wasted talents of these young people and in the hardships visited on their children.

As we have seen, many teenage mothers are disadvantaged in important ways that were not adjusted for in most of the Robin Hood studies. These disadvantages, which presumably would still be present if women delayed childbearing but nothing else changed in their lives, may be the real explanations for some teenage mothers' worse educational attainment, the greater school difficulties of their children, and so forth. These disadvantages may even explain some early childbearing itself, for it is possible that some teen mothers would fare even worse later in life if they delayed having children. With the publication of a number of studies that have failed to find any significant detrimental impacts of early childbearing on children or mothers once the disadvantaged circumstances of young mothers are fully accounted for, this alternative interpretation of teenage parenthood among some groups of young mothers has gained ground.

These new studies share the feature that the early and late childbearers who are compared have very similar backgrounds—they are sisters, for example—so the researchers are "comparing like with like." In one such study, Arline Geronimus compared children born to sisters, one of whom gave birth as a teenager and the other who gave birth later, on various health measures.[72] She found that although children born to teenagers have more health problems than do children with older mothers, most of the children's problems should be attributed to the family backgrounds of the teen mothers, rather than their youthfulness. Another study by Geronimus and Sanders Korenman, which focused on children's cognitive development rather than on their health, found only small differences within pairs of cousins. The children of teenage mothers actually scored higher than their cousins born to older women on several measures. Geronimus and Korenman conclude that they have found "little support for an adverse effect of young maternal age [on child outcomes]." They continue, "[Y]oung children of teen mothers appear to fare no worse on developmental indicators [for early childhood] than their cousins whose mothers postponed childbearing."[73]

A paper by Hotz, McElroy, and Sanders which reached parallel conclusions regarding the socioeconomic consequences of early childbearing for mothers was part of the Robin Hood report. These authors reasoned that the women most similar to teenage childbearers were women who would actually have had a child as a teen, except that they miscarried instead. Accordingly, they compared the educational levels, hours worked, earnings, and welfare utilization of early childbearers and of women who had miscarried prior to age eighteen and had their first child at age twenty or twenty-one.[74] These authors find that teenage mothers work *more* and earn *more* through age thirty-four than similar women who delayed their childbearing until age twenty or twenty-one.[75] Even more striking are these authors' findings on welfare costs: "Taxpayers would save virtually nothing if all of these women had delayed their first births by 2 to 2.5 years. In fact, we estimate that the total annual expenditures on public assistance would increase slightly . . . if all of these women had delayed their childbearing. . . . That getting teen mothers to delay their child-bearing would result in additional costs to government, rather than savings, is a direct consequence of our findings that . . . teen mothers would earn less over their lifetimes if they were forced to delay their first births."[76]

Hotz and colleagues do find that teenage motherhood has other, possibly detrimental, consequences, such as a lasting reduction in a teen mother's marriage prospects and an increase (by one-third of a child) in completed family size, and thus a larger number of children spending more time in a single-parent household. Nevertheless, the conclusions of the Hotz et al. study mirror a caution by Geronimus and Korenman that "policy makers may be overly optimistic about the ability of programs that (solely) encourage delayed childbearing to improve the socioeconomic status of poor women and their children"[77] or, we might add, to save government money.

Because the fact that a mother is a *teenager* may not be a central element in "the problem of teenage pregnancy," reducing the teen child-bearing rate should probably not be a goal that we try to achieve at any cost. If a teen mother is poor because of disadvantages she has carried with her through her childhood and adolescence, then even if she were persuaded or bullied by public policy to avoid giving birth until she was twenty, she might not be measurably better off, and neither would her children. Yet many policymakers are expressing just such a single-minded determination to reduce adolescent childbearing. Many seem to believe that legislative deterrents for early childbearing, combined with policies that emphasize teenagers' legal standing as minors and that communicate clear disapproval of teenage sex and childbearing, could change teenagers' behavior. Hence the push for school boards to prohibit contraceptive education for teenagers in their schools—it seems to legitimate teenage sex. Along the same lines, many states have passed legislation requiring an unmarried mother under eighteen to live with a parent or guardian in order to receive welfare. Most dramatically, the state of Iowa recently convicted Amanda Simsek, a pregnant high school student, of "criminal fornication," a violation of a little-known law dating from the 1920s and resurrected especially for this teenager, that prohibits sex between unmarried adults of any age.[78] Even harsher proposals have been discussed and may become law: for example, to make any child born to an unwed mother under eighteen ineligible for welfare assistance.

It is impossible to know in advance whether any of these policies will discourage teenagers from having children. However, the evidence in this chapter suggests that many teenagers become parents inadvertently, and that some do so in response to unrewarding or painful circumstances in their lives. In this teenagers are like many adults, who also have unplanned births (79 percent of unplanned births are to women over twenty)[79] and who also have children to bring meaning into their lives. Teenagers are similarly only a small part of a broad social trend in having sex and children outside marriage (69 percent of unwed births are to women over twenty). Given the larger social contexts within which teenagers live, these new policy deterrents may have only minimal effects on the adolescent birth rate, while they impose hardships on teen parents and their children.

## Public Policy: Three Complementary Approaches

Whether they subscribe to conservative perspectives on teenage childbearing or not, most observers agree that it is a serious social problem in the United States today. For the minority of teenage parents whose economic and educational prospects are relatively good before they give birth, early motherhood severely constrains their options just as the conventional wisdom claims. For many other teen mothers, early parenthood is a symptom of their (and their boyfriends') blighted opportunities and the harsh circumstances of their lives. The Robin Hood report argues that the costs of teenage (as opposed to later) childbearing are great, but also concludes that the costs of social, familial, and educational deficits that precede early childbearing—problems which will not vanish even if teenage childbearing is eliminated—are greater still. Consequently, policymakers need a three-pronged approach to the problem: support teenage parents in becoming economically stable and in raising their children; improve the skills, life circumstances, and prospects of disadvantaged teens who are not yet parents so they become as motivated to postpone parenthood as more advantaged teens are; and give all teenagers the information, skills, means, and consistent encouragement to avoid unwanted pregnancy and parenthood.

Special programs and services for pregnant and parenting teen mothers, and even occasionally for teen fathers, are springing up in schools, clinics, and community-based organizations. Typically they have three goals: to increase school completion among teenage parents; to improve their job skills and employability; and to promote the health and development of their children. California, like many other states, started a teen parent program—Cal-Learn—as part of welfare reform. Intended to increase graduation rates among teenage parents under nineteen, the program incorporates case management (each teen parent has a case manager to help her organize her schooling, child care, health care, and other needs) and education-related financial bonuses and sanctions (participants receive bonuses of $100 for each school report card indicating satisfactory progress in school and $500 upon graduation, and lose $100 from their welfare check for each report showing unsatisfactory progress or dropping out).

The evaluation of Cal-Learn showed that this two-pronged approach did increase graduation rates. The impact was concentrated among teen parents who had already dropped out of school and who, with case managers' encouragement and the inducement of a $500 bonus, then earned their GEDs.[80] Evaluations of other similar programs—the Teen Parent Demonstrations in Chicago, IL, Camden, NJ, and Newark, NJ; the LEAP (Learning, Earning and Parenting) project in Ohio, and the New Chance program in multiple sites nationally—have also yielded useful information on what is possible with large-scale programs for teenage parents. First, they showed that welfare programs can incorporate distinct provisions for special populations and still operate successfully. Given that many welfare programs had never even tried to identify who on their caseload was a teenage parent, let alone provide enhanced services or target sanctions or bonuses to them, this was an important finding. Second, the components of these programs—financial incentives and/or sanctions for schooling combined with funding for associated needs (child care, especially), and case management services—did improve graduation rates and attendance at educational or job-training programs, albeit only moderately, among the participants.[81,82] However, none of these programs increased the number of teenage parents who delayed having another child.

These evaluations showed that programs for teenage parents must include multiple services and be available to them over some period of time. In this very disadvantaged population, interruptions to school, training, and work are commonplace and programs need to be flexible in responding to clients' changing and diverse needs. Programs must also make special efforts to reach teen parents who dropped out of school before becoming pregnant. Financial incentives are not enough to bring these women, most of whom had failed repeatedly in school, back into the educational system. They also need counseling and specialized services. The new federal legislation that requires all welfare recipients to start working at least twenty hours a week (or be in high-school full time) within two years of first receiving assistance, and which places a five-year total lifetime limit on assistance for the family, are inappropriate for these women and their children. Given their academic and personal problems and their responsibilities caring for their young children, few of these young mothers are able to become economically self-sufficient and productive members of the labor force within these relatively brief periods of time.

But programs to help teenage parents and their children are not what most policymakers these days are looking for. They want to reduce the number of teenage parents. In this regard the United States may have something to learn from other countries. No Western European or developed English-speaking nation has rates of adolescent pregnancy and childbearing even close to those prevailing in the United States. While the United States had a teen pregnancy rate (computed as births and abortions to women aged fifteen to nineteen) of 116 per thousand in 1990,[83] the rate in England and Wales at about the same time was 47 per thou-

sand, in Canada 40 per thousand, in Norway 40 per thousand and in the
Netherlands 10 per thousand.[84] Compared with other developed countries, pregnancy rates are high among white U.S. teens as well as among
African-Americans and Latinas. And it is not that fewer teenagers in these
countries are sexually active. While the proportion of teens having sex
varies across countries, the United States is in the middle of the range.
Similarly, while the fraction of (viable) pregnancies carried to term in
those countries ranged from a low of 45 percent (Norway) to a high of
66 percent (England and Wales), the United States is again in the middle with, in 1997, 55 percent.

There is little systematic knowledge about what factors contribute to
lower teen pregnancy rates in other countries, but some contrasts with
the United States stand out. The countries just mentioned have substantially lower rates of child and adolescent poverty than the United States.
Many have more extensive educational systems that help non-college-
bound youth train for jobs and enter careers. All have universal health
care programs, which typically make contraceptives readily available to
teenagers at no cost. Some are more candid about sexuality in the public media than is true in the United States and offer more extensive and
explicit sex education in schools.[85] Whatever the particular combinations
of social circumstances and policies present in each of these countries,
their experiences—and those of Japan, Denmark, Finland, New Zealand,
Hungary, and Czechoslovakia, to mention only a few more—all indicate
that the United States could have a far lower teenage pregnancy rate than
it does.

The high teen birth rate in the United States suggests to many people that policies such as school-based sex education, clinics in schools,
and access for adolescents to abortion and contraception have failed. A
more accurate conclusion, however, is that over the past twenty years
these policies have reaped major benefits, but much remains to be done.[86]
From 1960 through 1987 the pregnancy rate for sexually active teenagers
fell by about 20 percent, indicating steady improvement in teenagers'
use of contraception. By 1988 two-thirds of sexually experienced
teenagers reported using a method of contraception at first intercourse
and about 80 percent reported using a method currently. The proportion of teenagers using a condom the first time they had sex doubled
between 1982 and 1988. Far from failing, policies to help adolescents
avoid unwanted pregnancies and births have helped maintain the rate of
teenage births at a roughly constant level despite substantial increases in
sexual activity among teens.

To be sure, our high rate of unplanned pregnancy among teenagers
demonstrates that there is plenty of room for improvement in helping
adolescents with sexual matters. Fortunately, some strategies do work.
School-based sex education leads to increased contraceptive use among
teenagers,[87] and there is no good evidence that it makes them more likely

to have sex. To be most useful, sex education should provide accurate information as well as develop students' skills in making responsible choices about sex.[88] Schools can also make it much easier for teens to get birth control, through school-based or school-affiliated health clinics. Many teenagers do not have a health-care provider that they feel comfortable asking about birth control, and some do not have health insurance. Many are deterred from going to a family-planning clinic because they do not know how to get there, they believe it would cost money, and they do not want to be examined by a male doctor whom they do not know. Health-care services associated with schools offer teenagers comprehensive primary care, including reproductive health care, in an unthreatening and familiar setting.

The United States' greatest underutilized resource in helping teens deal with sex, however, is parents. In a 1996 survey of U.S. adolescents aged twelve to eighteen, 26 percent of teenagers—including 23 percent of teens who had already had sex—said they had *never* discussed sex with their parents. A majority (54 percent) had never discussed birth control with their parents, and only 36 percent said they had learned "a lot" about pregnancy and birth control from them. Yet these teenagers wanted information. Asked whether "most teenagers have enough information about the following topics," 58 percent said "no" for "How to use different kinds of birth control" and 45 percent said "no" for "Where to get birth control." More than half (55 percent) said that they would trust their parents to give them the most complete and reliable information about birth control. A further 39 percent would trust nurses and doctors, and 24 percent would trust their teachers, school nurses, or classes at school (although, strikingly, 40 percent said they had learned "a lot" about pregnancy and birth control from teachers, school nurses, or classes in school). In contrast, only 8 percent would trust friends for the "most reliable" information, 6 percent would trust siblings, and 4 percent would trust adult relatives other than parents.[89] The message to parents of teenagers is clear: help your teenagers by making information about sex and birth control part of an ongoing conversation.

But improving sex education and access to birth control for teenagers will not solve the problems of our most disadvantaged teens, those who feel they do not have good reasons to postpone parenthood. Education and employment are key here. One approach is "Life Options" programs that seek to provide teenagers with visions of viable alternatives to early pregnancy and low-income work. Because so many teenagers who become pregnant do not have high aspirations, these programs attempt to instill and support higher educational and career goals. Various state-level and national policies are also geared to the needs of the non-college-bound or disadvantaged adolescent. The 1994 School-to-Work Opportunities Act may spur some improvements in this domain, if it is fully implemented. This legislation encourages substantial reforms in the ways schools, especially high schools, prepare young people for the job market. Where fully implemented, these initiatives have the potential to improve the prospects of many young people.

The larger picture, though, is one of growing inequality and persistent poverty among families raising children and adolescents. The problems facing the young women who are most inclined toward early motherhood do not lend themselves to quick fixes, and most will not be corrected with School-to-Work or Life Options programs. It would be far better to make sure that parents and communities are able to give all children the education, health care, housing, and adult attention they need to grow up with skills and hope for the future.

## Rewriting Jackie's Story

Imagine now what Jackie's story might be if these prevention policies—to improve the life options of low-income children and to prevent unplanned teenage pregnancies—had been in place over the past twenty years. What would her life look like now? We could assume that she has attended well-maintained schools with fairly small classes and after-school activities geared to her interests. Throughout her childhood, her family's income has been sufficient for their needs, whether her mother received welfare or was earning and receiving the Earned Income Tax Credit as a supplement. Her neighborhood is safe and offers a range of recreational activities for children and adolescents. From seventh grade on, she has been participating in a Career Academy geared to students interested in the legal profession. Now that she is a tenth-grader, she goes into the courtroom as an observer each week. She is developing a passionate interest in the law, recognizing that this profession might use her theatrical as well as her language skills. She has a "Big Sister" mentor, an attorney, with whom she spends much of each weekend as a break from her somewhat conflicted relationship with her own parents. With her mentor she has visited local community colleges and the state university. She knows that if she can make the good grades needed for admission, she will receive the necessary financial aid to go to college.

She has had several conversations with both her mother and her mentor about relationships, about sex, and about preventing pregnancy. Recognizing that early motherhood would interfere with her goal of becoming an attorney, and that HIV is a real and devastating risk facing her, she is cautious about having sex. With the support of the adults around her, she insists that she is not yet ready to start having sex with her new boyfriend. If the relationship lasts and the couple does start having sex, she will go on the pill and the couple will go for HIV tests well beforehand.

Pie in the sky? Such a childhood and adolescence are typical of middle-class teenagers in the United States, and common among teenagers in many European countries. Public policies, at least as much as parental luck and skill, create healthy and successful children and adolescents. The time is long past for the United States to invest in such policies.

## Notes

1. U.S. Census Bureau, Statistical Abstract of the United States, 2000. Tables 85, 88, 92. Available online at http://www.census.gov/prod/2001pubs/statab/sec02.pdf.

2. The Alan Guttmacher Institute, *Sex and America's Teenagers* (New York and Washington: The Alan Guttmacher Institute, 1994).

3. Child Trends, *Facts at a Glance 2001* (Washington DC). Available online at http://www.childtrends.org/factlink.asp.

4. The Alan Guttmacher Institute, *Sex and America's Teenagers.*

5. Andrew Greeley, Robert T. Michael, and Tom W. Smith, "Americans and Their Sexual Partners," *Society* 27(5):36–43, 1990.

6. Quoted in Alexander Cockburn's column printed in the *Oakland Tribune*, June 2, 1996.

7. Congressional Budget Office, *Sources of Support for Teenage Parents.* Washington, DC: U.S. Government Printing Office, 1990.

8. Rebecca Maynard (ed.), *Kids Having Kids: A Robin Hood Foundation Special Report on the Costs of Adolescent Childbearing* (New York: Robin Hood Foundation, June 1996).

9. Bureau of the Census, U.S. Department of Commerce, *Statistical Abstract of the United States 2000,* Table 748.

10. Kristin A. Moore, David Myers, D. F. Morrison, C. Nord, B. Brown, and B. Edmonston, "Age at First Childbirth and Later Poverty," *Journal of Research on Adolescence* 3(4):393–422, 1993.

11. Steven V. Cameron and James J. Heckman, "The Nonequivalence of High School Equivalents," *Journal of Labor Economics* 11(1):1–47, 1993.

12. R. Murnane, J. B. Willett, and K. P. Boudett, "Do High School Dropouts Benefit from Obtaining a GED?" *Educational Evaluation and Policy Analysis* 17(2):393–422, 1995.

13. Maynard, *Kids Having Kids.*

14. Author's estimates from the 1988 National Survey of Family Growth.

15. Maynard, *Kids Having Kids.*

16. The Alan Guttmacher Institute, *Sex and America's Teenagers.*

17. Ibid.

18. Letter from Mariana Moore; Letters to the Editor, *San Francisco Chronicle*, July 22, 1996.

19. Kathryn Kost and Jacqueline Forrest, "The Intention Status of U.S. Births in 1988: Differences by Mother's Socioeconomic and Demographic Characteristics," *Family Planning Perspectives* (January/February 1995).

20. Sarah S. Brown and Leon Eisenberg (eds.), *The Best Intentions: Unintended Pregnancy and the Well-Being of Children and Families* (Washington, DC: Institute of Medicine, National Academy Press, 1995).

21. U.S. Census Bureau, Current Population Report. P20–537, Tables A2, FG3, FG5.

22. Stanley Henshaw, "U.S. Teenage Pregnancy Statistics with Comparative Statistics for Women Aged 20–24," Alan Guttmacher Institute, March 5, 2001. Available online at http://www.agi-usa.org/pubs/teen_preg_sr_0699.html.

23. The Alan Guttmacher Institute, *Sex and America's Teenagers.*

24. Beatrix A. Hamburg and Sandra L. Dixon, "Adolescent Pregnancy and Parenthood," in Margaret K. Rosenheim and Mark F. Testa (eds.), *Early Parenthood and Coming of Age in the 1990s* (New Brunswick, NJ: Rutgers University Press, 1992).

25. National Center for Health Statistics, "Advance Report of Final Natality Statistics, 1987," *Monthly Vital Statistics Report* 38(3):1–48; "Advance Report of Final Natality Statistics, 1988," *Monthly Vital Statistics Report* 39(4):1–48; "Advance Report of Final Natality Statistics, 1989," *Monthly Vital Statistics Report* 40(8), 1–56, 1989, 1990, 1991.

26. Anne C. Case and Lawrence F. Katz, "The Company You Keep: The Effects of Family and Neighborhood on Disadvantaged Youth," *National Bureau of Economic Research.* Working Paper #3705, 1991.

27. Jeanne Brooks-Gunn, Greg J. Duncan, Pamela Kato Klebanov, and Naomi Sealand, "Do Neighborhoods Influence Child and Adolescent Development?" *American Journal of Sociology* 99(2):353–395, 1993.

28. Adolescent Pregnancy Project, *California Potential Project Areas for Adolescent Pregnancy Prevention Programs.* Maternal and Child Health Programs, School of Public Health, University of California, Berkeley. Jeffrey R. Gould, Director, 1996.

29. Douglas Massey and Nancy Denton, *American Apartheid: Segregation and the Making of the Underclass* (Cambridge: Harvard University Press, 1993).

30. Clea Sucoff and Dawn Upchurch, "Neighborhood Context and the Risk of Childbearing among Metropolitan-area Black Adolescents," *American Journal of Sociology* 63(4):571–585, 1998.

31. D.M. Upchurch, C.A. Aneshensel, C.A. Sucoff, and L. Levy-Storms, "Neighborhood and Family Contexts of Adolescent Sexual Activity," *Journal of Marriage and the Family* 61:920–933, 1999.

32. William Julius Wilson, *The Truly Disadvantaged* (Chicago: University of Chicago Press, 1987).

33. "Welfare" refers to the Temporary Assistance to Needy Families (TANF) program which provides a fixed amount of money (a "block grant") to each state to develop its own poverty-relief program for families with children. Prior to 1996 "welfare" referred to the Aid to Families with Dependent Children (AFDC) program.

34. Estimates based on data in the *1994 Green Book: Overview of Entitlement Programs.* Committee on Ways and Means, U.S. House of Representatives. Tables 10-24 and 10-27.

35. Maynard, *Kids Having Kids.*

36. Robert Moffitt, "Welfare Reform: An Economist's Perspective," *Yale Policy Review* 11(1):1993.

37. California Family Impact Seminar, California State Library Foundation, *Background Briefing Report: Teen Pregnancy and Parenting in California* (Sacramento: California State Library, 1994).

38. Sarah Ann Brown, "The Potential Effects of Welfare Reform Policies on Promoting Responsible Fatherhood," Doctoral Dissertation, University of California, Berkeley, 1995.

39. California Family Impact Seminar, *Background Briefing Report: Teen Pregnancy and Parenting in California.*

40. The Alan Guttmacher Institute, *Sex and America's Teenagers.*

41. Maris A. Vinovskis and Lindsey Chase-Lansdale, "Hasty Marriages or Hasty Conclusions?" *Public Interest* 90:128–132, 1988.

42. Frank Furstenberg, "Bringing Back the Shotgun Wedding," *Public Interest* 90:121–127, 1988.

43. Dawn M. Upchurch and James McCarthy, "The Timing of a First Birth and High School Completion." *American Sociological Review* 55:224–234, 1990.

44. Hamburg and Dixon, "Adolescent Pregnancy and Parenthood," p. 23.

45. Marilyn Benoit, "Intrinsic Psychological Issues in Teenage Pregnancy." Paper presented in "Programs for Unwed Teen Mothers," Seminar Series on Persistent Poverty, American Enterprise Institute. Washington, DC: 1994.

46. Unpublished research notes for Carol Chetkovich, Jane Mauldon, Claire Brindis, and Sylvia Guendelman, "Unappealing Choices and Limited Information: Low-Income Women's Experiences with Family Planning." Berkeley: University of California, UC DATA Working Paper #10, 1996.

47. The Alan Guttmacher Institute, *Sex and America's Teenagers.*

48. P. Roper and G. Weeks, "Child Abuse, Teenage Pregnancy and Welfare Dependency: Is There a Link?" Olympia: Washington State Institute for Public Policy, Evergreen State College, 1993.

49. Debra Boyer and David Fine, "Sexual Abuse as a Factor in Adolescent Pregnancy and Maltreatment," *Family Planning Perspectives* 24(1):4–11, 1992.

50. Judith Musick, *Child Poverty and Public Policy* (Washington, DC: Urban Institute, 1994).

51. Benoit, "Intrinsic Psychological Issues in Teenage Pregnancy."

52. Karen Pittman and Charles Govan, *Model Programs: Preventing Adolescent Pregnancy and Building Youth Self-Sufficiency* (Washington, DC: Children's Defense Fund, 1986).

53. Emmy Werner, *Overcoming the Odds: High-Risk Children from Birth to Young Adulthood* (Ithaca, NY: Cornell University Press, 1992).

54. Upchurch and McCarthy, "The Timing of a First Birth and High School Completion."

55. Janet C. Quint, Denise F. Polit, Hans Bos, and George Cave, *New Chance: Interim Findings on a Comprehensive Program for Disadvantaged Young Mothers and Their Children: Executive Summary* (New York: Manpower Demonstration Research Corporation, 1994).

56. The Alan Guttmacher Institute, *Sex and America's Teenagers.*

57. Allan F. Abrahamse, Peter A. Morrison, and Linda J. Waite, *Beyond Stereotypes: Who Becomes a Single Teenage Parent?* (Santa Monica, CA: Rand Corp., 1988).

58. Harrell R. Rodgers Jr., *Poor Women, Poor Children: American Poverty in the 1990s* (Armonk, NY: M. E. Sharpe, 1996).

59. Data for educational attainment and teenage births are available only for the three largest ethnicities in the United States: non-Hispanic whites, African-Americans, and Hispanics.

60. These proportions and the ones that follow are calculated by the author from tables in the *1995 Statistical Abstract of the United States.*

61. National Commission on Children, *Beyond Rhetoric: A New American Agenda for Children and Families. Final Report of the National Commission on Children* (Washington, DC: U.S. Government Printing Office, 1991).

62. Stephanie J. Ventura, Sally C. Curtin, and T.J. Matthews, "Variations in Teenage Birthrates 1991–1998: National and State Trends," *National Vital Sta-*

*tistics Reports.* vol. 48, no. 6. (Hyattsville MD: National Center for Health Statistics, 2000). Available online at http://www.cdc.gov/nchs/data/nvsr/nvsr48/nvs48_6.pdf.

63. Author's calculations based on data from Child Trends, *Facts at a Glance,* 1999.

64. Author's calculations based on household living arrangements data from Bureau of the Census, *1993 Current Population Reports.*

65. "Most people" in this context include older mothers who started having their children as teenagers. The low-income adult women who participated in the focus groups mentioned earlier expressed great concern about the teenagers they saw having children.

66. Frank Furstenberg, Jeannie Brooks-Gunn, and S. Philip Morgan, *Adolescent Mothers in Later Life* (Cambridge: Cambridge University Press, 1987).

67. Arline T. Geronimus, "On Teenage Childbearing and Neonatal Mortality in the United States," *Population and Development Review* 13:2 245–279, 1987.

68. Kristin Luker, *Dubious Conceptions* (Cambridge: Harvard University Press, 1996).

69. Beatrix Hamburg, "Subsets of Adolescent Mothers: Developmental, Biomedical and Psychosocial Issues," in J. Lancaster and B. Hamburg (eds.), *School-Age Pregnancy and Parenthood: Biosocial Dimensions* (New York: Aldine De Gruyter, 1986).

70. Carol Stack, *All Our Kin* (New York: Harper & Row, 1974).

71. Donna L. Franklin, "Early Childbearing Patterns among African Americans: A Socio-Historical Perspective," in Rosenheim and Testa (eds.), *Early Parenthood and Coming of Age in the 1990s.*

72. Arline Geronimus, "Maternal Youth or Family Background: On the Health Disadvantages of Infants with Teenage Mothers," *American Journal of Epidemiology* 137(2):213–225, 1993.

73. Arline T. Geronimus, Sanders Korenman, and Marianne M. Hellemeier, "Young Maternal Age and Child Development," *Population and Development Review* 20(3):585–609, 1994.

74. Joseph Hotz, Susan Williams McElroy, and Seth Sanders, "Mothers: Effects of Early Childbearing on the Lives of the Mothers," in Rebecca Maynard, (ed.), *Kids Having Kids: Economic Costs and Social Consequences of Teen Pregnancy* (Washington DC: Urban Institute Press, 1997).

75. These findings are from a paper by Hotz and colleagues published after the Robin Hood Report was issued. The report notes slightly lower earnings among teen mothers than older mothers because the comparisons are made over the first thirteen years of parenthood, not through a fixed age. After thirteen years of parenthood, teen mothers are younger than older mothers and have slightly lower lifetime earnings.

76. V. Joseph Hotz, Susan Williams McElroy, and Seth G. Sanders, "The Costs and Consequences of Teenage Childbearing for the Mothers and the Government," in Maynard (ed.), *Kids Having Kids: Economic Costs.*

77. Arline Geronimus and Sanders Korenman, "The Socioeconomic Consequences of Teen Childbearing Reconsidered." National Bureau of Economic Research. Working Paper #3701, 1991.

78. Reported in the *Wall Street Journal,* July 8, 1996.

79. The Alan Guttmacher Institute. *Sex and America's Teenagers.*

80. Jane Mauldon et al., *The Impact of California's Cal-Learn Demonstration Project: Final Report* (UC DATA, University of California Berkeley, June 2000). Availalbe online at http://ucdata.berkeley.edu/.

81. David Long, Robert G. Wood, and Hilary Kopp, *The Educational Effects of LEAP and Enhanced Services in Cleveland.* Manpower Demonstration Research Corporation (MDRC), October 1994.

82. Rebecca Maynard, "The Teenage Parent Demonstration Program." Paper presented in "Programs for Unwed Teen Mothers," Seminar Series on Persistent Poverty. Washington, DC: American Enterprise Institute, 1994.

83. Stephanie Ventura et al., "Trends in Pregnancy Rates for the United States, 1976–97: An Update." *National Vital Statistics Reports,* vol. 49, no. 4. (Hayattsville MD: National Center for Health Statistics, 2001). Available online at http://www.cdc.gov/nchs/data/nvsr/nvsr49/nvsr49_04.pdf.

84. The Alan Guttmacher Institute, *Sex and America's Teenagers.*

85. Elise F. Jones et al., *Teenage Pregnancies in Industrialized Countries* (New Haven and London: Yale University Press, 1986).

86. Jane Mauldon and Kristin Luker, "Does Liberalism Cause Sex?" *The American Prospect* 24:80–85, 1996.

87. Jane Mauldon and Kristin Luker, "The Effects of Contraceptive Education on Method Use at First Intercourse," *Family Planning Perspectives* (January/February 1996).

88. Douglas Kirby, L. Short, J. Collins, D. Rugg, L. Kolbe, M. Howard, B. Miller, F. Sonenstein, and L. Zabin, "School-Based Programs to Reduce Sexual Risk Behaviors: A Review of Effectiveness," *Public Health Reports* 109:3, 1994.

89. Kaiser Family Foundation, *The 1996 Kaiser Family Foundation Survey on Teens and Sex: What They Say Teens Today Need to Know, and Who They Listen To.* Princeton Survey Research Associates, June 1996.

# 4

# Children of Divorce: A Society in Search of Policy

## Judith S. Wallerstein

I first met Ellen when she was three and interviewed her for the fourth time when she was fourteen. Ellen is one of 130 children whose life experience I had decided to study during and after their parents' divorce in the early seventies. She was the only child of a professional couple who had been happily married, according to both parties' accounts, until the mother became pregnant against her husband's wishes. The marriage cascaded rapidly downward after Ellen was born. The father began to drink heavily, the mother's anger mounted, and she filed for divorce.[1]

When I interviewed Ellen at age fourteen, we were scarcely seated before she began. "Dr. Wallerstein, I have something very important to ask you. When will I be old enough that I don't have to visit my father? I feel like a stranger at my father's place, like I don't belong there."

"Why do you go?"

"Because I have to. The court said so, a long, long time ago. I have to go two weekends every month and all summer."

"Why does your father want you to come to him?"

"I don't know that, either."

"Do you feel that he loves you?"

"No," said the girl. "He doesn't love me. I know that because he doesn't respect me. People who love people respect them. He never asks me whether I want to come or what I want to do."

Her words came tumbling out with the urgency of her distress. "Every time I go to visit my father I get eczema on my hands. My hands get red and they begin to hurt and to blister, and the eczema starts on the Wednesday, or sometimes on Thursday, and usually goes away Sunday. Just on the weekends that I go there. My mom took me to the doctor. There was nothing they could do."

"Why do you think that happens?" I asked.

"I am very frightened of him. He has a terrible temper. I'm always afraid that he will hit me. He hasn't, but his yelling frightens me and he yells a lot."

"What happens," I asked, "if you ask him whether you can go to a school activity like a school dance or game on the weekend of your visit?"

Ellen grimaced. "I can't go. Once, I had a fever, and my mom called him and asked him whether I could stay home. He said he would drive down to see whether I really had a fever. So, I got out of bed when he came, and I met him in his car, and he said, 'Yes, you have a fever. All right, you can stay in bed.'" Her face clouded as she added, "When summer comes all the other kids in my class look forward to it. I dread it. It's terrible for me, I hate it so much. There are no kids where he lives. I'm all alone there."

"What would you like to do, Ellen, if you had your full choice in the whole, wide world?"

"I would like to be able to go to see him once a month, and sometimes not at all. My friends decide for themselves how they spend their time. Why can't I?"

I told Ellen that I would soon be talking to a group of judges and I wanted to help them to understand situations such as hers. How should I present her views? Should she, when she was six years old, have been told, then, that she did not need to visit her father? Ellen thought for a long time. Finally, she said, "I guess, when I was six, I wouldn't have known how much it would hurt him if I didn't visit. But now that I'm fourteen, I feel different."

The decisions regarding Ellen's life were made by the court when the child was very young. Doubtless, the court expected that her parents would be responsive to their child's developmental needs and wishes. I have found no evidence from my decades of work with divorced parents that this kind of flexibility is expectable, or that the amount of education parents have makes a difference. Rather, my observations are that the divorced family is not only more vulnerable than the intact family but often it is also brittle and relatively unresponsive to the changing needs of the children, especially so when visiting and custody were set by the court or negotiated in anger. Moreover, in this case, as in a great many divorces, the anger between the parents had not cooled, and they had not spoken civilly to each other in ten years.[2]

The court no doubt also assumed that Ellen would eventually raise a voice in her own behalf. But our evidence of many years has shown repeatedly that children in divorced families often feel weak and insecure, less able to assert their own wishes than their counterparts in intact families. The court order is a powerful, intimidating presence in their lives. Moreover, these children are often keenly aware of their role as pawn or battle trophy in the parental struggle, of not being loved or fought over for their own sake. Such children fear that if they speak up strongly for their own needs, there will be dire consequences for whichever parent they view as the most vulnerable. This concern is a heavy deterrent for a compassionate child.[3]

There is a widespread but erroneous notion that divorced families willingly return to court to seek changes in custody and visitation arrangements that are not working. Many do; more do not. When I asked Ellen's mother whether she had considered doing so, she said, "My former husband is rich and powerful. He will claim in court that I have brainwashed Ellen and he will ask for a change of custody. I have neither the money nor the emotional strength to fight him."

The widespread policy of court-ordered visits with the noncustodial parent is based on the court's belief that such visits promote the child's best interests by strengthening an affectionate bond between father and child. This is an unsupported proposition. There is no research evidence that either the frequency or the amount of contact between noncustodial parent and child is related to good outcome in the child. It is also the assumption of many judges that visiting will increase the father's willingness to provide economic support. This too is unsupported. Fathers who have good relationships with their children and are regularly employed are likely to pay child support, but there is no evidence that the visiting itself is causative.[4] It is, in fact, remarkable, considering the prominence of visiting in court orders and its importance in public policy discussions in family law, that there is not a single published study of what transpires during visits, court-ordered or voluntary. For Ellen and the other children in our study, the years of court-enforced visiting had none of the anticipated beneficial effects. Although she was his only child, her wealthy father paid only $150 a month toward her support, an amount which had been set when he was a struggling graduate student.

Now in her late twenties, Ellen has refused for many years to see him. She says firmly, "I have no relationship with my father." A recent national study accords with our findings regarding Ellen and the anger that she and many of her peers feel; it reports that many young adults from divorced families are angry at one or both parents, mostly at fathers, and warns that they can not be counted on to provide the emotional or economic support that their aging parents may someday need.[5]

The time frame of the court system and court policy is "the present." Court orders are shaped for the here and now in the life of the child and the family. But the time of childhood extends into a long future, and the child is ever changing. How to reconcile these two frames of reference in policies that will protect the growing child remains an unsolved issue in court policy and practice. And, just as important, how to develop policies that the growing child will view without bitterness, but as compassionate and just and as protective of her interests, is a serious, unresolved challenge.

I turn now to Steve, who was six years old when we met shortly after his parents separated. He too is a member of the same group of young people in the long-term study of children of divorce.[6] He and his two younger brothers were happy and well-parented in the predivorce family. At age thirty, he remembers their sandbox play and still recalls vividly the many bedtime stories his father told him and the wonderful times they shared. His mother sought divorce because of the father's alleged affair with the teenage baby-sitter, an accusation the father vehemently denied. Steve was thunderstruck by the marital breakup and did not speak at school, to his classmates or the teacher, for the entire year that followed.

At the time of my fourth follow-up interview with Steve, he was seventeen years old, working in a gas station, and hoping someday to go to college. Over the years, his father, who has held middle management positions in companies in several states, and who has remarried three times, seldom visited Steve and rarely paid the court-ordered child support. Steve grew up poor, without health insurance. To support her three children on her own, his mother held two jobs simultaneously, as a security guard climbing the catwalks of a deserted factory at night, and as a substitute teacher struggling against constant fatigue during the day.

During his childhood and adolescence, Steve remained preoccupied with thoughts about his father. He seemed unable to obtain relief from the pain of his father's abandonment or closure on the divorce which abruptly changed his world. Ten years after the divorce, when he was sixteen, he still spoke of his father with tears in his eyes. He said, "What I've realized is that my dad is selfish. It's like he's in quicksand. The more he struggles to have fun, the more selfish he becomes. It's like he didn't realize that I wanted to see him or that a letter from him was like a special reward. He doesn't understand that you can really hurt other people. To divorce is to leave them stranded." His hands began to shake as he added, "My dad loves life, but he has no heart for others." Like Ellen, Steve has had no relationship with his father during his adult years. But unlike Ellen, he continues to hope that his father will reach out lovingly to him and ease his pain.

Ellen and Steve stand at the opposite poles of public policy. The court remained a powerful, intrusive influence for many years in Ellen's young life. Her own, age-appropriate adolescent agenda was discouraged under a court order aimed at maintaining her solo time with her father—a court order that remained in place, unmodified, since she was a young child. Ellen's situation, and the millions like it, raises serious questions about the long-term psychological and social effects on the child of the widespread use of court orders to regulate the child's life, orders which are all too soon out of sync with the child's changing developmental needs and wishes. Do the policies employed by the courts, which intervene in the life of the child and the postdivorce family, achieve their goal of promoting the best interests of the child? Or are the more powerful and perhaps more lasting effects exactly those that were unintended and unforeseen?

Unlike Ellen, Steve has grown up under a social and legal policy of *laissez-faire*. For him, the court's time frame was "never." The social institutions such as the court and the government, like his father, took no interest in him and initiated no effective legal action in his behalf to secure regular child support. Nor did they provide any guidance for his father or help for the boy. Although Steve is the son of two college graduates, there is no provision for his college education. A sensitive, moral youngster, Steve comes to young manhood economically, socially, and psychologically disadvantaged. Five years after the divorce his mother said, "I feel dead inside." Steve, now age thirty, feels that he has paid dearly for his parents' divorce.

What responsibility, if any, does society bear for protecting Steve and the millions of other children who, like him, have suffered from parent's emotional and economic abandonment, often in favor of commitment to new children in subsequent marriages? What responsibility should the community have to provide economic and social support for the single parent whose exhausting jobs leave her with no time and no energy for her own life or for parenting her children? And, most of all, assuming that a moral community bears responsibility for the well-being of its children, what can society do? These are the central questions that we confront today which have haunted us since we first began to listen to the voices of our children.

## Demographics of Divorce

Divorce in the United States had been rising for more than a century. In the late sixties it began a steep climb, reaching an all-time high in the late seventies. One researcher concluded in 1992 that at least 40 percent of young adult women were likely to divorce, 30 percent to remarry, and 16 percent to divorce twice if current divorce rates continued. Although divorce levels decreased slightly in the eighties, demographers concur that there is no evidence of a significant downward trend.[7]

More than one million children each year have experienced their parents' divorce since the mid-1970s. Formal divorce statistics undercount the number of children who have separated parents, both because many couples separate without officially divorcing, and because many couples who are not married break up their relationship after they have had a child. In 1988, 15 percent (9.7 million) of all children under age eighteen lived with a divorced or separated parent. An additional 7.3 million (11 percent) lived with a stepparent. Overall, 26 percent of our nation's children have already experienced their parents' separation or divorce.[8]

The great majority of children live with their mothers after divorce. Approximately 13 percent of children live with their fathers. Although joint custody is a legal option in forty states, the number of children in joint physical custody varies widely from a high of 19 percent in a recent study of two California counties to an estimated low of 5 percent in Massachusetts.[9] The single mother or the remarried mother-stepfather family unit provides the dominant family structure for the child after the marital breakup. Because half of first divorces occur by the seventh year of the marriage, there is a preponderance of young children in the divorced population. Given the high incidence of remarried and redivorced families as well as the numerous brief and long-term informal liaisons that occur, many youngsters grow up in several different households with a changing cast of parents, stepparents, and live-in lovers.

## Research Findings

The assessment of the impact of divorce on any population has been rendered infinitely more difficult by the profound impact of the high divorce rate on society as a whole. The higher incidence of divorce has significantly raised levels of anxiety in relationships between men and women in courtship and marriage as well as between children and their parents in intact families.

There is little that is reassuring about the condition of children of divorce in single-parent or remarried homes. A range of longitudinal studies and national surveys shows that children in divorced and remarried families, when compared with those in intact families, demonstrate more antisocial acting out, more aggression directed toward authority figures, more difficulty with peers, more depression, more learning difficulties, and more school dropout. Social agencies, clinics, and inpatient psychiatric settings report a high incidence of child and adolescent patients from divorced families as compared to their representation in the general population. Analysis of national data from the National Center for Health Statistics tells us that, in 1988, children in single-parent and remarried families were two to three times more likely to have emotional and behavioral problems and learning difficulties than those in intact families.[10] The fact that these unhappy findings occur equally in children in single families and those in remarried families is important, because remarried families have significantly higher incomes and are socioeconomically equivalent to intact households.

One domain that has been little investigated until recently is the physical health of children from divorced families. Early reports show a concurrence of somatic and psychological illness including asthma. A significantly higher incidence of physical illness in children of divorce was also reported in a large recent public health study.[11]

A review of many studies also shows that parental divorce has a detrimental impact on the life-course. Compared with those raised in intact two-parent families, adults who experienced a parental divorce during their childhood have less sense of psychological well-being, more behavioral problems, less education, a lower standard of living, less marital satisfaction, heightened risk of divorce, heightened risk of being a single parent, and poorer psychological health. One recent public health report shows a shorter life span among adults whose parents divorced when they were children.[12]

The California Children of Divorce ten-year and fifteen-year longitudinal studies of children in a middle-class suburban community revealed a delayed (or sleeper) effect that appears at late adolescence. Young people from divorced families anticipate disappointment in their own adult relationships. Young women especially have difficulty at adolescence in separating psychologically from their mothers and fear both success, which will give them what many of their mothers failed to achieve, and failure, which would repeat their parents' experience.[13] Some, like Ellen, feel powerless in their relationships with men. Others say, "I never saw a good relationship between a man and a woman. Love and intimacy are strange ideas to me." Still others, like Steve, marry in haste, then divorce after a brief unhappy marriage, and go on with sad resignation to lead isolated, lonely lives. Steve's conclusion about himself would be familiar to many: "If a woman gets to know me she won't love me."

Parental divorce experienced in early childhood has been linked in national studies to early sexual activity, high levels of premarital sex and pregnancy, early marriage, and divorce. National statistics show that divorce runs 60 percent higher for white women (and 35 percent higher for white men) who are from divorced families than for those from intact families.[14] Some researchers claim that children of divorce have a lower commitment to marriage and are more likely to rush to divorce when they encounter marital difficulties. Other research findings reflect high impulsivity in the decision to marry.[15]

Most research on the psychological and social effects of divorce on children that has assessed children close at hand has examined white, middle-class populations; much less is known about the child's experience in other socioeconomic, ethnic, and racial groups. There are, however, findings which show that family disruption has especially harmful effects among Hispanics, somewhat less among blacks. McLanahan reports in a 1994 paper that "family disruption increases the risk of school failure by 24 percentage points among Hispanics, 17 percentage points among whites, and 13 percentage points among blacks." Family disruption raises the risk of dropping out of school by 150 percent for the average white child, 100 percent for the average Hispanic child, and 76 percent for the average black child.[16]

During the last decade of the century, there has been a convergence of research findings on the long-term effects of divorce on children that endure into adulthood.[17] Overall, findings from major studies are in accord that detrimental effects are long-lasting, and that adult children of divorce are less well-adjusted on a wide range of mental health measures than those raised in intact homes.

Some researchers claim that while these differences are significant, they are not a cause for serious worry. Others find them very troublesome and see them as a wake-up call for new interventions and policies. On examination, these seeming disagreements reflect the different methods and training of the researchers. Thus, as Lisa Laumann Billings and Robert E. Emery demonstrate,[18] sociologists who employ external measures of adjustment, such as school dropout, arrest records, teenage pregnancy, and clinical depression, report that while adult children of divorce are at greater risk of developing problems, most do not show these pathological behaviors. Researchers who rely on clinical interviews and projective tests with persons who grew up in divorced families find widespread emotional distress, troubled personal relationships, sad memories that intrude into their adult lives, and an enduring sense in adulthood that growing up was harder for them than for their peers in intact families. Their findings lead them to conclude that the suffering of children of divorce is serious and sufficient cause for grave concern and new interventions. Drawing several samples of young adults from different social classes Laumann-Billings and Emery find strong evidence for both sets of findings.

The specific sources of distress for adults in their twenties and thirties who experienced their parents' divorce as children is explicated in a 25-year longitudinal study that was published in 2000. It found that the distress among children is indeed long-lasting and, in fact, rises to crescendo as these young adults, confronting the challenges of love, sexual intimacy, and commitment, feel unprepared for adult relationships and are haunted by the ghosts of their parents' failed marriage. These findings put a human face on the troubling national statistics that continue to show a lower incidence of marriage, more early marriage, and a higher incidence of divorce among adult children of divorce compared with those raised in intact marriages.

Finally, one promising recent study takes yet another approach in examining the various subgroups in the divorce population. In an effort to distinguish outcomes, the researchers looked carefully at what the children had lost or gained from their parents' decision to divorce. Dividing the divorce population into those from high-conflict and those from low-conflict marriages, the researchers found that children from low-conflict marriages (who made up over one-half of the families in their study who divorced) suffered serious detrimental effects that lasted into adulthood. The divorce was, for them, a bolt out of the blue, which had no rational explanation and led only to the abrupt loss of the family they loved. By contrast, those who experienced relief because of the high parental conflict that existed during the marriage benefited from the divorce. The finding that many, perhaps most, divorces are not preceded by high parental conflict opens the door to exploring a wide range of parental relationships that precede the decision to divorce. These may, in turn, have a profound influence on the course of the child's adjustment during the post-divorce years.[19]

What has gone awry? Are such findings inevitable? Are distressed children and frightened young adults the price that we must pay for the freedom that adults desire? Or is there some way that the children can share in the benefits that one or both parents anticipate for themselves when they opt for divorce? What have we learned about the nature of divorce in our society that can shed light on the difficulties that so many children experience?

## The Nature of the Divorce Experience for the Child

What protects children during their growing-up years? To put aside economic factors for the moment, there are three major protective psychological factors for the child of divorce, just as there are for the child in the intact family. These are (1) the reasonably harmonious parental relationship in which parents support and spell each other through the rigors of parenting, (2) the sensitivity and commitment of each parent to the child, and (3) the psychological intactness and morality of each parent. If the child has two sensitive, committed, moral parents, who can coparent well (whether married or divorced), that child is doubly blessed. With only one such parent, many children do manage, although it is more difficult for both child and adult, whether mother or father.

Within the well-functioning two-parent or one-parent family, these three protective aspects of family life come together to provide an environment that is conducive to the healthy development of child and adult alike, a humane environment that continuously changes to support the ever-changing needs of all family members. Indeed, the mark of a healthy family is its capacity to bend, to adapt to the many changes in the adults and the continuous changes in the growing child as well as in the social surround.

Tragically, all three of these protective factors are subject to assault by divorce, during its overture, at the time of the breakup, and throughout its long aftermath. The coparenting relationship breaks apart and is frequently strife-ridden. The parenting capacity diminishes; one parent may even disappear from the child's life. The individual adult is often in crisis, sometimes temporarily, sometimes lastingly so, or is engaged in building a new adult relationship to replace that which was lost. The divorced family is often brittle and less sensitive to the child's needs. Thus what places the child of divorce at risk is not any single factor, but the overall weakening of the childrearing and protective functions of the family during critical and extended portions of the childhood years.

We have learned over many years of experience that divorce is not the brief circumscribed crisis in the life of adult and child that we anticipated. It is emphatically not a single event but a long-lasting process of radically changing family relationships that begins in the failing marriage, continues through the often chaotic period of the marital rupture and its immediate aftermath, and extends even further, often over many years of disequilibrium. Children are at risk at several points along the family breakdown and change continuum:

a. In the predivorce family where conditions may include marital abuse and violence as well as serious disruptions in parent-child relationships, which often include the inability or reluctance of the distressed adults to recognize severe problems in their children.[20]

b. At the time of the breakup, which is very frightening for most children, who react with a wide range of symptoms depending on their age, their gender, and the degree of anger and depression in the adults. The instability set into motion by the crumbling marriage is likely to include—specially for the child in the middle-class family—abrupt school change, loss of friends, and loss of community. Children describe the breakup period as the loneliest time of their lives. The great danger is that the child's acute symptoms, which arise in response to the crisis, will consolidate and endure. Thus difficulties in sleeping that occur frequently among preschool children at the time of the breakup, may become lasting and severe sleep disturbances if the fears that underlie the child's symptoms are not addressed.[21]

c. During the long years of the postdivorce, single-parent family, due to the multiple economic, social, and psycholgical stresses that arise, which often include a lowered standard of living, shrinking educational opportunities, radical alterations in parent-child relationships, with, perhaps, the loss of the continuing presence or the entire relationship with one parent, most often the father. Moreover, anger and conflict between the parents endure in an estimated one-third of divorced families. Postdivorce litigation reflects only a small part of the anger in mundane interactions between the parents that can surely dominate the child's experiences.[22]

d. In the remarried family because of the difficulty that the newly married couple confronts in integrating either spouse's previous children, especially older children, into the new family.[23]

e. In their adult relationships with the opposite sex, as children of divorce they are at risk for a range of sleeper or developmental effects when they confront serious commitments to relationships as they reach late adolescence and young adulthood.[24]

The anxieties inherent in these various postdivorce stages by no means always translate into unhappy or failed relationships or psychiatric illness. Many children and parents are successful in surmounting all of these hazards. Moreover, how the child responds at each of these critical stages is very much influenced by the age of the child amd the child's gender at these times and the psychological integrity of the custodial parent. But whether the child succeeds or fails, the child of divorce confronts a set of special and difficult psychological challenges superimposed on the normative challenges of growing up. Divorce changes the entire trajectory of childhood.

## Divorce-Related Changes in Parent-Child Relationships

Researchers have been surprised to discover major upheavals in parent-child relationships consequent to the marital breakup. The earlier notion of divorce as a short-lived crisis was predicated on the expectation that adults who separated without legally faulting each other would rebuild their separate lives and continue to be as responsive to their children as before. It is not clear, from psychological theory, why or how this expectation went awry. What is clear, however, is that the multiple changes and stresses of being a single or visiting or remarried parent, together with the unanticipated psychological reverberations of the broken marital contract, all too often combine to weaken the parent-child relationship. Parents suffer with a diminished capacity to parent as an expectable fallout of the marital breakup. There is abundant research documentation of this diminished capacity to parent as evidenced in the reduced time spent with the child, the greater chaos of the household, the lowered standards for behavior and discipline, and the increased irritability of the parent. It is also evident in a parent's increased emotional dependence on the child, with the consequent reduced capacity to hear the child's distinct voice and failure to separate the child's needs from those of the needy parent. This weakening of the integrity of the parent-child relationship, which is detrimental not only to the young child but to the adolescent as well may be temporary, or it may be lasting, but it goes with the territory of divorce.[25]

One striking change during recent years has been the rise of the fathers' movement, which has led to the long overdue recognition of the critical role of fathers in the emotional, moral, and social development of their children. An immediate result has been an increase in the number of fathers who reject the role of visiting parent as too marginal to their children's lives and who therefore request full or joint custody of their children, including infants. Studies indeed show that nonresident fathers' involvement with their children falls steadily over the postdivorce years, even for fathers who were initially heavily involved with their children.[26] By contrast, fathers who live with their children report enjoying close relationships that can continue into the adult years. How many couples will opt for dual-residence arrangements for their child, and how stable these arrangements will be, considering the high incidence of second marriages for men (which often include new children of that marriage as well as stepchildren), second divorces, and third marriages, is as yet unknown. An important issue is the attitude of the mother toward the father's continued contact. If the mother approves of the close contact between her child and its father, the child will benefit both from the continued affection of the father and from the parental harmony. If the mother disapproves of the father's influence, the child, feeling torn by conflicting loyalties, may fail to benefit. The mother's attitude, then, is critical, particularly her approval of the father's judgment and values, though not necessarily apparent in her overt behavior or even her verbal expression. These are the complex dynamics of life in the divorced family that shape the child's world.[27]

## Economic Issues

Mothers and children experience a significant decline in income following divorce. Fathers are less likely to suffer decline and often experience an increase, if one considers income relative to needs based on family size. Improvement in economic well-being for women and children after divorce is largely linked to remarriage.[28] Divorced mothers as a group earn significantly less than divorced fathers. Their lower earnings are not compensated for, either by private transfers from fathers in the form of child support or by public subsidies. In 1991, 39 percent of all divorced women with children and 55 percent of those with children under the age of six were living below the poverty level. Studies show that women and children who were in the upper economic group prior to the divorce suffer the most precipitous decline in income.[29] But the substantial increase in the percentage of families living below the poverty line following divorce results from the large number of families who lived close to the poverty line prior to disruption. Black and white women suffer a similar decline; but, because a greater number of intact black families have lower income levels than white families, a greater proportion of black women fall below the poverty level after the divorce.

Divorced women with children are likely not only to become poor after divorce but to remain poor for many years. During the late 1970s, female-headed families experienced an average poverty spell of seven years. Nor is the employment of divorced mothers always an effective buffer against poverty. Because of their handicaps in the marketplace, many divorced women, like Steve's mother, have no option but to take shift work or heavy, unpleasant work at minimum wages. This, of course, tragically diminishes their availability to their children and their capacity to provide the nurturance and protection that their children need.[30]

## Child Support

The primary public policy for care of children in divorced families has been that financial as well as social responsibility rests with the parents. Child support, mainly by the father, was the main mechanism by which continuing economic support was to be achieved. Unfortunately, the system has worked very poorly. Child support awards were traditionally set by the individual court in accord with a general standard of reasonableness as interpreted by the individual judge. This policy has led to inadequate awards, poorly enforced collection, and wide variations from case to case. Attempts to reform this system and improve the living condition of children resulted in federal legislation in 1984, and again in 1988, to facilitate collection especially across state lines. Court-ordered support has changed and is expected to conform to standardized guidelines.[31] Improved methods of collection have been implemented since 1994, including wage withholding.

Nevertheless, severe problems persist. Child support awards continue to be small. Payment is often irregular. The receipt of support declines over time, although the needs of children increase as they grow older. Twenty-five percent of those with awards receive no support. Forty-two percent of custodial mothers have no award to start with. The mean amount received by the custodial mother in 1989 was $3138 per year for an average of 1.5 children per family. Thus the average amount of child support, even when paid, is much less than the cost of raising a child.[32] The problems of collecting the award from a resistant father are daunting. These include locating the father, serving the papers, collecting arrears, and a range of time-consuming and costly legal and administrative processes. A serious issue is the large number of fathers who lack the economic means to pay, especially if they have established a second family or are not regularly or gainfully employed. In many families, the divorce was related to the father's unemployment or unreliability in providing economically for his family.

To complicate the issue further, how much fathers can and should be asked to provide for their former families is a debatable question. There are no objective criteria for its resolution; conflicting value systems and anger between the divorcing partners enter into the equation. Most estimates by economists agree, however, that the amount fathers can afford to provide far exceeds what is actually collected. One informed estimate is that fathers could contribute three or four times what they currently pay. This would raise the total amount of child support collected nationally from six billion dollars to between twenty-three and thirty billion dollars yearly. But even if these amounts were paid regularly, many women would remain in poverty because those mothers already better off would receive proportionately more. Thus, though the economic privation that children suffer would diminish, it would surely not disappear. Moreover, there is always the risk that an uncounted number of children in second families would newly sink into poverty.[33]

Finally, economic issues are not separate from psychological and social issues in the real world of the child and her family. After divorce, the economic issues include not only the deprivations of poverty but the detrimental effects of acute economic decline. They include the likelihood of a troubling discrepancy between the father's standard of living and that of the mother and children, of a wide and sometimes widening economic gap between the circumstances and opportunities available to the children in the second marriage as compared with those from the first marriage, and the chilling effects of narrowed economic and educational opportunities on the self-esteem and aspiration levels of adolescents and young adults who compare their shrinking opportunities with those of their classmates and peers whose families have remained intact.

There are also psychological and social consequences that attach to strict enforcement of child support, especially when these measures are resented by the father as arbitrary and unfair. The unintended consequences may be seriously detrimental to children. The finding that after the divorce many children in dual residential custody are cared for primarily by their mothers reveals that the increase in fathers' requests for joint custody in California is tied to a lower support award for the child who has joint residence in the two homes. More efficient collection of higher support awards has generated angry accusations against their former wives among organized groups of divorced fathers. And while the children benefit from higher economic support, they surely suffer if the price they must pay is greater anger between their parents or increased litigation.[34]

I turn briefly to some of the main policy remedies that have been essayed.

## Mediation as Remedy

A major concern all along has been the disastrous effect of parental conflict on the children, especially when fought within the courts in prolonged and repeated custody battles. From the viewpoint of judges and court-related personnel, the rise in civil litigation that has accompanied the steep rise in divorce represents an unforeseen, intolerable pressure for which the courts were, and remain, unprepared. Prominent researchers consider the bitterness between parents to be the central reason for the children's difficulties.[35]

Mediation of parental disputes in or outside the court system has gained much community and professional support within the past decade. Proposed as a preferred method for dispute resolution to the traditional court process, its proponents have held that the adversarial method of the court, which leads inevitably to emphasis on winning or losing, intensifies and even induces passionate conflicts between the parents. By polarizing their respective positions, the traditional court process diminishes the willingness and the capacity of parents to cooperate with each other in their continuing responsibility for their children during the postdivorce years. Additionally, many parents have found the high cost of attorneys, the crowded court calendars, and the brief hearings before judges, who often have little background in family issues, to be stressful and discouraging. Accordingly, for parents who disagree about visitation or custody, several states, including California, have built mandatory mediation into the court process with the expectation that, given an acceptable alternative, most parents would not choose to litigate their differences. Other states offer mediation as an option. Surveys following mediation show that most men and women are pleased with the mediation experience and do not go on to litigation, although this remains their legal option.[36]

Mediation in or outside the court has an important contribution to make in providing a safe and less costly forum for the resolution of those conflicts that can be resolved in this way. Research shows higher compliance by parents with mediated agreements than by those with agreements reached by traditional adversarial methods. A recent report shows that fathers are more likely to maintain their visitation schedule and their child support payments after mediation, over a nine-year follow-up period, as compared with fathers who participated in the traditional court process.[37] There is, however, no evidence in the various studies which have been reported that mediation is significantly related to better psychological outcome in children as compared to those in the traditional adversarial process. The failure of mediation to have a significant effect on children is a disappointing finding because the early proponents of mediation firmly believed that, via this approach, children's psychological condition would improve. They argued that the rewarding experience of the mediation process would generalize into the other domains of people's lives, especially into postdivorce coparenting. Apparently, this predicted spillover effect has not occurred.[38]

There are many relevant considerations. Although parental conflict is hurtful to children, the resolution of parental conflict, by itself, does not protect children. Settling conflict over legal issues, whether by mediation or court intervention, does not, for instance, banish from the child's life the fallout from parents' anger over past infidelity or abuse. When litigation or mediation ends, the quarrel between the parents may move out of the legal arena yet remain to dominate other domains of the child's life. Moreover, absence of legal conflict can reflect dislike, lack of interest, apathy, boredom, or fear of the other parent, as expressed by Ellen's mother. Absence of any overt conflict can be associated, as happens with tragic regularity, with economic, emotional, and physical abandonment. What protects children in the divorced family is cooperative, civilized coparenting. The resolution of conflict may represent a necessary step along that road, but resolution of legally defined conflict, alone, which has been the central concern of the courts and the mediation movement, is not sufficient to protect the child.

There is another aspect of the deficiency of mediation in safeguarding children which should be noted. The mediator, like the attorney, is unschooled in issues pertaining to children. Both mediation and negotiation in child-related matters are dependent on the parents' capacity to speak sensibly and sensitively for the needs of the child, because the attorney and the mediator rely on the parents' agendas. The parent, not the child, is the client. The extent to which the child's interests are served depends entirely on the motivation of the parents and their capacity to perceive the child's needs with reasonable accuracy, and to separate the child's needs and wishes from their own.[39] But at the time of the marital breakup, many parents, as already noted, can be temporarily or lastingly out of touch with what is troubling their children. Consequently, there may be a wide gulf between the condition of the children and the issues brought by parents to their attorneys or to the mediator.

For example, in one family, psychological assessment of one of the children showed her to be increasingly unable to distinguish her fantasies from reality. The other child, when asked to draw her family, drew only a scrawny black rat on a large empty page. Both children were by many psychiatric indications at high—even emergency level—risk. Yet the parents were engaged in mediating issues of diet during their repeated visits to the court-appointed mediator. The mother was strongly committed to the merits of one diet for the children and the father disagreed. There was no way that the mediator, or the attorney, no matter how skilled in conflict resolution, could have known how very troubled these children were, or about the grave lapses in parenting in this family. Diet was both a conscious and an unconscious smokescreen for the real issue, which neither parent could acknowledge, namely, that the children were emotionally starving and in desperate need of psychological nurturance.

## High-Conflict Families

There is mounting evidence that the high-conflict families for whom mediation was especially intended, couples who are locked into protracted, passionate disputes that often threaten to erupt into violence, are not good candidates for either the mediation method or the traditional court process.[40] These families, who represent a subgroup estimated at approximately 10 to 15 percent of divorcing families, challenge the full limits of psychological and psychiatric knowledge and clinical skill. Children in these troubled families are at high risk and are likely to remain so, because the rage between the parents does not appear to abate in the aftermath of the divorce. For these children, divorce offers little remedy; in fact, it may escalate the parental conflict and the child's fear and suffering.

Moreover, prolonged parental conflict has a high potential for invading and corroding the parent-child relationship. We have seen shocking examples of this, clinically, for many years. Johnston and Campbell demonstrated that intense conflict between the parents can impair the parent's most rudimentary judgment in caregiving.[41] They reported parental conflict running so counter to parental intuition that, for example, a mother was described as repeatedly ramming her car against the father's car, while the terrified child, who was the object of the custody dispute, was clinging to the seat beside her. In many of these families, the divorce represents an intolerable blow to one partner's self-esteem, which appears to trigger a serious, perhaps latent psychiatric disorder. Clinicians

are puzzled by the frequent observation that adults who are driven to irrational and violent behavior are often able to function with considerable
competence in other domains of their lives. Yet the passions, the rigid behaviors that all too often explode into violence, the distortions of reality
that characterize these parents' adjustment during lulls between the pre-
dictable disruptions and repeated litigations, continue to seriously threaten
the child's psychological development, even when the issues are not before the court or seem temporarily to have been resolved. Driven by inner turmoil, the tormented parent at the height of the struggle is truly
unable to stop fighting, or to distinguish his or her own ego boundaries
from those of the unfortunate child.[42]

People are quick to defend divorce for high-conflict families, arguing
that children and adults benefit from ending abusive and violent marriages. It is therefore ironic that these may be the families that are more
likely to reconcile. One major study in a large metropolitan area found
that 23 percent of the couples withdrew their divorce petition voluntarily. In comparing the group that withdrew their request for divorce with
those who divorced, the researchers found significantly higher physical violence among those who reconciled.[43] It may be, of course, that these
families are locked into repeated separations followed by reconciliations.
Informal reports from women's shelters confirm that a significant number of those who flee from violence return to their husbands. The women's
motives, of course, are mixed and include economic dependency, pity and
love for the man, fear of being alone, an internalized image that this is
what is expected in man-woman relationships, and fear of being stalked
and killed if they do not return.

Perhaps the most troubling aspect is that the divorce often fails to
rescue the children. What may in fact imperil the children more is that
the conflict which was preocccupied with real or imagined infidelity during the marriage may have shifted its main ground to fighting over the
children after the breakup. The training required to work with this group,
including the capacity to withstand the brutal emotional assault of the
parents' anguish and rage, and the skills to help their severely troubled
children, many of whom have a profound distrust of all adults and are
therefore very difficult to work with, are not within the province of the
mediator or the attorney. These families and their children require highly
sophisticated services, staffed by mental health practitioners who have the
particular interest, capacity, and specialized training to work with severely
disturbed adults and children, and who are interested in working at the
cutting edge of the field. Alas, the special needs of this subgroup, especially the children, have by and large not been recognized by the courts
or the community. Only a few pioneering outposts throughout the country have attempted to provide services.[44] Recognizing the enduring threat
that these parents pose to each other and to the psychological condition
of their children, some courts have made use of supervised visits and Special Masters to maintain a protective presence on behalf of the child in

the family long after the court proceedings have ended. These legal interventions may be a necessary long-term adjunct to psychotherapy.

## Joint Custody as Remedy

Joint custody has several different meanings. It can refer to legal authority shared equally by both parents, who are charged with joint decision making and shared responsibility for the child. It can refer to a dual residential arrangement in which the child spends a significant amount of time, usually at least one-third, in each of the two parental homes. Joint legal custody for the child was proposed in lieu of sole custody, because it was expected to make a significant difference to fathers that would lead to increased visiting and more regular payment of child support. Unfortunately, it has not fulfilled these expectations. Research shows no significant difference in visiting, support, or cooperation between the parents, as a result of being awarded joint legal custody.[45]

Dual residential custody has been proposed as a remedy for the child's sense of loss and abandonment by the visiting parent in the aftermath of divorce. The work of several researchers, including our own, has demonstrated that a child's relationships with both parents remain important during the postdivorce years, and that a good relationship with both, continuing over time, is related to good outcome in the children. This finding has fueled the hope that the creation of this essentially new family form would significantly ameliorate the negative consequences of divorce for children and the longing of noncustodial parents for regular contact with their children.[46]

Although there have been no long-term studies of shared physical custody, a number of researchers have examined children and parents in these arrangements over periods of up to four years. Summarizing six studies from the late 1980s and early 1990s, Johnston found few significant differences in the adjustment of children in the different custody arrangments. She reports that there was a tendency over time for a great deal of self-selection into the kind of custody arrangement that best suited the individual families. About one-third of the children changed their custody arrangements over a two-to-four-year period postdivorce. Children in dual residence tended to move back to the primary care of their mothers. Parents who chose and maintained dual residence arrangements were better educated and more affluent. There was a tendency for emotionally troubled children to be deposited in the primary care of fathers, especially during adolescence. In no group was a substantial amount of visiting in itself associated with better or worse outcomes among the children. The important predictors of good adjustment in the children were the parents' psychological functioning and the quality of the parent-child relationship, not the custody arrangement which mediators and attorneys had worked out with such care. There were consistent findings that children in the custody of anxious and depressed parents, or otherwise psychiatrically disturbed parents, themselves looked disturbed. This finding, also, was unrelated to custody arrangements.[47]

For a minority of divorcing parents, estimated variously at 10 percent to 15 percent of divorcing couples, who are caught up in intractable legal disputes and who are characterized by ongoing disagreements about day-to-day parenting, verbal abuse, or intermittent physical violence, joint custody appears to be contraindicated. In these families, studies by Johnston and her colleagues showed that frequent-visiting arrangements and dual residential schedules were likely to result in increased levels of verbal and physical aggression between parents. These outbreaks of rage and sometimes severe violence occurred mostly when the children were making the transition from one home to the other. Frequent transitions in this population were associated with more emotional and behavioral disturbance among the children, especially among the girls. The children were more likely to be depressed, withdrawn, aggressive, to suffer from physical symptoms, and to show poor social adjustment, as compared with peers in high-conflict families who were not required to make many transitions between the parents' homes and with those who were in sole custody.[48]

A report of an intervention study of expedited visitation services in Arizona sponsored under the Family Support Act of 1994 also noted that frequent access for children in high-conflict families was linked to increased observations of parental conflict and, in turn, to more aggressive behavior in the child. Unfortunately, it is precisely in these high-conflict situations that the policy of the courts has been to order dual residence over the objections of one or sometimes both parents.[49]

There are many motives that lead parents to choose dual residence for their children, including those that derive from love of the child and valuing the presence of the other parent for the child, and a sincere wish to maintain both parents in the life of the child; those that reflect the requirements of the workplace; those that derive primarily from one parent's yearning to restore the marriage, or from parental guilt, or from anger at the breakup and a wish to maintain a command post in the other parent's life; and those that derive from the parent's emotional dependence on the child.[50]

For the dual residence arrangement to work, parents have to help the child, especially the young child, with the many transitions. It requires parents who are able to set aside their grievances against each other and recognize the value of the child's contact with the other parent. It requires, as well, parents who do not depend on the child as a replacement for adult relationships. It requires parents who can agree on sleeping arrangements, toilet training, TV watching, and all the other critical management issues in a child's life. Dual residence also requires that the child have the flexibility to go back and forth and be able to maintain activities and peer relationships in two places. Not all children are able to achieve this. There are no studies on the percentage of children who can manage this kind of arrangement, at what developmental stages, with what kinds of support, and at what, if any, cost to their peer relationships and development.

The studies do show that, contrary to public policy in many jurisdictions, dual residence should be a viable option which parents can consider for its suitability to the particular child and the particular family, and enter into only if it can be modified flexibly to accommodate changes in the child's and the parents' lives. There is no basis in research for joint custody as a presumption in law, or as a policy that can provide a remedy for children. What is clear is that contrary to current policy in many jurisdictions, joint residence should not be ordered by the court or proposed by the mediator for the purpose of resolving disputes between parents.

## Parent Education as Remedy

In recent years, there has been a growing interest in educational programs under the aegis of the court or on referral from the court. The extent and long-lasting impact of such education for parents is as yet unexplored. Nevertheless, there is rising support for such programs throughout the country, bolstered by the argument that such programs will successfully modify parental attitudes and lead to diminished conflict, better parenting, and greater postdivorce cooperation between parents. The expectation is that the children will show evidence of improvement and that litigation over the children will diminish.[51]

There is, of course, something inherently compelling in the realization that divorced parents today must make major decisions about their child's future in the absence of essential information; that without this information, parents cannot provide truly informed consent or make informed choices. Such essential information includes access to the knowledge about different patterns of visiting, their difficulties, their advantages, and their consequences for the child and the parent. Nor can parents be expected to fine-tune these arrangements over the years, for the sake of the growing child and for their own changing needs, unless there is the understanding that these changes will occur.

Additionally, the average parent cannot be expected to provide the necessary support and clarification to the child regarding the causes of the breakup, at the time of the initial separation. Without information in hand about the child's expected reactions and concerns, how can the parent know what to say, or when, or how to deal with the many new ways in which separated parents must cooperate so the child's burdens can be eased as they go from home to home?

Courts that have traditionally been reluctant to order participation in educational programs have now, in a number of states, decided to do so. As a result, programs for parents have been established in a growing number of localities. The most common format consists of one to three lectures, averaging two hours each, offered by a mental health professional or mediator, and sometimes followed by small group discussions. By and large, the emphasis has been on calling attention to the children's expected distress and the ways that it becomes manifest at different ages (based largely on the findings from the California Children of Divorce Project), the importance of cooperation, and the avoidance of legal conflict between the parents.[52] In some courts or linked social agencies, the children have also met in groups for several sessions to discuss their parents' divorce with a teacher or mental health professional. Although many parents are initially reluctant to participate, evaluation forms completed immediately after final class meetings have shown predominantly positive responses. Unfortunately, there has been no evaluation of whether the information provided is actively employed by parents in their relationship with each other or with the child, or whether, indeed, there is any change in the child's well-being. Nor has there been any assessment of how much of the information is actually retained by the parents. Informal reports are that educational programs are associated with a decline in litigation over custody and visitation. The decline in litigation may or may not extend beyond the initial posteducation period, and may or may not be associated with improvement in the child. At this time, the policy and the hope that brief educational endeavors at the time of the breakup can make a difference in the child's condition remains untested.

## Conclusions

The impact of divorce on children is central to an increasingly strident public discourse on the state of the family in our society. Some decry the selfishness of men and women who allegedly place their wishes for self-realization ahead of the needs of other family members, and who seek divorce impulsively or without consideration of its impact on their children.[53] Others despair at the apparent forsaking of religious and moral values that traditionally provided the moral framework for marital stability. Organized women's groups blame the postdivorce impoverishment of mothers and children for the children's difficulties and deplore the economic abandonment of children by their divorced or remarried fathers. Organized men's groups complain of the economic burdens of supporting their former families, of being blocked by their former wives from access to their children, and of being assigned by court policy to the denigrated role of visitor in the lives of their children. Judges and court personnel complain of high pressure and understaffing and of the baffling family conflicts that come before them, which they are ill equipped to address. A range of community and church groups blame a deterioration of family values on the ease of obtaining a divorce and the lack of responsibility and morality that has been fostered by no-fault legislation. These groups have called for restricting legal access to divorce by limiting or eliminating no-fault and by building mandatory delays into the divorce process.

Each of the concerns has brought in its wake specific proposals for remedy, many of which have been reviewed and evaluated in the foregoing pages. These include calls for improved enforcement of child support and higher support awards, for expanding court-attached mediation services to undo the detrimental effects of the adversarial system, the push for joint legal custody and dual residential custody for children in order to create stronger bonds between fathers and children, and for mandating parent education to guide parents in providing the emotional support and understanding that the children need.[54]

Some of the proposals, as general policy, would undo or significantly mute the detrimental effects of divorce on children. Undoubtedly, there are millions of economically disadvantaged children, just like Steve, who would have benefited enormously had child support been enforced and had their fathers been ordered to contribute to their college education. Moreover, society as a whole would have been enriched by the creative labors of such young people and would have gained immeasurably from their view of the community as moral and caring. Surely the existence of a large group of embittered adolescents and young adults who feel they were abandoned by their parents and their communities is not in the interests of a good society. Similarly, it is likely that most parents would find parent education programs helpful, especially if these provided opportunities for interaction with trained people who could offer guidance in choosing custody and visitation plans that would be suitable to the child as well as to the parent.

Other proposals, such as dual residential custody and mediation programs, have merit if offered selectively to subgroups within the divorce population. These remedies focus attention on one troubling aspect within the divorcing and postdivorce family. Many of their supporters have little recognition that no one intervention suits all, and that no single set of guidelines benefits all. In the increasingly polarized political climate of the 1990s, each proposal for remedy has its political constituency, and there is little attempt to develop comprehensive programs that would encompass a diverse population. Yet, it is only when taken all together and applied with an understanding of their specific usefulness, their indications, and contraindications, that they represent a substantial advance that would benefit children.

All of the proposed programs homogenize the needs of children. All fail to distinguish children by age or developmental stage. Like current policy, they do not offer different guidelines that distinguish infants from younger or older children on issues of visiting, custody, or even child support. Nor do they distinguish high-conflict families from the majority of divorcing couples. Additionally, although divorce affects the entire trajectory of the child's growing-up years, the proposed policies are mostly front-loaded and deal with the family at the point of the breakup of the marriage and not with the developing child whose psychological, educational, social, and financial needs will inevitably continue to change and grow in complexity. Ellen's suffering and subsequent rejection of her father, which is similar to that experienced by many of her peers, argues for giving the adolescent the legal right to limit, or even refuse, visitation. Although it is always possible that a child's preference can be manipulated by an irate parent, that risk is less disturbing to the adolescent than the consequences of being rendered voiceless.

## Proposed Court and Legislative Reform

What is lacking is a mechanism for the differential use of policies and procedures and for their modification over time. The court and the legal system as traditionally structured lack the necessary flexibility to deal with families. It has been apparent for some time that there is a serious mismatch between the adversarial court system and the needs of divorcing families, which has contributed heavily to the difficulties encountered by children and parents.

The fact that each of the fifty states formulates its own policies and practices in family law, and that these are often widely divergent, is yet another source of confusion and often high expense. These differences were strikingly in evidence in a series of cases dealing with the right of the custodial parent to move away with the child from the vicinity of the noncustodial parent. The move-away issue affects thousands of children yearly because of the high mobility of American society. In 1996, the California Supreme Court and the New York Court of Appeals both issued decisions that took entirely different positions on this matter, with entirely different consequences for the families in these states. The California Supreme Court ruled that the custodial parent is presumptively entitled to change the child's residence subject to the court's power to restrain a move that would prejudice the rights and welfare of the child. Under the California ruling, the custodial parent does not have to prove that the move is necessary, although moves undertaken in bad faith to thwart the noncustodial parent's right to visit may be enjoined. The New York Court of Appeals did not include any such presumption; it requires that the moving parent demonstrate the "necessity" of the move. Thus it is more likely that parents in New York State will be unable to move or will have to return to court if the custodial parent wishes to move and this is opposed by the other parent.

Although there is no research about families that are permitted to move versus those who are restrained by the court, the arguments put forward in an amicus curiae brief filed in the California court case drew on relevant psychological research to support the importance of stability in the child's postdivorce family and the psychic hazards and suffering posed to parent and child of requiring the custodial parent to choose between a contemplated remarriage, or a plan to pursue economic and educational betterment, and having to relinquish the child to the custody of the noncustodial parent, if the noncustodial parent opposes the move. The California Supreme Court ruling was generally in accord with the opinion set forth in the submitted brief, which had emphasized the welfare of the child as the primary consideration over the visitation rights of the parent. These differing approaches taken by California and New York will undoubtedly serve as additional fuel in the ongoing national debate on child relocation following divorce.[55]

It may be useful to recall that the initial proposals in California for a change from fault to no-fault divorce were presented within the context of broad recommendations for establishing a family court staffed by specially trained judges with the authority and the funds to employ a permanent staff of highly trained mental health personnel.[56] Today, such a specialized court would surely offer a wider range of programs, which would include mediators for the simple disputes, highly specialized mental health professionals for the high-conflict cases, and a range of other services in and outside the courts to which families could be referred for education, guidance, and counseling.

## A Mandatory Waiting Period

Given a redesigned court, there might well be considerable benefit to parents and to children to introduce a mandatory waiting period between the filing and the granting of a divorce decree. Although some states already have this requirement, it tends not to be used in a purposeful, forward-looking way. Instead, there is either a vague hope of reconciliation or else the couple is largely marking time. But an appropriately used waiting period of one year could provide a moral context to the final chapter of the failing marriage. During this mandatory waiting period, models of custody and visiting could be explored and shaped not only to the parents' wishes but also to accord with the individual child's changing agenda over the years ahead.

This waiting period could provide time and opportunity to draw up plans for the economic support of the child into adulthood. These plans, in accord with proposals made by Glendon to the Massachusetts Bar Association's Commission on the Unmet Legal Needs of Children, might well include her proposal to divide the marital property only after funds had been allotted and set aside for the support of the children, including college education. Glendon has argued that the parents' legal duty to provide for minor children be given foremost consideration.[57] This would mean that the judge's main task would be to piece together from property, income, and in-kind personal care the best possible package to meet the needs of the children and their custodian. Until the welfare of the children had been adequately secured, there would be no debate about marital property. All property, no matter how acquired, would be subject to this first duty to provide for the child. Such a policy would not only change the economic condition of many children in middle-class or affluent homes, but it would also forcibly bring to the attention of the parents their continuing responsibility for their children and the priority accorded this responsibility under the law.

## *The Rights and Needs of Children*

There are many dilemmas that remain unresolved in the interface between the child of divorce and the legal system. How to build the individual voice of the child into the system is a challenge which has received increasing attention from scholars and practitioners, although it lacks a political constituency. What are the rights of the child, and how can these be implemented? Should we even talk of children's rights, or should the emphasis be on their needs or their broadly defined best interests? The various efforts to introduce into divorce proceedings an attorney for the children, a guardian *ad litem* or other representative, have been insufficiently defined in their potentialities and limitations, and the results have been almost entirely unevaluated. But without providing for the child's input, especially as the child gets older, how can we fashion policies that respect and protect the individual youngster?

Over and beyond creating appropriate mechanisms, building new structures and supports, and exercising restraint in intervening within the family system, we face a moral dilemma in formulating policies regarding divorce, which we have been reluctant to acknowledge. Divorce is a different experience for the adult than it is for the child. For the adult, divorce is a significant social remedy, which is welcomed because it brings an end to an unhappy life chapter and opens new opportunities. But the child seeks and needs continuity and protection within the family. Few children below midadolescence see any benefit to themselves in the divorce action. In the main, children hold their parents responsible for the unwelcome changes in their lives. Put succinctly, unlike other social ills such as poverty or community violence, where the interests of parents and children converge, in many divorcing families that which benefits one or even both adults is experienced by the children as detrimental to their needs, and indeed, it may be so. Our moral vision and our family laws have been built on the assumption of a convergence of interests between parents and children, except in the most aberrant circumstances. Divorce challenges this assumption. The rights and interests of divorcing parents may and often do collide with the interests of the child. How to formulate policies that will simultaneously address the legitimate goals of parents and the best interests of children is the overarching challenge that we have yet to address in its full complexity.

## Notes

1. Judith Wallerstein and Sandra Blakeslee, *Second Chances* (New York: Ticknor & Fields, 1989). See also the Cowans' chapter in this book.

2. Wallerstein and Blakeslee, *Second Chances*. Robert E. Emery, *Marriage, Divorce, and Children's Adjustment* (Beverly Hills: Sage, 1988).

3. Judith Wallerstein and Joan Kelly, *Surviving the Breakup* (New York: Basic Books, 1980).

4. Frank Furstenberg, "History and Current Status of Divorce in the United States," *The Future of Children* 4:29–43, 1994; Jessica Pearson and Jean Anhalt, "Examining the Connection between Child Access and Child Support," *Family and Conciliation Courts Review* 32:93–109, 1994.

5. Nicholas Zill, Donna Ruane Morrison, and Mary Jo Coiro, "Long-Term Effects of Parental Divorce on Parent-Child Relationships, Adjustment and Achievement in Young Adulthood," *Journal of Family Psychology* 7:1:91–103, 1993.

6. Wallerstein and Blakeslee, *Second Chances*.

7. Andrew Cherlin, *Marriage, Divorce, and Remarriage*, rev. ed. (Cambridge: Harvard University Press, 1992); Furstenberg, "History and Current Status of Divorce in the United States."

8. T. C. Martin and Larry Bumpass, "Recent Trends in Marital Disruption," *Demography* 26:37–51, 1989; Frank Furstenberg and Andrew Cherlin, *Divided Families: What Happens to Children When Parents Part* (Cambridge: Harvard University Press, 1991).

9. Eleanor Maccoby and Robert Mnookin, *Dividing the Child: Social and Legal Dilemmas of Custody* (Cambridge: Harvard University Press, 1992); Barbara Hauser and Robert Straus, "Legal and Psychological Dimensions of Joint and Sole Custody Agreements." Paper presented at the 68th annual meeting of the American Orthopsychiatric Association, Toronto, March 1991; Susan Kellum, "Child Custody and Support," *CQ Researcher* 5:25–48, Jan. 13, 1995; Patricia Shiono and Linda Quinn, "Epidemiology of Divorce," *The Future of Children* 4: 15–28, 1994.

10. Neil Kalter, "Children of Divorce in an Outpatient Psychiatric Population," *American Journal of Orthopsychiatry* 47:40–51, 1977; Nicholas Zill and Charlotte Schoenborn, "Developmental, Learning, and Emotional Problems: Health of Our Nation's Children, United States, 1988," *Advance Data, Vital and Health Statistics of the National Center for Health Statistics* (Washington, DC: National Center for Health Statistics no. 190, Nov. 16, 1990); Furstenberg and Cherlin, *Divided Families*.

11. Monica Cockett and John Tripp, *The Exeter Family Study: Family Breakdown and Its Impact on Children* (Exeter: University of Exeter Press, 1994); Ronald and Jacqueline Angel, "Physical Comorbidity and Medical Care Use in Children with Emotional Problems," *Public Health Reports* 111:140–145, 1996.

12. Paul Amato and Bruce Keith, "Parental Divorce and the Well-Being of Children: A Meta-Analysis," *Psychological Bulletin* 110:26–46, 1991; Joseph Schwartz, "Sociodemographic and Psychosocial Factors in Childhood as Predictors of Adult Mortality," *American Journal of Public Health* 85:1237–1245, 1995.

13. Wallerstein and Blakeslee, *Second Chances*. Neil Kalter, Barbara Riemer, Arthur Brickman, and Jade Chen, "Implications of Parental Divorce for Female Development," *Journal of the American Academy of Child Psychiatry* 24:538–544, 1985; Neil Kalter, "Long-Term Effects of Divorce on Children," *American Journal of Orthopsychiatry* 57:587–600, 1987.

14. Sara McLanahan, *Growing Up with a Single Parent: What Hurts, What Helps* (Cambridge: Harvard University Press, 1994); Sara McLanahan and Larry

Bumpass, "Intergenerational Consequences of Family Disruption," *American Journal of Sociology* 94:130–152, 1988; Norval D. Glenn and Kathryn Kramer, "The Marriages and Divorces of the Children of Divorce," *Journal of Marriage and the Family* 49:811–825, 1987.

15. Glenn and Kramer, "Marriages and Divorces of the Children of Divorce"; Wallerstein and Kelly, *Second Chances.*

16. Sara McLanahan, "The Consequences of Single Motherhood," *The American Prospect* 18:48–58, 1994, quotation on 49.

17. Paul Amato and Alan Booth, *A Generation at Risk: Growing Up in an Era of Family Upheaval* (Cambridge: Harvard University Press, 1997); P.L. Chase-Lansdale, Andrew Cherlin, and Kathryn Kiernan. "The Long-Term Effects of Parental Divorce on the Mental Health of Young Adults: A Development Perspective," *Child Development* 66:1614–1634, 1995; Judith Wallerstein, Julia Lewis, and Sandra Blakeslee, *The Unexpected Legacy of Divorce: Report of a 25-Year Landmark Study* (New York: Hyperion Press, 2000); Nicholas Zill, Donna Morrison, and Mary Jo Coiro, "Long-Term Effects of Parental Divorce on Parent-Child Relationships, Adjustment and Achievement in Young Adulthood," *Journal of Family Psychology* 7:91–103, 1993.

18. Lisa Laumann-Billings and Robert Emery, "Distress among Young Adults from Divorced Families," *Journal of Family Psychology* 14:4:671–687, 2000.

19. Alan Booth and Paul Amato, "Parental Predivorce Relations and Off-spring Postdivorce Well-Being," *Journal of Marriage and the Family* 64:197–212, February 2001.

20. Jeanne Block, Jack Block, and Per Gjerde, "The Personality of Children Prior to Divorce," *Child Development* 57:827–840, 1986; Andrew Cherlin, Frank Furstenberg, et al., "Longitudinal Studies of Effects of Divorce on Children in Great Britain and the United States," *Science* 252:1386–1389, 1991; Janet Johnston and Linda Campbell, *Impasses of Divorce: The Dynamics and Resolution of Family Conflict* (New York: Free Press, 1988).

21. E. Mavis Hetherington, Martha Cox, and Roger Cox, "The Aftermath of Divorce," in Joseph Stevens and Marilyn Mathews (eds.), *Mother-Child, Father-Child Relationships* (Washington, DC: National Association for the Education of Young Children, 1978), 149–176; Judith Wallerstein, "Changes in Parent-Child Relationships," in E. James Anthony and George Pollock (eds.), *Parental Influences in Health and Disease* (Boston: Little, Brown, 1985), 317–347.

22. Janet Johnston, "High-Conflict Divorce," *The Future of Children* 4: 165–182, 1994.

23. Kay Pasley and Marilyn Ihinger-Tallman, *Remarriage & Stepparenting: Current Research & Theory* (New York: Guilford, 1987); Cherlin, *Marriage, Divorce, and Remarriage.*

24. Wallerstein and Blakeslee, *Second Chances*; Glenn and Kramer, "Marriages and Divorces of the Children of Divorce"; Kalter, "Children of Divorce in an Outpatient Psychiatric Population."

25. Hetherington, Cox, and Cox, "The Aftermath of Divorce"; Wallerstein and Kelly, *Surviving the Breakup.*

26. Valarie King, "Non-Resident Father Involvement and Child Well-Being," *Journal of Family Issues* 15:78–96, 1994.

27. Adam Shapiro and James David Lambert, "Longitudinal Effects of Divorce on the Quality of the Father-Child Relationship and on Father's Psychological Well-Being," *Journal of Marriage and the Family* 61:2:397–408, 1999.

28. Richard Behrman and Linda Sandham Quinn, "Children and Divorce: Overview and Analysis," *The Future of Children* 4:4–14, 1994.

29. Jay Teachman and Kathleen Paasch, "Financial Impact of Divorce on Children and Their Families," *The Future of Children* 4:63–83, 1994; Paula Roberts, "Child Support Orders," *The Future of Children* 4:101–120, 1994.

30. Mary Jo Bane and David Ellwood, "Slipping Into and Out of Poverty: The Dynamics of Spells," *Journal of Human Resources* 21:1–23, 1986; Harriet Presser, "Shift Work among American Women and Child Care," *Journal of Marriage and the Family* 48:551–563, 1986.

31. Judith Seltzer, "Legal Custody Arrangements and Children's Economic Welfare," *American Journal of Sociology* 94:895–929, 1991; Irwin Garfinkel and Sara McLanahan, *Single Mothers and Their Children: A New American Dilemma* (Washington, DC: Urban Institute Press, 1986); Roberts, "Child Support Orders"; Robert Emery and Peter Dillon, "Divorce Mediation and Resolution of Child-Custody Disputes: Long-Term Effects," *American Journal of Orthopsychiatry* 66:131–140, 1996.

32. Teachman and Paasch, "Financial Impact of Divorce on Children and Their Families," 73.

33. Seltzer, "Legal Custody Arrangements and Children's Welfare"; Roberts, "Child Support Orders"; Irwin Garfinkel and D. Oellerich, "Noncustodial Fathers' Ability to Pay Child Support," *Demography* 26:219–233, 1989; Irwin Garfinkel, D. Oellerich, and Philip Robins, "Child Support Guidelines: Will They Make a Difference?" *Journal of Family Issues* 12:404–429, 1991; Ron Haskins, J. B. Schwartz, John Akin, and A. Dobelstein, "How Much Child Support Can Absent Fathers Pay?" *Policy Studies Journal* 14:201–222, 1985.

34. Maccoby and Mnookin, *Dividing the Child*.

35. Robert Emery, *Renegotiating Family Relationships: Divorce, Child Custody, and Mediation* (New York: Guilford Press, 1994); idem, "Interparental Conflict and the Children of Discord and Divorce," *Psychological Bulletin* 92:310–330, 1982.

36. Jessica Pearson and Nancy Thoennes, "Divorce Mediation: Reflections on a Decade of Research," in Kenneth Kressel and Dean Pruitt (eds.), *Mediation Research: The Process and Effectiveness of Third Party Intervention* (San Francisco: Jossey-Bass, 1989), 9–39; Robert Emery, Sheila Matthews, and Katherine Kitzmann, "Child Custody Mediation and Litigation: Parents' Satisfaction and Functioning One Year after Settlement," *Journal of Consulting and Clinical Psychology* 62:124–129, 1994; Robert Emery, "Divorce Mediation: Negotiating Agreements and Renegotiating Relationships," *Family Relations* 44:377–383, 1995; Joan Kelly, "A Decade of Divorce Mediation Research: Some Answers and Questions," *Family and Conciliation Courts Review* 34:373–385, 1996.

37. Emery and Dillon, "Divorce Mediation and Resolution of Child-Custody Disputes."

38. Emery and Dillon, "Divorce Mediation and Resolution of Child-Custody Disputes"; Pearson and Thoennes, "Divorce Mediation"; Joan Kelly, *Mediated and Adversarial Divorce Resolution Processes: An Analysis of Post-Divorce Outcomes.* Final report for the Fund for Research in Dispute Resolution. (Corte Madera, CA: Northern California Mediation Center, 1990).

39. Judith Wallerstein, "Psychodynamic Perspectives on Family Mediation," *Mediation Quarterly* 14/15: 7–21, Winter 1986/Spring 1987.

40. Kenneth Kressel, N. Jaffe, B. Tuchman et al., "A Typology of Divorcing Couples: Implications for Mediation and the Divorce Process," *Family Process*

19:101–116, 1980; Kenneth Kressel, *The Process of Divorce: How Professionals and Couples Negotiate Settlements* (New York: Basic Books, 1985).

41. Janet Johnston, Roberto Gonzalez, and Linda Campbell, "Ongoing Postdivorce Conflict and Child Disturbance," *Journal of Abnormal Psychology* 15: 493–509, 1987; Janet Johnston and Linda Campbell, *Impasses of Divorce: The Dynamics and Resolution of Family Conflict* (New York: Free Press, 1988); Janet Johnston, *High-Conflict and Violent Parents in Family Court: Findings on Children's Adjustment and Proposed Guidelines for the Resolution of Custody and Visitation Disputes.* Final report to the Judicial Council of the State of California, Statewide Office of Family Court Services (San Francisco: Judicial Council, 1992); idem, "High-Conflict Divorce"; Janet Johnston, Marsha Kline, and Jean Tschann, "Ongoing Postdivorce Conflict in Families Contesting Custody: Effects on Children of Joint Custody and Frequent Access," *American Journal of Orthopsychiatry* 59: 576–592, 1989.

42. Johnston, *High-Conflict and Violent Parents in Family Court*; idem, "Gender, Violent Conflict, and Mediation," *Journal of the National Association of Family Mediation and Conciliation Services* 3:9–13, 1993; Janet Johnston and Linda Campbell, "Parent-Child Relationships in Domestic Violence Families Disputing Custody," *Family and Conciliation Courts Review* 31:282–298, 1993.

43. Gay Kitson, "Couples Who File for Divorce but Change Their Minds," *American Journal of Orthopsychiatry* 54:469–489, 1984.

44. Vivienne Roseby and Janet Johnston, "Clinical Interventions with Latency-Age Children of High Conflict and Violence." *American Journal of Orthopsychiatry* 65:48–59, 1995; Janet Johnston with Vivienne Roseby, *In the Name of the Child* (New York: Free Press, 1997).

45. Catherine Albiston, Eleanor Maccoby, Christy Buchanan, Robert Mnookin, and Sanford Dornbusch, "Postdivorce Roles of Mothers and Fathers in the Lives of Their Children," *Journal of Family Psychology* 7:24–28, 1993.

46. Ross Thompson, "The Role of the Father after Divorce," *The Future of Children* 4:210–235, 1994.

47. Janet Johnston, "Research Update: Children's Adjustment in Sole Custody Compared to Joint Custody. Families and Principles for Custody Decision Making," *Family and Conciliation Courts Review* 33:415–425, 1995; Marsha Kline, Jeanne Tschann, Janet Johnston, and Judith Wallerstein, "Children's Adjustment in Joint and Sole Physical Custody Families," *Developmental Psychology* 25:430–438, 1989.

48. Johnston, Kline, and Tschann, "Ongoing Postdivorce Conflict"; Johnston, "Research Update: Children's Adjustment in Sole Custody Compared to Joint Custody."

49. Cheryl Lee, John Shaughnessy, Joel Bankes, "Impact of Expedited Visitation Services, a Court Program That Enforces Access: Through the Eyes of Children," *Family and Conciliation Courts Review* 33:495–505, 1995.

50. Rosemary McKinnon and Judith Wallerstein, "Joint Custody and the Preschool Child," *Behavioral Sciences and the Law* 4:169–183, 1986; idem, "A Preventive Intervention Program for Parents and Young Children in Joint Custody Arrangements," *American Journal of Orthopsychiatry* 58:168–178, 1988.

51. Virginia Petersen and Susan Steinman, "Helping Children Succeed after Divorce: A Court-Mandated Educational Program for Divorcing Parents," *Family and Conciliation Courts Review* 32:27–39, 1994; Larry Lehner, "Education for Parents Divorcing in California," *Family and Conciliation Courts Review*

32:50–54, 1994. This "peace program" is associated most prominently with Andrew Shepherd.

52. As reported in Wallerstein and Kelly, *Surviving the Breakup.*

53. See, e.g., David Popenoe, *Life without Father: Compelling New Evidence that Fatherhood and Marriage Are Indispensable for the Good of Children and Society* (New York: Free Press, 1996).

54. See, e.g., Maggie Gallagher, *The Abolition of Marriage: How We Destroy Lasting Love* (Washington, DC: Regnery, 1996).

55. Judith Wallerstein and Tony Tanke, "To Move or Not to Move: Psychological and Legal Considerations in the Relocation of Children Following Divorce," *Family Law Quarterly* 30:305–332, 1996. This article was adapted from an *amica curiae* brief filed by Mr. Tanke on behalf of Dr. Wallerstein in the California case *In re* Marriage of Burgess (Apr. 15, 1996) 96 SF Daily Journal, Daily App. Rpt. 4375, 1996 CAL. LEXIS 1573. The New York case is Tropea v. Tropea 1996 N.Y. LEXIS.

56. *Report of the Governor's Commission on the Family*, Dec. 1966. (Sacramento, CA: Government Printing Office, 1966).

57. *Report of the Governor's/Massachusetts Bar Association's Commission on the Unmet Needs of Children.* Massachusetts Bar Association, 1988; for the "children first" policy, see Mary Ann Glendon, *Abortion and Divorce in Western Law* (Cambridge: Harvard University Press, 1987).

# 5

# The Modern American Stepfamily: Problems and Possibilities

### Mary Ann Mason

Cinderella had one, so did Snow White and Hansel and Gretel. Our traditional cultural myths are filled with the presence of evil stepmothers. We learn from the stories read to us as children that stepparents, particularly stepmothers, are not to be trusted. They may pretend to love us in front of our biological parent, but the moment our real parent is out of sight they will treat us cruelly and shower their own children with kindnesses. Few modern children's tales paint stepparents so harshly, still the negative image of stepparents lingers in public policy. While the rights and obligations of biological parents, wed or unwed, have been greatly strengthened in recent times, stepparents have been virtually ignored. At best it is fair to say that as a society we have a poorly formed concept of the role of stepparents and a reluctance to clarify that role.

Indeed, the contrast between the legal status of stepparents and the presumptive rights and obligations of natural parents is remarkable. Child support obligations, custody rights, and inheritance rights exist between children and their natural parents by virtue of a biological tie alone, regardless of the quality of social or emotional bonds between parent and child, and regardless of whether the parents are married. In recent years policy changes have extended the rights and obligations of natural parents, particularly in regard to unwed and divorced parents, but have not advanced with regard to stepparents. Stepparents in most states have no obligation during the marriage to support their stepchildren, nor do they enjoy any right of custody or control. Consistent with this pattern, if the marriage terminates through divorce or death, they usually have no rights to custody or even visitation, however longstanding their relationship with their stepchildren. Conversely, stepparents have no obligation to pay child support following divorce, even if their stepchildren have depended on their income for many years. In turn, stepchildren have no right of inheritance in the event of the stepparent's death (they are, however, eligible for Social Security benefits in most cases).[1]

Policymakers who spend a great deal of time worrying about the economic and psychological effects of divorce on children rarely consider the fact that about 70 percent of mothers are remarried within six years. Moreover, about 28 percent of children are born to unwed mothers, many of whom eventually marry someone who is not the father of their child. In a study including all children, not just children of divorce, it was estimated that one-fourth of the children born in the United States in the early 1980s will live with a stepparent before they reach adulthood.[2] These numbers are likely to increase in the future, at least as long as the number of single-parent families continues to grow. In light of these demographic trends, federal and state policies affecting families and children, as well as policies governing private-sector employee benefits, insurance, and other critical areas of everyday life, may need to be adapted to address the concerns of modern stepfamilies.

In recent years stepfamilies have received fresh attention from the psychological and social sciences but little from legal and policy scholars. We now know a good deal about who modern stepfamilies are and how they function, but there have been few attempts to apply this knowledge to policy. This chapter first of all reviews the recent findings on the everyday social and economic functioning of today's stepfamilies, and then examines current state and federal policies, or lack of them in this arena. Finally, the sparse set of current policy recommendations, including my own, are presented. These proposals range from active discouragement of stepfamilies[3] to a consideration of stepparents as de facto parents, with all the rights and responsibilities of biological parents during marriage, and a limited extension of these rights and responsibilities following the breakup of marriage or the death of the stepparent.[4]

## The Modern Stepfamily

The modern stepfamily is different and more complex than Cinderella's or Snow White's in several important ways. First, the stepparent who lives with the children is far more likely to be a stepfather than a stepmother, and in most cases the children's biological father is still alive and a presence, in varying degrees, in their lives. Today it is divorce, rather than death which usually serves as the background event for the formation of the stepfamily, and it is the custodial mother who remarries (86 percent of stepchildren live primarily with a custodial mother and stepfather),[5] initiating a new legal arrangement with a stepfather.[6]

Let us take the case of the Jones-Hutchins family. Sara was eight and Josh five when their mother and father, Martha and Ray Jones divorced. Three years later Martha married Sam Hutchins, who had no children. They bought a house together and the children received health and other benefits from Sam's job, since Martha was working part time at a job with no benefits.

Theoretically, this new parental arrangement was a triangle, since Ray was still on the scene and initially saw the children every other weekend. In most stepfamilies the noncustodial parent, usually the father, is still alive (only in 25 percent of cases is the noncustodial parent dead, or his whereabouts unknown). This creates the phenomenon of more than two parents, a situation that conventional policymakers are not well equipped to address. However, according to the National Survey of Families and Households (NSFH), a nationally representative sample of families, contact between stepchildren and their absent natural fathers is not that frequent. Contact falls into four broad patterns: roughly one-quarter of all stepchildren have no association at all with their fathers and receive no child support; one-quarter see their fathers only once a year or less often and receive no child support; one-quarter have intermittent contact or receive some child support; and one-quarter may or may not receive child support but have fairly regular contact, seeing their fathers once a month or more. Using these data as guides to the quality and intensity of the father-child relationship, it appears that relatively few stepchildren are close to their natural fathers or have enough contact with them to permit the fathers to play a prominent role in the children's upbringing. Still, at least half of natural fathers do figure in their children's lives to some degree.[7] The presence of the noncustodial parent usually precludes the option of stepparent adoption, a solution that would solve the legal ambiguities, at least, of the stepparent's role.

In size, according to the National Survey of Families and Households, modern residential stepfamilies resemble modern nondivorced families and single-parent families, with an average of two children per family. Only families with two stepparents (the rarest type of stepfamily, in which both parents had children from previous relationships, and both are the custodial parents) are larger, with an average of 3.4 children per household. In part because divorce and remarriage take time, children are older. In the NSFH households, the youngest stepchildren in families are, on average, aged eleven, while the youngest children in nondivorced families are six and a half.[8]

There are also, of course, nonresidential stepparents (the spouses of noncustodial parents), usually stepmothers. In our case, Ray married again, the year after Martha married Sam. Ray's new wife, Leslie, was the custodial parent of Audrey, age twelve. This marriage complicated the weekend visits. The Jones children were resentful of their new stepmother, Leslie, and her daughter, Audrey. Ray found it easier to see them alone, and his visits became less frequent.

Some children may spend a good deal of time with nonresidential stepparents, and they may become significant figures in the children's lives, unlike Leslie in our example. But for our purpose of reassessing the parental rights and obligations of stepparents, we will focus only on residental stepparents, since they are more likely to be involved in the everyday support and care of their stepchildren. Moreover, the wide variety of benefits available to dependent children, like Social Security and health insurance, are usually attached only to a residential stepparent.

The modern stepfamily, like those of Cinderella and Snow White, also has stresses and strains. This was certainly true for the Jones-Hutchins family. Sara was eleven and Josh seven when their mother married Sam. At first Sara refused to talk to Sam and turned her face away when he addressed her. Josh was easier. He did not say much, but was willing to play catch or go an on errand with Sam if encouraged by Sam to do so. Sara grew only slightly more polite as she developed into adolescence. She spoke to Sam only if she needed something. But, as her mother pointed out to Sam, she hardly spoke to her either. Josh continued to be pleasant, if a little distant, as he grew older. He clearly preferred his mother's attention.

The classic longitudinal studies by Heatherington and colleagues,[9] spanning the past two decades, provide a rich source of information on how stepfamilies function. Heatherington emphasizes that stepchildren are children who have experienced several marital transitions. They have usually already experienced the divorce of their parents (although the number whose mothers have never before wed is increasing) and a period of life in a single-parent family before the formation of the stepfamily. In the early stages of all marital transitions, including divorce and remarriage, child-parent relations are often disrupted and parenting is less authoritative than in nondivorced families. These early periods, however, usually give way to a parenting situation more similar to nuclear families.[10]

The Heatherington studies found that stepfathers vary in how enthusiastically and effectively they parent their stepchildren, and stepchildren also vary in how willingly they permit a parental relationship to develop. Indeed, many stepfather-stepchild relationships are not emotionally close. Overall, stepfathers in these studies are most often disengaged and less authoritative as compared with nondivorced fathers. The small class of residential stepmothers exhibits a similar style.[11] Conversely, adolescent children tend to perceive their stepfathers negatively in the early stages of remarriage, but over time, they too become disengaged. In an interesting twist on fairy tale lore, adolescent children in stepfamilies experience less conflict with their residential stepmothers than do children in nondivorced families with their own mothers.[12]

The age and gender of the child at the time of stepfamily formation are critical in his or her adjustment. Early adolescence is a difficult time in which to have remarriage occur, with more sustained difficulties in step-father-stepchild relations than in remarriages where the children are younger. Young (preadolescent) stepsons, but not necessarily stepdaughters, develop a closer relationship to their stepfathers after a period of time; this is not as likely with older children.[13]

Other researchers have found that in their lives outside the family, stepchildren do not perform as well as children from nondivorced families, and look more like the children from single-parent families. It seems that divorce and remarriage (or some factors associated with divorce and remarriage) increase the risk of poor academic, behavioral, and psychological outcomes.[14]

The difficulties of the stepfamily relationship are evident in the high divorce rate of such families. About one-quarter of all remarrying women separate from their new spouses within five years of the second marriage, and the figure is higher for women with children from prior relationships. A conservative estimate is that between 20 percent and 30 percent of stepchildren will, before they turn eighteen, see their custodial parent and stepparent divorce.[15] This is yet another disruptive marital transition for children, most of whom have already undergone at least one divorce.

Other researchers look at the stepfamily more positively. Amato and Keith analyzed data comparing intact, two-parent families with stepfamilies and found that while children from two-parent families performed significantly better on a multifactored measure of well-being and development, there was a significant overlap. A substantial number of children in stepfamilies actually perform as well or better than children in intact two-parent families. As Amato comments, "Some children grow up in well-functioning intact families in which they encounter abuse, neglect, poverty, parental mental illness, and parental substance abuse. Other children grow up in well-functioning stepfamilies and have caring stepparents who provide affection, effective control and economic support."[16] Still other researchers suggest that it may be the painful transitions of divorce and economically deprived single-parenthood which usually precede the formation of the stepfamily that explain the poor performance of stepchildren.[17]

Perhaps a fairer comparison of stepchildren's well-being is against single-parent families. Indeed, if there were no remarriage, (or first marriage, in the case of unmarried birth mothers), these children would remain a part of a single-parent household. On most psychological measures of behavior and achievement, stepchildren look more like children from single-parent families than children from never-divorced families, but on economic measures it is a different story. The National Survey of Families and Households (NSFH) data show that stepparents have slightly lower incomes and slightly less education than parents in nuclear families, but that incomes of all types of married families with children are three to four times greater than the incomes of single mothers. Custodial mothers in stepfamilies have similar incomes to single mothers (about

$12,000 in 1987). If, as seems plausible, their personal incomes are about the same before they married as after, then marriage has increased their household incomes more than threefold. Stepfathers' incomes are, on average, more than twice as great as their wives', and account for nearly three-fourths of the family's income.[18]

In contrast to residential stepparents, absent biological parents only rarely provide much financial or other help to their children. Some do not because they are dead or cannot be found; about 26 percent of custodial, remarried mothers and 28 percent of single mothers report that their child's father is deceased or of unknown whereabouts. Yet even in the three-quarters of families where the noncustodial parent's whereabouts are known, only about one-third of all custodial mothers (single and remarried) receive child support or alimony from former spouses, and the amounts involved are small compared to the cost of raising children. According to NSFH data, remarried women with awards receive on average $1780 per year, while single mothers receive $1383. Clearly, former spouses cannot be relied on to lift custodial mothers and their children out of poverty.[19]

The picture is still more complex, as is true with all issues relating to stepfamilies. Some noncustodial fathers, like Ray Jones in our scenario, have remarried and have stepchildren themselves. These relationships, too, are evident in the NSFH data. Nearly one-quarter (23 percent) of residential stepfathers have minor children from former relationships living elsewhere. Two-thirds of those report paying child support for their children.[20] In our case, Ray Jones did continue his child support payments, but he felt squeezed by the economic obligation of contributing to two households. This is a growing class of fathers who frequently feel resentful about the heavy burden of supporting two households, particularly when their first wife has remarried.

In sum, although we have no data that precisely examine the distribution of resources within a stepfamily, it is fair to assume that stepfathers' substantial contributions to family income improve their stepchildren's material well-being by helping to cover basic living costs. For many formerly single-parent families, stepfathers' incomes provided by remarriage are essential in preventing or ending poverty among custodial mothers and their children. (The data are less clear for the much smaller class of residential stepmothers.)

While legal dependency usually ends at eighteen, the economic resources available to a stepchild through remarriage could continue to be an important factor past childhood. College education and young adulthood are especially demanding economic events. The life-course studies undertaken by some researchers substantiate the interpersonal trends seen in stepfamilies before the stepchildren leave home. White reports that viewed from either the parent's or the child's perspective, relationships over the life-course between stepchildren and stepparents are substantially weaker than those between biological parents and children. These rela-

tionships are not monolithic, however; the best occur when the stepparent is a male, there are no step siblings, the stepparent has no children
of his own, and the marriage between the biological parent and the stepparent is intact.[21] On the other end, support relationships are nearly always cut off if the stepparent relationship is terminated because of divorce
or the death of the natural parent.

The Jones children were fortunate. Martha and Sam enjoyed a good
marriage, in spite of the stress of stepparenting, and Sam was glad to help
them with college expenses. Their biological father, Ray, felt he had his
own family to support; his stepdaughter, Audrey, also needed money for
college. As Sara grew older she grew more accepting of Sam. And after
her first child was born, she seemed happy to accept Sam as a grandfa-
ther for her child. Josh continued on good terms with Sam.

Again, one might ask to compare these findings to single-parent
households where there are no stepparents to provide additional support.
The data here are less available. While we do know that stepchildren leave
home earlier and are less likely to attend college than children from intact families, the comparison with single-parent families is not clear.[22]
One study of perceived normative obligation to stepparents and stepchildren suggests that people in stepfamilies have weaker, but still important,
family ties than do biological kin.[23] In terms of economic and other forms
of adult support, even weak ties cannot be discounted. They might, instead, become the focus of public policy initiatives.

## Stepfamilies in Law and Public Policy

Both state and federal law set policies that affect stepfamilies. Overall,
these policies do not reflect a coherent policy toward stepparents and
stepchildren. Two competing models are roughly evident. One, a
"stranger" model, followed by most states, treats the residential stepparent as if he or she were a legal stranger to the children, with no rights
and no responsibilites. The other, a "dependency" model, most often followed by federal policymakers, assumes the residential stepfather is, in
fact, supporting the stepchildren and provides benefits accordingly. But
there is inconsistency in both state and federal policy. Some states lean at
times toward a dependency model and require support in some instances,
and the federal government sometimes treats the stepparent as if he or
she were a stranger to the stepchildren, and ignores them in calculating
benefits.

State law governs the traditional family matters of marriage, divorce, adoption, and inheritance, while federal law covers a wide range
of programs and policies that touch on the lives of most Americans,
including stepfamilies. As the provider of benefits through such programs as Temporary Aid for Needy Families (TANF) and Social Security, the federal government sets eligibility standards that affect the economic well-being of many stepfamilies. In addition, as the employer of

the armed forces and civil servants, the federal government establishes employee benefits guidelines for vast numbers of American families. And in its regulatory role, the federal government defines the status of stepfamilies for many purposes ranging from immigration eligibility to tax liability.

Not covered in this chapter or, to my knowledge, yet systematically investigated are the wide range of private employee benefit programs, from medical and life insurance through educational benefits. These programs mostly take their lead from state or federal law. Therefore, it is fair to guess that they suffer from similar inconsistencies.

## State Policies

State laws generally give little recognition to the dependency needs of children who reside with their stepparent; they are most likely to treat the stepparent as a stranger to the children, with no rights or obligations. In contrast to the numerous state laws obligating parents to support natural children born out of wedlock or within a previous marriage, only a few states have enacted statutes which specifically impose an affirmative duty on stepparents The Utah stepparent support statute, for example, provides simply that, "A stepparent shall support a stepchild to the same extent that a natural or adoptive parent is required to support a child."[24] This duty of support ends upon the termination of the marriage. Most states are silent on the obligation to support stepchildren.[25]

A few states rely on common law, the legal tradition stemming from our English roots. The common law tradition leans more toward a dependency model. It dictates that a stepparent can acquire the rights and duties of a parent if he or she acts *in loco parentis* (in the place of a parent). Acquisition of this status is not automatic; it is determined by the stepparent's intent. A stepparent need not explicitly state the intention to act as a parent; he or she can "manifest the requisite intent to assume responsibility by actually providing financial support or by taking over the custodial duties."[26] Courts, however, have been reluctant to grant *in loco* parental rights or to attach obligations to unwilling stepparents. In the words of one Wisconsin court, "A good Samaritan should not be saddled with the legal obligations of another and we think the law should not with alacrity conclude that a stepparent assumes parental relationships to a child."[27]

At the extreme, once the status of *in loco parentis* is achieved, the stepparent "stands in the place of the natural parent, and the reciprocal rights, duties, and obligations of parent and child subsist." These rights, duties, and obligations include the duty to provide financial support, the right to custody and control of the child, immunity from suit by the stepchild, and, in some cases, visitation rights after the dissolution of the marriage by death or divorce.

Yet stepparents who qualify as *in loco parentis* are not always required to provide support in all circumstances. A subset of states imposes obligation only if the stepchild is in danger of becoming dependent on public assistance. For example, Hawaii provides that:

> A stepparent who acts in loco parentis is bound to provide, maintain, and support the stepparent's stepchild during the residence of the child with the stepparent if the legal parents desert the child or are unable to support the child, thereby reducing the child to destitute and necessitous circumstances.[28]

Just as states do not regularly require stepparents to support their stepchildren, they do not offer stepparents the parental authority of custody and control within the marriage. A residential stepparent generally has fewer rights than a legal guardian or a foster parent. According to one commentator, a stepparent "has no authority to make decisions about the child—no authority to approve emergency medical treatment or even to sign a permission slip for a field trip to the fire station"[29]

Both common law and state statutes almost uniformly terminate the stepparent relationship upon divorce or the death of the custodial parent. This means that the support obligations, if there were any, cease, and that the stepparent has no rights to visitation or custody. State courts have sometimes found individual exceptions to this rule, but they have not created any clear precedents. Currently only a few states authorize stepparents to seek visitation rights, and custody is almost always granted to a biological parent upon divorce. In the event of the death of the stepparent's spouse, the noncustodial, biological parent is usually granted custody even when the stepparent has, in fact, raised the child. In one such recent Michigan case, *Henrickson* v. *Gable*,[30] the children, aged nine and ten when their mother died, had lived with their stepfather since infancy and had rarely seen their biological father. In the ensuing custody dispute, the trial court left the children with their stepfather, but an appellate court, relying upon a state law that created a strong preference for biological parents, reversed this decision and turned the children over to their biological father.

Following the stranger model, state inheritance laws, with a few complex exceptions, do not recognize the existence of stepchildren. Under existing state laws, even a dependent stepchild whose stepparent has supported and raised the child for many years is not eligible to inherit from the stepparent if there is no will. California provides the most liberal rule for stepchild recovery when there is no will, but only if the stepchild meets relatively onerous qualifications. Stepchildren may inherit as the children of a deceased stepparent only if "it is established by clear and convincing evidence that the stepparent would have adopted the person but for a legal barrier."[31] Very few stepchildren have been able to pass this test. Similarly a stepchild cannot bring a negligence suit for the accidental death of a stepparent. In most instances, then, only a biological child will inherit or receive legal compensation when a stepparent dies.

## Federal Policies

The federal policies that concern us here are of two types: federal benefit programs given to families in need, including TANF and Supplemental Security Income (SSI), and general programs not based on need, including Social Security was well as civil service and military personnel employee benefits. Most of these programs follow the dependency model. They go further than do most states in recognizing or promoting the actual family relationship of residential stepfamilies. Many of them (although not all) assume that residential stepparents support their stepchildren and accordingly make these children eligible for benefits equivalent to those afforded to other children of the family.

Despite the fact that federal law generally recognizes the dependency of residential stepchildren, it remains wanting in many respects. There is a great deal of inconsistency in how the numerous federal programs and policies treat the stepparent-stepchild relationship, and the very definitions of what constitutes a stepchild are often quite different across programs. Most of the programs strive for a dependency-based definition, such as living with or receiving 50 percent of support from a stepparent. However, some invoke the vague definition, "actual family relationship," and some do not attempt any definition at all, thus potentially including nonresidential stepchildren among the beneficiaries. In some programs the category of stepchild is entirely absent or specifically excluded from the list of beneficiaries for some programs.

Even where program rules permit benefits for dependent stepchildren as for natural children, the benefits to stepchildren are typically severed by death or divorce.[32] While Social Security does cover dependent stepchildren in the event of death, several programs specifically exclude stepchildren from eligibility for certain death benefits. Under the Federal Employees' Retirement System, stepchildren are explicitly excluded from the definition of children in determining the default beneficiary, without concern for the stepchild's possible dependency. All stepchildren are similarly excluded from eligibility for lump-sum payments under the Foreign Service Retirement and Disability System and the CIA Retirement and Disability program.[33]

Stepchildren are even more vulnerable in the event of divorce. Here the stranger model is turned to. As with state law, any legally recognized relationship is immediately severed upon divorce in nearly all federal programs. The children and their stepparents become as strangers. Social Security does not provide any cushion for stepchildren if the deceased stepparent is divorced from the custodial parent. Under Social Security law, the stepparent-stepchild relationship is terminated immediately upon divorce and the stepchild is no longer eligible for benefits even if the child has in fact been dependent on the insured stepparent for the duration of a very long marriage.[34] If the divorce were finalized the day before the stepparent's death the child would receive no benefits.

In sum, current federal policy goes part way toward defining the role of the stepparent by assuming a dependency model in most programs, even when state law does not, and providing benefits to stepchildren based on this assumption of stepparent support. However, as described, existing federal stepparent policy falls short in several critical areas. And state laws and policies fall far short of federal policies in their consideration of stepfamilies, for the most part treating stepparents as strangers with regard to their stepchildren.

## New Policy Proposals

Proposals for policy reform regarding stepfamilies are scant in number and, so far, largely unheard by policymakers. Most of the proposals come from legal scholars, a few from social scientists. Stepparents have not been organized to demand reform, nor have child advocates. All the reforms have some disagreements with the existing stranger and dependency models, but few offer a completely new model.

All of the proposals I review base their arguments to a greater or lesser degree on social science data, although not always the same data. The proposers may roughly be divided into three camps. The first, and perhaps smallest camp, I call *negativists*. These are scholars who view stepfamilies from a sociobiological perspective, and find them a troublesome aberration to be actively discouraged. The second, and by far largest group of scholars, I term *voluntarists*. This group acknowledges both the complexity and the often distant nature of stepparent relationships, and largely believes that law and policy should leave stepfamilies alone, as it does now. If stepparents wish to take a greater role in their stepchildren's lives, they should be encouraged to do so, by adoption or some other means. The third camp recognizes the growing presence of stepfamilies as an alternate family form and believes they should be recognized and strengthened in some important ways. This group, I call them *reformists*, believes the law should take the lead in providing more rights or obligations to stepparents. The few policy initiatives from this group range from small specific reforms regarding such issues as inheritance and visitation to my own proposal for a full-scale redefinition of stepparents' rights and obligations.

The negativist viewpoint on stepparenting, most prominently represented by sociologist David Popenoe, relies on a sociobiological theory of reproduction. According to this theory, human beings will give unstintingly to their own biological children, in order to promote their own genes, but will be far less generous to others. The recent rise in divorce and out-of-wedlock births, according to Popenoe, has created a pattern of essentially fatherless households that cannot compete with the two-biological-parent families.

Popenoe believes the pattern of stepparent disengagement revealed by many researchers is largely based on this biological stinginess.

> If the argument . . . is correct, and the family is fundamentally rooted in biology and at least partly activated by the "genetically selfish" activities of human beings, childbearing by non relatives is inherently problematic. It is not that unrelated individuals are unable to do the job of parenting, it is just that they are not as likely to do the job well. Stepfamily problems, in short, may be so intractable that the best strategy for dealing with them is to do everything possible to minimize their occurrence.

Moreover, Popenoe cites researchers on the greatly increased incidence of child abuse by stepfathers over natural fathers, who suggest that "stepchildren are not merely 'disadvantaged' but imperiled."[35] This argument is not so farfetched, he claims, in fact it is the stuff of our folk wisdom. Snow White and Hansel and Gretel had it right; stepparents are not merely uncaring, they may be dangerous.

Popenoe goes beyond the stranger model, which is neutral as to state activity, and suggests an active discouragement of stepparent families. He believes the best way to obstruct stepfamilies is to encourage married biological two-parent families. Premarital and marital counseling, a longer waiting period for divorce, and a redesign of the current welfare system so that marriage and family are empowered rather than denigrated are among his policy recommendations. He is heartened by what he calls the "new familism," a growing recognition of the need for strong social bonds, which he believes can best be found in the biological two-parent family.[36]

The second group of scholars, whom I call voluntarists, generally believe that the stepparent relationship is essentially voluntary and private and the stranger model most clearly reflects this. The legal bond formed by remarriage is between man and wife—stepchildren are incidental; they are legal strangers. Stepparents may choose, or not choose, to become more involved with everyday economic and emotional support of their stepchildren; but the law should not mandate this relationship, it should simply reflect it. These scholars recognize the growth of stepfamilies as a factor of modern life and neither condone nor condemn this configuration. Family law scholar David Chambers probably speaks for most scholars in this large camp when he says,

> In most regards, this state of the law nicely complements the state of stepparent relationships in the United States. Recall the inescapable diversity of such relationships—residential and non-residential, beginning when the children are infants and when they are teenagers, leading to comfortable relationships in some cases and awkward relationships in others, lasting a few years and lasting many. In this context it seems sensible to permit those relationships to rest largely on the voluntary arrangements among stepparents and biologic parents. The current state of the law also amply recognizes our nation's continuing absorption with the biologic relationship, especially as it informs our sensibilities about enduring financial obligations.[37]

Chambers is not enthusiastic about imposing support obligations on stepparents, either during or following the termination of a marriage, but is interested in promoting voluntary adoption. He would, however, approve some middle ground where biological parents are not completely cut off in the adoption process.

Other voluntarists are attracted by the new English model of parenting, as enacted in the Children Act of 1989. Of great attraction to American voluntarists is the fact that under this model a stepparent who has been married at least two years to the biological parent may voluntarily petition for a residence order for his or her spouse's child. With a residence order the stepparent has parental responsibility toward the child until the age of sixteen. But this order does not extinguish the parental responsibility of the noncustodial parent.[38] In accordance with the Children Act of 1989, parents, biological or otherwise, no longer have parental rights, they have only parental responsibilities, and these cannot be extinguished upon the divorce of the biological parents. In England, therefore, it is possible for three adults to claim parental responsibility. Unlike biological parental responsibility, however, stepparent responsibility does not usually extend following divorce. The stepparent is not normally financially responsible following divorce, but he or she may apply for a visitation order.

The third group, whom I call reformists, believe that voluntary acts on the part of stepparents are not always adequate, and that it is necessary to reform the law in some way to more clearly define the rights and responsibilities of stepparents. The American Bar Association Family Law Section has been working for some years on a proposed Model Act to suggest legislative reforms regarding stepparents' obligations to provide child support and rights to discipline, visitation, and custody. A Model Act is not binding anywhere; it is simply a model for all states to consider. Traditionally, however, Model Acts have been very influential in guiding state legislative reform. In its current form, the ABA Model Act would require stepparents to assume a duty of support during the duration of the remarriage only if the child is not adequately supported by the custodial and noncustodial parent. The issue is ultimately left to the discretion of the family court, but the Model Act does not require that the stepparent would need to have a close relationship with a stepchild before a support duty is imposed. The Model Act, however, does not describe what the rule should be if the stepparent and the custodial parent divorce.

The proposed statute is rather more complete in its discussion of stepparent visitation or custody rights following divorce. It takes a two-tiered approach, first asking if the stepparent has standing (a legal basis) to seek visitation and then asking if the visitation would be in the best interests of the child. The standing question is to be resolved with reference to five factors, which essentially examine the role of the stepparent in the child's life (almost an *in loco parentis* question), the financial support offered by the stepparent, and the detriment to the child from denying visitation. The court, if it finds standing, then completes the analysis with the best interests standard of the jurisdiction. The Model Act's section on physical custody also requires a two-tiered test, requiring standing and increasing the burden on the stepparent to present clear and convincing proof that he or she is the better custodial parent.

The ABA Model Act is a worthwhile start, in my opinion, but it is little more than that. At most it moves away from a stranger model and provides a limited concept of mandatory stepparent support during a marriage, acknowledging that stepchildren are at least sometimes dependent. It also gives a stepparent a fighting chance for visitation or custody following a divorce. It fails to clarify stepparents' rights during the marriage, however, and does not deal with the issue of economic support at the period of maximum vulnerability, the termination of the marriage through death and divorce. Moreover, the Model Act, and, indeed, all the existing reform proposals, deal only with traditional legal concepts of parenthood defined by each state and do not consider the vast range of federal programs, or other public and private programs, that define the step parent-stepchild relationship for purposes of benefits, insurance, or other purposes.

I propose, instead, a new conceptualization of stepparent rights and responsibilities, a de facto parent model, that will cover all aspects of the stepparent-stepchild relationship and will extend to federal and private policy as well. My first concern in proposing a new framework is the welfare of the stepchildren, which is not adequately dealt with in either the stranger or the dependency model. The failure of state and, to a lesser extent, federal policy to address coherently the financial interdependencies of step relationships, described earlier in this chapter, means that children dependent upon a residential stepparent may not receive adequate support or benefits from that parent during the marriage, and they may not be protected economically in the event of divorce or parental death.

The longitudinal studies of families described earlier in this chapter suggest that the most difficult periods for children are those of marital transition, for example, divorce and remarriage. Families with a residential stepfather have a much higher family income than mother-headed single families; indeed, their household incomes look much like nuclear families.[39] However, research demonstrates that stepfamilies are fragile and are more likely to terminate in divorce than biological families. The event of divorce can quite suddenly pull the resources available for the children back to the single-parent level. Currently children are at least financially cushioned by child support following the divorce of their biological parents, but have no protective support following the breakup of their stepfamily. Nor are they protected in the event of the death of the stepparent, which is certainly another period of vulnerability (as discussed earlier, only a small minority continue to receive support from noncustodial parents).

A second reason for proposing a new framework is to strengthen the relationship of the stepparent and stepchildren. While research generally finds that stepparents are less engaged in parenting than natural parents, research studies do not explain the causes; others must do so. In addition to the sociobiologists' claim for stingy, genetically driven behavior, sociologists have posited the explanation of "incomplete institutionalization."[40] This theory is based on the belief that, by and large, people act as they are expected to act by society. In the case of stepfamilies, there are unclear or absent societal norms and standards for how to define the remarried family, especially the role of the stepparent in relation to the stepchild.

Briefly, my new model requires, first of all, dividing stepparents into two subclasses: those who are de facto parents and those who are not. De facto parents would be defined as "those stepparents legally married to a natural parent who primarily reside with their stepchildren, or who provide at least 50 percent of the stepchild's financial support." Stepparents who do not meet the de facto parent requirements would, in all important respects, disappear from policy.

For the purposes of federal and state policy, under this scheme, a de facto parent would be treated virtually the same as a natural parent during the marriage. The same rights, obligations, and presumptions would attach vis-à-vis their stepchildren, including the obligation of support. These rights and duties would continue in some form, based on the length of the marriage, following the custodial parent's death or divorce from the stepparent, or the death of the stepparent. In the event of divorce the stepparent would have standing to seek custody or visitation but the stepparent could also be obligated for child support of a limited duration. Upon the death of a stepparent, a minor stepchild would be treated for purposes of inheritance and benefits as would a natural child.

So far this proposal resembles the common law doctrine of *in loco parentis,* described earlier, where the stepparent is treated for most purposes (except inheritance) as a parent on the condition that he or she voluntarily agrees to support the child. In the de facto model, however, support is mandatory, not voluntary, on the grounds both that it is not fair to stepchildren to be treated by the law in an unequal or arbitrary manner, and that child welfare considerations are best met by uniform support of stepchildren. Furthermore, in the traditional common law *in loco parentis* scenario, the noncustodial parent had died, and was not a factor to be reckoned with. Under this scheme, creating a de facto parent category for stepparents would not invalidate the existing rights and obligations of a noncustodial biological parent. Rather, this proposal would empower a stepparent as an additional parent.

Multiple parenting and the rights and obligations of the stepparent and children following divorce or death are controversial and difficult policy matters that require more detailed attention than the brief exposition that can be offered here. Multiple parenting is the barrier upon which many family law reform schemes, especially in custody and adoption, have foundered. It is also one of the reasons that there has been no consistent effort to reformulate the role of stepparents. Working out the details is critical. For instance, mandating stepparent support raises a central issue of fairness. If the stepparent is indeed required to support the child, there is a question about the support obligations of the noncustodial parent. Traditionally, most states have not recognized the stepparent contribution as an offset to child support.[41] While this policy promotes administrative efficiency, and may benefit some children, it may not be fair to the noncustodial parent. An important advance in recognizing the existence of multiple parents in the nonlinear family is to recognize multiple support obligations. The few states that require stepparent obligation have given limited attention to apportionment of child support obligations, offering no clear guidelines. I propose that state statutory requirements for stepparent obligation as de facto parents also include clear guidelines for apportionment of child support between the noncustodial natural parent and the stepparent.

Critics of this proposal may say that if the custodial parent's support is reduced, the child will have fewer resources. For some children, this may be true, but as discussed earlier in this chapter, only about 25 percent of all stepchildren receive child support and the average amount is less than $2000 per year.[42] Therefore, a reduction of this small amount of support to a minority of stepchildren would not have a large overall effect compared with the increased resources of living with a stepparent that most stepchildren enjoy. And, certainly, the additional safety net of protection in the event of the death of the stepparent or divorce from the custodial parent would benefit all stepchildren. In addition, under the de facto scheme, the reduction of the support payment for the noncustodial parent may help to sweeten the multiple parenting relationship.

Let us apply this model to the Jones-Hutchins family introduced earlier. If Ray Jones, the noncustodial parent, were paying $6000 a year support for his two children (on the high end for noncustodial parents according to the National Survey for Children and Families), his payments could be reduced by as much as half, since Sam Hutchins's income is $50,000 per year and he has no other dependents. It should be emphasized, however, that in most stepfamilies there would be no reduction in support, because the noncustodial parent is paying no support. In the Jones-Hutchins family the $3000 relief would certainly be welcome to Ray, who is also now living with and helping to support his new wife's child. The relief would likely make him somewhat friendlier toward Sam, or at least more accepting of his role in his children's lives. It also might make him more likely to continue support past eighteen, since he would not feel as financially pinched over the years. More important, while the children would lose some support, they would have the security that if Sam died they would be legal heirs and default beneficiaries to his life insurance. They could also ask for damages if his death were caused by negligence or work-related events. And if he and their mother divorced, they could continue for a time to be considered dependents on his health and other benefits and to receive support from him.

Another facet of multiple parenting is legal authority. If stepparents are required to accept parental support obligations, equal protection and fairness concerns dictate that they must also be given parental rights. Currently, state laws, as noted earlier, recognize only natural or adoptive parents; a stepparent currently has no legal authority over a stepchild, even to authorize a field trip. If stepparents had full parental rights, in some cases, as when the parents have shared legal custody, the law would be recognizing the parental rights of three parents, rather than two. While this sounds unusual, it is an accurate reflection of how many families now raise their children. Most often, however, it would be only the custodial parent and his or her spouse, the de facto parent, who would have authority to make decisions for the children in their home.

In the Jones-Hutchins family this policy would give Sam more recognition as a parent. Schools, camps, hospitals, and other institutions that require parental consent or involvement would now automatically include him in their consideration of the children's interests. Since Sam is the more day-to-day parent, their biological father, Ray, may not mind at all. If he did mind, the three of them would have to work it out (or in an extreme event, take it to mediation or family court). In fact, since only a minority of noncustodial dads see their children on a regular basis, three-parent decision making would be unusual.

Critics of this scheme may argue that adoption, not the creation of the legal status of de facto parent, is the appropriate vehicle for granting a stepparent full parental rights and responsibilities.[43] If, as discussed earlier, nearly three-quarters of stepchildren are not being supported by their noncustodial parents, policy initiatives could be directed to terminating the nonpaying parents' rights and promoting stepparent adoption. Adoption is not possible, however, unless the parental rights of the absent natural parent have been terminated—a difficult procedure against a reluctant parent. Normally, the rights of a parent who maintains contact with his or her child cannot be terminated even if that parent is not contributing child support. And when parental rights are terminated, visitation rights are terminated as well in most states. It is by no means clear that it is in the best interests of children to terminate contact with a natural parent, even if the parent is not meeting his or her obligation to support.[44] As discussed earlier, a large percentage (another 25 percent or so), of noncustodial parents continue some contact with their children, even when not paying support.[45] And while stepparent adoption should be strongly encouraged when it is possible, this solution will not resolve the problem of defining the role of stepparents who have not adopted.

Extending, in some form, the rights and obligations following the termination of the marriage by divorce or death is equally problematical. Currently, only a few courts have ruled in favor of support payments following divorce, and these have been decided on an individual basis. Only one state, Missouri, statutorily continues stepparent support obligations following divorce.[46] It would clearly be in the best interests of the child to experience continued support, since a significant number of children may sink below the poverty line upon the dissolution of their stepfamily.[47]

Since the de facto model is based on dependency, not blood, a fair basis for support following divorce or the death of the custodial parent might be to require that a stepparent who qualified as a de facto parent for at least one year must contribute child support for half the number of years of dependency until the child reached majority. If a child resided with the stepparent for four years, the stepparent would be liable for support for two years. If the biological noncustodial parent were still paying support payments, the amount could be apportioned. While it may be said that this policy would discourage people from becoming stepparents by marrying, it could also be said to discourage divorce once one has become a stepparent. Stepparents might consider working harder at maintaining a marriage if divorce had some real costs.

Conversely, stepparents should have rights as well as responsibilities following divorce or the death of the custodial parent. Divorced or widowed stepparents should be able to pursue visitation or custody if they have lived with and supported the child for at least one year. Once again, multiple parent claims might sometimes be an issue, but these could be resolved, as they are now, under a primary caretaker, or a best interest standard.

The death of a stepparent is a particular period of vulnerability for stepchildren for which they are unprotected by inheritance law. While Social Security and other federal survivor benefits are based on the premise that a stepchild relies on the support of the residential stepparent and will suffer the same hardship as natural children if the stepparent dies, state inheritance laws, notoriously archaic, decree that only biology, not dependency, counts. State laws should assume that a de facto parent would wish to have all his dependents receive a share of his estate if he died without a will. If the stepchildren are no longer dependent, that assumption would not necessarily prevail. The same assumption should prevail for insurance policies and compensation claims following an accidental death. A dependent stepchild, just as a natural child, should have the right to sue for loss of support.

On the federal front, a clear definition of stepparents as de facto parents would eliminate the inconsistencies regarding stepparents which plague current federal policies and would clarify the role of the residential stepparent. For the duration of the marriage, a stepchild would be treated as a natural child for purposes of support and the receipt of federal benefits. This treatment would persist in the event of the death of the stepparent. The stepchild would receive all the survivor and death benefits that would accrue to a natural child.[48]

In the case of divorce, the issue of federal benefits is more complicated. Stepchildren and natural children should not have identical coverage for federal benefits following divorce, again, but neither is it good policy to summarily cut off children who have been dependent, sometimes for many years, on the de facto parent. A better policy is to extend federal benefits for a period following divorce, based on a formula that matches half the number of years of dependency, as earlier suggested for child support. For instance, if the stepparent resided with the stepchild for four years, the child would be covered by Social Security survivor benefits and other federal benefits, including federal employee benefits, for a period of two years following the divorce. This solution would serve children by at least providing a transitional cushion. It would also be relatively easy to administer. In the case of the death of the biological custodial parent, benefits could be similarly extended, or continued indefinitely if the child remains in the custody of the stepparent.

All other private benefits programs would similarly gain from the application of a clear definition of the rights and obligations of residential stepparents. While these nongovernmental programs, ranging from eligibility for private health and life insurance and annuities to access to employee child care, are not reviewed in this chapter, they almost surely reflect the same inconsistencies or silences evident in federal and state policies.

Ultimately, state law defines most of these stepfamily relationships, and it is difficult, if not impossible to achieve uniform reform on a state-by-state basis. In England it is possible to pass a single piece of national legislation, such as the Children Act of 1989, which completely redefines parental roles. In America, the process of reform is slower and less sure. Probably the first step in promoting a new policy would be for the federal government to insist all states pass stepparent general support obligation laws requiring stepparents acting as de facto parents (by my definition) to support their stepchildren as they do their natural children. This goal could be accomplished by making stepparent general support obligation laws a prerequisite for receiving federal welfare grants. Federal policy already assumes this support in figuring eligibility in many programs, but it has not insisted that states change their laws. Precedent for this strategy has been set by the Family Support Acts of 1988 in which the federal government mandated that states set up strict child support enforcement laws for divorced parents and unwed fathers at TANF levels in order to secure AFDC funding.[49] The second, larger step would be to require limited stepparent support following divorce, as described previously. Once the basic obligations were asserted, an articulation of basic rights would presumably follow.

## Conclusion

Stepfamilies compose a large and growing sector of American families that is largely ignored by public policy. Social scientists tell us that these families have problems. Stepparent-stepchildren relationships, poorly defined by law and social norms, are not as strong or nurturing as those in nondivorced families, and stepchildren do not do as well in school and in other outside settings. Still, stepfamily relationships are important in lifting single-parent families out of poverty. When single or divorced mothers marry, the household income increases by more than threefold, rising to roughly the same level as nuclear families. A substantial portion of these families experiences divorce, however, placing the stepchildren at risk of falling back into poverty. It makes good public policy sense then, both to strengthen these stepfamily relationships and to cushion the transition for stepchildren should the relationship end.

## Notes

1. Mary Ann Mason and David Simon, "The Ambiguous Stepparent: Federal Legislation in Search of a Model," *Family Law Quarterly* 29:446–448, 1995.
2. E. Mavis Heatherington and Kathleen M. Jodl, "Stepfamilies as Settings for Child Development," in Alan Booth and Judy Dunn (eds.), *Stepfamilies: Who Benefits? Who Does Not?* (Hillsdale, N.J.: L. Erlbaum 1994), 55; E. Mavis Heatherington, "An Overview of the Virginia Longitudinal Study of Divorce and Remarriage: A Focus on Early Adolescence," *Journal of Family Psychology* 7:39–56, 1993.
3. David Popenoe, "Evolution of Marriage and Stepfamily Problems," in Booth and Dunn (eds.), *Stepfamilies,* 3–28.
4. Mason and Simon, "The Ambiguous Stepparent," 467–482; Mary Ann Mason and Jane Mauldon, "The New Stepfamily Needs a New Public Policy," *Journal of Social Issues* 52(3), Fall 1996.
5. U.S. Bureau of Census, 1989.
6. Divorce is not always the background event. An increasing, but still relatively small number of custodial mothers have not previously wed.
7. Mason and Mauldon, "The New Stepfamily," 5.
8. Ibid., 6.
9. Heatherington and Jodl, "Stepfamilies," 55–81.
10. Ibid., 76.
11. E. Mavis Heatherington and William Clingempeel, "Coping with Marital Transitions: A Family Systems Perspective," *Monographs of the Society for Research in Child Development* 57:2–3, Serial No. 227, New York: 1992; E. Thomson, Sara McLanahan, and R. B. Curtin, "Family Structure, Gender, and Parental Socialization," *Journal of Marriage and the Family* 54:368–378, 1992.
12. Heatherington and Jodl, "Stepfamilies," 69.
13. Ibid., 64–65.
14. Thomson, McLanahan, and Curtin, "Family Structure," 368–378.
15. L. Bumpass and J. Sweet, *American Families and Households* (New York: Russell Sage Foundation, 1987), 23.
16. Paul Amato, "The Implications of Research Findings on Children in Stepfamilies," in Booth and Dunn (eds.), *Stepfamilies,* 84.
17. Nicholas Zill, "Understanding Why Children in Stepfamilies Have More Learning and Behavior Problems Than Children in Nuclear Families," in Booth and Dunn (eds.), *Stepfamilies,* 89–97.
18. Mason and Mauldon, "The New Stepfamily Needs a New Public Policy," 7.

19. Ibid., 8.

20. Ibid.

21. Lynn White, "Stepfamilies over the Lifecourse: Social Support," in Booth and Dunn (eds.), *Stepfamilies,* 109–139.

22. Ibid., 130.

23. A. S. Rossi and P. H. Rossi, *Of Human Bonding: Parent-Child Relations Across the Life Course* (New York: A. de Gruyter, 1990).

24. Utah Code Ann. 78-45-4.1.

25. Margaret Mahoney, *Stefamilies and the Law* (Ann Arbor: University of Michigan Press, 1994), 13–47.

26. Miller v. United States, 123 F.2d 715, 717 (8th Cir, 1941).

27. Niesen v. Niesen, 157 N. W.2d 660 664(Wis. 1968).

28. Hawaii Revised Stat. Ann., Title 31, Sec. 577-4.

29. David Chambers, "Stepparents, Biologic Parents, and the Law's Perceptions of 'Family' after Divorce," in S. Sugarman and H. H. Kay (eds.), *Divorce Reform at the Crossroads* (New Haven: Yale University Press, 1990), 102–129.

30. Henrickson v. Gable.

31. Cal. Prob. Code, Sec. 6408.

32. Mason and Simon, "The Ambiguous Stepparent: Federal Legislation in Search of a Model," 449.

33. Ibid., p. 460–466.

34. 42 U.S.C. sec. 416(e), 1994.

35. M. Daly and M. Wilson, *Homicide* (New York: Aldine de Gruyter, 1988), 230.

36. Barbara Whitehead, "A New Familism?" *Family Affairs* Summer, 1992.

37. Chambers, "Stepparents, Biologic Parents, and the Law's Perceptions of 'Family' after Divorce," 26.

38. Mark A. Fine, "Social Policy Pertaining to Stepfamilies: Should Stepparents and Stepchildren Have the Option of Establishing a Legal Relationship?" in Booth and Dunn (eds.), *Stepfamilies,* 199.

39. Mason and Mauldon,"The New Stepfamily," 5.

40. Andrew Cherlin, "Remarriage as an Incomplete Institution," *American Journal of Sociology* 84:634–649, 1978.

41. S. Ramsey and J. Masson, "Stepparent Support of Stepchildren: A Comparative Analysis of Policies and Problems in the American and British Experience," *Syracuse Law Review* 36:649–666, 1985.

42. Mason and Mauldon,"The New Stepfamily," 7.

43. Joan Hollinger (ed.) et al., *Adoption Law and Practice* (New York: Matthew Bender, 1988).

44. Katherine Bartlett, "Re-thinking Parenthood as an Exclusive Status: The Need for Alternatives When the Premise of the Nuclear Family Has Failed," *Virginia Law Review* 70:879–903, 1984.

45. Mason and Mauldon, "The New Stepfamily," 5.

46. Vernon's Ann. Missouri Stats. 453.400, 1994.

47. Mason and Mauldon, "The New Stepfamily," 5.

48. Mason and Simon, "The Ambiguous Stepparent," 471.

49. 100 P.L. 485; 102 Stat. 2343 (1988).

# 6

# Ambiguous-Father Families

## Ira Mark Ellman

Our image of the traditional family includes a husband who also fulfills the role of father. He provides a substantial portion of the child's financial support, lives with the child, spends at least some time in direct care of the child, and shares with the mother the major decisions of parenthood. Both he and the child view him as father, and third parties do as well. We can call this man the child's social father. Of course, one can imagine cases in which dispute is possible over whether a particular man is the child's social father. While that is one kind of paternal ambiguity, the focus of this chapter is on two other kinds of cases. In the first, there is no dispute about the child's social father, but there is ambiguity about the legal father because the social father is not the biological father, and no formal adoption has taken place to align the two. In the second, the child has no social father, and questions arise about whether the biological father can be considered the legal father.

## Introduction

When a married woman bears a child, both social conventions and legal presumptions have long treated her husband as the father. That was once how the rights and responsibilities of legal fatherhood was established for nearly all children, with little cost, contention, or complication. During the final quarter of the twentieth century, however, things became more complex. The complexity arose from three developments, two social and one scientific. The two social developments were the increasing proportion of children born out-of-wedlock and the increasing determination of policymakers to collect child support from absent fathers. Because of the first, there were more children whose father was not identified by the social conventions and legal presumptions applicable to marital children. Because of the second, identifying the legal father (and thus, the man responsible to provide support) became more important. The scientific development was the ability to establish biological paternity through genetic tests of the child and adults. This scientific development seemed to provide an answer to the problem created by the social developments. Legal paternity could be established by biology. But a new set of problems has been created by the possibility of establishing legal paternity in the absence of, or even in opposition to, social indicators of paternity.

Prior to the development of genetic tests, it was usually impossible to determine biological paternity. In consequence, the law usually relied upon presumptions that typically attributed legal paternity to the child's social father—most importantly, to the mother's husband. States had varying rules concerning the admissibility of evidence to rebut the presumption of the husband's paternity. Some restricted such evidence very severely, while others might allow it.[1] But even when courts accepted such evidence, it was not often persuasive. The primitive blood tests then available were unlikely to exclude a man as the child's biological father even when he in fact was not.[2] Under these conditions, husbands were almost always identified as the legal father of their wife's children. Since as recently as 1970, about 90 percent of all children were born to married mothers, the "marital presumption," as it is called, settled the question of legal paternity in the vast majority of cases. The presumption also identified as the legal father a man who was nearly always the children's social father. He was probably their biological father as well, but if he was not, few knew, at least not for certain. In short, the law did not then often face a forced choice between social and biological paternity.

For the relatively small proportion of children then born to unmarried women, the absence of the marital presumption usually left the child with no legally established father. A paternity action could be brought, of course. But prior to the advent of modern genetic testing, the typical paternity case consisted of conflicting testimony over the alleged father's sexual "access" to the mother during the probable period of conception and over whether the mother had sexual relations during the same time period with other men.[3] The latter question was relevant because under the usual legal rule, the mother's sexual relations with more than one man during the probable period of conception prevented her from showing that any one of them was probably the father.[4] That rule encouraged perjury by both sides, and the encouragement was effective.[5] In these muddied waters, the mother seeking to establish paternity was unlikely to meet her burden of proof, and her claim would fail. Doubtless many unmarried mothers never brought a paternity claim in the first place, anticipating this result. It would seem that this state of affairs ill served nonmarital children, who were deprived of the financial support that a finding of paternity would promise. On the other hand, it might not have mattered much because child support orders, and especially those obtained against unmarried fathers, rarely fulfilled that promise anyway. This was the era before child support enforcement became a national policy priority.[6]

While the outcomes for children born to married and unmarried mothers were thus very different, they were also consistent in one important respect: In both cases the attribution of legal paternity paralleled the reality of social paternity. The husband was the legal and social father of the marital child. And while no one was the legal father of the nonmarital child, typically no one was the child's social father either. Indeed, a nonmarital biological father who was the social father of his children was thought sufficiently rare that the law did not need to consider the possibility of his existence. For example, single mothers alone could consent to the adoption of their child, a core parental right. It was 1972 before American constitutional law recognized that the nonmarital father had any parental rights at all. In that year, the Supreme Court came to the assistance of Mr. Stanley, a nonmarital father who, rather atypically, had lived with his children and their mother for years. Illinois law did not recognize him as a parent, so when the mother died the children were legal orphans who became wards of the state, available for adoption. As a legal stranger to his children, Stanley had no particular priority among those seeking to adopt them.[7] While not necessarily disagreeing with the state's factual claims that nonmarital fathers like Stanley were unusual, the Court held that the state must afford Stanley a chance to show that he was different, before giving his children to strangers. In a famous footnote justifying to skeptics this recognition of nonmarital fathers, the Court observed that the cost of protecting them would be minimal if most did not show up to demand the hearings to which the new rule now entitled them.[8]

The Court ultimately decided four more cases on this general topic of nonmarital fathers' rights. Between the first and the last of these five cases (from 1972 to 1989), a sea change occurred in the science of paternity testing (and it has advanced even further since).[9] In later cases, the Court therefore had to confront a question that *Stanley* never raised, whether the constitutional rights it had recognized arose from social paternity, biological paternity, or both. Its later decisions suggest that the Constitution guarantees the biological father some opportunity to establish a social connection with his offspring, but does not guarantee full paternal rights to the man who declines that opportunity.[10] And the Court's decisions also suggest that state policymakers may treat a child's social father as the legal father, in preference to the biological father, although the Constitution does not require them to make this choice.[11] So answers to the important questions were left largely to state policymakers.

Choosing the appropriate rule for assigning paternity becomes more difficult when social and biological paternity diverge. The newly devel-

oped reliability in assessing biological paternity forces attention to this issue because it makes our knowledge of such divergence more likely. At
the same time, the recent legislative determination to collect child support from absent fathers gives assignment of legal paternity enhanced importance in public policy. Moreover, a legal parent is not only obliged to
provide support, but can also seek custody and is usually guaranteed at
least some time with the child. Support duties and custody rights are in
this way legally connected.[12] Parents intuit the connection, and both custodial parents considering claims for support and noncustodial parents
considering claims for custody sometimes forego their claim to avoid triggering the corresponding claim back from the other parent. The two also
have a social connection: The biological father who has enjoyed a parental
relationship with a child is more likely to pay support, and to want assured access, than the biological father who has not.[13] So, in allowing the
law to identify genetic fathers who have never known their child, modern science has given the law a challenge as well as a tool.

    This chapter provides an illustrative discussion of some of the more
common cases in which discrepancies between biological and social paternity can arise. It deals with some social fathers who are not the child's
biological father—primarily, cuckholded husbands—and with some biological fathers who are not the child's social father.

## Cuckolded Husbands and other Fine Fellows

Reliable estimates of the frequency with which married women bear children not biologically their husband's (called "paternal discrepancy") are,
for obvious reasons, difficult to obtain. Many of the published studies
that attempt a direct measure of the paternal discrepancy rate predate the
availability of the most precise biological tests. The results of these studies also seem to vary considerably with the local population examined.[19]
Less direct data provide conflicting indicators. On one hand, it appears
that married American couples are relatively monogamous. A 1990s study
of American sexual behavior found that more than 90 percent of wives
reported that they were sexually faithful during their marriage; women in
unmarried cohabiting unions were slightly more likely to report having
had sexual relations with a man other than their regular partner.[14] On
the other hand, it appears that women engaging in "extrapair"[15] sexual
relations are more likely to do so during the most fertile period of their
cycle,[16] and less likely to use contraceptives,[17] than when engaging in sexual relations with their regular partner.[18]

    In the aggregate, one might therefore expect a rate of paternal dis-
crepancy that was steady if not high, although higher perhaps than most
men think. It appears that the professional consensus is that the rate of
paternal discrepancy for couples in stable unions, whether legally married
or cohabiting, is from 10 to 15 percent.[20] If the rate among married couples were 10 percent, then 260,000 of the 2.6 million marital children

born in 1997[21] were not the husband's, whether he knows it or not. How should the law treat this possibility? Consider first a simple case in which the biological father is not on the scene:

## *Illustration 1*

Bob and Roberta marry in 1995. Roberta delivers a child, Rob, in 1998. Ralph, Roberta's former employer, is actually the biological father of Rob, as a result of a brief affair that Bob never knew about. Ralph moved to another state shortly after Roberta became pregnant. He never knew of Roberta's pregnancy and has had no contact with Roberta since moving. When Rob is six years old, Bob files for divorce.

Suppose Bob and Roberta now find themselves in a nasty custody dispute. Roberta claims for the first time that Bob is not Rob's biological father and that he therefore is not his legal father either. Were that so, Bob would have no legal claim to custody or visitation. Of course, if he is not Rob's legal father, Bob has no child support obligation either. But suppose Roberta is willing to accept that result as the price of total victory in the custody dispute. (Perhaps she is comfortably employed herself, or plans to remarry a generous man with a reliable income.) Bob objects to the genetic tests because he doesn't expect to change his feelings toward Rob, and is prepared to pay child support, no matter the outcome.

To many people, this would seem an easy case. There is good reason to believe that biological paternity should be irrelevant here—that Bob, Rob's social father, should also be declared his legal father in any event. That surely must be the right result from Rob's perspective: How could he be better off by the law's refusing to recognize the only father he has ever known, who desires to remain his father, especially when there is no other man he had known who could fulfill that role? And if that is our conclusion, then there is no reason to order genetic tests over Bob's opposition: It is a pointless intrusion to force the biological information on the parties if the legal attribution of paternity will not turn upon it.

Notice too how much we can vary this story without changing our conclusion, so long as our focus stays on the child. Suppose, for example, Bob hadn't been deceived throughout the marriage but knew of Ralph's biological paternity when Rob was born, yet chose to treat Rob as his son anyway. Or suppose Roberta was already pregnant when she and Bob married, and either Bob knew then that the child was not his biological offspring, or he did not, but in either event treated Rob as his son over the next six years. Or suppose Bob and Roberta had never married at all, but simply lived together with Rob in an informal family unit for six years. From the child's perspective, these are all distinctions without a difference: Bob has always been his father, and he is best off if the law recognizes him as such. He has no other.

Now consider a different version of the story. This time, Bob, not Roberta, asks the court to order genetic tests, so that he can avoid liability for child support. From the adults' perspective, a fair ruling on Bob's claim might now depend upon which factual variation is before us. For example, we might think that if Bob knew from the outset that Rob was not his biological child, but had agreed to treat him as though he were, then he cannot now renege, but that if he had been deceived then he should perhaps be allowed to withdraw when he learns the truth. But once again, from the child's perspective these distinctions may have no importance. Rob is probably better off having Bob declared his father whether or not Bob had been deceived. Of course, the law probably cannot enforce Bob's paternal affection, and with these facts that affection may be less likely to continue than in the first version of our story (in which Bob wished to remain his father). But the law can enforce Bob's child support obligation, and perhaps the continuing obligation to pay support will influence Bob to remain emotionally involved with Rob as well.[22] In any event, the only alternative is to treat Ralph as Rob's legal father instead. But Ralph has no relationship with Rob, so he hardly seems a better bet to assume the role of Rob's social father, and he may offer more resistance than Bob to paying support.

All in all, it would seem to make sense, in the cases we have considered so far, to treat Bob as we treat any other divorcing dad regardless of whether it is Bob or Roberta who seeks to deny his fatherhood and regardless of whether or not he was deceived about his biological paternity. Bob's social paternity should establish his legal paternity no matter which spouse claims otherwise.

One can imagine, however, a third factual variation that might matter: Suppose Bob and Roberta end their relationship when Rob is six months old rather than six years old, and the challenge to Bob's paternity is made then? This temporal variation has more bite because it bears on the assumption that Bob is Rob's social father. Social paternity takes time to establish, and six months may not be long enough to develop a relationship upon which the law can pin the next $17\frac{1}{2}$ years of rights and obligations. Moreover, it is not too late for Ralph, the biological father, to become Rob's social father as well, if he has both inclination and opportunity. A judicial determination that Ralph was Rob's legal father might yield both. Even if it does not, Ralph's biological paternity, combined with judicial recognition of his right to pursue social paternity, may provide a firmer foundation upon which to rest his child support obligation than could be found to explain a support order against Bob. After all, Bob is not established as Rob's social father either.

So it should matter whether the husband's paternity is challenged when the child is six months old or six years old. The importance of the child's age in analyzing these cases lies behind California's well-known rule barring belated challenges to the husband's paternity of a child born to his wife: Any challenge must be brought within two years of the child's birth.[23] California has explained this bar on belated challenges as "based upon a determination by the Legislature as a matter of overriding social policy, that given a certain relationship between the husband and wife, the husband is to be held responsible for the child, and that the integrity of the family unit should not be impugned."[24] The two-year window is a mechanical rule meant to distinguish, in an administratively convenient fashion, cases in which the husband has developed the requisite parental relationship with the child, from those in which he has not. California believes that "[t]his social relationship is much more important, to the child at least, than a biological relationship of actual paternity."[25]

Unfortunately, most states do not have a provision like California's. In 1973, the Commissioners on Uniform State Laws recommended to the states the Uniform Parentage Act. Adopted in about nineteen states,[26] it requires that an action to challenge the husband's paternity of his wife's child be brought "within a reasonable time after obtaining knowledge of the relevant facts." That means, for example, that Bob could raise a challenge when Rob was ten or twelve, if that is when he first learned of the doubts about his biological paternity.[27] Whether the husband acted promptly after learning the facts may seem relevant if we are focused on fairness to him, but has little bearing on the child's interests, which are affected by the passage of time whether or not the husband knew the biological facts as the time passed. Another clause of the Parentage Act, however, does recommend that challenges to a husband's paternity be subject to an outer time limit of five years from the child's birth, no matter when the facts were discovered. Unfortunately, few states adopted this provision.[28] The Commissioners proposed a new version of the Uniform Parentage Act in 2000 that has an improved formulation barring challenges to the husband's paternity more than two years after the child's birth, so long as the birth occurred during his marriage to the mother, or within 300 days of its dissolution.[29] The bar on delayed challenges also applies when the child was born before the mother's marriage, if the man she later marries had "voluntarily asserted his paternity of the child" in a writing or by agreeing to be named as the child's father on the birth certificate.[30] It remains to be seen how many states accept these recommendations.

States that do not set an absolute time limit on challenges to the husband's paternity often rely upon another legal doctrine, called *estoppel*, to reach a sensible result in the most compelling cases. This general legal principle can bar persons from bringing an otherwise valid legal claim when the surrounding facts make it very unfair for them to press it. For example, while A has the legal right to keep adjoining landowner B from crossing his land, a court might find A "estopped" from asserting that right if B had built a house on his land in reliance on A's normally unenforceable oral promise to allow B to cross.

The estoppel doctrine, unlike a simple two-year rule, necessarily requires a case-by-case examination of the facts, with far more variable results. Some courts apply the doctrine flexibly to bar either spouse from denying the husband's paternity whenever they have both treated the children as the husband's over a significant time period, if the disavowal has the potential for causing the children harm.[31] But other courts adhere to the doctrine's technical requirements and therefore focus on facts that are irrelevant to the child's interests, such as whether the husband knew he was not the children's biological father when he treated them as his own.[32] A narrow technical analysis leads still other courts to reject a claim that the husband is estopped from denying his paternity, no matter how long he treated the children as his, unless he is directly responsible for the biological father's unavailability a source of support.[33] For example, these courts treat the mother's husband as the children's father if she sought severance of the biological father's parental status in reliance upon her husband's promise to support them, but will allow the husband to deny paternity, despite having treated the children as his throughout their life, if the biological father is unavailable because he is dead or cannot be found. Overall, then, from the child's perspective the estoppel doctrine is poorly equipped as a general approach to these cases, although it can serve as a useful stopgap when better statutory provisions are not available.

For example, the estoppel doctrine might benefit the children of unmarried couples who get nothing from a statutory rule barring belated challenges to a *husband*'s paternity. Unfortunately, many courts do not apply estoppel in this context, despite compelling facts, as a recent decision of the Michigan Supreme Court illustrates. The mother cohabited with Van for five years, and continued to see him after that. She led him to believe he was the father of the two children born to her during their relationship, and Van treated them as his children. When the children were seven and three, the couple's relationship ended. The mother now denied Van all access to them. When he sought legal relief she alleged, for the first time, that he was not their biological father. Tests confirmed her claim. The court refused to apply estoppel to protect Van because he was not married to the mother. The court conceded that the case presented "tragic circumstances":

> [T]he children were suddenly separated from Mr. Van, the only father they had known; Mr. Van lost contact with the children whom he helped raise and support; and Ms. Zahorik only belatedly introduced the biological father into the picture. However, the current state of child custody law simply provides no means for Mr. Van, who is not related to the children . . . either biologically or by marriage, to pursue parental rights under . . . equitable estoppel. In short, he has no legal right to continue a relationship with the children.[34]

Recent law reform efforts take conflicting positions on the treatment of unmarried couples. The original Uniform Parentage Act established a presumption of paternity, analogous to the marital presumption, in favor of the man who, "while the child is under the age of majority, [receives] the child into his home and openly holds out the child as his natural child."[35] But unlike the marital presumption, this "nonmarital presumption" could be challenged at any time. Nonetheless, like the marital presumption, it could only be rebutted by "clear and convincing evidence," a difficult barrier prior to the age of reliable genetic tests. But with their advent, the draftsman had to choose between strengthening the nonmarital presumption or dropping it, since there was little point to retaining it in this form. The provision was dropped. Under the new Parentage Act, Mr. Van would have neither parental claims nor support obligations. In contrast, the American Law Institute, a prestigious private organization whose recommendations are often followed by courts, recommends no distinction between married and unmarried couples in the estoppel doctrine's application. It also allows application of the estoppel doctrine to protect the relationship of a child and a long-term social father in cases in which some courts, as explained above, would reject it on technical grounds.[36] The Institute's approach seems the better policy. About one-third of all births today are to unmarried women, but only about one-half of unmarried mothers are cohabiting with the child's biological father at the time of the birth.[37] To invest legal paternity in the absent biological father, rather than in the social father on the scene with whom the child enjoys a paternal relationship, seems unlikely to be in the child's interest.

Now consider a more complicated case: What if the biological father *is* on the scene, and wants to assert his paternity of the wife's child?

### Illustration 2

Harry and Sally are married and have a child, Edgar, who is eight. Vince, with whom Sally had a brief affair, is actually Edgar's biological father. But after some difficult times, Harry and Sally's marriage survived, and they have always treated Edgar as their marital child. Vince, who remains in town, has on occasion seen the child as "Uncle Vince," but has recently been turned away by Harry and Sally. He now seeks to establish his legal paternity of Edgar, so that he can see him regularly. He is prepared to pay child support. Harry and Sally oppose his petition.

The California rule barring challenges to the husband's paternity more than two years after the child's birth would doom Vince's claim. But in the majority of states that do not have a rule like California's, Vince could prevail unless the court found him estopped from asserting paternity, and many courts would not.[38] Some take an intermediate position. Massachusetts, for example, has held that a third party can offer genetic evidence to establish his legal paternity of a married woman's child if he can show that he and the child already have "a substantial parent-child relationship."[39] In one Massachusetts case, the mother was living with C.C., the putative father, when she gave birth, although she reunited with her husband before C.C. brought this suit. It is plausible to argue that these facts should lead to a different result from our illustration, at least if the mother and C.C. lived together long enough for him to establish the parental relationship that Massachusetts requires. By contrast, it seems clear in our second illustration that Edgar's interests lie in protecting the only parental relationships he has ever known from Vince's potentially troublesome intrusion. The advantage of California's approach is that its unambiguous exclusion of Vince's claim may deter him from bringing it in the first place. Its disadvantage, compared with the Massachusetts rule, is its potential for excluding claims by biological fathers such as C.C.

Some courts have suggested a third party's challenge to the husband's paternity ought to be allowed if made after the mother's marriage has ended, believing the marital dissolution leaves no reason to bar the biological father's claim.[40] But others realize that if one focuses on the child's interests, the dissolution of the mother's marriage is not as important as whether the claim is brought soon after the child's birth (*before* the husband has established a parental relationship with the child) or years later (*after* he probably has).[41] The dissolution does not change the preferred principle, which is to preserve the child's relationship with the social father, if there is one. In deciding upon the best legal rule by which to implement this principle, we must choose, as we often must, between a rule like Massachusetts',[42] which inquires closely into the facts of each case in the hope of reaching the right result in every one, and a rule like California's, which sorts the cases more mechanically (via the two-year window), in the belief that while some may be treated incorrectly, most will be better handled by a clear rule that deters litigation over the identity of the child's legal father.

The key things we learn from all these cases, however, is that the rights and obligations of parentage arise from relationships, not just from biology. But what then of children who have no social father—no man with whom they have a parental relationship? We hardly want to say that none of these men should have parental obligations. Those are the cases to which we now turn.

## Disappearing Dads and other Suspect Fellows

### *The Absent Father of the Child Born to an Unmarried Woman*

Between 1970 and 1992, nonmarital births increased from 10.7 percent of all births to 30 percent. There was a smaller increase, to 33 percent, by 1999.[43] This increased proportion of nonmarital births resulted from both a substantial increase in the birth rate of unmarried women and a decline in the birth rate of married women.[44] As a result, unmarried mothers (as compared with divorced or separated mothers) grew from 17 percent of all single mothers in 1976, to 46 percent in 1997.[45] The increased birth rate for unmarried women could arise from an increased number of nonmarital pregnancies, an increased proportion of nonmarital pregnancies that continue to term, or a reduced proportion of nonmarital pregnancies in which the mother marries before the birth—what were once called "shotgun" marriages. It is difficult to tease apart the separate contributions made by each of these three factors to the final result, but some researchers believe a large decline in shotgun marriages has been important.[46] When parents do not marry, their children do not begin life with a particular man clearly identified as their father by virtue of the marital presumption. It is true, as mentioned earlier, that the 1973 Uniform Parentage Act includes a kind of "nonmarital presumption" that identifies as the father of a child born to an unmarried woman a man who "receives the [minor] child into his home and openly holds out the child as his natural child". Another clause of the 1973 Act extends the presumption to the man who acknowledged his paternity of the child in a writing filed with the appropriate local agency, if the mother does not contest the acknowledgment within a reasonable time.[47] These presumptions, rebuttable only by "clear and convincing evidence," originally provided an important basis for assigning legal paternity of a nonmarital child who had a social father. But for the majority who did not have a social father, paternity was not easily established. In 1979, only 11 percent of never-married custodial mothers had child support orders.[48] The great majority of nonmarital children had no legal father.

In succeeding decades, most states changed their parentage acts to reflect the availability of the new genetic tests. The new 2000 revision of the Uniform Parentage Act reflects these developments. It deletes entirely the presumption arising from the nonmarital father's having received the child into his home,[49] providing instead that genetic tests conclusively establish legal paternity for most nonmarital children, rebuttable only if a second genetic test gives a different result.[50] The only important exception to this otherwise exclusive reliance upon biology arises from the provision of the 1996 federal welfare reform act[51] requiring states, with narrow exceptions, to treat an acknowledgement of paternity signed by the mother and putative father as establishing legal paternity.[52] Massachusetts pioneered this technique before 1996, obtaining such acknowledgments, before the mother and child left the hospital, in an astonishing 70 percent of all nonmarital births.[53] Its success has apparently now been replicated elsewhere under the press of the new federal law.[54] But this program is of course dependent upon the father's knowledge that resistance is futile because genetic tests are available to establish paternity, if needed. The 1996 welfare reform act requires states, with narrow exceptions, to authorize their child support enforcement agency to compel tests administratively if the agency receives a sworn statement of facts establishing "a reasonable possibility" of the requisite sexual contact.[55] While earlier reforms substantially improved the collection of child support for nonmarital children,[56] the 1996 reforms promise much greater success.

Yet exclusive reliance upon biological paternity in the invigorated campaign to collect child support from unmarried fathers may sometimes yield problematic results. In some cases, as we have already seen in con-

nection with marital children, biology chooses the wrong man to treat as
the child's legal father.[57] In other cases, however, it is not clear whether
*any* man should be called a child's legal father for support purposes. Consider, for example, the case of *Brad v. Lee*.[58] Brad was born to Catherine
in 1977; she was unmarried and never sought to establish Brad's paternity. She changed her mind in 1992. Brad was now fifteen, and she became concerned about paying for his college education. She wrote Lee,
asking for help. When he didn't reply she sought help from the county
child support enforcement office, which obtained blood tests confirming
Lee's paternity.

All agreed that Lee never knew of Brad's existence before receiving
Catherine's 1992 letter. But Lee, the court explained, was always liable
for Brad's support; he just didn't know that he was. He was therefore ordered to pay retroactive support—arrearages—for the past fifteen years,
as well as current support during the next three. During his fifteen years
of ignorance, Lee had married, fathered two children, and ran a farm and
logging business with his wife. Perhaps he had been setting aside college
money for the two marital children he knew about; perhaps he would
have made some life decisions differently during the past fifteen years if
he had known he was responsible for a third child. But while expressing
some sympathy for these concerns, the court concluded that Brad was
nonetheless entitled to the money, for "the child cannot be held responsible . . . simply because the father was not aware of his child's birth."[59]

There are a surprising number of cases like *Brad v. Lee* involving
claims for retroactive support from men who never knew they had a
child.[60] A few courts have been sympathetic to the father's claim that he
should not have to pay because the delay denied him any opportunity to
develop a relationship with the child he is belatedly asked to support,[61]
but most, as in *Brad* itself, reject this defense.[62] They sometimes observe
that the father could have found out about the child had he taken the
initiative and sought genetic tests himself to learn whether the child was
his, a response that is sometimes more plausible than it would have been
for Lee.[63] In *Brad v. Lee*, the son received the payments; in other cases
the court has directed that the payments go to the custodial mother as
reimbursement for the child support expenses she incurred during the
child's minority.[64]

Why are paternity actions sometimes brought so late? It is not always
the mother's doing: if she assigns the claim to the local welfare agency,
the agency may be tardy.[65] When the delay is hers, the explanations vary.
The U.S. Census Bureau tells us that 6.6 million custodial parents in 1997
had no formal, legal agreement for support payments.[66] When asked why,
32 percent said they "did not feel need to make legal" (as characterized
by the Bureau's truncated descriptions of the parents' responses). Perhaps
the father was contributing informally to the child's support in amounts
the mother believed appropriate. Clearly she should be allowed to bring
a formal support claim later if the voluntary payments become unreliable.

Another group said the other parent "provides what they can" (23%) or "could not afford to pay" (25%), and in fact researchers have estimated that 30 percent of the nonpaying fathers of nonmarital children are "poor" or "near-poor."[67] Perhaps some of these mothers change their mind later because the father's income goes up. Most of these fathers probably know about their children, and presumably would have the opportunity to establish a relationship with them if they sought it. So we might conclude that if they are not the child's social father, it is as likely to be their own responsibility as anyone else's.

Of greatest relevance, however, are the 19 percent who responded that they "did not want other parent to pay," and the 16 percent who said they "did not want to have contact with other parent." One imagines that this too is a diverse group. It must include some women who do not want contact with the father because they are afraid of him, including some who have been threatened explicitly with physical abuse if a support order is sought. But it must also include others who simply prefer to live their lives free of the father's presence and believe that they can get by well enough without his financial assistance. Mothers receiving welfare benefits may be denied this choice by the relevant public agency, which will require their cooperation in locating the father unless persuaded the mother has "good cause" to refuse.[68] But those not receiving welfare benefits will have more freedom of choice. They may be employed, have assistance from family members, or have established a relationship with another man who provides support. If these mothers successfully exclude the child's biological father from the child's life during most of the child's minority, should we nonetheless treat him as the child's legal father when they make a belated support request?

We cannot justify imposing child support obligations upon such men by reference to their parental relationship with the child, because they have none. So if a parental relationship is the only basis upon which a support obligation can rest, then Lee has no such obligation. Yet because support is often collected from biological fathers who have little relationship with their children, the law clearly assumes an alternative basis for the obligation: the belief that men *should* take social responsibility for the children they sire. Men who take no responsibility for their children may still be treated differently from those who do: Their conduct may justify limiting their custodial rights because they are not true parents. But while people may forfeit rights by not fulfilling their duties, they cannot forfeit their obligations. The law's underlying moral proposition is that biological fathers have a duty to try to become the child's social father, and they may not avoid the obligations of social paternity by evading this duty. A more pragmatic explanation for the prevailing legal rule would appeal to the law's instrumental value: Placing a support obligation on the socially unconnected biological father may deter some men from having children they do not intend to nurture, and may induce others to care about the children they are required to support.

But neither the moral argument nor the instrumental rationale can explain collecting support arrearages from men like Lee who were denied any opportunity to be responsible fathers. Furthermore, when it is the mother herself whose choice has denied the biological father the opportunity to become the child's social father, instrumental considerations argue against allowing her a child support claim, and especially a claim for arrearages. Permitting the arrearage claim gives mothers the wrong incentive by assuring them that foregone support can always be collected later, after the biological father has been excluded from the child's life. (Of course, many mothers will feel they cannot afford to delay collecting support, but there are others, like Catherine in *Brad v. Lee*, who believe they can.) This concern about providing mothers the wrong incentive helps justify judicial decisions holding that men are not liable for child support when their children are actively concealed from them by the mother, despite their efforts to find them.[69] The best rationale for these decisions would also seem to apply to men like Lee, whom one could call an "excluded parent."

Some courts are understandably reluctant to permit this concealment defense, for fear that it will jeopardize the child's interests.[70] The child's interests are obvious when a low-income custodial mother of an eight-year old makes a belated request for current child support. But that is hardly the exclusive pattern. For example, the child's interests are not implicated when the mother of a grown child seeks arrearages as reimbursement for the expenses she incurred during the child's minority. Even when an arrearage claim is formally made on the child's behalf, its justification on grounds of the child's interests may be questionable. The mother who concealed the child presumably had alternative arrangements for his support. And if there were deprivations arising from her choice, they can hardly be undone by a windfall arrearage award years later. Moreover, while money is always convenient to have, a child support decree must be justified as serving a purpose for which child support is ordered. Arrearages received when the child is near or beyond the age of majority may well be applied to expenses for which child support is not ordinarily allowed.[71] They certainly should not be demanded of a man who was never allowed to be the child's father.

### Involuntary Absence Arising from the Child's Move

Moving is a relatively common experience for American families. Between March 1997 and March 1998, 16 percent of all Americans moved.[72] About 43 percent of them moved to a different Metropolitan Statistical Area.[73] The adults most likely to move are those between 20 and 34 years old, ages at which they are likely to have young children.[74] Undoubtedly for that reason, children are, on average, more likely to move than are adults. Between March 1997 and March 1998, 23.5 percent of all children between one and four years of age moved. Children between five and six moved at an annual rate of 17.9 percent. Rates for older children were a bit lower.[75] It is generally believed that people are especially likely to move after their marriage fails. A 1986 study of divorcing couples with children in the Phoenix, Arizona, metropolitan area found that 3 percent of the custodial parents that researchers could locate moved out of the area within twelve weeks of the divorce filing, 10 percent moved away within a year, and 17 percent within two years.[76] Almost certainly, even higher percentages of the residential parents that the researchers were *not* able to locate had moved out of the county. Presumably, most of these moves were not surreptitious, but done with the knowledge and acceptance of the other parent. Moreover, recent legal trends have favored residential parents who seek to move out of state with the child, even when the other parent objects. The increasingly common approach, reflected in the recommendations of the American Law Institute, assumes that a parent with primary residential custody can usually choose where the custodial household should live. The court will try to adjust the visitation schedule to reflect the realities of the parents' new addresses. The nonmoving parent can try to show that the child's interests require changing the child's primary residence to his household from that of the moving parent. But he usually won't have the facts to make out that claim, and the child's move will take place.

A move occurring when the child is ten or twelve will not keep the nonmoving father from maintaining his social paternity of the relocating child. But consider this example, adapted from a recent California decision, involving the move of a very young child:[77]

### Illustration 3

Steven and Phyllis divorce after five years of marriage, when their only child, Ryan, is about two months old. Phyllis has primary physical custody of Ryan; Steven has custody of Ryan on alternate weekends. A year after divorce, Phyllis is offered a good job as an aeronautical engineer, but requiring her to move from California to Syracuse, N.Y. The divorce court, applying local law, confirms Phyllis's right to take Ryan with her to Syracuse, over Steven's objection. In an effort to allow Steven to preserve a relationship with Ryan, the court also orders Phyllis to bring Ryan back to California for weekend visits with Steven once a month. Ryan is fourteen months old at the time of her move.

Maintaining a parental relationship can be difficult for the father who no longer lives regularly with the child,[78] but it is possible. However, significant physical separation that makes weekly or even monthly visits impractical and may add considerably to the difficulty. Even then we might assume it is still possible for the determined father to maintain a parental relationship. But with very young children—e.g., those less than two years old at the time of separation—the problem for the father becomes much greater, because his parental relationship with the child must be established, not just maintained. The father in the intact family, even the traditional one with only secondary parenting responsibilities, establishes that relationship by seeing his children nearly every day. This process can never occur if the family unit dissolves when the child is young. When there is not only dissolution but great physical distance between father and child, substitute strategies for establishing social paternity seem unpromising. Courts may pretend otherwise when they approve revised visitation plans, but the plans will often not work.[79] Frequent cross-country trips may not be logistically or financially feasible, and they impose their own burdens on the young child. Weekend stays are likely too short to justify the travel time, and longer stays may become impractical as the child develops roots and routines in the new city. Fathers like Steven may then find they have no paternal relationship with their child, whatever their desire. If Phyllis remarries, Steven's problem may get worse. Her new husband (call him Stan) may develop a parental relationship with Ryan. Stan and Phyllis may have additional children, whom Ryan treats as his siblings. Steven's occasional appearance in Ryan's life may seem increasingly irrelevant to his "real family," none of the rest of whom treat Steven as a family member.

There may be men in Steven's position so uninterested in their children that they would never have developed a relationship with them had they lived next door. And some may manage to establish a parental relationship with their child despite the mother's long-distance move, perhaps by moving themselves to her new location. But there will surely be many who resist relocation for reasons at least as compelling as those that led the mother to choose it. In sum, there will be men in Steven's position who find themselves rendered strangers to their children, despite their desire and best efforts to the contrary, by virtue of their child's distant relocation at a very young age. In approving the child's relocation under such circumstances, the court may create ambiguity about the biological father's legal parenthood by denying him an essential incident of parental status, the opportunity to develop a relationship with the child. And as with the biological father in *Brad v. Lee*, who also involuntarily lost the opportunity to become the child's social father, the basis for requiring the biological father to pay child support is then put in doubt. The moral argument for requiring support from the biological father becomes uncertain when the mother's actions deprive him of any chance to be the child's social father, and the instrumental rationale for requiring support obviously has no application to the biological father whose desire to be the child's social father was frustrated by decisions made by others that he could not influence despite his objections.

There is nonetheless a difference between this case and *Brad v.Lee* that may color our attitude toward it: We sympathize with Phyllis who has good reasons for her move, and proceeds with it openly, more than with the mother who, without compelling reason (such as fear of physical abuse), conceals a child's very existence from the child's father. But Phyllis's good faith cannot explain requiring Steven to pay support, any more than the arguable bad faith of the mother in *Brad v. Lee* is our reason for excusing that biological father's support obligation. The biological father's support obligation depends upon his relationship with the child, or upon his responsibility for the absence of any relationship, not upon the mother's good or bad faith. That is why, for example, no defense to the child support obligation should arise from the arguable bad faith of the wife who deceives her husband into believing the child born during their marriage was his, even when he objects promptly after learning the truth. While his objection upon learning the truth is perhaps understandable, and we may sympathize with him, he must still be treated as the child's legal father if his objection comes after his social paternity of his wife's child has become established. The same principle leads to the conclusion that the biological father's objection to supporting a child removed to a distant location, before he has any chance to become its social father, should not fail just because the mother has understandable reasons for her move.

Not long ago, a husband in Steven's position might simply stop paying child support in this situation, and effective enforcement would be unlikely. Or the parties might reach an informal understanding relieving him of support payments in exchange for his acquiescence to the move. Modern child support rules, however, render such arrangements increasingly difficult to make. A court is not likely to approve an agreement waiving support,[80] and without the court's approval there can be no change in the usual order deducting Steven's support payments directly from his wages.[81] Nor would the parents' agreement to waive or reduce support payments bar Phyllis or Ryan from later claiming arrearages for the difference between the court-ordered support and what Steven actually paid: The parties' informal agreement to ignore the support order would not usually provide him with any defense.[82] These inflexible rules were designed to improve the enforcement of support orders from the larger group of fathers whose moral obligation is clear, but apply equally to Steven, whose moral obligation is more ambiguous. Perhaps the rules should be changed.

Changes in the child support obligation would be appropriate, if at all, primarily in the case of very young children. But the best approach to changing the rules applicable to move-away cases is not clear. To be entirely excused from support obligations, it would seem the biological father should relinquish all parental rights, severing permanently his status as the child's legal father. But he may not wish to do so, perhaps in the hope that despite the hurdles he will somehow manage to establish his social paternity of the child. Another possibility might be a reduction in his support obligation, roughly reflecting, perhaps, the impairment in his access to the child. That arrangement might lead to an ultimate severance of the legal parentage, were the father's hopes dashed, or it might continue indefinitely. We may be reluctant to go down this road if we believed the child's welfare depended upon the biological father's financial support. But that dependence is unlikely in some of the very cases in which courts increasingly endorse move-aways: where the custodial mother moves because she, or her new husband, can thereby obtain or retain a good job. If the adequacy of the child's financial well-being is not put in jeopardy, one might well conclude that the reduction is appropriate because the mother should share the economic advantage of the move with the biological father whose relationship with the child is compromised on account of it.

## Conclusion

Legal paternity and biological paternity have never been identical. That was once inevitable; today it is a matter of choice. Particularly as policymakers have become more determined to enforce child support obligations, the choice becomes more important. Even though the law's historical emphasis on social paternity owed much to scientific ignorance, it often produced sensible results. Those results should not be displaced by our new-found ability to establish biological paternity.

Biological fathers have a moral duty to try to become the child's social father, or to cooperate in providing the child with another suitable parent. A biological father who does not fulfill this duty may in consequence lose his paternal rights, but his own failure will not excuse him from his paternal obligations. Both the rights and obligations of fatherhood may be assumed, however, by a child's social father, displacing the biological father. Social paternity, once established over time, should prevail over biological paternity, and for that reason time limits should be set upon biological challenges to the legal paternity of a child's social father. Belated biological challenges to a husband's paternity should not be allowed, with a possible exception for the unusual case in which the biological father is also the social father, and the husband is not.

When children have no social father, the law's treatment of the biological father should depend upon why he has not fulfilled that role. As a general matter, legal rights and responsibilities arise from relationships and not from genes. At the same time, both a moral argument and a deterrence rationale justify imposing support obligations on men whose own choices explain their lack of any relationship with their biological child. Neither morals nor deterrence applies, however, when the biological father's lack of social paternity is involuntary, the result of choices by others that the biological father could not affect. No legal rule can induce a man to care for a child that is taken from him, or that he did not know he had. Particularly when it is also true that the child's welfare does not depend on collecting support—as is typically the case for arrearages, or when the custodial mother is financially capable on her own of providing reasonable support—it is difficult to justify imposing such support duties upon an objecting, excluded, biological father. Legal paternity is most firmly grounded on actual relationships and should be adjusted when the law alters them.

## Notes

1. See Ira Ellman, Paul Kurtz, and Elizabeth Scott, *Family Law: Cases, Text, Problems*, 3rd. ed., (Charlottesville: Lexis Law Publishing 1998), 1041–1043.

2. Before modern genetic tests became available, tests that relied upon the division of human blood types into A, B, AB, and O were all there were to refute a paternity allegation. But the ABO tests are not very useful for this purpose because they type individuals for characteristics that are so common that on average they fail to exclude 86.6 percent of the male population. See Ira Mark Ellman and David Kaye, *Probabilities and Proof: Can HLA and Blood Group Testing Prove Paternity?* 54 N.Y.U.L.Rev. 1131, 1135 (1979).

3. See Ellman, Kurtz, and Scott, *Family Law*, 1047–1048.

4. The defense had a Latin name, *exceptio plurium concubentium*. A contrasting approach, once followed in Denmark, made all such men liable for child support, which could be apportioned among them; such offspring were called "company children." See Lodgberg, "The Reform of Family Law in the Scandanavian Countries," in A.G. Chloros, (ed.), *The Reform of Family Law in Europe* (Boston: Kluwer, 1978), 201, 217.

5. The rule encouraged friends of the putative father to testify falsely that they also had sexual relations with the mother, since that concession, if believed, would shield him without making them liable for support. A classic study found that when confronted with a lie detector test, 57 percent of men who had testified to intercourse with the mother to establish the *exceptio plurium* defense admitted that they had lied. On the other hand, 48 percent of the mothers admitted having lied in their denial of such intercourse. See Arthur and Reid, "Using the Lie Detector to Determine the Truth In Disputed Paternity Cases," *Journal of Criminal Law, Criminology and Police Science* 45:213 1954.

6. It was also a time when having children out of wedlock was still deviant behavior, and some men might accept a quiet settlement to avoid the social embarrassment of a paternity suit, even one they could win. Their payment of a single lump sum, with no concession of paternity and no continuing financial obligation, could often settle the case and shield the putative father from later claims. Today it probably would not, because federal law now disallows lump sum settlements that bar marital children from making later claims for support, and several courts have held that the Equal Protection Clause requires extending the same principle to nonmarital children. See Ellman, Kurtz, and Scott, *Family Law*, 1059–1060.

7. Stanley v. Illinois, 405 U.S. 645 (1972).

8. Id., at note 9.

9. By 1999, over 95 percent of accredited American blood banks routinely used DNA technologies in performing paternity tests; less than 10 percent did so in 1990. American Association of Blood Banks, *Annual Report Summary for 1999*. Press Release. October 12, 2000, 6. See also Ellman, Kurtz and Scott, *Family Law*, 1049–1057.

10. See Lehr v. Robertson, 463 U.S. 248 (1983) (mother may terminate the rights of the biological father without notice to him, giving effective consent

to the child's adoption by her husband, where the father did not place himself on a state registry established for the purpose of notifying interested parties of his desire to maintain a connection with the child); Quilloin v. Walcott, 434 U.S. 246 (1978) (similar). Still undecided is the extent to which the Constitution protects the biological father who fails to establish a social connection only because he is thwarted by the mother's resistance or her concealment of the child. See Ellman, Kurtz and Scott, *Family Law*, 1083–1086.

11. Michael H. v. Gerald D., 491 U.S. 1094 (1989). In this case, the Court sustained California's decision to treat the mother's husband as the legal father of her child, over the objection of the child's biological father, who sought to establish his own legal paternity. The case was more difficult because the mother had left her husband and lived with the biological father for some time after the child's birth, although the mother and her husband had reconciled by the time of this lawsuit and were united in their opposition to the biological father's claim. Nonetheless, the child had known both men in a paternal role.

12. The idea that the two are not connected arises from a different legal rule, that each parent's legal obligation to pay support, and permit access, continues without regard to the other's fulfillment of his or hers, until a court decides otherwise. See *Principles of the Law of Family Dissolution: Analysis and Recommendations* (Dayton: Lexis-Nexis, 2002) § 3.21. The only way to effect a permanent denial of a parent's right of access to a child is to sever his parental rights, and severance also typically ends the child support obligation. See e.g., City of Ventura v. Gonzales, 106 Cal.Rptr.2d 461 (App. 2001) (the termination of parental "rights" construed to mean the termination of both parental rights and parental responsibilities).

13. Judith Seltzer, "Child Support and Child Access: Experiences of Divorced and Nonmarital Families," in Thomas Oldham and Marygold Melli, (eds.), *Child Support: The Next Frontier* (Ann Arbor: University of Michigan Press, 2000), 69, 81. As Seltzer points out, it is not clear that the connection is causal, just that it exists.

14. Edward O. Laumann, John H. Gagnon, Robert T. Michael, and Stuart Michaels, *The Social Organization of Sexuality: Sexual Practices in the United States* (Chicago: University of Chicago Press 1994), 214. Seventy-five percent of men report sexual faithfulness during their marriage. Id.

15. This is the term behavioral biologists appear to prefer to describe sexual relations with someone other than a person's regular partner.

16. R. Robin Baker and Mark A. Bellis, *Human Sperm Competition: Copulation, Masturbation, and Infidelity* (London: Chapman & Hall, 1995), 160–161.

17. David C. Geary, *Male, Female: The Evolution of Human Sex Differences* (Washington, DC: American Psychological Association, 1998), 135.

18. While such data may seem surprising, they were predicted by evolutionary theorists who suggest that natural selection favored a woman inclined to become pregnant through clandestine extrapair relations with men whose attributes promise a chance to improve the genetic quality of her children. See the sources cited in the prior two notes. Of course, the same evolutionary logic also predicts that natural selection would favor men inclined to "mate-guarding" strategies that reduce their partner's chance of deceiving them into devoting resources to another's man's child, and women inclined to extrapair relations only when the risk of detection was low. See David M. Buss, *The Dangerous Passion: Why Jealousy Is as Necessary as Love and Sex* (New York: Free Press, 2000). The obvious argu-

ment for the male strategy is that in the prehistoric era during which our genes were forged, access to scarce resources was an important factor in a child's survival, so that the genes of men who successfully focused their resources on their genetic children were more likely to survive to the next generation then the genes of men deceived into dispersing their resources among unrelated children as well. The obvious argument for female deception is that women whose infidelity was discovered risked the loss of access to their long-term mate's resources for their children, so that the genes of women who were successfully deceptive were more likely to survive to the next generation than the genes of women who were not.

19. One set of studies shows rates varying from 1.4 percent (a 1963 study in Michigan) to 30 percent (studies from the 1970s in England). Baker and Bellis, *Human Sperm Competition*, 200.

20. Medical students are routinely taught that the rate is 10 to 15 percent, and standard genetics texts use a figure of 10 percent. Baker and Bellis, *Human Sperm Competition*, 199. A journalist reported that genetic counselors he interviewed believed, apparently from their own experience with paternity data uncovered in genetic tests conducted for other reasons, that 10 percent of American marital children are not in fact the genetic offspring of their mother's husband. Nicholas Wade, *Birds Do It, Bees Do It, Some People Do, Too, The New York Times*, May 22, 2001, in Westlaw at 2001 WL-NYT 0114200001. In actual paternity tests performed in 1999 by American blood banks, 28 percent of the putative fathers were excluded as the child's biological father. American Association of Blood Banks, *Annual Report Summary for 1999*. Press release. October 12, 2000, 5. These aggregate data include unmarried putative fathers as well as husbands, and the data are not broken down by marital status. But one expects that the majority of paternity tests are conducted on unmarried partners, since paternity disputes among married couples are far less common. These data therefore suggest that among unmarried couples, about a quarter of the men identified as the likely father, presumably on the basis of their relationship with the mother during the probable period of conception, in fact were not.

21. Stephanie J. Ventura, Joyce A. Martin, Sally C. Curtin, and T.J. Mathews, *Births: Final Data for 1997*. National Center for Health Statistics, Centers for Disease Control and Prevention, *National Vital Statistics Reports*, V. 47, no. 18 (Washington, DC: Government Printing Office. April 29, 1999).

22. There is of course a correlation between a nonresident fathers' paying support and spending time with the child, but that does not mean that enhanced support enforcement will also increase the absent fathers' time commitment. The correlation might arise because involved fathers are more likely both to pay support and spend time with their child. Efforts to find a causal link between support and time spent with the child have not been able to uncover any strong connection; "the effect of payments on visits is modest at best when other factors are taken into account." Seltzer, "Child Support and Child Access," 81.

23. Actually, the rule has some exceptions. California's two-year limit applies only when the spouses were cohabiting at the time of conception and the husband "is not impotent or sterile." California Family Code § 7540. The exception for impotence and sterility is difficult to reconcile with the statute's accepted rationale: Why allow belated challenges based upon biological nonpaternity arising from the husband's impotence or sterility, while otherwise rejecting the relevance of biological nonpaternity? California courts have held that any live sperm is enough to render a man fertile under this section, even if well below the

amount medical experts believe necessary for fertility, because "biology is not the predominant consideration in determining parental responsibility once a child has reached his or her third year of life." Marriage of Freeman, 53 Cal.Rptr.2d 439, 447 (App. 1996).

24. Vincent B. v. Joan R., 179 Cal.Rptr. at 10.

25. Estate of Cornelious, 198 Cal.Rptr. 543, 546, 35 Cal.3d 461, 465, 674 P.2d 245, 248 (1984), quoting "Recent Developments, California's Tangled Web: Blood Tests and the Conclusive Presumption of Legitimacy," *Stanford Law Review* 20:754, 761-765, 1968. The court explained further that "adoption of a statute of limitations in lieu of [a] tangle of evidentiary rules offers the obvious advantage of greatly simplifying the law and at the same time molding the law to closer conformity with the relevant policies. . . ."

26. The notes in Uniform Laws Annotated report its adoption in nineteen states as of January 2001.

27. UNIFORM PARENTAGE ACT §§ 4, 6(a)(2), 9B Uniform Laws Annotated 298–299, 302 (1973).

28. An examination of the statutes of the states adopting the Parentage Act found five that included this provision: Alabama and New Jersey adopted the recommended five-year limit; Hawaii, Minnesota, and North Dakota require that the action be brought within three years of the child's birth.

29. Sections 204 and 607 of the new Uniform Parentage Act. Exceptions permit a challenge to the husband's paternity if (a) the mother and presumed father neither cohabited nor engaged in sexual intercourse during the probable period of conception, *and* (b) the presumed father never openly treated the child as his own. In other words, challenges can be allowed only when the person making the challenge can show that the husband was *neither* the social nor the biological father of the child.

30. Ibid.

31. Cases extending custodial or visitation rights to an individual because others are estopped from denying their parentage include Jean Maby H. v. Joseph H., 676 N.Y.S.2d 677 (App. Div. 1998) (mother who married defendant when they both knew she was pregnant with another man's child and who held out defendant as the child's father to neighbors, friends, and the child, is equitably estopped from precluding defendant from seeking custody or visitation with the child at their divorce); In the Matter of Sleeper, 929 P.2d 1028 (Or. App. 1996), aff'd on other grounds, 982 P.2d 1126 (Or. 1999) (mother estopped from denying husband's paternity of her children whom both knew were biologically his where he relied on her representations to develop a parental relationship with the children and both spouses represented to others that he was their father).

32. See, e.g., Sekol v. Delsantro, 763 A.2d 405 (Pa. Super. 2000).

33. For example, the Alaska Supreme Court held the husband could be estopped from denying his paternity of his wife's child only if the trial court found that the child had suffered "financial prejudice" from the husband's having treated the child as his own during the first three years of the marriage. B.E.B. v. R.L.B., 979 P.2d 514, 519 (Alaska 1999).

34. Van v. Zahorik, 597 N.W.2d 15, 23 (Mich. 1999). See also Price v. Howard, 484 S.E.2d 528 (N.C. 1997) (although man lived together with child's mother from the time of her birth, held himself out as the child's father and was the child's primary caretaker at the time of the action, although mother represented to the man and to others that he was the father, and although the child

believed that he was her father, parental rights doctrine requires award of sole custody to child's biological mother, absent a finding of her unfitness or that she engaged in conduct "inconsistent with the constitutionally protected status of a natural parent") and Petition of Bruce, 522 N.W.2d 67 (Iowa 1994) (similar).

35. Uniform Parentage Act § 4(a)(4).

36. American Law Institute, *Principles of the Law of Family Dissolution*, §§ 2.03 and 3.03.

37. Sara McLanahan, Irwin Garfinkel, Nancy Reichman, Julien Teitler, Marcia Carlson & Christina Audigier, *The Fragile Families and Child Wellbeing Study: Baseline Report*, August 2001, Table 2. Available online at ⟨http://crew.princeton.edu/fragilefamilies/nationalreport.pdf⟩. Earlier studies suggested that the percentge was lower, about one-quarter. Larry Bumpass, R. Kelly Raley, and James A. Sweet, "The Changing Character of Stepfamilies: Implications of Cohabitation and Nonmarital Childbearing," *Demography* 32:425–436, 1995, 426. Of the 3.8 million heterosexual couples who identified themselves to the Census Bureau in March 2000 as unmarried partners, more than 1.5 million, or 41 percent had minor children living with them. Jason Fields and Lynne Casper, *America's Families and Living Arrangements*, Current Population Reports P20–537, U.S. Census Bureau, U.S. Department of Commerce (2001), at 12–14. Available online at ⟨http://www.census.gov/prod/2001pubs/p20-537.pdf⟩.

38. Decisions permitting third-party paternity claims over the united opposition of husband and wife include Witso v. Overby, 627 N.W.2d 63 (Minn. 2001) (young child, precise age at time of suit not provided; majority cautions that while third party is entitled to show his biological paternity the trial court is not necessarily bound to provide him access to the child); In re J.W.T., 872 S.W.2d 189 (Tex. 1994) (finding that the state constitution protects the biological father's right to assert his paternity); K.S. v. K.S., 669 N.E.2d 399 (Ind. 1996) (neighbor permitted to bring action asserting his paternity of the youngest child of the married couple's three children, under the plain language of the state's parentage act).

39. C.C. v. A.B., 550 N.E.2d 365, 372 (Mass. 1990).

40. E.g., In re Paternity of S.R.I., 602 N.E.2d 1014 (Ind. 1992); Weidenbacher v. Duclos, 661 A.2d 988, 998 (Conn. 1995) (after the divorce, "there is no 'family integrity' left to be maintained").

41. E.g., Susan H. v. Jack S., 37 Cal.Rptr.2d 120 (App. 1994). And in *Duclos*, the child in fact had apparently developed a more significant relationship with the biological father than with the mother's husband, from who she became separated during the child's first year.

42. Followed in other states as well, see, e.g., Allen v. Stone, 474 S.E.2d 554 (W.Va. 1996).

43. Centers for Disease Control and Prevention, National Center for Health Statistics, *National Vital Statistics Report*, vol. 48, no. 16, October 18, 2000, at Table 1, 17. Available online at ⟨http://www.cdc.gov/nchs/data/nvs48_16.pdf⟩.

44. The birth rate per 1000 unmarried women ages 15 to 44 increased from 26.4 in 1970 to a peak of 46.9 in 1994, retreating slightly to 43.9 in 1999. The corresponding rate for married women was 121.1 in 1970, declining rapidly to 94.7 by 1973. Since then it has been much more steady, bottoming out 1996 at 83.7 percent and rebounding to 87.3 percent in 1999. Ibid.

45. Elaine Sorenson and Ariel Halpern, *Child Support Enforcement Is Working Better than We Think*, Urban Institute Report No. A-31 (March, 1999). Available online at ⟨http://newfederalism.urban.org/html/anf_31.html⟩.

46. George Akerlof, Janet Yellen, and Michael Katz, "An Analysis of Out-of-Wedlock Childbearing in the United States," *Quarterly Journal of Economics,* 111:277–317, 1996. They believe that from three-fifths (for blacks) to three-fourths (for white) of the increased proportion of nonmarital births between the four-year periods 1965–1969 and 1985–1989 are accounted for by the reduced shotgun marriage rate. They define a "shotgun marriage" as any marriage occurring within the seven-month period prior to the child's birth. Their conclusion is subject to some quibble. The enormous increase in the abortion rate between these two time periods (it was not until 1972 that Roe v. Wade was decided) is probably concentrated among single women. Franklin Zimring, "Of Doctors, Deterrence, and the Dark Figure of Crime: A Note on Abortion in Hawaii," *University of Chicago Law Review* 39:699, 1972. Zimring argues that many of the "missing" shotgun marriages during the later time period did not really yield additional nonmarital births because the corresponding pregnancy was aborted rather than changed from a marital to a nonmarital birth. Personal discussion with F. Zimring, June 1, 2001. Akerloff et al. put a different spin on the same observation. They believe the reason that the availability of abortion contributes to the decline in shotgun marriages is that men feel less obligation to marry the pregnant woman who has the choice to abort, even if she declines to abort. They therefore believe the availability of abortion changes marital births to nonmarital births by encouraging a reduced shotgun marriage rate even when the pregnancy is not aborted.

47. Section 4(a). This summary glosses over some details not relevant here.

48. Daniel Meyer, "Fathers and the Child Support System," in Oldham and Melli (eds.), *Child Support,* 88, 90. Meyer gets this figure from the Census data, which in turn relies upon the mother's report.

49. Section 204 of the new Uniform Act.

50. Section 505.

51. Known as PRWORA, for Personal Responsibility and Work Opportunity Reconciliation Act, 110 Stat. 2105 (1996).

52. 42 U.S.C. § 666(a)(1)(C).

53. Marilyn Rae Smith, "Child Support Reform in Action: New Strategies and New Frontiers in Massachusetts," in Martin Whyte (ed.), *Marriage in America: A Communitarian Perspective* (Lanham: Rowman & Littlefield Publishers, 2000), 269, 275.

54. Paul Legler, President Clinton's Assistant Commissioner in the Office of Child Support Enforcement, reported "astounding success" in the initial results from the new federal laws. Paul Legler, "The Impact of Welfare Reform on the Child Support Enforcement System," in Oldham and Melli, *Child Support,* 46, 48.

55. 42 U.S.C. § 666(a)(1)(B).

56. The proportion of never-married mothers reporting receipt of any child support payments increased from 4 percent in 1976 to 18 percent in 1997—much greater than the gains reported by divorced mothers. Elaine Sorenson and Ariel Halpern, *Child Support Enforcement Is Working Better Than We Think,* Urban Institute Report No. A-31 (March 1999). Available online at ⟨http://newfederalism.urban.org/html/anf_31.html⟩.

57. Tedford v. Gregory, 959 P.2d 540 (N.M.App. 1998), is a bizarre example of such a case. After their 1975 divorce, Tedford paid support for all four children born to Nina during their marriage, including Jeanne, the youngest, who

was fourteen months old when the marriage ended. When Jeanne was sixteen, Nina told her that Gregory was her biological father, which neither she nor Tedford had known. When she was twenty, Jeanne sought child support arrearages from Gregory. After genetic tests confirmed his biological paternity, he was ordered to pay eighteen years' support. Left unresolved was whether Tedford could claim reimbursement from Jeanne for funds collected from Gregory.

58. Brad Mitchell v. Lee D., 564 N.W.2d 354 (Wisc.App. 1997).

59. Id. at 360. Wisconsin later decided that in such cases a court could order less support than specified by the applicable guidelines. See Brenton T.C. v. Patrick G.B., 2001 WL 101588 (Wis.App.).

60. The cases are collected at Anno, *Liability of Father for Retroactive Child Support on Judicial Determination of Paternity*, 87 A.L.R.5th 361 (2001).

61. In re Loomis, 587 N.W.2d 427 (S.D. 1998). The daugher was fourteen when her mother filed the action. The court ordered current support, but denied any claim for arrearages. It noted that Loomis had two children to support in his current marriage, and that "had he known all along that [the daughter] was his, he would have . . . been able to develop some sort of relationship with her." Id. at 430. Some states limit such arrearages by statute. California goes the furthest, barring support arrearages for periods preceding the filing (or sometimes the service) of the initial pleading establishing the child support obligation. California Family Code § 4009 (Westlaw 2002). See Marriage of Goosmann, 31 Cal.Rptr.2d 613 (App. 1994) and Cty. of Santa Clara v. Perry, 956 P.2d 1191 (Cal. 1998) (§ 4009 held to also apply to paternity actions brought by the district attorney).

62. E.g., Golden v. Lewis, 647 So.2d 979 (Fla.App. 1994) and Donovan v. Zajac, 708 N.E.2d 254 (Ohio App. 1998).

63. Courts making this observation include Donovan v. Zajac, 708 N.E.2d 245 (Ohio App. 1998) and Brenton v. Patrick, 2001 WL 101588 (Wis App). In *Donovan*, the biological father knew of the child's existence, but did not know he was the child's biological father (although he presumably knew he could be). The child was nearly eighteen when the action was brought, and the defendant was assessed $54,450 in retroactive support, which he was ordered to pay off within ten years, even though he was supporting three children in his current marriage on an income that was limited by his being on sick leave. Donavan v. Zajac, 2000 WL 816249 (Ohio App. 2000) (unpublished). In *Brenton* the father knew he was one of four men who might be the child's biological father. When the child was ten the mother brought a paternity action. She named Patrick only after her first two defendants were excluded by genetic tests. At the time of the suit the defendant was married with two other children. He was ordered to pay retroactive support.

64. E.g., Donovan v. Zajac, 708 N.E.2d 245, 253 (Ohio App. 1998)

65. E.g., Dept of Human Services v. Bell, 711 A.2d 1292 (Me. 1998).

66. U.S. Bureau of the Census, *Child Support for Custodial Mothers and Fathers, 1997,* Current Population Reports P60–212 (2000). Available online at ⟨http://www.census.gov/hhes/www/childsupport/cs97.html⟩. Of course, these data are based upon a sample, not a count of the entire population.

67. Irwin Garfinkel, Sara McClanahan, and Thomas Hanson, "A Patchwork Portrait of Nonresident Fathers," in Irwin Garfinkel, Sara McLanahan, Daniel Meyer, and Judith Seltzer (eds.), *Fathers under Fire: The Revolution in Child Support Enforcement* (New York: Russell Sage Foundation, 1998), 31, 51.

68. Section 332 of the 1996 federal welfare reform legislation, PRWORA,

gave the states broad flexibility to define "cooperation" and "good cause" and to determine the penalty for noncooperation.

69. Admittedly, such a rule requires the court to make some factual distinctions; the father may claim concealment while the mother may claim he made himself impossible to find, or threatened abduction of the child, or threatened her. See, e.g., Damico v. Damico, 7 Cal.4th 673, 872 P.2d 126, 29 Cal.Rptr.2d 787 (1994) (mother may not collect child support arrearages from father after child's majority if she actively concealed child from him; remanded to determine whether she did). Courts have often been very cautious in adopting the "concealment defense" rule. For example, in Comer v. Comer, 14 Cal.4th 504, 927 P.2d 265, 59 Cal.Rptr.2d 155 (1996), California limited *Damico* by allowing claims for arrearages arising during a period of concealment, if the claim is brought while the children are still minors. (The concealment in *Comer* began when the mother took the children from the marital jurisdiction when they were five and two years old, and continued for seven years until the older son contacted the father.) *Comer* also held that the county agency's right of reimbursement for the public support it provided the mother during the concealment period could be enforced in an arrearage action. That decision, in particular, seems like puzzling public policy, unless the agency found the mother had "good cause" for declining to cooperate in enforcement actions during the concealment period. In the absence of such a good cause finding, it would seem that the mother herself, rather than the father, would be the appropriate person from whom the agency should have a theoretical right of reimbursement, on both moral and instrumental grounds. The agency's understandable reluctance to go against the mother hardly provides a good basis for seeking reimbursement from the excluded father.

70. E.g., New Mexico v. Roybal, 963 P.2d 548 (N.M.App. 1998) (district court's child support order was not an abuse of discretion because one should not "remove a benefit from Son because of Mother's selfish actions"). This line of reasoning seemed particularly inapt in *Roybal*, where the arrearage action was brought when the son was twenty years old, and the court conceded that the son had been provided for during his minority.

71. For example, in *Roybal*, id., there was apparently reason to believe that the ordered arrearages would be applied to support the son's college education—a worthy use, certainly, but not one which New Mexico law allowed as the basis for a child support order.

72. Geographical Mobility, U.S. Department of Commerce, Bureau of the Census, Current Population Reports P20-520 (January 2000). Available online at ⟨http://www.census.gov/prod/2000pubs/p20-520.pdf⟩.

73. The percentage of the population moving within a given year varies widely by region. Westerners are the most likely to move (19.4 percent moved during this time period) while those in the Northeast are least likely (11.5 percent). Ibid.

74. Adults between twenty and twenty-four moved more frequently (34.2 percent) than adults in any other age range, with those from twenty-five to twenty-nine (31 percent) and thirty to thirty-four (22 percent) next most likely.

75. Of those ten to fourteen, 14.7 percent moved; and fifteen to nineteen, 15.9 percent. Id.

76. Personal communication from Professor Sanford Braver, Department of Psychology, Arizona State University. These figures do not include residential parents who moved from the family home but remained within the county.

77. These facts are adapted from Marriage of Whealon, 61 Cal.Rptr.2d 559 (App. 1997).

78. There is certainly plenty of evidence that children have impaired relationships with the noncustodial parent. Of course, the relationship may have been suboptimal before the marital separation ever took place. Nonetheless, it is also true that children of divorce report having had a a lower-quality relationship with the noncustodial parent the longer they have lived apart from that parent, suggesting, not surprisingly, that the separation itself contributes to the relationship's deterioration—or, to the put matter another way, the younger the child at the time of separation, the greater its impact upon the relationship. Diane N. Lye, Daniel H. Klepinger, Patricia Davis Hyle, and Anjanette Nelson, "Childhood Living Arrangements and Adult Children's Relations with Their Parents," *Demography* 32:261–280, 1995. Children of divorce are less likely, as adults, to give or receive financial assistance to or from their fathers, than are children of intact families—but divorce has no analogous impact on the likelihood of such transfers between children and their mothers. Frank F. Furstenberg, Jr., Saul D. Hoffman, Laura Shrestha, "The Effect of Divorce on Intergenerational Transfers: New Evidence," *Demography* 32:319–333, 1995.

79. Mavis Heterington found that contact between children and non-residential fathers declined significantly when the father lived more than 75 miles from the child. E. Mavis Hetherington and John Kelly, *For Better or For Worse.* New York: W.W. Norton & Co., 2002, 134.

80. E.g., Kelley v. Kelley, 449 S.E.2d 55 (Va. 1994) (husband ordered to pay support despite the parties' agreement at divorce waiving child support payments in recognition of husband's lump sum payment $40,000; agreement held void); Reimer v. Reimer, 502 N.W.2d 231 (N.D. 1993) (similar).

81. 42 U.S.C. § 666(b) requires states to impose automatic wage withholding in all child support orders unless one of the parties demonstrates there is good cause not to require it, or the parties by written agreement provide for an alternative arrangement; these exceptions are not available if there is any arrearage.

82. Indeed, even the parents' agreement to change custody provides no defense if they do not also obtain a formal change in the support order. Without it, the former custodial parent can later claim arrearages for the payments the support obligor did not make while the child lived with him pursuant to the parents' agreement. See, e.g., Price v. Price, 912 S.W.2d 44 (Ky. 1995) (two years' arrearage); Houser v. Houser, 535 N.W.2d 882 (S.D. 1995) (ten years' arrearage). Some courts have relied upon the estoppel doctrine in such cases to prevent enforcement of the support order. See Ellman, Kurtz and Scott, *Family Law,* 572.

# 7

# Gay and Lesbian Families:
# Queer Like Us

Judith Stacey

Until recently, gay and lesbian families seemed quite a queer concept, if
not oxymoronic, not only to scholars and the general public but even to
most lesbians and gay men. The grass roots movement for gay liberation
of the late 1960s and early 1970s struggled along with the militant feminist movement of that period to liberate gays and women *from* perceived
evils and injustices represented by "the family," rather than *for* access to
its blessings and privileges. Early marches for gay pride and women's liberation flaunted provocative, countercultural banners, like "Smash the
Family" and "Smash Monogamy." Their legacy is a lasting public association of gay liberation and feminism with family subversion. Today, however, gays and lesbians are in the thick of a vigorous profamily movement
of their own.

Gay and lesbian families are indisputably here. By the late 1980s an
astonishing "gay-by" boom had swelled the ranks of children living with
at least one gay or lesbian parent.[1] *Family Values*, the title of a popular
1993 book by and about a lesbian's successful struggle to become a legal second mother to the son she and his biological mother have coparented since his birth,[2] is also among the most popular themes of contemporary Gay Pride marches. In 1989, Denmark became the first nation
in the world to legalize a form of gay marriage, termed "registered partnerships," and its Nordic neighbors, Norway and Sweden, soon followed
suit. In April 2001, the Netherlands leap-frogged ahead to become the
first nation in the world to grant full legal marriage rights to same-sex
couples. Meanwhile, in 1993, thousands of gay and lesbian couples par-

ticipated in a mass wedding ceremony on the Washington Mall during the largest demonstration for gay rights in U.S. history. That same year, the Hawaiian state supreme court issued a ruling that raised the prospect that Hawaii would become the first state in the United States to legalize same-sex marriage. As a result, controversies over gay and lesbian families began to receive center stage billing in U.S. electoral politics.

Gay and lesbian families come in different sizes, shapes, ethnicities, races, religions, resources, creeds, and quirks, and even engage in diverse sexual practices.[3] The gay and lesbian family label primarily marks the cognitive dissonance, and even emotional threat, that much of the nongay public experiences upon recognizing that gays can participate in family life at all. What unifies such families is their need to contend with the particular array of psychic, social, legal, practical, and even physical challenges to their very existence that institutionalized hostility to homosexuality produces. Paradoxically, the label "gay and lesbian family" might become irrelevant if the nongay population could only "get used to it."

In this chapter I hope to facilitate such a process of normalization, ironically, perhaps, to make using the marker "gay and lesbian" to depict a family category seem queer—as queer, that is, as it now seems to identify a *family*, rather than an individual or a desire, as heterosexual.[4] I will suggest that this historically novel category of family crystallizes widespread processes of family diversification and change that characterize the postmodern family condition.[5] Gay and lesbian families represent such a new, embattled, visible, and, necessarily, self-conscious genre of kinship, that they help to expose the widening gap between the complex reality of contemporary family forms and the dated family ideology that still undergirds most public rhetoric, policy, and law concerning families. Nongay families, family scholars, and policymakers alike can learn a great deal from examining the experience, struggles, conflicts, needs, and achievements of contemporary gay and lesbian families.

## Brave New Family Planning

History rarely affords a social scientist an opportunity to witness during her own lifetime the origins and evolution of a dramatic and significant cultural phenomenon in her field. For a family scholar, it is particularly rare to be able to witness the birth of a historically unprecedented variety of family life. Yet the emergence of the "genus" gay and lesbian family as a distinct social category, and the rapid development and diversification of its living species, have occurred during the past three decades, less than my lifetime. Same-sex desire and behavior, on the other hand, have appeared in most human societies, including all Western ones, as well as among most mammalian species; homosexual relationships, identities, and communities have much longer histories than most Western heterosexuals imagine; and historical evidence documents the practice of sanctioned and/or socially visible same-sex unions in the West, as well as elsewhere, since ancient times.[6] Nonetheless, the notion of a gay or lesbian family is decidedly a late-twentieth-century development, and several particular forms of gay and lesbian families were literally "inconceivable" prior to recent developments in reproductive technology.

Indeed, before the Stonewall rebellion in 1969, the family lives of gays and lesbians were so invisible, both legally and socially, that one can actually date the appearance of the first identifiable species of gay family life—a unit that includes at least one self-identified gay or lesbian parent and children from a former heterosexual marriage. Only one U.S. child custody case reported before 1950 involved a gay or lesbian parent, and only five more gays or lesbians dared to sue for custody of their children between 1950 and 1969. Then, immediately after Stonewall, despite the predominantly antifamily ethos of the early gay liberation period, gay custody conflicts jumped dramatically, with fifty occurring during the 1970s and many more since then.[7] Courts consistently denied parental rights to these early pioneers, rendering them martyrs to a cause made visible by their losses. Both historically and numerically, formerly married lesbian and gay parents who "came out" after marriage and secured at least shared custody of their children represent the most significant genre of gay families. Such gay parents were the first to level a public challenge against the reigning cultural presumption that the two terms, "gay" and "parent" are antithetical. Their family units continue to comprise the vast majority of contemporary gay families and to manifest greater income and ethnic diversity than newer categories of lesbian and gay parents. Moreover, studies of these families provide the primary data base of the extant research on the effects of gay parenting on child development.

It was novel, incongruous, and plain brave for lesbian and gay parents to struggle for legitimate family status during the height of the antinatalist, antimaternalist, antifamily fervor of grass roots feminism and gay liberation in the early 1970s. Fortunately for their successors, such fervor proved to be quite short-lived. Within very few years many feminist theorists began to celebrate women's historically developed nurturing capacities, not coincidentally at a time when aging, feminist baby-boomers had begun producing a late-life boomlet of their own.[8] During the middle to late seventies, the legacy of sexual revolution and feminist assertions of female autonomy combined with the popularization of alternative reproductive technologies and strategies to embolden a first wave of "out" lesbians to join the burgeoning ranks of women actively choosing to have children outside of marriage.

Fully intentional childbearing outside of heterosexual unions represents one of the only new, truly original, and decidedly controversial genres of family formation and structure to have emerged in the West during many centuries. While lesbian variations on this cultural theme include some particularly creative reproductive strategies, they nonetheless represent not deviant, but vanguard manifestations of much broader late-twentieth-century trends in Western family life. Under postmodern conditions, processes of sexuality, conception, gestation, marriage, and parenthood, which once appeared to follow a natural, inevitable progression of gendered behaviors and relationships, have come unhinged, hurtling the basic definitions of our most taken-for-granted familial categories—like mother, father, parent, offspring, sibling, and, of course, "family" itself—into cultural confusion and contention.

The conservative turn toward profamily and postfeminist sensibilities of the Reagan-Bush era, combined with the increased visibility and confidence of gay and lesbian communities, helped to fuel the "gay-by" boom that escalated rapidly during the 1980s. It seems more accurate to call this a "lesbaby" boom, because lesbians vastly outnumber the gay men who can, or have chosen to, become parents out of the closet. Lesbian "planned parenthood" strategies have spread and diversified rapidly during the past two decades. With access to customary means to parenthood denied or severely limited, lesbians necessarily construct their chosen family forms with an exceptional degree of reflection and intentionality. They have been choosing motherhood within a broad array of kinship structures. Some become single mothers, but many lesbians choose to share responsibility for rearing children with a lover and/or with other coparents, such as sperm donors, gay men, and other friends and relatives. Several states expressly prohibit adoptions and/or foster care by lesbians and gay men, and many states and adoption agencies actively discriminate against them. Consequently, independent adoption provided the first, and still traveled, route to planned lesbian maternity, but increasing numbers of lesbians have been choosing to bear children of their own. In pursuit of sperm, some lesbians resort quite instrumentally to heterosexual intercourse—with or without the knowledge of the man involved—but most prefer alternative insemination strategies, locating known or anonymous donors through personal networks or through private physicians or sperm banks.

Institutionalized heterosexism and married-couple biases pervade the medically controlled fertility market. Many private physicans and many sperm banks in the United States, as well as the Canadian and most European health services, refuse to inseminate unmarried women in general, and lesbians particularly. More than 90 percent of U.S. physicians surveyed in 1979 denied insemination to unmarried women, and a 1988 federal government survey of doctors and clinics reported that homosexuality was one of their top four reasons for refusing to provide this service.[9] Thus, initially, planned lesbian pregnancies depended primarily upon donors located through personal networks, very frequently involving gay men or male relatives who might also agree to participate in child rearing, in varying degrees. Numerous lesbian couples solicit sperm from a brother or male relative of one woman to impregnate her partner, hoping to buttress their tenuous legal, symbolic, and social claims for shared parental status over their "turkey-baster babies."

Despite its apparent novelty, "turkey-baster" insemination for infertility dates back to the late eighteenth century, and, as the nickname implies, is far from a high-tech procedure requiring medical expertise.[10] Nonetheless, because the AIDS epidemic and the emergence of child custody conflicts between lesbians and known sperm donors led many lesbians to prefer the legally sanitized, medical route to anonymous donors, feminist health care activists mobilized to meet this need. In 1975 the Vermont Women's Health Center added donor insemination to its services, and in 1980 the Northern California Sperm Bank opened in Oakland expressly to serve the needs of unmarried, disabled, or nonheterosexual women who want to become pregnant. The clinic ships frozen semen throughout North America, and more than two-thirds of the clinic's clients are not married.[11]

The absence of a national health system in the United States commercializes access to sperm and fertility services. This introduces an obvious class bias into the practice of alternative insemination. Far more high-tech, innovative, expensive, and, therefore, uncommon is a procreative strategy some lesbian couples now are adopting in which an ovum from one woman is fertilized with donor sperm and then extracted and implanted in her lover's uterus. In June 2000, one such couple in San Francisco became the first to receive joint recognition as the biological and legal co-mothers of their infant. The irony of deploying technology to assert a biological, and thereby a legal, social, and emotional claim to maternal and family status throws the contemporary instability of all the relevant categories—biology, technology, nature, culture, maternity, family—into bold relief.

While the advent of AIDS inhibited joint procreative ventures between lesbians and gay men, the epidemic also fostered stronger social and political solidarity between the two populations and stimulated gay men to keener interest in forming families. Their ranks are smaller and newer than those of lesbian mothers, but by the late eighties gay men were also visibly engaged in efforts to become parents, despite far more limited opportunities to do so. Not only do men still lack the biological capacity to derive personal benefits from most alternative reproductive technologies, but social prejudice also severely restricts gay male access to children placed for adoption, or even into foster care. Ever since Anita Bryant's "Save the Children" campaign against gay rights in 1977, rightwing mobilizations in diverse states, including Florida, Utah, New Hampshire, and Massachusetts, have successfully cast gay men, in particular, as threats to children and families and denied them the right to adopt or foster the young. In response, some wishful gay fathers have resorted to private adoption and surrogacy arrangements, accepting the most difficult-to-place adoptees and foster children, or entering into shared social parenting arrangements with lesbian couples or single women. During the 1990s, "Growing Generations," the world's first gay and lesbian-owned surrogacy agency, opened in Los Angeles to serve an international constituency of prospective gay parents.

Compelled to proceed outside conventional channels, lesbian and gay male planned parenthood has become an increasingly complex, creative, and politicized, self-help enterprise. Because gays forge kin ties without established legal protections or norms, relationships between gay parents and their children suffer heightened risks. By the mideighties many lesbians and gays found themselves battling each other, as custody conflicts between lesbian coparents or between lesbian parents and sperm donors and/or other relatives began to reach the dockets and to profoundly challenge family courts.[12] Despite a putative "best interests of the child" standard, a bias favoring the heterosexual family guided virtually all the judges who heard these early cases. Biological claims of kinship nearly always trumped those of social parenting, even in heartrending circumstances of custody challenges to bereaved lesbian "widows" who, with their deceased lovers, had jointly planned for, reared, loved, and supported children since their birth.[13] Likewise, judges routinely honored fathers' rights arguments by favoring parental claims of donors who had contributed nothing more than sperm to their offspring over those of lesbians who had coparented from the outset, *even when these men had expressly agreed to abdicate paternal rights or responsibilities.* The first, and still rare, exception to this rule involved a donor who did not bring his paternity suit until the child was ten years old.[14] While numerous sperm donors have reneged on their prenatal custody agreements with lesbian parents, thus far no lesbian mother has sued a donor to attain parental terms different from those to which he first agreed. On the other hand, in the first case in which a lesbian biological mother sought financial support from her former lesbian partner, a New York court found the nonbiological coparent to be a parent. Here, the state's fiduciary interest rather than gay rights governed the decision.[15]

Perhaps the most poignant paradox in gay and lesbian family history concerns how fervently many lesbians and gay men have had to struggle for family status precisely when forces mobilized *in the name of The Family* conspire to deny this to them. The widely publicized saga of the Sharon Kowalski case, in which the natal family of a lesbian who had been severely disabled in a car crash successfully opposed her guardianship by her chosen life-companion, proved particularly galvanizing in this cause, perhaps because all of the contestants were adults. After eight years of legal and political struggle, Sharon's lover, Karen Thompson, finally won a reversal, in a belated, but highly visible, landmark victory for gay family rights.[16]

Gay family struggles rapidly achieved other significant victories, like the 1989 *Braschi* decision by New York State's top court, which granted protection against eviction to a gay man by explicitly defining family in inclusive, social terms, to rest upon

> the exclusivity and longevity of the relationship, the level of emotional and financial commitment, the manner in which the parties have conducted their everyday lives and held themselves out to society, and the reliance placed upon one another for daily family services . . . it is the totality of the relationship as evidenced by the dedication, caring and self-sacrifice of the parties which should, in the final analysis, control.[17]

More recently, in 2000, Vermont became the first state in the United States to grant same-sex couples the right to enter a civil union, a status that confers all of the legal benefits of marriage except those denied by federal law, and numerous state legislatures will be considering similar proposals. The struggle for second-parent adoption rights, which enable a lesbian or gay man to adopt a lover's children without removing the lover's custody rights, represents one of the most active, turbulent fronts in the struggle for gay family rights. In more than half of the 50 states, individual lesbian and gay male couples have won petitions for second-parent adoptions at the trial court level. However, many trial judges deny such petitions, and only a handful of states have granted this right at the appeals court level. In 2000, a Pennsylvania appeals court decision denied such an appeal, thereby setting back the drive for gay parental rights in that state. Even the Nordic countries explicitly excluded adoption rights when they first legalized gay registered partnerships, but since then the Netherlands, Denmark, and Iceland have granted these rights, and other European and Commonwealth countries are beginning to follow suit.

The highly politicized character of family change in the United States renders struggles for gay parenting rights painfully vulnerable to unfavorable political winds. For example, state barriers to lesbian and gay second-parent adoptions in California rise and fall with the fortunes of Republican and Democratic gubernatorial campaigns. The National Center for Lesbian Rights considers second-parent adoptions right to be so crucial to the lesbian "profamily" cause that it revoked its former policy of abstaining from legal conflicts between lesbians over this issue. Convinced that the long-term, best interests of lesbian parents and their children depend upon defining parenthood in social rather than biological terms, the center decided to represent lesbian parents who are denied custody of their jointly reared children when their former lovers exploit the biological and homophobic prejudices of the judiciary.[18]

Here again, gay family politics crystallize, rather than diverge from, pervasive cultural trends. Gay second-parent adoptions, for example, trek a kin trail blazed by court responses to families reconstituted after divorce and remarriage. Courts first allowed some stepparents to adopt their new spouses' children without terminating the custody rights of the children's former parents. Gay family rights law also bears a kind of second cousin tie to racial kin case law. Gay and lesbian custody victories rely heavily on a milestone race custody case, *Palmore* v. *Sidoti* (1984), which restored the custody rights of a divorced, white mother who lost her children after she married a black man. Even though *Palmore* was decided on legal principles governing race discrimination, which do not yet apply to gender or sexual discrimination, several successful gay and lesbian custody decisions rely on its logic. The first successful second-parent adoption award to a lesbian couple actually was a "third-parent" adoption on the new model of stepparent adoption after divorce, which Mary Ann Mason discusses in her chapter on stepparents in this volume. The court granted coparent status to the nonbiological mother without withdrawing it from the sperm donor father, a Native American, in order to honor the shared desires of all three parents to preserve the child's bicultural inheritance.[19]

As U.S. tabloid and talk show fare testify daily, culturally divisive struggles over babies secured or lost through alternative insemination, in vitro fertilization, ovum extraction, frozen embryos, surrogacy, transracial adoption, not to mention mundane processes of divorce and remarriage are not the special province of a fringe gay and lesbian minority. We now inhabit a world in which technology has upended the basic premises of the old nature-nurture debate by rendering human biology more amenable to intervention than human society. Inevitably, therefore, contests between biological and social definitions of kinship, such as depicted in the chapters on adoption and stepfamilies, will continue to proliferate and to rub social nerves raw.

Thus while one can discern a gradual political and judicial trend toward granting parental and family rights to gays, the legal situation in the fifty states remains uneven, volatile, and replete with major setbacks for gay and lesbian parents.[20] Forces opposed to gay parenting continue to introduce statewide initiatives and regulations to rescind such rights. The crucial fact remains that numerous states still criminalize sodomy, supported by the 1986 U.S. Supreme Court decision in *Bowers* v. *Hardwick*, which upheld the constitutionality of this most basic impediment to civil rights for gay relationships. One decade later, however, in May 1996, the court struck down a Colorado antigay rights initiative in *Romer* v. *Evans*," raising the hopes of gays and lesbians that it might soon reconsider the detested *Bowers* ruling. As of 2002, however, such wishes remain unfulfilled.

## A More, or Less, Perfect Union?

Much nearer at hand, however, than most ever dared to imagine is the momentous prospect of legal gay marriage. The idea of same-sex marriage used to draw nearly as many jeers from gays and lesbians as from nongays. As one lesbian couple recalls,

> In 1981, we were a very, very small handful of lesbians who got married. We took a lot of flak from other lesbians, as well as heterosexuals. In 1981, we didn't know any other lesbians, not a single one, who had had a ceremony in Santa Cruz, and a lot of lesbians live in that city. Everybody was on our case about it. They said, What are you doing, How heterosexual. We really had to sell it.[21]

Less than a decade later, gay and lesbian couples would proudly announce their weddings and anniversaries, not only in the gay press, which now includes specialized magazines for gay and lesbian couples and parents, like *Partners Magazine*, but even in such mainstream, midwestern newspapers as the Minneapolis *Star Tribune*.[22] Jewish rabbis, Protestant ministers, Quaker meetings, and even some Catholic priests regularly peform gay and lesbian wedding or commitment ceremonies, and the phenomenon has become a fashionable pop culture motif. In December 1995, the long-running, provocative TV sitcom program *Roseanne* featured a gay male wedding, and one month later, the popular sitcom *Friends* aired a lesbian wedding on primetime television. A few years later, a high profile made-for-TV HBO movie starring Vanessa Redgrave, Michelle Williams, Ellen DeGeneres, and Sharon Stone, *If These Walls Could Talk 2*, expanded on the theme by highlighting difficulties experienced by lesbian couples who cannot be legally married. Such popular culture breakthroughs have helped normalize what once seemed inconceivable to gay and straight audiences alike.

Gradually, major corporations, universities, and nonprofit organizations are providing spousal benefits to the domestic mates of their gay and lesbian employees, and a small but growing number of U.S. municipalities, states, and increasing numbers of European and Commonwealth nations have legalized domestic partnerships, which grant legal status and varying rights and responsibilities to cohabiting couples, irrespective of gender or sexual identity.

When the very first social science research collection about gay parents was published in 1987, its editor concluded that however desirable such unions might be, "it is highly unlikely that marriages between same-sex individuals will be legalized in any state in the foreseeable future."[23] Yet, almost immediately thereafter, precisely this specter began to exercise imaginations across the political spectrum. A national poll reported by the *San Francisco Examiner* in 1989 found that 86 percent of lesbians and gay men supported legalizing same-sex marriage.[24] A few years later, the Hawaiian supreme court issued a ruling that made such a prospect seem imminent. Amidst rampant rumors that thousands of mainland gay and lesbian couples were stocking their hope chests with Hawaiian excursion fares, posied to fly to tropical altars the instant the first gay matrimonial bans falter, right-wing Christian groups began actively to mobilize resistance. Utah became the first state to pass legislation refusing recognition to same-sex marriages if they were performed in other states. Soon a majority of states were considering similar bills.

On May 8, 1996, gay marriage galloped onto the nation's center political stage when Republicans introduced the Defense of Marriage Act (DOMA) to define marriage in exclusively heterosexual terms as "a legal union between one man and one woman as husband and wife." Introduced primarily as a "wedge" issue in the Republican 1996 electoral strategy, DOMA passed both houses of Congress in a landslide vote, and President Clinton promptly signed it, despite his personal support for gay rights.

As with child custody, the campaign for gay marriage clings to legal footholds planted by racial justice pioneers. It is startling to recall how recent it was that the Supreme Court finally struck down antimiscegenation laws. Not until 1967, that is only two years before the Stonewall rebellion, did the high court, in *Loving* v. *Virginia*, find state restrictions on interracial marriages to be unconstitutional. (Twenty states still had such restrictions on the books in 1967, a greater number than currently prohibit sodomy.) A handful of gay couples quickly sought to marry in the 1970s through appeals to this precedent, but until three lesbian and gay male couples sued Hawaii in *Baehr* v. *Lewin* for equal rights to choose marriage partners without restrictions on gender, all U.S. courts had dismissed the analogy. In a historic ruling in 1993, the Hawaii Supreme Court remanded this suit to the trial court, requiring the state to demonstrate a "compelling interest" in prohibiting same-sex marriage, a strict scrutiny standard that the state was unable to meet when the case was retried. Significantly, the case was neither argued nor adjudicated as a gay rights issue. Rather, just as ERA opponents once had warned and advocates had denied, passage of an equal rights amendment to Hawaii's state constitution in 1972 paved the legal foundation for *Baehr*.[25]

Although backlash forces succeeded in preventing the legalization of gay marriage in Hawaii, this global struggle keeps achieving milestone victories at a breathless pace. Marriage rights in all but name are now available throughout most of Western Europe and Canada, as well as in Vermont. In 2001, the Netherlands assumed world leadership in fully legalizing same-sex marriage at the national level, and similar developments appear imminent in the Nordic nations, Canada, and perhaps in South Africa. Clearly this issue is on the historical agenda for the twenty-first century. Not all gay activists or legal scholars embrace this prospect with enthusiasm. Although most of their constituents desire the right to marry, gay activists and theorists continue to debate vigorously the politics and effects of this campaign. An articulate, vocal minority seeks not to extend the right to marry, but to dismantle an institution they regard as inherently, and irredeemably, hierarchical, unequal, conservative, and repressive.[26] A second perspective supports legal marriage as one long-term goal of the gay rights movement but voices serious strategic objections to making this a priority before there is sufficient public support to sustain a favorable ruling in any state or the nation. Such critics fear that a premature victory will prove pyrrhic, because efforts to defend it against the vehement backlash it has already begun to incite are apt to fail, after sapping resources and time better devoted to other urgent struggles for gay rights. Rather than risk a major setback for the gay movement, some leaders advocate an incremental approach to establishing legal family status for gay and lesbian kin ties through a multifaceted struggle for "family diversity."[27]

However, the largest, and most diverse, contingent of gay activist voices now supports the marriage rights campaign, perhaps because gay marriage can be perceived as harmonizing with virtually every hue on the gay ideological spectrum. Progay marriage arguments range from profoundly conservative to liberal humanist to radical and deconstructive. Conservatives, like those radicals who still oppose marriage, view it as an institution that promotes monogamy, commitment, and social stability, along with interests in private property, social conformity, and mainstream values.[28] Liberal gays support legal marriage, of course, not only to affirm the legitimacy of their relationships and help sustain them in a hostile world but as a straightforward matter of equal civil rights. They also recognize the social advantages of divorce law. "I used to say, 'Why do we want to get married? It doesn't work for straight people,'" one gay lawyer comments. "But now I say we should care: They have the privilege of divorce and we don't. We're left out there to twirl around in pain."[29]

Some feminist and other critical gay legal theorists craft more radical defenses of gay marriage. Nan Hunter, for example, rejects feminist colleague Nancy Polikoff's belief that marriage is an unalterably sexist and heterosexist institution. Hunter argues that legalized same-sex marriage would have "enormous potential to destabilize the gendered definition of marriage for everyone."[30] Likewise, Evan Wolfson, director of the Marriage Project of the gay legal rights organization Lambda Legal Defense, who served as co-counsel in *Baehr*, argues that marriage is neither inherently equal nor unequal, but depends upon an ever-changing cultural and political context.[31] (Anyone who doubts this need only consider such examples as polygamy, arranged marriage, or the same-sex unions in early Western history documented by the late Princeton historian John Boswell.)

Support for gay marriage, not long ago anathema to radicals and conservatives, gays and nongays alike, now issues forth from ethical and political perspectives as diverse, and even incompatible, as these. The cultural and political context has changed so dramatically since Stonewall that it now seems easier to understand why marriage has come to enjoy overwhelming support in the gay community than to grasp the depth of resistance to the institution that characterized the early movement.

Gay marriage, despite its apparent compatibility with mainstream "family values" sentiment, raises far more threatening questions than does military service about gender relations, sexuality, and family life. Few contemporary politicians, irrespective of their personal convictions, display the courage to confront this contradiction, even when urged to do so by gay conservatives. Gay marriage would strengthen the ranks of those endangered two-parent, "intact," married-couples families whose praises conservative, "profamily" enthusiasts tirelessly sing. Unsurprisingly, however, this case has won few nongay conservative converts to the cause. After all, homophobia is a matter of passion, politics, and prejudice, not logic.

Surveys suggest, however, that while a majority of citizens still oppose legalizing gay marriage, the margin of opposition is declining slowly but surely. In a 1994 *Time* magazine/CNN poll, 64 percent of respondents did not want to legalize gay marriages.[32] A *Newsweek* poll conductd right after the DOMA was introduced in May 1996 reported that public opposition to gay marriage had declined to 58 percent, and a Gallup poll conducted June 2001 indicated a further drop to 52 percent.[33]

Despite the paucity of mainstream political enthusiasm for legalizing gay marriage, there are good reasons to believe that gays and lesbians will eventually win this right and to support their struggle to do so. Legitimizing gay and lesbian marriages would promote a democratic, pluralist expansion of the meaning, practice, and politics of family life in the United States, helping to supplant the destructive sanctity of *The Family* with respect for diverse and vibrant *families*. To begin with, the liberal implications of legal gay marriage are far from trivial, as the rush to nullify them should confirm. For example, legal gay marriage in one state could begin to threaten antisodomy laws in all the others. Policing marital sex would be difficult to legitimate, and differential prosecution of conjugal sex among same-sex couples could violate equal protection legislation. Likewise, if gay marriage were legalized, the myriad of state barriers to child custody, adoption, fertility services, inheritance, and other family rights that lesbians and gay men currently suffer could also become subject to legal challenge. Moreover, it seems hard to overestimate the profound cultural implications for the struggle against the injurious effects of legally condoned homophobia that would ensue were lesbian and gay relationships to be admitted into the ranks of legitimate kinship. In a society that forbids most public school teachers and counselors even the merest expression of tolerance for homosexuality, while lesbian and gay youth attempt suicide at rates estimated to be at least three times greater than other youth,[34] granting full legal recognition to lesbian and gay relationships could have dramatic, and salutary, consequences.

Moreover, while it is unlikely that same-sex marriage can in itself dismantle the patterned gender and sexual injustices of the institution, I believe it could make a potent contribution to those projects, as the research on gay relationships I discuss later seems to indicate. Admitting gays to the wedding banquet invites gays and nongays alike to consider the kinds of place settings that could best accommodate the diverse needs of all contemporary families. Subjecting the conjugal institution to this sort of heightened democratic scrutiny could help it to assume varied, creative, and adaptive contours. If we begin to value the meaning and quality of intimate bonds over their customary forms, people might devise marriage and kinship patterns to serve diverse needs. For example, the "companionate marriage," a much celebrated, but less often realized, ideal of modern sociological lore, could take on new life. Two friends might decide to "marry" without basing their bond on erotic or romantic attachment, as Dorthe, a prominent Danish lesbian activist who had initially opposed the campaign for gay marriage, fantasized after her nation's parliament approved gay "registered partnerships": If I am going to marry it will be with one of my oldest friends in order to share pensions and things like that. But I'd never marry a lover. That is the advantage of being married to a close friend. Then, you never have to marry a lover![35]

While conservative advocates of gay marriage scoff at such radical visions, they correctly realize that putative champions of committed relationships and children who oppose gay marriage can be charged with gross hypocrisy on this score. For access to legal marriage not only would promote long-term, committed intimacy and economic security among gay couples but also would afford invaluable protection to the children of gay parents. Public legitimacy for gay relationships would also provide indirect protection to closeted gay youth who reside with nongay parents. Clearly, only through a process of massive denial of the fact that millions of children living in gay and lesbian families are here, and here to stay, can anyone genuinely concerned with the best interests of children deny their parents the right to marry.

## In the Best Interests of Whose Children?

The most cursory survey of the existing empirical research on gay and lesbian families reveals the depth of sanctioned discrimination they continue to suffer and the absence of evidence to justify this iniquity. To be sure, substantial limitations mar the social science research on this subject, which is barely past its infancy. Mainstream journals, even those specializing in family research, warmed to this subject startlingly late and little, relegating the domain primarily to sexologists, clinicians, and a handful of movement scholars and their sympathizers and opponents. In 1995, a survey of the three leading journals of family research in the United States found only 12 of the 2598 articles published between 1980 and 1993, that is less than .05 percent, focused on the families of lesbians and gay men, which, even by conservative estimates make up at least 3 percent of U.S. families.[36] The research that does exist, moreover, has deficiencies that skew results so as to exaggerate rather than understate any defects of gay and lesbian families. Until very recently, most investigators began with a deviance perspective, seeking, whether homophobically or defensively, to "test" the validity of the popular prejudice that gay parenting is harmful to children. In other words, the reigning premise has been that gay and lesbian families are dangerously, and *prima facie,* "queer" in the pejorative sense, unless proven otherwise. Taking children reared by nongay parents as the unquestioned norm, most studies asymmetrically ask whether lesbian and gay parents hinder their children's emotional, cognitive, gender, or sexual development. Because lesbian and gay "planned parenthood" is so new, and its progeny so young, nearly all of the studies to date sample the ranks of formerly married parents who had children before they divorced and came out of the closet. The studies are generally small-scale and draw disproportionately from urban, white, middle-class populations. Frequently they make misleading comparisons between divorced lesbian and nongay, single-mother households by ignoring the presence or absence of lesbian life partners or other caretakers in the former.[37]

Despite such limitations, psychologists, social psychologists, and sociologists have by now conducted dozens of studies which provide overwhelming support for the "proven otherwise" thesis. Almost without exception they conclude, albeit in defensive tones, that lesbian and gay parents do not produce inferior, nor even particularly different kinds of children than do other parents. Generally they find no significant differences in school achievement, social adjustment, mental health, gender identity, or sexual orientation between the two groups of children. As Joan Laird's overview of research on lesbian and gay parents summarizes:

> a generation of research has failed to demonstrate that gays or lesbians are any less fit to parent than their heterosexual counterparts. Furthermore, a substantial number of studies on the psychological and social development of children of lesbian and gay parents have failed to produce any evidence that children of lesbian or gay parents are harmed or compromised or even differ from, in any significant ways along a host of psychosocial developmental measures, children raised in heterosexual families.[38]

The rare small differences between gay and nongay parents reported tend to favor gay parents, portraying them as somewhat more nurturant and tolerant, and their children, in turn, more tolerant and empathic, and less aggressive than those reared by nongay parents.[39] In April 1995, British researchers published the results of their unusual sixteen-year-long study which followed twenty-five children brought up by lesbian mothers and twenty-one brought up by heterosexual mothers from youth to adulthood. They found that the young adults raised in lesbian households had better relationships with their mothers' lesbian partners than the young adults brought up by heterosexual single mothers had with their mothers' male partners.[40] Published research to date seems to vindicate one ten-year-old girl who, rather apologetically, deems herself privileged to be the daughter of two lesbian parents: "But I think you get more love with two moms. I know other kids have a mom and a dad, but I think that moms give more love than dads. This may not be true, but it's what I think." Her opinion is shared by a six-year-old girl from another lesbian family: "I don't tell other kids at school about my mothers because I think they would be jealous of me. Two mothers is better than one."[41]

In light of the inhospitable, often outrightly hostile climate which gay families typically encounter, this seems a remarkable achievement. One sign that mainstream social scientists have begun to recognize the achievement is the inclusion of Laird's chapter, "Lesbian and Gay Families," in the 1993 edition of a compendium of research, *Normal Family Processes*, whose first edition, in 1982, ignored the subject.[42] Researchers have begun to call for, and to initiate, a mature, creative, undefensive approach to studying the full range of gay and lesbian families. Coming to terms with the realities of the postmodern family condition, such studies begin with a pluralist premise concerning the legitimacy and dignity of diverse family structures. They ask whether and how gay and lesbian families differ, rather than deviate, from nongay families; they attend as much to the differences among such families as to those dividing them from nongays; and they explore the particular benefits as well as the burdens such families bestow on their members.[43]

This kind of research has begun to discover more advantages of gay and lesbian family life for participants and our society than have yet been explored. Most obvious, certainly, are mental health rewards for gay and lesbian youth fortunate enough to come of age in such families. Currently most youth who experience homosexual inclinations either conceal their desires from their immediate kin or risk serious forms of rejection. State hostility to gay parents can have tragic results. In 1994, for example, the Nebraska Department of Social Services adopted a policy forbidding lesbian or gay foster homes, and the next day a seventeen-year-old openly gay foster child committed suicide, because he feared he would be removed from the supportive home of his gay foster parents.[44]

Of course, this speaks precisely to the heart of what homophobes most fear, that public acceptance of lesbian and gay families will spawn an "epidemic" of gay youth. As Pat Robertson so crudely explained to a Florida audience: "That gang of idiots running the ACLU, the National Education Association, the National Organization of Women, they don't want religious principles in our schools. Instead of teaching the Ten Commandments, they want to teach kids how to be homosexuals."[45] Attempting to respond to such anxieties, most defenders of gay families have stressed the irrelevance of parental sexual identity to that of their children. Sympathetic researchers repeatedly, and in my view misguidedly, maintain that lesbian and gay parents are no more likely than nongay parents to rear lesbian and gay children. Laird, for example, laments:

> One of the most prevalent myths is that children of gay parents will themselves grow up gay; another that daughters will be more masculine and sons more feminine than "normal" children. A number of researchers have concluded that the sexual orientations/preferences of children of gay or lesbian parents do not differ from those whose parents are heterosexual.[46]

Increasingly this claim appears illogical, unlikely, and unwittingly antigay. Ironically, it presumes the very sort of fixed definition of sexuality that the best contemporary gay and lesbian scholarship has challenged. Although it is clearly true that, until now, nearly all "homosexuals," like almost everyone else, have been reared by nongays, it is equally clear that sexual desire and identity do not represent a singular fixed "trait" that expresses itself free of cultural context. However irresolvable eternal feuds over the relative weight of nature and nurture may forever prove to be, historical and anthropological data leave no doubt that culture profoundly influences sexual meanings and practices. Homophobes are quite correct to believe that environmental conditions incite or inhibit expressions of homosexual desire, no matter its primary source. If culture had no influence on sexual identity, there would not have emerged the movement for gay and lesbian family rights that inspired me to write this chapter.

Contrary to what most current researchers claim, public acceptance of gay and lesbian families should, in fact, slightly expand the percentage of youth who would dare to explore their same-sex desires. In fact, a careful reading of the studies does suggest just this.[47] Children reared by lesbian or gay parents feel greater openness to homosexuality or bisexuality. In January 1996, the researchers who conducted the long-term British study conceded this point, after issuing the obligatory reassurance that, "the commonly held assumption that children brought up by lesbian mothers will themselves grow up to be lesbian or gay is not supported by the findings." Two of the twenty-five young adults in the study who were reared by lesbians grew up to identify as lesbians, but none of the twenty-one who were reared in the comparison group of heterosexual mothers identify as lesbian or gay. More pertinent, in my view, five daughters and one son of lesbian mothers, but none of the children of heterosexual mothers, reported having had a same-sex erotic experience of some sort, prompting the researchers to acknowledge that, "It seems that growing up in an accepting atmosphere enables individuals who are attracted to same-sex partners to pursue these relationships."[48] This prospect should disturb only those whose antipathy to homosexuality derives from deeply held religious convictions or irrational prejudice.

The rest of us could benefit from permission to explore and develop sexually free from the rigid prescriptions of what Adrienne Rich memorably termed "compulsory heterosexuality."[49] Currently, lesbian and gay parents grant their children such permission much more generously than do other parents. Not only do they tend to be less doctrinaire or phobic about sexual diversity than heterosexual parents, but, wishing to spare their children the burdens of stigma, some gay parents actually prefer that their youngsters do not become gay. Indeed, despite the ubiquity of Pat Robertson's sort of alarmist, propagandistic warnings, "advice on how to help your kids turn out gay," as cultural critic Eve Sedgwick sardonically puts it, "not to mention your students, your parishioners, your therapy clients, or your military subordinates, is less ubiquitous than you might think."[50]

Heterosexual indoctrination is far more pervasive and far the greater danger. Contemporary adolescent culture is even more mercilessly homophobic, or perhaps less hypocritically so, than most mainstream adult prejudices countenance. Verbal harrassment, ridicule, hazing, and ostracism of "faggots," "bull-dykes," and "queers"—quotidien features of our popular culture—are particularly blatant among teens. "Sometimes I feel like no one really knows what I'm going through," one fifteen-year-old daughter of a lesbian laments: "Don't get me wrong. I really do love my mom and all her friends, but being gay is just not acceptable to other people. Like at school, people make jokes about dykes and fags, and it really bothers me. I mean I bite my tongue, because if I say anything, they wonder, Why is she sticking up for them?"[51] In a 1995 survey, nearly

half the teen victims of reported violent physical assaults identified their
sexual orientation as a precipitating factor. Tragically, family members inflicted 61 percent of these assaults on gay youth.[52]

Little wonder such disproportionate numbers of gay youth commit
suicide. Studies claim that gay youth commit one-third of all teenage suicide attempts.[53] To evade harassment, most of the survivors suffer their
clandestine difference in silent isolation, often at great cost to their self-
esteem, social relationships, and to their very experience of adolescence
itself. One gay man bought his life partner a Father's Day card, because
he "realized that in a lot of ways we've been brother and father to each
other since we've had to grow up as adults. Because of homophobia, gay
people don't have the same opportunity as heterosexuals to be ourselves
when we are teenagers. A lot of times you have to postpone the experiences until you're older, until you come out."[54]

The increased social visibility and community-building of gays and
lesbians have vastly improved the quality of life for gay adults. Ironically,
however, Linnea Due, author of a book about growing up gay in the
nineties, was disappointed to find that this improvement has had contra-
dictory consequences for gay teens. Due expected to find conditions much
better for gay youth than when she grew up in the silent sixties. Instead,
many teens thought their circumstances had become more difficult, because, as one young man put it, "now they know we're here."[55]

While most youth with homosexual desires will continue to come of
age closeted in nongay families into the foreseeable future, they would
surely gain some comfort from greater public acceptance of gay and lesbian families. Yet in 1992, when the New York City Board of Education
tried to introduce the Rainbow multicultural curriculum guide which advocated respect for lesbian and gay families in an effort "to help increase
the tolerance and acceptance of the lesbian/gay community and to de-
crease the staggering number of hate crimes perpetrated against them,"
public opposition became so vehement that it contributed to the dismissal
of Schools Chancellor Joseph Fernandez.[56]

Indeed, the major documented special difficulties that children in gay
families experience derive directly from legal discrimination and social prejudice. As one, otherwise well-adjusted, sixteen-year-old son of a lesbian
puts it: " If I came out and said my mom was gay, I'd be treated like an
alien."[57] Children of gay parents are vicarious victims of homophobia and
institutionalized heterosexism. They suffer all of the considerable economic, legal, and social disadvantages imposed on their parents, sometimes even more harshly. They risk losing a beloved parent or coparent at
the whim of a judge. They can be denied access to friends by the parents
of playmates. Living in families that are culturally invisible or despised, the
children suffer ostracism by proxy, forced continually to negotiate conflicts between loyalty to home, mainstream authorities, and peers.

However, as the Supreme Court belatedly concluded in 1984, when
it repudiated discrimination against interracial families in *Palmore* v. *Sidoti*,

and as should be plain good sense, the fact that children of stigmatized parents bear an unfair burden provides no critique of their families. The sad *social* fact of prejudice and discrimination indicts the "family values" of the bigoted society, not the stigmatized family. In the words of the Court: "private biases may be outside the reach of the law, but the law cannot, directly or indirectly, give them effect."[58] Although the strict scrutiny standards that now govern race discrimination do not apply to sexual discrimination, several courts in recent years have relied on the logic of *Palmore* in gay custody cases. These decisions have approved lesbian and gay custody awards while explicitly acknowledging that community disapproval of their parents' sexual identity would require "greater than ordinary fortitude" from the children, but that in return they might more readily learn that, "people of integrity do not shrink from bigots." The potential benefits that children might derive from being raised by lesbian or gay parents which a New Jersey court enumerated could serve as child-rearing ideals for a democracy:

> emerge better equipped to search out their own standards of right and wrong, better able to perceive that the majority is not always correct in its moral judgments, and better able to understand the importance of conforming their beliefs to the requirements of reason and tested knowledge, not the constraints of currently popular sentiment or prejudice.[59]

The testimony of one fifteen-year-old daughter of a lesbian mother and gay father indicates just this sort of outcome:

> I think I am more open-minded than if I had straight parents. Sometimes kids at school make a big deal out of being gay. They say it's stupid and stuff like that. But they don't really know, because they are not around it. I don't say anything to them, but I know they are wrong. I get kind of mad, because they don't know what they are talking about.[60]

However, literature suggests that parents and children alike who live in fully closeted lesbian and gay families tend to suffer more than members of "out" gay families who contend with stigma directly.[61] Of course, gay parents who shroud their families in closets do so for compelling cause. Some judges still make the closet an explicit condition for awarding custody or visitation rights to gay or lesbian parents, at times imposing direct restrictions on their participation in gay social or political activity.[62] Or, fearing judicial homophobia, some parents live in mortal terror of losing their children, like one divorced lesbian in Kansas City whose former, violent husband has threatened an ugly custody battle if anyone finds out about her lesbianism.[63]

Heroically, more and more brave new "queer" families are refusing the clandestine life. If the survey article, "The Families of Lesbians and Gay Men: A New Frontier in Family Research,"[64] is correctly titled, then research on fully planned lesbian and gay families is its vanguard outpost. Researchers estimate that by 1990, between five thousand and ten thousand lesbians in the United States had given birth to chosen children, and the trend has been increasing ever since.[65] Although this represents a small fraction of the biological and adopted children who live with lesbian parents, planned lesbian births, as Kath Weston suggests, soon, "began to overshadow these other kinds of dependents, assuming a symbolic significance for lesbians and gay men disproportionate to their numbers."[66] Lesbian "turkey-baster" babies are equally symbolic to those who abhor the practice. "National Fatherhood Initiative" organizer David Blankenhorn, for example, calls for restricting sperm bank services to infertile married couples in order to inhibit the production of such "radically fatherless children," and similar concerns have been expressed in such popular publications as *U.S. News and World Report* and *Atlantic Monthly*.[67] (Interestingly, restrictions that limit access to donor sperm exclusively to married women remain widespread in Europe, even in most of the liberal Nordic nations.) Because discrimination against prospective gay and lesbian adoptive parents leads most to conceal their sexual identity, it is impossible to estimate how many have succeeded in adopting or fostering children, but this, too, has become a visible form of gay planned parenthood.[68]

Research on planned gay parenting is too young to be more than suggestive, but initial findings give more cause for gay pride than alarm. Parental relationships tend to be more cooperative and egalitarian than among heterosexual parents, child rearing more nurturant, children more affectionate.[69] On the other hand, lesbian mothers do encounter some particular burdens. Like straight women who bear children through insemination, they confront the vexing question of how to negotiate their children's knowledge of and relationship to sperm donors. Some progeny of unknown donors, like many adopted children, quest for contact with their genetic fathers. One ten-year-old girl, conceived by private donor insemination, explains why she was relieved to find her biological father: "I wanted to find my dad because it was hard knowing I had a dad but not knowing who he was. It was like there was a missing piece."[70]

Lesbian couples planning a pregnancy contend with some unique decisions and challenges concerning the relationship between biological and social maternity. They must decide which woman will try to become pregnant and how to negotiate feelings of jealousy, invisibility, and displacement that may be more likely to arise between the two than between a biological mother and father. Struggling to equalize maternal emotional stakes and claims, some couples decide to alternate the childbearing role, others attempt simultaneous pregnancies, and some, as we have seen, employ reproductive technology to divide the genetic and gestational components of procreation. Some nongestational lesbian mothers stimulate lactation, so that they can jointly breastfeed the babies their partners bear, some assume disproportionate responsibility for child care to compensate for their biological "disadvantage," and others give their surnames to their partners' offspring.

Planned lesbian and gay families, however, most fully realize the early Planned Parenthood goal, "every child a wanted child," as one twelve-year-old son of a lesbian recognized: "I think that if you are a child of a gay or lesbian, you have a better chance of having a great parent. If you are a lesbian, you have to go through a lot of trouble to get a child, so that child is really wanted."[71] Disproportionately "queer" families choose to reside in and construct communities that support family and social diversity. Partly because fertility and adoption services are expensive and often difficult to attain, intentional gay parents are disproportionately white, better educated, and more mature than other parents. Preliminary research indicates that these advantages more than offset whatever problems their special burdens cause their children.[72] Clearly, it is in the interest of all our children to afford their families social dignity and respect.

If we exploit the research with this aim in mind, deducing a rational wish list for public policy is quite a simple matter. A straightforward, liberal, equal rights agenda for lesbians and gays would seem the obvious and humane course. In the best interests of all children, we would provide lesbian and gay parents equal access to marriage, child custody, adoption, foster placements, fertility services, inheritance, employment, and all social benefits. We would adopt "rainbow" curricula within our schools and our public media that promote the kind of tolerance and respect for family and sexual diversity that Laura Sebastian, an eighteen-year-old reared by her divorced mother and her mother's lesbian lover, advocates:

> A happy child has happy parents, and gay people can be as happy as straight ones. It doesn't matter what kids have—fathers, mothers, or both—they just need love and support. It doesn't matter if you are raised by a pack of dogs, just as long as they love you! It's about time lesbians and gays can have children. It's everybody's right as a human being.[73]

## Our Queer Postmodern Families

Far from esoteric, the experiences of diverse genres of gay and lesbian "families we choose" bear on many of the most feverishly contested issues in contemporary family politics. They can speak to our mounting cultural paranoia over whether fathers are expendable, to nature-nurture controversies over sexual and gender identities and the gender division of labor, to the meaning and purpose of voluntary marriage, and, most broadly, to those ubiquitous "family values" contests over the relative importance for children of family structure or process, of biological or "psychological" parents.

From the African-American "Million Man March" in October 1995, the stadium rallies of Christian male "Promise Keepers" that popularized the subject of responsible fatherhood in evangelical churches across the nation, and the National Fatherhood Initiative, to congressional hearings on the Father's Responsibility Act in 2001, the nation seems to be gripped by cultural obsession over the decline of dependable dads. Here research on lesbian families, particularly on planned lesbian couple families, could prove of no small import. Thus far, as we have seen, such research offers no brief for Blankenhorn's angst over "radically fatherless children." Also challenging to those who claim that the mere presence of a father in a family confers significant benefits on his children are surprising data reported in a study of youth and violence commissioned by Kaiser Permanente and Children Now. The study of 1000 eleven to seventeen-year-olds and of 150 seven to ten-year-olds found that, contrary to popular belief, 68 percent of the "young people exposed to higher levels of health and safety threats" were from conventional two-parent families. Moreover, poignantly, fathers were among the last people these troubled teens would turn to for help, even when they lived in such families. Only 10 percent of the young people in these two-parent families said they would seek their fathers' advice first, compared with 44 percent who claimed they would turn first to their mothers, and 26 percent who would first seek help from friends. Many more youth were willing to discuss concerns over their health, safety, and sexuality with nurses or doctors.[74] Thus, empirical social science to date, like the historical record, gives us impeccable cause to regard fathers and mothers alike as "expendable." The quality, not the gender, of parenting is what truly matters.

Similarly, research on the relationships of gay male and lesbian couples depicts diverse models for intimacy from which others could profit. "Freed" from normative conventions and institutions that govern heterosexual gender and family relationships, self-consciously "queer" couples and families, by necessity, have had to reflect much more seriously on the meaning and purpose of their intimate commitments. Studies that compare lesbian, gay male, and heterosexual couples find intriguing contrasts in their characteristic patterns of intimacy. Gender seems to shape domestic values and practices more powerfully than sexual identity, so that same-sex couples tend to be more compatible than heterosexual couples. For example, both lesbian and straight women are more likely than either gay or straight men to value their relationships over their work. Yet both lesbian and gay male couples agree that both parties should be employed, while married men are less likely to agree with wives who wish to work. Predictably, same-sex couples share more interests and time together than married couples. Also unsurprising, lesbian couples have the most egalitarian relationships, and married heterosexual couples the least. Lesbian and gay male couples both share household chores more equally and with less conflict than married couples, but they share them differently. Lesbian couples tend to share most tasks equally, while gay males more frequently assign tasks "to each according to his abilities," schedules, and preferences.[75] Each of these modal patterns for intimacy has its particular strengths and vulnerabilities. Gender conventions and gender fluidity alike have advantages and limitations, as Blumstein and Schwartz and other researchers have discussed. Accepting queer families does not mean converting to any characteristic patterns of intimacy, but coming to terms with the collapse of a monolithic cultural regime governing our intimate bonds. It would mean embracing a genuinely pluralist understanding that there are diverse, valid ways to form and sustain these.

Perhaps what is truly distinctive about lesbian and gay families is how unambiguously the substance of their relationships takes precedence over their form, emotional and social commitments over genetic claims. Compelled to exercise "good, old-fashioned American" ingenuity to fulfill familial desires, gays and lesbians improvisationally assemble a patchwork of "blood" and intentional relations—gay, straight, and other—into creative, extended kin bonds.[76] Gay communities more adeptly integrate singles into their social worlds than does mainstream heterosexual society, a social "skill" quite valuable in a world in which divorce, widowhood, and singlehood are increasingly normative. Because "queer" families must continually, self-consciously migrate in and out of the closet, they hone bicultural skills particularly suitable for life in a multicultural society.[77] Self-identified queer families serve on the front lines of the postmodern family condition, commanded directly by its regime of improvisation, ambiguity, diversity, contradiction, self-reflection, and flux.

Even the distinctive, indeed the definitional, burden that pervasive homophobia imposes on lesbian and gay families does not fully distinguish them from other contemporary families. Unfortunately, prejudice, intolerance, and disrespect for "different" or "other" families is all too commonplace in the contemporary world. Ethnocentric familism afflicts the families of many immigrants, interracial couples, single mothers (be they unwed or divorced, impoverished or affluent) remarried couples, childless "yuppie" couples, bachelors and "spinsters," househusbands, working mothers, and the homeless. It even places that vanishing, once-hallowed breed of full-time homemakers on the ("I'm-just-a-housewife") defensive.

Gay and lesbian families simply brave intensified versions of ubiquitous contemporary challenges. Both their plight and their pluck expose the dangerous disjuncture between our family rhetoric and policy, on the one hand, and our family and social realties, on the other. In stubborn denial of the complex, pluralist array of contemporary families and kinship, most of our legal and social policies atavistically presume to serve a singular, "normal" family structure—the conventional, heterosexual, married-couple, nuclear family. In the name of children, politicians justify decisions that endanger children, and in the name of *The Family*, they cause grave harm to our families. It is time to get used to the queer, postmodern family condition we all now inhabit.

## Notes

1. An estimate that at least six million children would have a gay parent by 1985 appeared in J. Schulenberg, *Gay Parenting* (New York: Doubleday, 1985) and has been accepted or revised upwards by most scholars since then. See, for example, F. W. Bozett (ed.), *Gay and Lesbian Parents* (New York: Praeger, 1987),

39; C. Patterson, "Children of Lesbian and Gay Parents," *Child Development* 63:1025–1042; K. R. Allen and D. H. Demo, "The Families of Lesbians and Gay Men: A New Frontier in Family Research," *Journal of Marriage and the Family* 57 (February 1995):111–127. Nevertheless, these estimates are based upon problematic assumptions and calculations, so the actual number could be considerably lower—especially if we exclude children whose parents have not acknowledged to anyone else in the family that they are gay or lesbian. Still, even a conservative estimate would exceed one million.

2. P. Burke, *Family Values: A Lesbian Mother's Fight for Her Son.* (New York: Random House, 1993).

3. For a sensitive discussion of the definitional difficulties involved in research on gay and lesbian families, see Allen and Demo, "Families of Lesbians and Gay Men," 112–113.

4. Many gay activist groups and scholars, however, have begun to reclaim the term "queer" as a badge of pride, in much the same way that the black power movement of the 1960s reclaimed the formerly derogatory term for blacks.

5. In J. Stacey, *Brave New Families* (New York: Basic Books, 1990). I provide a book-length, ethnographic treatment of postmodern family life in the Silicon Valley.

6. For historical and cross-cultural treatments of same-sex marriages, relationships, and practices in the West and elsewhere, see J. Boswell, *Same-Sex Unions in Premodern Europe* (New York: Villard Books, 1994) and W. N. Eskridge Jr., "A History of Same-Sex Marriage," *Virginia Law Review* 79:1419–1451, 1993.

7. R. R. Rivera, "Legal Issues in Gay and Lesbian Parenting," in Bozett, ed., *Gay and Lesbian Parents.*

8. Among the influential feminist works of this genre were: N. Chodorow, *The Reproduction of Mothering* (Berkeley and Los Angeles: University of California Press, 1978); C. Gilligan, *In a Different Voice* (Cambridge: Harvard University Press, 1982); and S. Ruddick, *Maternal Thinking* (Boston: Beacon Press, 1989).

9. See R. Rosenbloom (ed.), *Unspoken Rules: Sexual Orientation and Women's Human Rights* (San Francisco: International Gay and Lesbian Human Right Commission, 1995), 226 (fn22); and L. Benkov, *Reinventing the Family.* (New York: Crown, 1994), 117.

10. D. Wikler and N. J. Wikler, "Turkey-baster Babies: The Demedicalization of Artificial Insemination," *Milbank Quarterly* 69(1):10, 1991.

11. Ibid.

12. The first known custody battle involving a lesbian couple and a sperm donor was *Loftin* v. *Flournoy* in California. For a superb discussion of the relevant case law, see N. Polikoff, "This Child Does Have Two Mothers," *Georgetown Law Journal* 78(1990):459–575.

13. Polikoff, "Two Mothers" provides detailed discussion of the most significant legal cases of custody contests after death of the biological lesbian co-mother. In both the most prominent cases, higher courts eventually reversed decisions that had denied custody to the surviving lesbian parent, but only after serious emotional harm had been inflicted on the children and parents alike. See pp. 527–532.

14. V. L. Henry, "A Tale of Three Women," *American Journal of Law & Medicine* XIX, 3:297, 1993.

15. Ibid., 300; Polikoff, "This Child Does Have Two Mothers," 492.

16. J. Griscom, "The Case of Sharon Kowalski and Karen Thompson," in P.S. Rothenberg (ed.), *Race, Class, and Gender in the United States* (New York: St. Martin's Press, 1992).

17. See W. B. Rubenstein (ed.), *Lesbians, Gay Men, and the Law*, (New York: New Press, 1993), 452.

18. National Center for Lesbian Rights, "Our Day in Court—Against Each Other," in Rubenstein, 561–562.

19. M. Gil de Lamadrid, "Expanding the Definition of Family: A Universal Issue," *Berkeley Women's Law Journal* v. 8:178, 1993.

20. The Sharon Bottoms case in Virginia is the most prominent of current setbacks. In 1994, Sharon Bottoms lost custody of her two-year-old son because the trial court judge deemed her lesbianism to be immoral and illegal. In April 1995, the Virginia state supreme court upheld the ruling, which at this writing is being appealed to the U.S. Supreme Court.

21. Quoted in S. Sherman (ed.), *Lesbian and Gay Marriage* (Philadelphia: Temple University Press, 1992), 191.

22. Ibid., 173.

23. Bozett, epilogue to *Gay and Lesbian Parents*, 232.

24. Cited in Sherman, *Lesbian and Gay Marriage*, 9 (fn. 6). A more recent poll conducted by *The Advocate* suggests that the trend of support for gay marriage is increasing. See E. Wolfson, "Crossing the Threshhold," *Review of Law & Social Change* XXI, 3:583, 1994–95.

25. The decision stated that the sexual orientation of the parties was irrelevant because same-sex spouses could be of any sexual orientation. It was the gender discrimination involved in limiting one's choice of spouse that violated the state constitution. See Wolfson, "Crossing the Threshold," 573.

26. See, for example, Nancy Polikoff, "We Will Get What We Ask For: Why Legalizing Gay and Lesbian Marriage Will Not 'Dismantle the Legal Structure of Gender in Every Marriage.'" *Virginia Law Review* 79:1549–1550, 1993.

27. Law professor Thomas Coleman, executive director of the "Family Diversity Project" in California, expresses these views in Sherman, 128–129. Likewise, Bob Hattoy, a gay White House aide in the Clinton administration, believed that "to support same-sex marriage at this particular cultural moment in America is a loser." Quoted in Francis X. Clines, "In Gay-Marriage Storm, Weary Clinton Aide Is Buffeted on All Sides." *New York Times*, May 29, 1996, A16.

28. A. Sullivan, "Here Comes the Groom: A Conservative Case for Gay Marriage," *New Republic* 201 (9):20–22, August 28, 1989; J. Rauch, "A Pro-Gay, Pro-Family Policy," *Wall Street Journal*, November 29; 1995, A22.

29. Kirk Johnson, quoted in Wolfson, 567.

30. N. D. Hunter, "Marriage, Law and Gender: A Feminist Inquiry," *Law & Sexuality* 1(1):12, 1991.

31. Wolfson, "Crossing the Threshhold,"

32. "Some Progress Found in Poll on Gay Rights," *San Francisco Chronicle*, June 20, 1994.

33. Support for Clinton's Stand on Gay Marriage," *San Francisco Chronicle*, May 25, 1996, A6; Available online at www.gallup.com/poll/releases/pr010604.asp.

34. G. Remafedi (ed.), *Death by Denial* (Boston: Alyson Publications, 1994).

35. Quoted in Miller, *Out in the World*, 350.

36. The three journals were *Journal of Marriage and the Family, Family Relations,* and *Journal of Family Issues;* Allen and Demo, "Families of Lesbians and Gay Men," 119.

37. For overviews of the research, see Patterson, "Children of Lesbian and Gay Parents"; J. Laird, "Lesbian and Gay Families," in Walsh (ed.), *Normal Family Processes* 2nd ed. (New York: Guilford Press, 1993), 282–328; Allen and Demo, "Families of Lesbians and Gay Men."

38. Laird, "Lesbian and Gay Families," 316–317.

39. Ibid., 317; D. H. Demo and K. Allen, "Diversity within Lesbian and Gay Families," *Journal of Social and Personal Relationships* 13 (3):26, 1996; F. Tasker and S. Golombok, "Adults Raised as Children in Lesbian Families," *American Journal of Orthopsychiatry,* 65:203–215, 1998.

40. Tasker and Golombok, "Adults Raised as Children in Lesbian Families."

41. Quoted in L. Rafkin, *Different Mothers* (Pittsburgh: Cleis Press, 1990), 34.

42. Laird, "Lesbian and Gay Families."

43. See, for example, Patterson; Demo and Allen; Benkov; K. Weston, *Families We Choose* (New York: Columbia University Press, 1991); and L. Peplau, "Research on Homosexual Couples: An Overview," in J. P. De Cecco (ed.), *Gay Relationships* (New York: Hayworth Press, 1988).

44. S. Minter, "U.S.A.," in Rosenbloom (ed.), *Unspoken Rules,* 219.

45. Quoted in Maralee Schwartz & Kenneth J. Cooper, "Equal Rights Initiative in Iowa Attacked," *Washington Post,* Aug 23, 1992, A15.

46. Laird, 315–316.

47. See, for example, Judith Stacey and Timothy Biblarz, "Does the Sexual Orientation of Parents Matter?" *American Sociological Review* 66(2):159–183, April 2001.

48. As Tasker and Golombok concede, "Young adults from lesbian homes tended to be more willing to have a sexual relationship with someone of the same gender if they felt physically attracted to them. They were also more likely to have considered the possibility of developing same-gender sexual attractions or relationships. Having a lesbian mother, therefore, appeared to widen the adolescent's view of what constituted acceptable sexual behavior to include same-gender sexual relationships," 212.

49. A. Rich, "Compulsory Heterosexuality and the Lesbian Continuum," *Signs* 5(4):Summer 1980:631–660.

50. Eve Sedgwick, "How to Bring Your Kids Up Gay," in Warner (ed.), *Fear of a Queer Planet* (Minneapolis: University of Minnesota Press, 1993), 76.

51. Quoted in Rafkin, *Different Mothers,* 64–65.

52. Minter, "U.S.A.," 222.

53. Remafedi, *Death by Denial.*

54. Quoted in Sherman, 70.

55. L. Due, *Joining the Tribe* (New York: Doubleday, 1996).

56. See J. M. Irvine, "A Place in the Rainbow: Theorizing Lesbian and Gay Culture," *Sociological Theory* 12(2):232, July 1994.

57. Quoted in Rafkin, *Different Mothers,* 24.

58. Quoted in Polikoff, "This Child Does Have Two Mothers," 569–570.

59. Quoted in Polikoff, 570.

60. Quoted in Rafkin, 81.

61. Benkov, *Reinventing the Family,* chap. 8.

62. L. Kurdek and J. P. Schmitt, "Relationship Quality of Gay Men in Closed or Open Relationships," *Journal of Homosexuality* 12(2):85–99, 1985; and F. R. Lynch, "Nonghetto Gays: An Ethnography of Suburban Homosexuals," In Herdt (ed.), *Gay Culture in America* (Boston: Beacon Press, 1992), 165–201.

63. Rafkin, 39.

64. Allen and Demo.

65. Polikoff, "This Child Does Have Two Mothers," 461 (fn.2).

66. Weston, "Parenting in the Age of AIDs," 159.

67. D. Blankenhorn, *Fatherless America* (New York: Basic Books, 1995), 233; J. Leo, "Promoting no-dad families," *U.S. News and World Report*, May 15, 1995: 26; and S. Seligson, "Seeds of Doubt," *Atlantic Monthly*, March 1995:28.

68. Bozett, p.4 discusses gay male parenthood strategies. Also, available on-line at www.growinggenerations.com.

69. Stacey and Biblarz, "Does the Sexual Orientation of Parents Matter?"; Maureen Sullivan, "Rozzie and Harriet?: Gender and Family Patterns of Lesbian Coparents," *Gender & Society* 10(6):747–767, December 1996.

70. Quoted in Rafkin, 33.

71. Ibid., 53.

72. Stacey and Biblarz "Does the Sexual Orientation of Parents Matter?" 176.

73. Rafkin, 174.

74. T. Moore, "Fear of Violence Rising among 1990s Youth," *San Francisco Chronicle*, December 7, 1995, A1, A15.

75. L. Kurdek, "The Allocation of Household Labor in Gay, Lesbian, and Heterosexual Married Couples," *Journal of Social Issues* 49 (3):127–139, 1993; P. Blumstein and P. Schwartz, *American Couples* (New York: William Morrow, 1983); Peplau, 193; Stacey and Biblarz, "Does the Sexual Orientation of Parents Matter," 173–174; Sullivan, "Rozzie and Harriet?"; Gillian Dunne, "Opting into Motherhood: Lesbians Blurring the Boundaries and Transforming the Meaning of Parenthood and Kinship," *Gender & Society* 14(1):11–35, 2000.

76. See Weston, *Families We Choose*, for an ethnographic treatment of these chosen kin ties.

77. As Allen and Demo suggest, "An aspect of biculturalism is resilience and creative adaptation in the context of minority group oppression and stigma," and this "offers a potential link to other oppressed groups in American society." "Families of Lesbians and Gay Men," 122.

# 8

# A Sign of Family Disorder?
# Changing Representations
# of Parental Kidnapping

### Paula S. Fass

In the summer of 1873, "a gentleman of high social position" in Williamstown, New York, hired a "fast livery team" and carried off both his children. He presumably fled with them to Europe, since as "a man of means," he would "spare no money to cover up the trail." Although the courts had given this man, a Mr. Neil, custody of one of his daughters in the "decree of separation on the ground of incompatibility of temperment," the other daughter, whom he also took with him, had been awarded to his wife, who now suffered "fearfully over the theft."[1] Recorded in the *New York Times* more than 100 years ago, Mr. Neil's abduction of his daughter was an example of what is known today as parental kidnapping. That episode, and others like it, while unusual and newsworthy, were hardly unknown more than a century ago, because then, as today, husbands and wives fought over the custody of their children. And children were even then pawns in an uncertain legal struggle among the mother, the father, and the state.[2]

An especially vivid glimpse of the parental tug-of-war over a child took place in New York in 1879 when Henry Coolidge and his former wife, Belthiede, were found quarreling on West Sixteenth Street in Manhattan over possession of their daughter. "The woman had the child by one arm and the man by the other arm and they were pulling the little girl hither and thither." Pending the outcome of the divorce instituted by Henry, the judge had ordered one of their daughters to be placed in the custody of the maternal grandmother and the other with a friend of the family. Henry had taken the older girl from the grandmother's house, "ostensibly for a walk," but he had not returned her. The mother, with the assistance of her own father, had retaken the girl and had just met Coolidge on the street where he attempted once again to take the child. This was the background for the little drama that was enacted on the street in New York. When brought before the local magistrate, Coolidge did not deny his wife's story, but noted that he was rescuing his daughter from being subjected to "immoral influences," a charge strenuously denied by Mrs. Coolidge and her mother. The judge ordered the child returned in accordance with the original determination of temporary custody.[3]

For the Coolidges and for many divorcing couples in the nineteenth century, the court had rendered a judgment that at least one of the contending parties found painful, harmful, or unjust, and it led to personal attempts to correct the situation. As with the Coolidges too, many cases involved extended kin who became actively involved in the dispute over the children. Then, as now, the cost of these disputes was often best expressed in the striking visual image of "pulling the little girl hither and thither."

These two episodes from the 1870s are an important reminder that the kidnapping of children by their parents or other family members is not a new social experience. Indeed, few of the essential *human* elements have changed very much in the more than 100 years since the Coolidges struggled over their daughter on a New York street. Certain issues have changed, however. Two are of primary significance: in sheer numbers, these abductions have increased together with the enormous rise in divorce. And they have been given a dramatic new public prominence and visibility as the public lamentations over the state of the family and its trustworthiness as a source of child welfare has grown. These two issues are obviously related to each other, but that relationship is not simple. On the contrary, in this chapter I suggest that parental kidnapping, as the most extreme instance of individual family disorder and one of its most hostile expressions, has, over the last twenty-five years, been portrayed as an ominous social problem because of its symbolic power as a sign of the erosion of contemporary family life. Indeed, in the past twenty-five years the horror that we have associated with child kidnapping has become an effective means to dramatize the extreme disintegration which is presumed now to characterize much of family life in the United States and increasingly elsewhere in the Western world. During the decade of the 1990s, parental kidnapping has also been used seriously to question the intrusive and insensitive role of the state in regulating family relationships. Thus parental kidnapping is both a real experience and a form of cultural representation which gives us a revealing glimpse of how divorce, custody, and child abuse issues have come together in the vivid portrayal of the crime of parental kidnapping. As the following pages show, parental kidnapping has literally come to haunt a culture caught in a paralyzing vision of family disintegration, gender conflict, and judicial incompetence.

## The Historical Absence of Laws

In 1993, a federal appeals court in Richmond, Virginia, ruled that a natural mother was exempt from federal kidnap law (the Lindbergh Act). In this case, a woman, with the aid of two friends, had tied, gagged, roughed up, and robbed her children's foster parents and then abducted the children from their new home in Missouri. In excluding the mother alone (the others had already been sentenced to prison), the justices noted that the Lindbergh Act exempted parents from the crime of kidnapping. The ruling further asserted that the state court could "not alter the identity of a biological parent," even though it could end a parent's right to custody. The case suggests some of the legal complications implicit in the very concept of parental kidnapping.[4]

The Lindbergh Act was the first federal kidnapping legislation in the United States, but its predecessors both in England and the American states had also excluded parents either entirely or from the full force of kidnapping penalties. In England, the first legislation, "An Act for the More Effectual Prevention of Child Stealing," enacted in 1814, specifically *excluded* "any Person who shall have claimed to be the Father of an illegitimate Child," effectively excluding all natural or legal fathers from kidnapping. Since the law declared that the child was being stolen to "deprive its Parent or Parents . . . of the Possession of such Child," it presumed that fathers of legitimate children could not possibly be violators, since a father could not steal what was already his. The updated Act of 1892 excluded all those "claiming in good faith a right to the possession of the child," thus bringing mothers under the protective umbrella, commensurate with their newly gained status as potential custodians. The law effectively remained the same until the 1980s when the Child Abduction Act of 1984 made it an offense for a parent or guardian given custody to remove a child from Great Britain without appropriate legal consent, or for a person not having custody or guardianship to take such a child or "to keep him out of lawful control of any person entitled to his control." This updated vision of custody, as we shall see, corresponded to a growing recognition in the West of the explosive possibilities of child custody cum kidnapping offenses. The English Custody Act of 1985 brought English law into compliance with new protocols in international custody disputes.[5]

In the United States, through most of the nineteenth century, case law had evolved erratically concerning parental kidnapping by drawing upon the English common law definition of kidnapping—the forcible carrying of a child to another location (initially out of the country) without consent. In a Massachusetts case of 1862, the court ruled that "A child of the age of nine years is incapable of giving a valid assent to a forcible transfer of him by a stranger from the legal custody of his father to the custody of his mother, who had no right thereto; and evidence of such assent is incompetent in defense to an indictment of an assault and battery upon him in making such transfer." In another case, the theft of a four-year-old by his father was defined as "unlawfully and forcibly carrying the child out of the state," in accordance with the kidnapping definition. But in Georgia, in 1894, the court ruled that "A father cannot be charged with kidnapping his minor child, where he has not parted with his parental right to its custody." And in Kansas, in 1889, the court ruled that even a third party "who assists a mother in leaving her husband and taking away the infant child of herself and husband is *not guilty* of kidnapping, since she is as much entitled to the custody of the child as its father." In these last cases, both parents were absolved of guilt in child stealing. But these rulings, like their enforcement in the nineteenth century, were vague, erratic, and changeable.[6]

Starting in the early twentieth century, as more and more state legislatures began to institute or beef up laws against kidnapping, they often found it necessary specifically to distinguish abductions perpetrated by strangers from those by parents. In so doing, they sometimes also instituted punishments for parental kidnappings. When in 1911 New York specifically exempted parents from the newly harsh penalties called for in kidnap legislation (though they were not entirely excluded from all penalty), one legislator noted that it was "pretty generally recognized that there are extenuating circumstances where, through affection and love, a parent tries to get possession of his child." This view reflected the dominant contemporary perspective on children as priceless emotional assets rather than possessions or investments, and assumed that parental action was ultimately based on affection. And for a long time, both social attitudes and criminal justice proceedings reflected this belief. Just as nineteenth-century English law assumed that no father could steal what was already his, most American courts and police through most of the twentieth assumed that parental kidnapping bespoke an act of love, which could hardly be a serious crime.[7]

The distinction between kidnapping by strangers and by parents begun in state laws at the beginning of the century and subsequently enshrined (by excluding parents) in the federal statutes of the 1930s remained in place until the 1970s and 1980s when, as we shall see, the astronomical increase in divorce and the resulting custody and jurisdictional disputes projected parental kidnapping into the center of a much larger public discourse over family breakdown. That discourse eroded the sharp boundaries between parental and stranger kidnapping earlier put in place. The strong move to criminalize parental kidnapping in the 1980s marked a new public posture toward family life. Until then, while the courts could intrude in extreme detail in the relations between parents and children as families exposed themselves to state supervision through breakup, parental kidnapping remained largely a social rather than a legal issue.

## Parental Kidnapping in the First Half of the Twentieth Century

In the first decades of the twentieth century, the divorce rate had already begun the rise that would accelerate rapidly with the unfolding century. And that rise naturally increased the momentum for aggrieved parents to attempt to resolve custody disputes and unhappiness over custody decrees through child snatching. Besides the sharp rise in divorce, perhaps the most notable social change to influence parental kidnapping was the introduction of the automobile. Just as the automobile put the lives of young children, especially in the cities, at risk generally, it increased the risk of abduction to children of feuding, separated, or divorced parents. Starting in the early twentieth century, children were whisked away, sometimes within sight of their other parent, in an automobile. "Boy Spirited Away By Five Men in Auto," read one headline that recounted a parental abduction; "Boy Kidnapped By Woman in Auto," read another.[8]

Despite the potential for suffering by parents and children involved in these events, newspapers adopted a tone of amusement when they described parental kidnappings. Thus when nine-year-old Dean McLaughlin was abducted in an automobile, the *New York Times* observed, "The boy has been kidnapped so many times by his father and his mother that he appears to be enjoying the experience." This attitude prevailed even though the abductions were deadly serious for the parents and sometimes involved physical force or the use of threatening weapons. In abducting Beverly Lorraine Whitgreave, eighteen months of age and great-granddaughter of a local Chicago hero, the mother was reported by the *Chicago Tribune* to have announced: "I've come for my baby. . . . I've got a revolver and I'll kill you if you don't give her up." This was the fourth time that the baby had been kidnapped. "The first time she was taken by her father, the second time by her mother, and the last time by her father." Even this phrasing in the *New York Times* turned the experience into a game or contest.[9]

The view of parental snatchings as somehow part of the droll battle between the sexes or a drawing room comedy was exaggerated in the 1920s and 1930s by the fact that most of the news stories involved custody disputes among the socially prominent. In the late nineteenth century, and to some extent even in the early twentieth, the domestic disputes of poorer folks also made news, and children were reported as abducted even in the absence of divorce decrees, the situation that prevailed among the poor. After the First World War, the press largely restricted its coverage of these issues to the rich. Through the peephole of parental abduction, the public could enter into the unsavory domestic affairs of the socially prominent who were thereby shown to be in no way morally superior. As a result of this selective coverage, parental kidnapping was portrayed as unusual rather than ordinary, and appeared to be mostly confined to those whose lives were in all ways exceptional and morally suspect. The public representations of the problem of parental abductions thus gave the impression that parental kidnapping was hardly a general social problem. When, in the 1970s and 1980s, the media shifted their vision to dramatically report on the prevalence of parental abductions among all classes and in escalating numbers fed by increased divorce, the phenomenon seemed new and unprecedented. In fact, parental abductions have been firmly a feature of twentieth-century domestic relations among all classes, with deep roots in the nineteenth century.

The San Francisco press riveted the attention of its readers in the mid-1920s with the exploits of the fantastically beautiful socialite Milo Abercrombie Swenson, whom Charles Dana Gibson had called "one of the most beautiful girls in America." The dissolution of Milo's second marriage to Navy Lieutenant Lyman Knute Swenson, in 1925, led to a tangled and extended controversy over the visitation rights Swenson had to his two children and eventually to Milo losing custody of the children. In 1929, rather than surrender custody, Milo disappeared with her children. Similarly, in 1924, newspapers in the Midwest were full of the abduction by oil and real-estate magnate Charles Bliss of his son from the Chicago hotel room of his beautiful opera star wife, Beryl Brown Bliss. In these headline-grabbing cases certain features of the controversy stood out. Above all, parents who kidnapped their children often accused the other parent of gross misconduct, especially sexual impropriety. In the Swenson case, Milo accused her husband of sexually molesting her four-year-old daughter Cecelia, while Charles Bliss accused his wife of being too "modern" and caring more for her career than for a settled family life. When Josephine Sullivan Kieffer snatched her daughter from her husband, a prominent New York attorney with a Harvard and Rhodes scholar pedigree, she not only accused him of infidelity but noted that he "neglected and has at times slapped, beaten and otherwise abused the said child." The Swensons, Blisses, and Kieffers had each found just the right lever to push in their contentious quarrels over custody. The kidnapping of their children was an extension of those quarrels.[10]

Impugning the reputation of the opposing party was only one of the means used in custody battles that could serve to legitimate kidnappings and to reverse custody decisions. The other tactic was to use the power that came from divergent jurisdictions. When Charles Bliss kidnapped his son from his wife's hotel room in Chicago, he took the boy back to Tulsa, Oklahoma. Bliss's possession of the child in Tulsa helped him to obtain temporary custody of his son. The judge allowed him to keep Charles, Jr., in "the jurisdiction of the Tulsa county court until after a settlement of the divorce case." Having the child within the jurisdiction of one of the contending parties often resulted in at least temporary orders acknowledging that parent's right. In this context, it was not uncommon for the other parent to attempt to rekidnap a child and thereby achieve a legal victory in another jurisdiction. Because custody came within the exclusive jurisdiction of each state, the courts were quite impotent beyond their own borders, and conflicting orders were often in place.[11]

## A New Perspective and New Laws

Fifty years later, the domestic issues in parental kidnapping had changed very little, but the public problem and its representation had been utterly transformed. The source of society sensations had become the democratic "Agony of the 80s," in the words of *USA Today*, and parental kidnapping was often described as an epidemic—a rapidly spreading and terrifying illness of the society. Newspapers, women's magazines, and news journals, as well as novels and personal memoirs focused on the problem and gave it extensive popular exposure. Parents who had lost their children testified in the press and at congressional hearings and told their stories on television talk shows. Americans still occasionally learned about the snatches of the rich and famous, but these had receded in the enormous waves of the perceived problem. Starting in the 1970s, the media portrayed the painful experiences of middle Americans, and circulated statistics which defined parental kidnapping as a problem for thousands, even hundreds of thousands of families. The new profile of the kidnapping family was composed not of the society swells and their beautiful but unconventional wives, but of ordinary people whose lives were seared when their spouses or former spouses kidnapped their children. Precisely because it was so ordinary, parental kidnapping suggested that even families that seemed normal might hide some deep pathology.[12]

Certainly, the dimensions of the phenomenon had changed. Although we have no figures for parental abductions in the nineteenth century (or for most of the twentieth century, either), the breathtaking increase in divorce, and especially of divorce where children were involved, after 1960, created a vastly larger potential for abductions. And just as the automobile had changed abductions in the early twentieth century, the democratization of plane travel in the period after the 1960s made escape to other states and even to foreign countries accessible to more than the rich.

Initially, indeed, it was this new mobility and its potential for jurisdictional disputes in custody that rang the alarm bells and called for action. Snatching seemed to be a by-product of jurisdictional shopping, as a disaffected parent, unhappy with the custody ruling in one state, took the child to another where he was granted custody in the absence of the other parent. With an appropriate court order, the parent could feel himself or herself comfortably in compliance with the law. Although the child had been snatched, the custody decree in a new jurisdiction seemed to legitimize the action. And if shopping for custody was the problem, the remedy seemed simple—a stricter enforcement of the initial decree and compliance by sister states. In fact, rationalizing custody procedures was not simple, since the Supreme Court imposed the full faith and credit clause of the United States Constitution only to a limited degree to custody cases, and because state courts, according to an expert observer, "believed strongly that flexibility was necessary to best protect children's interests."[13]

Throughout the 1970s, much attention and energy, both in the popular media and among legal experts, was directed to enforcing custody decrees across state lines, and most discussion took as its objective the enactment by the fifty states of the model laws proposed in the Uniform Child Custody Jurisdiction Act (UCCJA), a voluntary agreement to which states could subscribe. Initially approved by the National Conference of Commissions on Uniform State Laws in 1968, by the mid 1980s, almost all the states had subscribed to the agreement.[14]

It soon became apparent that the UCCJA was not the solution many had foreseen. Although reliable statistics about the problem were still not available, the publicity surrounding parental kidnapping remained clamorous and the problem seemed far from solved. In part because many parents abducted their children before any custody order was in place (as they always had); in part because communications and enforcement between states was slipshod; in part because police were not eager to be bothered by what they saw as "domestic disputes," the new state agreements on mutual enforcement seemed to have only a marginal impact on the perceived incidence of the problem or the sense of social malfunction caused by that perception.

In 1980, in response to growing media attention, the federal government finally took note of the problem, and with much fanfare and publicity, Congress passed, and President Jimmy Carter signed, the Parental Kidnapping Prevention Act (PKPA). The PKPA did not reverse the protection offered to parents by the Lindbergh Act, and did not make parental kidnapping a federal offense. The new law was intended to enhance the UCCJA, by requiring states to give full faith and credit to custody decrees of other states, and made the Federal Parent Locator Service available to parents trying to find their children. It also facilitated the work of state and local agencies in enforcing their own parental kidnapping laws. Throughout the period of the 1970s and 1980s, states were enacting legislation that made parental kidnapping a criminal offense. Although these laws differed among themselves, with some states defining parental abductions as felonies and others merely as misdemeanors, by 1991, every state and the District of Columbia had a criminal statute prohibiting parental kidnapping.[15]

In 1982 and 1984, the federal government increased its role in parental kidnapping cases (and other forms of child disappearance) by passing the Missing Children's Act and the Missing Children's Assistance Act. Both provided informational and material assistance to parents and local governments in their attempts to locate children. These acts also, for the first time, made the FBI available as a resource of information. By 1984, the federal government had authorized the establishment of a national clearinghouse for information about missing children and a toll-free hot line for reporting abductions. The United States had also been instrumental in negotiating the Hague Convention on the Civil Aspects of International Child Abduction, and became, in 1988, one of only a handful of signatories who voluntarily agreed to surrender children brought into their jurisdiction in international custody disputes. Throughout the 1980s, therefore, the federal government had taken note of and responded to the growing sense of alarm about parental kidnapping.[16]

In good part, federal action was a response to an already flourishing grass roots movement of private self-help agencies, like Child Find and Children's Rights, Inc., which offered information and tools to help parents locate children lost to all kinds of abductions and mischance. Hardly an article, pamphlet, or book published on the subject in the last twenty-five years failed to give parents advice on how to respond in the event that they had a child snatched or how to prevent such a snatching. Parents were often urged to seek assistance from these private organizations. A substantial part of the federal response was also the result of the fact that these organizations had mobilized public opinion and congressional action by conflating the problem of parental kidnapping with that of stranger abduction as they dedicated themselves to finding abducted children of all kinds. In so doing, they had increased the sense of alarm and fear associated with parental snatching by blending it with the even more frightening forms of stranger abductions. The federal government had now added another layer to a burgeoning industry based in a deeply rooted network of information and alarm. In addition to the work of these organizations and their spokespeople and in part as a result of the attention they drew to the problem, throughout the 1970s and 1980s, popular news journals, as well as women's and parents' magazines, were full of haunting pictures of children stolen from, and presumably forever lost to, their parents, together with searing stories of their parents' anguish. Altogether, private organizations, federal and state laws, and the media had turned parental kidnapping into a major public problem.[17]

## Parental Kidnapping and the Social Agendas of the 1970s, 1980s, and 1990s

As parental kidnapping became widely denominated as a serious social problem, it became part of other contemporary agendas, especially the feminist critique of the family and its patriarchal social supports. The question of child custody had always been deeply a woman's issue. Since the last half of the nineteenth century, unless they were judged unfit or they were incapable of caring for them, women were considered the proper custodians of their children. By the 1980s, however, the widespread commitment to granting mothers custody of their children except when unfit had faded with older stereotypes of women, as most states replaced earlier presumptions in favor of maternal custody with a gender-neutral standard. By then, thirty-seven states had adopted rules which facilitated the adoption of joint custody in child dispositions. Even though the original feminist agenda helped to underwrite changes in custodial determinations that stressed greater paternal involvement, women increasingly saw the difficulties for themselves and the conflicts for their children that resulted from the need to continue negotiating with former spouses in matters concerning their children (see Wallerstein). Less immediately apparent but just as significant for parental kidnapping was the fact that joint custody often rendered new laws concerning parental abduction inoperative. As a 1989 Justice Department pamphlet to parents observed, "Ironically the increased use of joint or shared custody—often pursuant to newer State statutes establishing a legislative preference for joint custody arrangement—has had the unintended side effect of hindering successful prosecution of some parental kidnapping cases. . . . in several cases . . . defendants have successfully argued that an accused parent cannot, by virtue of his or her joint custodial rights, be guilty of criminal custodial interference."[18]

Because it was portrayed as the most dramatic manifestation of the destabilization of the American family and as an index of family disorder, parental kidnapping rapidly became laced into almost every conceivable issue related to the contemporary family, from child custody to wife battering and sexual abuse. And it became a kind of talisman of contemporary anxiety about the family. By the 1980s, what had been in the 1920s and 1930s a window on other people's misbehavior and figured in a psychology of *schadenfreude*, became an index of social pathology and a reflection of the state of the family itself.

The issue which even as recently as the 1970s seemed a simple matter of getting states to comply with the custody decrees of other states became ever less simple and clear. What had once had a straightforward objective—returning the child to its custodial parent—became in the 1990s deeply contested. Indeed, as the state became an object of suspicion, public sympathy often turned to parents who kidnapped their children in order to rescue them from conditions where they were exposed to sexual abuse or physical neglect, situations in which the state had placed them when it granted custody or visitation rights to the other parent. That basis for snatching was not new. As we have seen, earlier in the century Milo Abercrombie and Josephine Sullivan Kieffer abducted children from situations they believed to be abusive. By the 1990s, however, these abductions were supported by an underground network which thrived on images of widespread family dysfunction. By then, too, the government's role, initially sought after, became much murkier and problematic, especially as the federal government became more visibly involved. A bureaucratic and rule-driven government which seemed once to provide solutions to a problem of national dimensions seemed ever more distant and impersonal. As a government pamphlet noted, "Parental kidnapping is not the right answer; but it is an anwer to which many parents resort in desperation. To the degree that judges and law enforcement officials can pay closer attention to parents with serious and apparently well-grounded fears for the physical, mental, and emotional well being of their children, one important part of the overall parental kidnapping problem may be eliminated at its source." The issue had come full circle as the officials became not the saviors but suspects in the problem.[19]

In the 1990s, as the state and government at all levels came in for increasingly harsh scrutiny, the state's role as an arbiter of family feelings and relationships became ever more suspect. Thus, ironically, just at the time when the family was viewed as unstable and pathological, the state, too, was increasingly seen as incompetent to come to the rescue of children.

## Personal Kidnap Narratives: The Heroic Mode in a Democratic Society

Parental kidnapping in the last twenty-five years has been defined and articulated as a social pathology through a huge and variegated literature and media presentations. These include news reports; expert social science analyses and conference reports; novels and television programs based on true stories and fictions; and personal snatch narratives. Together, these forms of popular and expert testimony have defined parental abduction as a massive problem and as a measure of family change and dysfunction.[20]

Probably the most socially revealing of these forms are the snatch narratives. These are witness to the unique combination of the common and the extraordinary which has come to define the public representation of parental kidnapping as a contemporary experience. The narratives testify to the stunning, even heroic, experiences of ordinary people as their lives are transformed by the loss of a child and propelled into articulation. The experience of child loss creates the need to share with other victims and potential victims the understanding, techniques, and personal wisdom gained from this experience.

The narratives are based on the assumption that the problem is widespread because family breakup is a familiar part of the social landscape. Where parental kidnap narratives end with the child successfully recaptured, they usually close with the healing provided by a new family created out of the painful death of the old. Thus the typical parental kidnapping narrative is the memoir not only of wrenching loss and victimization but of family disenchantment and a new dependence on alternative family forms, usually involving extended kin and often a new mate. (See Mason.) Parental kidnapping narratives thus testify to the decline of the conventional family and propose that the family changes of the 1970s and 1980s are healthful and therapeutic.

The personal narrative is a variation and extension of the human interest stories developed in many magazines in the 1970s and 1980s to publicize the phenomenon of parental kidnapping. "It was a cool evening in March 1977 when Robin Reiss, her parents and two-and-a-half-year-old son, Kevin, walked away from a friendly diner in Brooklyn, N.Y.," one such article in the *Ladies' Home Journal* began. "The boy was giggling when Robin felt her grip on his hand suddenly tighten. It was at that moment that a horrible, ongoing nightmare began. From across the street, six burly thugs were sprinting toward her family.... Kevin screamed 'Mama,' and Robin saw the toddler reaching his arms toward her before she was blinded and silenced by a faceful of burning mace." Here the violent abduction on the father's behalf plays on, and the article specifically alludes to, fears about stranger abductions as it attempts to create an emotional equivalence between the two. The authors, Sally Abrahms and Joseph Bell, go on to tell several similar stories, and later expanded their efforts in a book. This article, like many others, escalates the level of terribleness with each successive segment, selectively choosing the most harrowing details and combining them into a tale of horror.[21]

Individual narratives like that of Eileen Crowley in *Good Housekeeping* usually began much less dramatically than that of Abrahms and Bell. The problems began for Crowley two years after her divorce, when her daughter, Robyn, did not return after an ordinary visit with her father. Crowley recounts her problems with the authorities who did not want to get involved in "a domestic matter." She hires lawyers and detectives, the usual devices of stunned parents. None of these legal means work. Neither do *habeus corpus* writs and court orders. Friends and family provide support, assistance, and comfort. The child, as in most such narratives, is eventually found through a happy coincidence, almost never through the work of law enforcement agencies. In Crowley's case, "on Friday, June 4, 1982 [seven years after the abduction], I received a letter from an old friend on Long Island. 'Yesterday I heard a girl yell out 'Robyn,' ... I turned around and saw a miniature you as I remember you from our childhood together." Crowley and her new husband immediately make plans to retrieve the girl, now almost twelve years old. Crowley, her husband and their son, together with Robyn, now form a new kind of family. There are brief problems of adjustment, but the story ends happily: "Mommy, I love you."[22]

Crowley's story reflects the general pattern of such accounts—loss, a desperate search, the help of kin and friends, the impotence and incompetence of authorities, a new family, and then an almost miraculous reunion. But while Crowley obviously blames her former husband for the loss of her child, she does not characterize him as anything more than a snatcher. Other narratives develop the evil and vindictive possibilities of the snatching husband in great detail.[23]

As the alarum over parental kidnapping increased in the late 1970s and early 1980s, this theme of parental selfishness came to the fore. Traditionally, the legal distinction between stranger abductions and parental kidnapping hinged on the belief that parents stole their children out of love. As part of the effort to paint parental kidnapping as a real crime, many of the arguments used by participants and activists in the evolving public discourse and in the personal narratives began to paint a very different picture, not of a loving parent, but of a vindictive husband who kidnapped his children to punish his former wife. Since this was the period in which the women's movement peaked, this portrayal dovetailed with feminist pictures of family dynamics. In a *Ms* magazine article, abducting mothers were almost completely ignored as Lindsy Van Gelder concluded that "Many of the abducting fathers are newly spurned husbands, reacting to the news that their wives want a divorce." Van Gelder used parental kidnapping to attack "the myth that the cornerstone of American life and law is 'the sanctity of the family,'" arguing instead that the family was balanced on women's pain and that the law was not available to women. "In the course of researching this article I found one case in which the law *voluntarily* went after a child-snatcher: here the offender was a *woman*." Similarly, Adrienne Rich's introduction to Anna Demeter's *Legal Kidnapping* turns the story into a feminist exposé. "The mother-child relationship can be seen as the first relationship violated by patriarchy. Mother and child, as objects of possession by the fathers, are reduced to pieces of property and to relationships in which men can feel in control, powerful, wherever else they feel impotent." Rich argues that "Legally, economically, and through unwritten sanctions, including the unlegislated male-bonding network documented in this book, the mother and child live under male control although males assume a minimal direct responsibility for children." Thus the snatch narratives that gave a dramatic face to the most extreme kinds of family disintegration in this decade incorporated many of that period's most challenging issues.[24]

Whether the tales have a feminist twist or not, most of the snatch narratives describe the snatcher as emotionally unstable and depict children as painfully exposed to the brutality that results from parental selfishness. *Child Snatched: The Danny Strickland Story* by Margaret Strickland provides a homey account of one family's experiences, which poignantly exposes the pathological possibilities. David Strickland and Joan O'Brien were a couple of kids when they were married in 1971 in Cocoa Beach, Florida. She was a high school dropout; he, a student in a local community college. Joan was already pregnant. Not long after the child's birth, Joan left David for one of David's coworkers, and took Danny with her.[25]

David Strickland and his parents soon became concerned over Danny's welfare. Joan puts her own interests above the needs of the child, leaving him in parked cars until late at night while she cavorts with men or visits bars. She leaves him in the care of irresponsible sitters who are often drunk. She is a forger, a shoplifter, and involved in drugs. Joan is obviously an irresponsible mother and the court eventually gives permanent custody to David Strickland and visitation rights of one week every month to Joan. The visits with the mother are not successful and Danny begins to bring home tales of his other "daddy," whose many sexual antics he has observed. Danny draws indecent pictures of sex acts and takes his clothes off whimsically. "During his short, one week stay with Joan, Danny had undergone a complete change in personality. He was no longer the normal, spirited boy one knew so well." Worse is to follow. His body has a series of scabs ("Mama Joan did it with a knife"); he has a large head wound. Finally, he pleads not to have to "go with Mama Joan again," and he warns them "they're going to keep me."[26]

Joan had become the daugher-in-law from hell—irresponsible, abusive, foul-mouthed, erratic, untrustworthy, sexually permissive—even before the day that two cars with several large men and their barely concealed weapons accompany Joan when she collects her son for his usual noncustodial visit. Although the Stricklands do not want to believe it at first, it soon becomes plain that Danny is not coming back.[27]

The Stricklands follow all the rules: they get contempt motions, writs of attachment, and orders terminating visitation. They deliver these to the State Attorney General's office, which ignores them. They can't even get the sheriff to file a missing person's report. "If this child is with a relative, now mind you, I did not say *mother*, I can't help you." They appeal to the governor of Florida, who replies, "Depend on your local law enforcement agency." Margaret's response is "What a joke!" They run up massive legal expenses, requiring the sale of valued property. They hire a detective. To pay him, Margaret keeps his children for the summer at no cost while his wife attends nursing school. The Stricklands have a down home attitude and values. They learn to do what they do best—draw upon their own resources and their friends for aid and comfort. The courts, the state, the local police, are a "joke."[28]

In the end they are lucky. Following through on an FBI lead on the most recent man with whom Joan was living and the fact that Joan is pregnant, a wild set of coincidences puts Margaret Strickland's good friend Kathryn Case in the same Colorado Springs maternity waiting room with little Danny Strickland. "Only God," Case notes, "could have produced and arranged such a logical sequence of events, such happiness."[29]

The Strickland's happiness was not complete and was to be severely tried by the challenge mounted by the O'Briens (Joan's family) in the courts and in the press. "After Danny's return, we were on a legal merry-go-round that never stopped. Seldom did Danny go two consecutive days without court ordered activities." Their lives and the life of the child are not normal. In Strickland's narrative, the state, the police, and the courts only seem to make matters worse. In the end, this narrative and the final decree, which kept Danny in his father's custody, was their vindication.[30]

The divorce, the abduction, the pursuit, the reunion, and the acrimonious court battles were not the only costs of the experience. Little Danny Strickland, only six years old when he is finally returned to the

Stricklands, had been the object of it all, and he became its real victim. He was, according to David Strickland, "an innocent child caught in the web of legal jargon." He suffers emotional wounds. Even the final custody order provides no real closure. The child is quoted as saying "he did not like himself—would like to kill himself." Confused and unable to keep up at school, Danny was assigned a court counselor but he "had precious little peace of mind."[31]

This narrative, despite its down-to-earth tone, is shot through with a vision of personal pathology and child endangerment, court interference in tandem with official incompetence. It all culminates in the need for psychological intervention and anticipates the most recent perspectives on parental kidnapping. Danny's story had in fact helped to change the laws, as the publicity about the case finally forced Florida (long a holdout) to subscribe to the UCCJA. In an addendum to her story, Margaret discusses how this lightened the burden for others who followed. But the passage of the new laws also shifted the center of gravity of the problem. With its emphasis on emotional disorder and its innuendos of sexual abuse, the Strickland story highlighted family pathology rather than legislation as the central issue in parental kidnapping cases.

## Measuring the Problem

In 1990, in fulfillment of the requirements of the 1984 Missing Children's Act, the Justice Department published the first ever statistical analysis of the missing children's problem. The study was a response to the general furor over missing children that had been created in the 1970s and 1980s of which parental kidnapping was one significant part. In the attempt to criminalize parental kidnapping, advocates and the media had associated it with the even more fearsome anxieties about stranger abduction and they had conflated the statistics of the two, at once making stranger abductions seem more common and parental abductions more frightening. As a result, wild figures for the prevalence of stranger abductions were floated in newspapers and congressional hearings. These statistics eventually resulted in more careful examinations, which attempted to deflate the balloon. Many of these cast serious doubt on the scope of the problem and raised important methodological questions about the manner in which different kinds of phenomena had been juxtaposed to inflame popular feelings. One of these examinations, a series in the *Denver Post*, garnered headlines and approval when it won the Pulitzer Prize.[32]

The Justice Department study first of all refined definitions, treating different categories of missing children as distinct and separate issues, and then gave two kinds of numbers within each category. For a long time, advocates of government intervention had inflated numbers by downplaying distinctions and by counting every possible incident or attempted occurrence as part of the phenomenon. In first distinguishing among five different kinds of child loss, and then differentiating what it called "broad scope" problems, which included all incidents (even very minor ones), from more serious ones, the study provided a more realistic profile of the problem. The second set of numbers was usually from one-half to one-fifteenth the size of the broad scope numbers.[33]

The Justice Department study made clear that most kidnapped children were abducted by their parents. Using only the narrower definitions, family abductions accounted for the most numerous group of missing children in 1988. The 163,200 cases suggested a very significant problem. By the more flexible definition, which included every instance when a child was taken "in violation of a custody agreement or decree, or a child was not returned on time from an agreed upon overnight visit," there were 354,100 cases, a number even greater than proposed by most vocal advocates of federal action. But this kind of violation of agreements hardly met the image of parental kidnapping created in the media—an abrupt rupture in parent-child relations, and a long-term disappearance where one parent did not know the child's whereabouts. The broad focus abductions were usually only defined as abductions at all because they conformed to a strictly "legal conception."

The 163,200 cases that met the more stringent definition were large enough, however. These cases met the criterion of "intentional concealment"; and included cases where attempts were made to prevent contact with the child; or the child was transported out of the state; or "there was evidence that the abductor had the intent to keep the child indefinitely or to permanently alter custodial privileges." Statistically, at least, parental kidnapping was a real and substantial social problem, larger than most had imagined.[34]

The Justice Department study created a careful, focused picture of the parental kidnapping phenomenon. The most common times for abductions were January and August during periods of extended visitations. They were rarely long term: "Most of the episodes lasted two days to a week, with very few, 10 percent, a month or more. In only a tiny fraction, 1 percent or less, was the child still being held by the abductor."[35] In other words, most parental kidnappings were resolved in fairly short order. While the numbers seemed to substantiate the furor over parental kidnapping that began in the early 1970s, many of the specific facts did not. Most articles in the 1970s and 1980s had claimed that only about 10 percent of all children abducted by parents would ever be returned. In the personal narratives where children were recovered, the period of loss ranged from many months to many years. Danny Strickland had been gone for three years; Robyn Crowley, for seven. The Justice Department study made it clear that only 10 percent of all children were gone even a month or more and that very few were never returned. In only one-half of all the cases, did the caretaking parent not know *at all times* the child's whereabouts. The media representations of parental kidnapping were hardly representative.

It is always important not to confuse numbers with significance. Each of the abductions was a serious loss and a wrenching and painful experience no matter its duration. Parents were victimized when their children did not come home, even for a few days, or a few hours. In some cases, the children may have been at risk for some physical harm, though in many others they had merely overstayed an otherwise normal visit with one parent. But it is also important not to read the statistics without the specific qualifications to which they were attached, or to confuse them with the picture of children lost all over America, with parents responsible for their lasting disappearance, which had circulated in stories since the 1970s.

To those who had attached themselves to the missing children's phenomenon these official numbers became a kind of holy grail. Indeed, the agency most directly affected, the National Center for Missing and Exploited Children (NCMEC), which had been assigned the information clearinghouse functions required by the federal law in 1984, began to redefine its own agenda after 1990, shifting from an emphasis on stranger abduction to dedicate itself to parental abductions (increasingly called family abductions), in the light of these statistics. Its director, Ernie Allen, now identified parental kidnapping as monumental and still growing at "an alarming rate." Allen and the NCMEC used the much larger, broad focus figures in their public statements and analyses. In its pamphlet, "The Kid is with a Parent. How Bad Can it Be?" the NCMEC called the situation "a crisis" and boldly pronounced that it was very bad indeed, when 4 percent of all these children experienced serious physical harm, 4 percent physical abuse, 1 percent sexual abuse, and 16 percent mental abuse. In absolute numbers, the children affected in this way were greater than those who suffered from measles or Lyme disease. In calculating the number of children presumably at risk for harm, the pamphlet assumed that the number of children who suffered from each type of abuse could be added, rather than that many of these abuses were experienced by the same children.[36] The Justice Department numbers were now available for those who had all along been committed to using parental kidnapping as a window on contemporary family abuse and dysfunction, or for those who had a stake in portraying the problem of abduction (of any variety) as rampant.

## Parental Kidnapping in a New Global Perspective

All through the discussions of the 1970s and 1980s, wildly fluctuating statistics had been accompanied in the public portrait of parental kidnapping by personal stories of emotional distress and family disorder. As the statistics were stabilized and made "official," the center of discussion shifted to an examination of the psychological dimensions of the kidnap experience. While the newspapers earlier in the century had portrayed the problem of parental kidnapping as a game in which the children participated, by the late twentieth century, social science and psychology transformed the experience into childhood trauma. At the turn of the millennium, this perspective has become the basis for outrage and action. Initially, these conclusions were conjecture or based on very small samples of individuals who came to the attention of therapists in clinical practice.[37]

In 1993, however, the first comprehensive profile of abducted children and their families was published based on interviews with people discovered through an innovative sampling technique that captured a far larger and more diverse group. The authors, Geoffrey Greif and Rebecca Hegar, worked hard to diffuse the sensationalism that had come to mark most of the publicity surrounding parental kidnapping; they accepted few of the common stereotypes, and their conclusions are temperate and even-handed. Not all abducted children are abused or traumatized or unhappy. Unlike earlier feminist accounts, Greif and Hegar showed that both mothers and fathers kidnap their children; parents who kidnap are often loving and caring as well as vindictive and abusive. The authors shrewdly understand that many of the charges and countercharges about abuse come from escalated conflicts in custody disputes. Nevertheless, as clinicians oriented to issues of pathology, Greif and Hegar's varied stories are similar in the commonness of the overall family pathology that they detail. There are an enormous number of drug- or drink-addicted parents, a startling amount of violence between parents, and many of the homes from which abducted children come can only be described as chaotic. And they implicitly raise questions about how children can be rescued from abuse, the issue which has come to define the problem and increasingly also to legitimate parental kidnapping since the 1990s.[38]

One of Greif and Hegar's most compelling findings is that a significant disproportion of *serious* family kidnappings are international or intercultural. This conclusion correlates with mounting evidence that the UCCJA could hardly help many parents whose children had been abducted, because they had been taken overseas and beyond the jurisdiction of American courts. Many of the most intransigent (and long-term) cases of parental kidnapping are of this type. While any abducted child might be transported abroad (as even Mr. Neil's daughters were presumably transported in 1873), in fact many of these children are abducted by parents who were nationals of other countries and who now shed American citizenship and return to earlier cultural identities. As the issues of globalization have become prominent, so too have the global dimensions of parental kidnapping. Indeed, the matter has been injected into the highest levels of international diplomacy.[39] In the absence of cooperation from the country to which a child has been abducted, his or her retrieval is beyond the *legal* means available to parents. Nations in the Balkans and Middle East often do not recognize a mother's right to her child, and since these countries are not affiliated with the Hague Convention, fathers who abduct their children to these locations are usually home free. But even among the almost fifty countries that have now become signatories to the Hague Convention, differences in interpretation and domestic laws have created snags and often serious impediments to full implementation of its provisions. Lady Catherine Meyer discovered this when her children were not returned to Great Britain from Germany, even though both countries have signed the Hague Convention. So serious is the problem of international abductions that the State Department published a self-help pamphlet advising parents of their rights and options. In October 1996, the Departments of State and Justice announced that the U.S. government would help defray the expenses of needy parents who traveled abroad to recover children abducted by spouses.[40] In May 2000 the U.S. Senate and House unanimously passed resolutions calling for enforcement of the Hague Convention, while one month later President Bill Clinton raised the issue with German Chancellor Gerhard Schroeder. Most press and media attention in the last several years has focused on these cases.

The newspapers and other media have also highlighted the vigilante groups that have developed in response. Trained as a Delta Force Commando, Don Feeney and others in the North Carolina group he organized, Corporate Training Unlimited, have had several spectacular successes "rescuing" children from Iraq, Bangladesh, Jordan, Tunisia, and elsewhere. Their successful adventure in reabducting a girl from Jordan even became the subject of an NBC television movie. The members of the group are portrayed as both American freedom fighters and dedicated to parental justice. Don Feeney and his wife, Judy, who works with him, have become modern day frontier gunslingers, fighting along the boundary between law and justice. Operating along this erratic line, they rekidnap children and break the laws of other countries.[41]

In this way, the public image of parental kidnapping has become global and taken a new turn, emphasizing individual righteousness operating outside any law. What had begun in the 1970s as a drive to bring the laws into line with changing social conditions, twenty-five years later centers on desperate acts in opposition to law. Just as the Feeney Commandos operate outside of American law to kidnap children from foreign countries and break the laws of those countries, recent stories about parental kidnapping often focus on parents who become heros by kidnapping their own children in the United States. When Dr. Elizabeth Morgan, with the assistance of her parents, kidnapped her daughter to New Zealand to prevent her dentist husband from exercising his visitation rights, she accused him of child molestation. She went to jail for her defiance of the court, only to emerge a media star and the subject of a very sympathetic 1992 television movie. In Marin County, California, Paula Oldham repeated the Morgan kidnap saga and became a local heroine in 1994. When popular columnist Anna Quindlen featured her in one of Quindlen's last *New York Times* pieces, Oldham became a national figure and a new feminist champion. Quindlen accepts her story as fact, and not only justifies the abduction but condemns the courts and the law which put Oldham in jail and then sent "the child . . . to live with the man Paula believed was a pedophile: her daughter's father, who denies the allegation." Oldham's husband not only denied the charge but refused to be identified in the media, knowing the fate of those who are even vaguely associated with such behavior. He has strong allies among law enforcement authorities. According to Marin County Deputy District Attorney Al Dair, "Oldham simply made up the allegation to punish and deny custody rights to her former husband, whom he has labeled the victim in the case."[42]

In the past, it was usually a mother's access to her children that was threatened by aspersions about immoral sexual behavior, and this was the basis upon which she could be judged "unfit." Today, a father's visitation rights, or custody, can most effectively be threatened by accusations of sexual abuse of the child. The charges are not new. Milo Abercrombie had used them against Lyman Swenson in 1925. But the contemporary reverberations are more extensive. Now linked up with spreading allegations about the prevalence of incest and questions about how common child sexual abuse is even in the most "respectable" families, and how often repressed memories of this abuse are recalled later in life under therapeutic conditions, parental kidnapping has become attached to radiating circles linked to a general discourse of family pathology and an increasing focus on the family as the source of many modern social ills.

And just as the Feeney Commandos have become famous for rescuing children from the clutches of foreign countries to which they were abducted by their parents, an underground woman's network most visibly represented by Faye Yager has emerged to save women and their children from male violence and the American legal system. Yager, and the Children's Underground Network which she founded, is part of a growing self-help movement aimed at rescuing women and their children from abusive and sexually depraved husbands and fathers. Yager, whose own daugher was raped by Yager's first husband, has become a female Rambo, meting out justice where law has misfired. Described as having "nothing but contempt for the judiciary; and . . . comfortable in the role of avenger . . . she is obsessive in pressing her case that America has given up its children not merely to individual deviates but to a conspiracy of satanists— preachers and politicians and mafiosi and Masons—bent on stealing souls." In painting her as a Bible Belt paranoid, *Life* magazine's hostile portrait of Yager shows her to be relentless. "If she believes that you have sexually molested your own brood, she will accuse you loudly and fearlessly, on TV and in print, oblivious to lawsuits for libel and slander, pointing a finger until she has divested you not only of your children but also of what remains of your reputation." Yager is a sharp thorn in the side of officals. But she has a devoted following who help her to relocate women and their children by providing them with safe houses and new identities. Accused by police of hiding and browbeating children into making accusations against their fathers, she was herself tried and acquitted on kidnapping charges in Atlanta in 1990, an event that served loosely as the basis of a television *Law and Order* episode. Speaking "with the passion of an abolitionist," Yager reports that she has helped "about half of the 2,000 families she has counseled to go into hiding."[43]

Yager has come to represent the unmet needs of America's abused children and the failures of American courts. At her trial, the defense, "was able to discuss child abuse in general and . . . turned the trial into an emotional, at times horrifying, evocation of children betrayed by abuse and perversion." One juror told Mrs. Yager afterward that she'd made her want to start a "safe house for such children." As the *New York Times* concluded, Yager's trial "and those attending it provide a glimpse into the *darkest edges of domestic disorder*, in which truth can be exceedingly difficult to ascertain."[44]

Today, this tangle of sexual innuendo and its justification for law breaking is often at the heart of parental kidnapping as a public issue. Even the National Center for Missing and Exploited Children has been forced to take a public position. Noting that "less than 1 per cent," of all parental abductions involve "allegations of child sexual assault," the center insists that "the key is to work within the legal system . . . **not to advocate that parents take the law in their own hands and flee.**" But the legal system has increasingly come to be seen as a serious part of the problem. No longer an infraction that results from inadequate laws, parental kidnapping has become a recourse *against family pathology* that is assumed by many to be the essence of contemporary family life and a struggle against the corrupt laws that support it.[45]

## Conclusion

I have examined parental kidnapping historically to show that while it is not a new problem, contemporary concerns about family breakdown and pathology have transformed domestic child stealing into a powerful sign and symptom of family distress. We simply do not know how prevalent parental kidnappings were in the past. Unquestionably, the incidence has increased over the course of the twentieth century and especially in the last twenty-five years, as divorce has increased dramatically. But defining the exact nature of the problem, let alone solving it, is not simple, since its public portrayal and elevation into a compelling social issue is a form of social commentary and has become a means to lament the conditions of contemporary family life. Parental kidnapping is not new, as many modern commentators seem to believe, but it has become laden with new meanings. Even in the recent past, those meanings have changed: from defining the inadequacy of national standards and laws protecting custody determinations to providing a means to question the legitimacy and sensitivity of custody decrees and the safety provided within the family. Increasingly, the depictions of parental kidnapping have helped to portray the family as a pathological environment in which children are hostage to parental selfishness. As a means for Americans to comment on other family problems, parental kidnapping is a vehicle for expressing wider anxieties and concerns about the family. This does not mean that parental kidnapping is not a serious issue, especially in light of the large number of abductions that take place each year. It does mean that we must understand how family abduction is embedded in a wide web of representation and advocacy, perception and portrayal.

As a result, designing effective social policies in relation to parental kidnapping is tricky. Historians, even more than other social analysts, are aware of the multiple and ambiguous consequences of change, including purposive policy changes. With parental kidnapping, especially, the problem itself exists as a by-product of other social policy decisions, in areas of divorce and custody above all, and it is possible to argue that parental kidnapping (since the passage of the laws in the 1980s) requires no direct action itself. As we have seen, even laws meant to protect the rights of custodial parents have not entirely quelled the issue, since custodial parents may themselves kidnap their children to protect them from what they believe or imagine to be abuse during noncustodial visits.

Nevertheless, a two-pronged response as a minimum policy seems clearly desirable: The first would aim to clarify and enforce existing domestic and international laws. The second is for the courts to be more quickly prepared to abrogate visitation by some parents. The courts might also be asked to pay more careful attention to serious clues to potentials for abuse by either parent and alert to possible mental imbalance. (See Barth, Wallerstein.) Clearly this may infringe on the rights of the noncustodial parent, but it is in line with other suggestions in this book which put the interests and needs of the child first (Skolnick and Wallerstein). More broadly, parental kidnapping may force us to reevaluate imposed joint custody, especially as a solution in cases where both parents are fighting hard for custody, because this disposition may actually increase the level of parental conflict and lead one parent to try to put the other out of the picture either by kidnapping or by child abuse accusations. Neither of these will entirely ensure that every problem will be effectively addressed, but some cases, at least, will be eliminated through more effective enforcement and more consistent and clear laws. As we have seen, the courts have hardly been equal to the many challenges that surround the issues of divorce today, and they (as well as other officials) have often been suspect among families who resort to kidnapping. It is not especially realistic to believe that the courts will be able to prevent (or rectify) the more than 163,000 serious parental kidnappings that occur annually. We should also be aware that a court-ordered abrogation of the rights of a noncustodial parent may lead to more parental kidnapping as a last and heroic attempt is made to continue contact with the child or for other motives. Kidnapping could also increase as parents disapprove of new and unfamiliar relationships and arrangements established by former spouses. (See Mason, Stacey.) And the most terrifying and legally ir-remediable forms of abduction, those to foreign countries outside the aegis of the Hague protocols, may increase as a natural by-product of our increasingly multicultural society, and one that exists in a shrinking world.

In a larger historical sense, however, policy may be the least signifi-cant implication of this chapter, since I have focused more on a history of perceptions and public portrayals than on behavior. What parental kid-napping means has changed over time as the public's vision of who the problem families are has changed. In other words, the public issue un-derlying parental kidnapping concerns not primarily the theft of children but our modern visions of the family. As a crime against its own children, family kidnapping is, in some sense, a contradiction (bizarre, one of our coauthors called it), and we have been legally struggling with this contra-diction for the greater part of the twentieth century. As long as children were understood to belong to the family, to both mother and father since the late nineteenth century, how could they be stolen by either parent? How could parents who loved their children harm them? King Solomon, after all, depended on the fact that a "real" mother would protect her child from harm even at the cost of losing that child. However, as soon as the family ceased to be viewed as a stable and dependable unit of social space (first among the rich and then much more generally), and more recently as the family was no longer assumed to be a safe haven, parental kidnap-ping became a possible offense. It has, indeed, become a symbolic crime, a product of selfish, feuding parents who prey on each other and on their own children. It is not surprising, therefore, that at a time when all bets are off, when we find it difficult even to say what the family is, let alone how it is constituted or when it is a better or worse instrument of child rearing, our public imagination fills with pictures of parents stealing their own children. Parental kidnapping is certainly an extreme expression of contemporary life, but maybe it is also an uncanny symbol of our am-biguous perspectives on family life today.

## Notes

1. *New York Times*, August 13, 1873, 2.

2. Mary Ann Mason, *From Father's Property to Children's Rights* (New York: Columbia University Press, 1994), 59.

3. *New York Times*, December 10, 1879, 3.

4. *New York Times*, April 2, 1993, 11.

5. E. G. Ewaschuk, "Abduction of Children by Parents," *The Criminal Law Quarterly* 21:176–177, 1978–79; Margaret R. De Haas, *Domestic Injunc-tions* (London: Sweet & Maxwell, 1987), 52–53.

6. Commonwealth v. Nickerson, 87 Mass. 5 (Allen) 518; State v. Farrar, 41 N. H. 53; Hunt v. Hunt, 94 Ga. 257, 21 S. E. 515; State v. Angel, 42 Kan. 216 21 Pac. 1075. The cases are summarized in *Century Edition of the Ameri-can Digest* 31: St. Paul: 1902 (my emphasis).

7. *New York Times*, July 9, 1911, 4, April 14, 1911, 10; Viviana A. Zelizer, *Pricing the Priceless Child: The Changing Social Value of Children* (New York: Basic Books, 1985).

8. *New York Times*, June 11, 1927, 24, June 28, 1910, 7. For the dangers to children from automobiles, see Zelizer, *Pricing the Priceless Child*.

9. *New York Times*, November 11, 1910, 9; *Chicago Tribune*, August 28, 1916, 1; *New York Times*, August 28, 1916, 9.

10. *San Francisco Chronicle*, July 18, 1966, 24, July 10, 1935, 15; *New York Times*, July 12, 1921, 17, July 11, 1921, 1.

11. *Chicago Tribune*, September 14, 1924, 1, September 17, 1924, 2.

12. *USA Today*, July 15, 1983, 4d. For the language of epidemic, see, for example, *U.S. News and World Report* 87:57, September 3, 1979; Bruce W. Most, "The Child Stealing Epidemic," *Nation* 224:559, May 7, 1977.

13. Sanford N. Katz, *Child Snatching: The Legal Response to the Abduction of Children*. Section of Family Law, American Bar Association, American Bar Association Press: 1981, 3, 11–12.

14. Katz, *Child Snatching*, 15.

15. David Finkelhor, Gerald Hotaling, and Andrea Sedlak, *Missing, Abducted, Runaway, and Thrownaway Children in America: First Report: Numbers and Characteristics National Incidence Studies*. Executive Summary, May 1990, U.S. Department of Justice, Office of Juvenile Justice and Delinquency Prevention, 40; Katz, *Child Snatching*, 123.

16. U.S. Department of State, Bureau of Consular Affairs, *International Parental Abduction*, 3rd ed. 1989, 21. See also, *National Law Journal* 12:3, 34, October 9, 1989.

17. The *Denver Post* featured a scathing analysis of the numbers and the hype; see Louis Kitzer, and Diana Griego, "The Truth About Missing Kids," *Sunday Denver Post*, May 12, 1985, 1A, 13A, the follow-up *Denver Post*, May 13, 1985, 1A, 10A, and the editorial, May 19, 1985, 6H. Probably the most influential social science critique is Joel Best, *Threatened Children: Rhetoric and Concern about Child-Victims* (Chicago: University of Chicago, 1990). For an excellent discussion of how issues of this kind are created and disseminated, see Cynthia Gentry, "The Social Construction of Abducted Children as a Social Problem," *Sociological Inquiry* 58:413–425, 1988.

18. Mason, *From Father's Property to Children's Rights*, 130; U.S. Department of Justice, Office of Juvenile Justice and Delinquency Prevention, U.S. Attorney General's Advisory Board on Missing Children, 1988, *Missing and Exploited Children: The Challenge Continues* (Washington, DC: 1988), 42.

19. *Missing and Exploited Children: The Challenge Continues*, 49.

20. One mother was able to locate her child when her abducting husband appeared on the *Donahue* show on child snatching. When Donahue refused to disclose vital information about her husband, she sued and won a 5.9-million-dollar court settlement; see *Newsweek* 101:101, May 30, 1983.

21. Sally Abrahms and Joseph N. Bell, "Have You Seen These Children? Child Snatching: The Cruelest Crime," *Ladies' Home Journal* 98:77, April 1981; Abrahms and Bell, *Children in the Crossfire: The Tragedy of Parental Kidnapping* (New York: Atheneum, 1983).

22. Eileen Crowley, as told to Karen Freifeld, "I Found My Kidnapped Daughter," *Good Housekeeping* 197:117,180, 182, August 1983.

23. Among other narratives, see Bonnie Black, *Somewhere Child* (New York: Viking, 1981); Anna Demeter, *Legal Kidnapping: What Happens to a Family When the Father Kidnaps Two Children* (Boston: Beacon, 1977); Thomas Froncek, *Take Away One* (New York: St. Martin's, 1985); and the novel by Joy Fielding, *Kiss Mommy Goodbye* (New York: New American Library, 1981), which closely parallels the personal narrative form.

24. Lindsy Van Gelder, "Beyond Custody: When Parents Steal Their Own Children," *Ms.* 5:52, 94, May 1978 (emphasis in original); Adrienne Rich, introduction, *Legal Kidnapping*, xiv–xv.

25. Margaret Strickland, "Child Snatched: The Danny Strickland Case," In *How to Deal with a Parental Kidnapping*, compiled by Margaret Strickland (Moorehaven, FL: 1983), originally published 1979.

26. Ibid., 193, 194–195, 202–203, 204, 207.

27. Ibid., 210.

28. Ibid., 212 (emphasis in original).

29. Ibid., 232–233, 234.

30. Ibid., 237, 248.

31. Ibid., 187, 250, 248.

32. *Denver Sunday Post*, May 13, 1985, A1. For other studies that question the statistics and the exaggerated alarm, see Best, *Threatened Children*; Martin L. Forst and Martha-Elin Blomquist, *Missing Children: Rhetoric and Reality* (New York: Lexington Books, 1991).

33. Finkelhor, Hotaling, and Sedlak, *Missing, Abducted, Runaway, and Thrownaway Children in America*, Executive Summary, 5.

34. Finkelhor, Hotaling, Sedlak, *Missing, Abducted, Runaway, and Thrownaway Children in America: First Report*, 45; Finkelhor, Hotaling, and Sedlak, *Missing, Abducted, Runaway, and Thrownaway Children in America*, Executive Summary, 6.

35. Finkelhor, Hotaling, Sedlak, *Missing, Abducted, Runaway, and Thrownaway Children in America*, Executive Summary, 6.

36. Ernie Allen, "The Crisis of Family Abductions in America," *FBI Law Enforcement Bulletin* 61:18–19, August 1992; Allen, "The Kid Is with a Parent, How Bad Can it Be?" Washington, D.C.: National Center for Missing and Exploited Children, no date, 2–3.

37. For clinical studies, Diane H. Sehetky and Lee H. Haller, "Child Psychiatry and Law: Parental Kidnapping," *Journal of the American Academy of Child Psychiatry* 22:279–285, 1983; Neil Senior, Toba Gladstone, and Barry Nurcombe, "Child Snatching: A Case Report," *Journal of the American Academy of Child Psychiatry* 21:578–583, 1982; Finkelhor, Hotaling, Sedlak, *Missing, Abducted, Runaway, and Thrownaway Children in America*, First Report, 60.

38. Geoffrey L. Greif and Rebecca L. Hegar, *When Parents Kidnap: The Families Behind the Headlines* (New York: Free Press, 1993), vii, 34, 32 and *passim*.

39. Greif and Hegar, *When Parents Kidnap*, 179–195. This international theme is the basis for the narratives in Black, *Somewhere Child* and Froncek, *Take One Away*.

40. U.S. Department of State, Bureau of Consular Affairs, *International Parental Abduction*, 3rd ed. 1989, and "Child Custody Unit Helps Parents Keep Track," *U.S. Department of State Dispatch* 2:49, January 21, 1991; *San Francisco Chronicle* (October 11, 1996), 11. Lady Meyer is the wife of the British Ambassador to the United States and has become a notable activist in this area. See,

Catherine Meyer, *They Are My Children too: A Mother's Struggle For Her Sons* (New York: Public Affairs, 1999).

41. *New York Times*, September 5, 1994, 1; *Los Angeles Times*, November 13, 1994, A1. For the Feeneys, see *Newsweek* 118: July 8, 1993, 31; *New York Times*, September 5, 1994, 1; *Los Angeles Times*, November 13, 1994, A1, A30; "The Search for Lauren," *Readers' Digest* 135:77–84, August, 1987. The movie, "Desperate Rescue: The Cathy Mahone Story," was first broadcast on NBC on January 28, 1993, and starred Mariel Hemingway.

42. "The Elizabeth Morgan Story" was aired on ABC, November 29, 1992. For Paula Oldham, *New York Times*, December 10, 1994, 15; *SF Weekly*, June 22, 1994, 7. For a very sympathetic portrayal of Oldham, see the appropriately titled, "Kidnap or Rescue?" *SF Weekly*, April 6, 1994, 11–14.

43. Tom Junod, "The Last Angry Woman," *Life* 14:65, April, 1991; *New York Times*, April 27, 1992, A1; *New York Times*, May 16, 1992, A6; *Atlanta Constitution*, May 16, 1992, B5; *New York Times*, April 27, 1992, A1, B10. The *Law and Order* segment was aired on NBC, January 6, 1993.

44. *New York Times*, May 16, 1992, A6, April 27, 1992, B10, (my emphasis); *Atlanta Constitution*, May 16, 1992, B5.

45. "Position Statement of the National Center for Missing and Exploited Children on the 'Underground Railroad,'" no date (boldface in original).

# 9

# New Families: Modern Couples as New Pioneers

Philip Cowan and Carolyn Pape Cowan

Mark and Abby met when they went to work for a young, ambitious candidate who was campaigning in a presidential primary. Over the course of an exhilarating summer, they debated endlessly about values and tactics. At summer's end they parted, returned to college, and proceeded to forge their individual academic and work careers. When they met again several years later at a political function, Mark was employed in the public relations department of a large company and Abby was about to graduate from law school. Their argumentative, passionate discussions about the need for political and social change gradually expanded to the more personal, intimate discussions that lovers have.

They began to plan a future together. Mark moved into Abby's apartment. Abby secured a job in a small law firm. Excited about their jobs and their flourishing relationship, they talked about making a long-term commitment and soon decided to marry. After the wedding, although their future plans were based on a strong desire to have children, they were uncertain about when to start a family. Mark raised the issue tentatively, but felt he did not have enough job security to take the big step. Abby was fearful of not being taken seriously if she became a mother too soon after joining her law firm.

Several years passed. Mark was now eager to have children. Abby, struggling with competing desires to have a baby *and* to move ahead in her professional life, was still hesitant. Their conversations about having a baby seemed to go nowhere but were dramatically interrupted when they suddenly discovered that their birth control method had failed: Abby was unmistakably pregnant. Somewhat surprised by their own reactions, Mark and Abby found that they were relieved to have the timing decision taken out of their hands. Feeling readier than they anticipated, they became increasingly excited as they shared the news with their parents, friends, and coworkers.

Most chapters in this book focus on high-risk families, a category in which some observers include all families that deviate from the traditional two-parent, nonteenage, father-at-work–mother-at-home "norm." The increasing prevalence of these families has been cited by David Popenoe, David Blankenhorn, and others[1] as strong evidence that American families are currently in a state of decline. In the debate over the state of contemporary family life, the family decline theorists imply that traditional families are faring well. This view ignores clear evidence of the pervasive stresses and vulnerabilities that are affecting most families these days—even those with two mature, relatively advantaged parents.

In the absence of this evidence, it appears as if children and parents in traditional two-parent families do not face the kinds of problems that require the attention of family policymakers. We will show that Abby and Mark's life, along with those of many modern couples forming new families, is less ideal and more subject to distress than family observers and policymakers realize. Using data from our own and others' studies of partners becoming parents, we will illustrate how the normal process of becoming a family *in this culture, at this time* sets in motion a chain of potential stressors that function as risks that stimulate moderate to severe distress for a substantial number of parents. Results of a number of recent longitudinal studies make clear that if the parents' distress is not addressed, the quality of their marriages and their relationships with their children are more likely to be compromised. In turn, conflictful or disengaged family relationships during the family's formative years foreshadow later problems for the children when they reach the preschool and elementary school years. This means that substantial numbers of new two-parent families in the United States do not fit the picture of the ideal family portrayed in the family decline debate.

In what follows we: (1) summarize the changing historical context that makes life for many modern parents more difficult than it used to be; (2) explore the premises underlying the current debate about family decline; (3) describe how conditions associated with the transition to parenthood create risks that increase the probability of individual, marital, and family distress; and (4) discuss the implications of this family strain for American family policy. We argue that systematic information about the early years of family life is critical to social policy debates in two ways: first, to show how existing laws and regulations can be harmful to young families, and second, to provide information about promising interventions with the potential to strengthen family relationships during the early childrearing years.

## Historical Context: Changing Families in a Changing World

From the historical perspective of the past two centuries, couples like Mark and Abby are unprecedented. They are a modern, middle-class couple attempting to create a different kind of family than those of their parents and grandparents. Strained economic conditions and the shifting ideology about appropriate roles for mothers and fathers pose new challenges for these new pioneers whose journey will lead them through unfamiliar terrain. With no maps to pinpoint the risks and hardships, contemporary men and women must forge new trails on their own.

Based on our work with couples starting families over the past twenty years, we believe that the process of becoming a family is more difficult now than it used to be. Because of the dearth of systematic study of these issues, it is impossible to locate hard evidence that modern parents face more challenges than parents of the past. Nonetheless, a brief survey of the changing context of family life in North America suggests that the transition to parenthood presents different and more confusing challenges for modern couples creating families than it did for parents in earlier times.

### *Less Support = More Isolation*

While 75 percent of American families lived in rural settings in 1850, 80 percent were living in urban or suburban environments in the year 2000. Increasingly, new families are created far from grandparents, kin, and friends with babies the same age, leaving parents without the support of those who could share their experiences of the ups and downs of parenthood. Most modern parents bring babies home to isolated dwellings where their neighbors are strangers. Many women who stay home to care for their babies find themselves virtually alone in the neighborhood during this major transition, a time when we know that inadequate social support poses a risk to their own and their babies' well-being.[2]

### *More Choice = More Ambiguity*

Compared with the experiences of their parents and grandparents, couples today have more choice about whether and when to bring children into their lives. In addition to the fact that about 4.5 percent of women now voluntarily remain forever childless (up from 2.2 percent in 1980), partners who do become parents are older and have smaller families— only one or two children, compared to the average of three, forty years ago. The reduction in family size tends to make each child seem especially precious, and the decision about whether and when to become parents even more momentous. Modern birth control methods give couples more control over the timing of a pregnancy, in spite of the fact that many methods fail with some regularity, as they did for Mark and Abby. Although the legal and moral issues surrounding abortion are hotly debated, modern couples have a choice about whether to become parents, even after conception begins.

Once the baby is born, there are more choices for modern couples. Will the mother return to work or school, which most were involved in before giving birth, and if so, how soon and for how many hours? Whereas only 18 percent of women with a child under six were employed outside the home in 1960, according to the 2000 census, approximately 55 percent of women with a child *under one* now work at least part time. Will the father take an active role in daily child care, and if so, how much? Although having these new choices is regarded by many as a benefit of modern life, choosing from among alternatives with such far-reaching consequences creates confusion and uncertainty for both men and women—which itself can lead to tension within the couple.

### New Expectations for Marriage = New Emotional Burdens

Mark and Abby, like many other modern couples, have different expectations for marriage than their forebears. In earlier decades, couples expected marriage to be a working partnership in which men and women played unequal but clearly defined roles in terms of family and work, especially once they had children. Many modern couples are trying to create more egalitarian relationships in which men and women have more similar and often interchangeable family and work roles.

The dramatic increase of women in the labor force has challenged old definitions of what men and women are expected to do inside and outside the family. As women have taken on a major role of contributing to family income, there has been a shift in *ideology* about fathers' greater participation in housework and child care, although the *realities* of men's and women's division of family labor have lagged behind. Despite the fact that modern fathers are a little more involved in daily family activities than their fathers were, studies in every industrialized country reveal that women continue to carry the major share of the burden of family work and care of the children, even when both partners are employed full time.[3] In a detailed qualitative study, Arlie Hochschild notes that working mothers come home to a "second shift." She describes vividly couples' struggle with contradictions between the values of egalitarianism and traditionalism, and between egalitarian ideology and the constraints of modern family life.

As husbands and wives struggle with these issues, they often become adversaries. At the same time, they expect their partners to be their major suppliers of emotional warmth and support.[4] These demanding expectations for marriage as a haven from the stresses of the larger world come naturally to modern partners, but this comfort zone is difficult to create, given current economic and psychological realities and the absence of helpful models from the past. The difficulty of the task is further compounded by the fact that when contemporary couples feel stressed by trying to work and nurture their children, they feel torn by what they hear from advocates of a "simpler," more traditional version of family life. In sum, we see Abby and Mark as new pioneers because they are creating a new version of family life in an era of greater challenges and fewer supports, increased and confusing choices about work and family arrangements, ambiguities about men's and women's proper roles, and demanding expectations of themselves to be both knowledgeable and nurturing partners and parents.

## Political Context: Does Family Change Mean Family Decline?

A number of writers have concluded that the historical family changes we described have weakened the institution of the family. One of the main spokespersons for this point of view, David Popenoe,[5] interprets the trends as documenting a "retreat from the traditional nuclear family in terms of a lifelong, sexually exclusive unit, with a separate-sphere division of labor between husbands and wives." He asserts, "Nuclear units are losing ground to single-parent families, serial and stepfamilies, and unmarried and homosexual couples."[6] The main problem in contemporary family life, he argues, is a shift in which familism as a cultural value has lost ground to other values such as individualism, self-focus, and egalitarianism.[7]

Family decline theorists are especially critical of single-parent families whether created by divorce or out-of-wedlock childbirth.[8] They assume that two-parent families of the past functioned with a central concern for children that led to putting children's needs first. They characterize parents who have children under other arrangements as putting themselves first, and they claim that children are suffering as a result.

The primary index for evaluating the family decline is the well-being of children. Family decline theorists repeatedly cite statistics suggesting that fewer children are being born, and that a higher proportion of them are living with permissive, disengaged, self-focused parents who ignore their physical and emotional needs. Increasing numbers of children show signs of mental illness, behavior problems, and social deviance. The remedy suggested? A social movement and social policies to promote "family values" that emphasize nuclear families with two married, monogamous parents who want to have children and are willing to devote themselves to caring for them. These are the families we have been studying.

Based on the work of following couples starting families over the past twenty years, we suggest that there is a serious problem with the suggested remedy, which ignores the extent of distress and dysfunction in this idealized family form. We will show that in a surprisingly high proportion of couples, the arrival of the first child is accompanied by increased levels of tension, conflict, distress, and divorce, not because the parents are self-centered but because it is inherently difficult in today's world to juggle the economic and emotional needs of all family members, even for couples in relatively "low-risk" circumstances. The need to pay more attention to the underside of the traditional family myth is heightened by the fact that we can now (1) identify in advance those couples most likely to have problems as they make the transition to parenthood, and (2) intervene to reduce the prevalence and intensity of these problems. Our concern with the state of contemporary families leads us to suggest remedies that would involve active support to enable parents to provide nurturance and stability for their children, rather than exhortations that they change their values about family life.

## Real Life Context: Normal Risks Associated with Becoming a Family

To illustrate the short-term impact of becoming parents, let us take a brief look at Mark and Abby four days after they bring their daughter, Lizzie, home from the hospital.

> It is 3 A.M. Lizzie is crying lustily. Mark had promised that he would get up and bring the baby to Abby when she woke, but he hasn't stirred. After nudging him several times, Abby gives up and pads across the room to Lizzie's cradle. She carries her daughter to a rocking chair and starts to feed her. Abby's nipples are sore and she hasn't yet been able to relax while nursing. Lizzie soon stops sucking and falls asleep. Abby broods silently, the quiet broken only by the rhythmic squeak of the rocker. She is angry at Mark for objecting to her suggestion that her parents come to help. She fumes, thinking about his romantic image of the three of them as a cozy family. "Well, Lizzie and I are cozy all right, but where is Mr. Romantic now?" Abby is also preoccupied with worry. She is intrigued and drawn to Lizzie but because she hasn't experienced the "powerful surge of love" that she thinks "all mothers" feel, she worries that something is wrong with her. She is also anxious because she told her boss that she'd be back to work shortly, but she simply doesn't know how she will manage. She considers talking to her best friend, Adrienne, but Adrienne probably wouldn't understand because she doesn't have a child.
>
> Hearing what he interprets as Abby's angry rocking, Mark groggily prepares his defense about why he failed to wake up when the baby did. Rather than engaging in conversation, recalling that Abby "barked" at him when he hadn't remembered to stop at the market and pharmacy on the way home from work, he pretends to be asleep. He becomes preoccupied with thoughts about the pile of work he will face at the office in the morning.

We can see how two well-meaning, thoughtful people have been caught up in changes and reactions that neither has anticipated or feels able to control. Based on our experience with many new parent couples, we imagine that, if asked, Abby and Mark would say that these issues arousing their resentment are minor; in fact, they feel foolish about being so upset about them. Yet studies of new parents suggest that the stage is set for a snowball effect in which these minor discontents can grow into more troubling distress in the next year or two. What are the consequences of this early disenchantment? Will Mark and Abby be able to prevent it from triggering more serious negative outcomes for them or for the baby?

To answer these questions about the millions of couples who become first-time parents each year, we draw on the results of our own longitudinal study of the transition to parenthood and those of several other investigators who also followed men and women from late pregnancy into the early years of life with a first child.[9] The samples in these studies were remarkably similar: the average age of first-time expectant fathers was about thirty years, of expectant mothers approximately one year younger. Most investigators studied urban couples, but a few included rural families. Although the participants' economic level varied from study to study, most fell on the continuum from working class, through lower-middle, to upper-middle class. In 1995 we reviewed more than twenty longitudinal studies of this period of family life; we included two in Germany by Engfer and Schneewind[10] and one in England by Clulow,[11] and found that results in all but two reveal an elevated risk for the marriages of couples becoming parents.[12] A more recent study and review comes to the same conclusion.[13]

We talk about this major normative transition in the life of a couple in terms of risk, conflict, and distress for the relationship because we find that the effects of the transition to parenthood create disequilibrium in each of five major domains of family life: (1) the parents' sense of self; (2) parent-grandparent relationships; (3) the parent-child relationships; (4) relationships with friends and work; and (5) the state of the marriage. We find that "fault lines" in any of these domains before the baby arrives amplify marital tensions during the transition to parenthood. Although it is difficult to determine precisely when the transition to parenthood begins and ends, our findings suggest that it encompasses a period of more than three years, from before conception until at least two years after the first child is born. Since different couples experience the transition in different ways, we rely here not only on Mark and Abby but also on a number of other couples in our study to illustrate what happens in each domain when partners become parents.

## Parents' Sense of Self

Henry, aged 32, was doing well in his job at a large computer store. Along with Mei-Lin, his wife of four years, he was looking forward to the birth of his first child. Indeed, the first week or two found Henry lost in a euphoric haze. But as he came out of the clouds and went back to work, Henry began to be distracted by new worries. As his coworkers kept reminding him, he's a father now. He certainly feels like a different person, though he's not quite sure what a new father is supposed to be doing. Rather hesitantly, he confessed his sense of confusion to Mei-Lin, who appeared visibly relieved. "I've been feeling so fragmented," she told him. "It's been difficult to hold on to my sense of *me*. I'm a wife, a daughter, a friend, and a teacher, but the Mother part seems to have taken over my whole being."

Having a child forces a redistribution of the energy directed to various aspects of parents' identity. We asked expectant parents to describe themselves by making a list of the main aspects of themselves, such as son, daughter, friend, worker, and to divide a circle we called *The Pie* into pieces representing how large each aspect of self feels. Men and women filled out *The Pie* again six and eighteen months after their babies were born. As partners became parents, the size of the slice labeled *parent* increased markedly until it occupied almost one-third of the identity of mothers of eighteen-month-olds. Although men's *parent* slice also expanded, their sense of self as father occupied only one-third the "space" of their wives'. For both women and men, the *partner* or *lover* part of their identities got "squeezed" as the *parent* aspect of self expanded.

It is curious that in the early writing about the transition to parenthood, which E. E. LeMasters claimed constituted a crisis for a couple,[14] none of the investigators gathered or cited data on postpartum depression—diagnosed when disabling symptoms of depression occur within the first few months after giving birth. Accurate epidemiological estimates of risk for postpartum depression are difficult to come by. Claims about the incidence in women range from .01 percent for serious postpartum psychosis to 50 percent for the "baby blues." Results of a study by Campbell and her colleagues suggest that approximately 10 percent of new mothers develop serious clinical depressions that interfere with their daily functioning in the postpartum period.[15] There are no epidemiological estimates of the incidence of postpartum depression in new fathers. In our study of 100 couples, one new mother and one new father required medical treatment for disabling postpartum depression. What we know, then, is that many new parents like Henry and Mei-Lin experience a profound change in their view of themselves after they have a baby, and some feel so inadequate and critical of themselves that their predominant mood can be described as depressed.

### Relationships with Parents and In-Laws

Sandra, one of the younger mothers in our study, talked with us about her fear of repeating the pattern from her mother's life. Her mother gave birth at sixteen, and told her children repeatedly that she was too young to raise a family. "Here I am with a beautiful little girl, and I'm worrying about whether I'm really grown up enough to raise her." At the same time, Sandra's husband, Daryl, who was beaten by his stepfather, is having flashbacks about how helpless he felt at those times: "I'm trying to maintain the confidence I felt when Sandra and I decided to start our family, but sometimes I get scared that I'm not going to be able to avoid being the kind of father I grew up with."

Psychoanalytically oriented writers[16] focusing on the transition to parenthood emphasize the potential disequilibration that is stimulated by a reawakening of intrapsychic conflicts from new parents' earlier relation-ships. There is considerable evidence that having a baby stimulates men's and women's feelings of vulnerability and loss associated with their own childhoods, and that these issues play a role in their emerging sense of self as parents. There is also evidence that negative relationship patterns tend to be repeated across the generations, despite parents' efforts to avoid them;[17] so Sandra and Daryl have good reason to be concerned. How-ever, studies showing that a strong, positive couple relationship can pro-vide a buffer against negative parent-child interactions suggest that the repetition of negative cycles is not inevitable.[18]

We found that the birth of a first child increases the likelihood of contact between the generations, often with unanticipated consequences. Occasionally, renewed contact allows the expectant parents to put years of estrangement behind them if their parents are receptive to renewed contact. More often, increased contact between the generations stimu-lates old and new conflicts—within each partner, between the partners, and between the generations. To take one example: Abby wants her mother to come once the baby is born but Mark has a picture of begin-ning family life on their own. Tensions between them around this issue can escalate regardless of which decision they make. If Abby's parents do visit, Mark may have difficulty establishing his place with the baby. Even if Abby's parents come to help, she and Mark may find that the grand-parents need looking after too. It may be weeks before Mark and Abby have a private conversation. If the grandparents do not respond or are not invited, painful feelings between the generations are likely to ensue.

## The Parent-Child Relationship

Few parents have had adequate experience in looking after children to feel confident immediately about coping with the needs of a first baby.

> Tyson and Martha have been arguing, it seems, for days. Eddie, their six-month-old, has long crying spells every day and into the night. As soon as she hears him, Martha moves to pick him up. When he is home, Tyson ob-jects, reasoning that this just spoils Eddie and doesn't let him learn how to soothe himself. Martha responds that Eddie wouldn't be crying if something weren't wrong, but she worries that Tyson may be right; after all, she's never looked after a six-month-old for more than an evening of baby-sitting. Al-though Tyson continues to voice his objections, he worries that if Martha is right, *his* plan may not be the best for his son either.

To make matters more complicated, just as couples develop strategies that seem effective, their baby enters a new developmental phase that calls for new reactions and routines. What makes these new challenges difficult to resolve is that each parent has a set of ideas and expectations about how parents should respond to a child, most based on experience in their fam-ilies of origin. Meshing both parents' views of how to resolve basic questions about child rearing proves to be a more complex and emotionally draining task than most couples had anticipated.

## Work and Friends

Dilemmas about partners' work outside the home are particularly salient during a couple's transition to parenthood.

> Both Hector and Isabel have decided that Isabel should stay home for at least the first year after having the baby. One morning, as Isabel is washing out José's diapers and hoping the phone will ring, she breaks into tears. Life is not as she imagined it. She misses her friends at work. She misses Hector, who is working harder now to provide for his family than he was before José was born. She misses her parents and sisters who live far away in Mexico. She feels strongly that she wants to be with her child full time, and that she should be grateful that Hector's income makes this possible, but she feels so unhappy right now. This feeling adds to her realization that she has always contributed half of their family income, but now she has to ask Hector for household money, which leaves her feeling vulnerable and dependent.
>
> Maria is highly invested in her budding career as an investment counselor, making more money than her husband, Emilio. One morning, as she faces the mountain of unread files on her desk and thinks of Lara at the child care center almost ready to take her first steps, Maria bursts into tears. She feels confident that she and Emilio have found excellent child care for Lara, and reminds herself that research has suggested that when mothers work outside the home, their daughters develop more competence than daughters of mothers who stay home. Nevertheless, she feels bereft, missing milestones that happen only once in a child's life.

We have focused on the women in both families because, given current societal arrangements, the initial impact of the struggle to balance work and family falls more heavily on mothers. If the couple decides that one parent will stay home to be the primary caretaker of the child, it is almost always the mother who does so. As we have noted, in contemporary America, about 50 percent of mothers of very young children remain at home after having a baby and more than half return to work within the first year. Both alternatives have some costs and some benefits. If mothers like Isabel want to be home with their young children, and the family can afford this arrangement, they have the opportunity to participate fully in the early day-to-day life of their children. This usually has benefits for parents and children. Nevertheless, most mothers who stay home face limited opportunities to accomplish work that leads them to feel competent, and staying home deprives them of emotional support that coworkers and friends can provide, the kinds of support that play a significant role in how parents fare in the early postpartum years. This leaves women like Isabel at risk for feeling lonely and isolated from friends and family.[19] By constrast, women like Maria who return to work are able to maintain a network of adults to work with and talk with. They may

feel better about themselves and "on track" as far as their work is concerned, but many become preoccupied with worry about their children's
well-being, particularly in this age of costly but less than ideal child care.
Furthermore, once they get home, they enter a "second shift" in which
they do the bulk of the housework and child care.[20]

We do not mean to imply that all the work-family conflicts surrounding the transition to parenthood are experienced by women. Many
modern fathers feel torn about how to juggle work and family life, move
ahead on the job, and be more involved with their children than their fathers were with them. Rather than receive a reduction in workload, men
tend to work longer hours once they become fathers, mainly because they
take their role as provider even more seriously now that they have a child.[21]
In talking to more than 100 fathers in our ongoing studies, we have become convinced that the common picture of men as resisting the responsibilities and workload involved in family life is seriously in error. We
have become painfully aware of the formidable obstacles that bar men
from assuming more active roles as fathers and husbands.

First, parents, bosses, and friends often discourage men's active involvement in the care of their children ("How come you're home in the
middle of the day?" "Are you really serious about your work here?" "She's
got you baby-sitting again, huh?"). Second, the economic realities in
which men's pay exceeds women's, make it less viable for men to take
family time off. Third, by virtue of the way males and females are social-
ized, men rarely get practice in looking after children and are given very
little support for learning by trial and error with their new babies.

> In the groups that we conducted for expectant and new parents, to which
> parents brought their babies after they were born, we saw and heard many
> versions of the following: we are discussing wives' tendency to reach for the
> baby, on the assumption that their husbands will not respond. Cindi de-
> scribes an incident last week when little Samantha began to cry. Cindi waited.
> Her husband, Martin, picked up Samantha gingerly, groped for a bottle, and
> awkwardly started to feed her. Then, according to Martin, within about sixty
> seconds, Cindi suggested that Martin give Samantha's head more support
> and prop the bottle in a different way so that the milk would flow without
> creating air bubbles. Martin quickly decided to hand the baby back to "the
> expert" and slipped into the next room "to get some work done."

The challenge to juggle the demands of work, family, and friendship
presents different kinds of stressors for men and women, which propels
the spouses even farther into separate worlds. When wives stay at home,
they wait eagerly for their husbands to return, hoping the men will go
"on duty" with the child, especially on difficult days. This leaves tired
husbands who need to unwind facing tired wives who long to talk to an
adult who will respond intelligibly to them. When both parents work outside the family, they must coordinate schedules, arrange child care, and
decide how to manage when their child is ill. Parents' stress from these
dilemmas about child care and lack of rest often spill over into the work-

day—and their work stress, in turn, gets carried back into the family atmosphere.[22]

## *The Marriage*

It should be clearer now why we say that the normal changes associated with becoming a family increase the risk that husbands and wives will experience increased marital dissatisfaction and strain after they become parents. Mark and Abby, and the other couples we have described briefly, have been through changes in their sense of themselves and in their relationships with their parents. They have struggled with uncertainties and disagreements about how to provide the best care for their child. Regardless of whether one parent stays home full or part time or both work full days outside the home, they have limited time and energy to meet conflicting demands from their parents, bosses, friends, child, and each other, and little support from outside the family to guide them on this complex journey into uncharted territory. In almost every published study of the transition conducted over the last four decades, men's and women's marital satisfaction declined. Belsky and Rovine found that from 30 percent to 59 percent of the participants in their Pennsylvania study showed a decline between pregnancy and nine months postpartum, depending on which measure of the marriage they examined.[23] In our study of California parents, 45 percent of the men and 58 percent of the women showed declining satisfaction with marriage between pregnancy and eighteen months postpartum. The scores of approximately 15 percent of the new parents moved from below to above the clinical cutoff that indicates serious marital problems, whereas only 4 percent moved from above to below the cutoff.

Why should this optimistic time of life pose so many challenges for couples? One key issue for couples becoming parents has been treated as a surefire formula for humor in situation comedies—husband-wife battles over the "who does what?" of housework, child care, and decision making. Our own study shows clearly that, regardless of how equally family work is divided before having a baby, or of how equally husbands and wives *expect* to divide the care of the baby, the roles men and women assume tend to be gender-linked, with wives doing more family work than they had done before becoming a parent and substantially more housework and baby care than their husbands do. Furthermore, the greater the discrepancy between women's predicted and actual division of family tasks with their spouses, the more symptoms of depression they report. The more traditional the arrangements—that is, the less husbands are responsible for family work—the greater fathers' *and* mothers' postpartum dissatisfaction with their overall marriage.

Although theories of life stress generally assume that *any* change is stressful, we found no correlation between sheer *amount* of change in the five aspects of family life and parents' difficulties adapting to parenthood.

In general, parenthood was followed by increasing discrepancies between husbands' and wives' perceptions of family life and their descriptions of their actual family and work roles. Couples in which the partners showed the greatest increase in those discrepancies—more often those with increasingly traditional role arrangements—described increasing conflict as a couple and greater declines in marital satisfaction.

These findings suggest that whereas family decline theorists are looking at statistics about contemporary families through 1950 lenses, actual families are responding to the realities of life in the twenty-first century. Given historical shifts in men's and women's ideas about family roles and present economic realities, it is not realistic to expect them to simply reverse trends by adopting more traditional values and practices. Contemporary families in which the parents' arrangements are at the more traditional end of the spectrum are *less* satisfied with themselves, with their relationships as couples, and with their role as parents, than those at the more egalitarian end.

## Do We Know Which Families Will Be at Risk?

The message for policymakers from research on the transition to parenthood is not only that it is a time of stress and change. We and others have found that there is predictability to couples' patterns of change: this means that it is possible to know whether a couple is at risk for more serious problems before they have a baby and whether their child will be at risk for compromised development. This information is also essential for purposes of designing *preventive* intervention. Couples most at risk for difficulties and troubling outcomes in the early postpartum years are those who were in the greatest individual and marital distress before they became parents. Children most at risk are those whose parents are having the most difficulty maintaining a positive, rewarding relationship as a couple.

### The "Baby-Maybe" Decision

Interviews with expectant parents about their process of making the decision to have a baby provide one source of information about continuity of adaptation in the family-making period. By analyzing partners' responses to the question, "How did the two of you come to be having a baby at this time?" we found four fairly distinct types of decision making in our sample of lower-middle- to upper-middle-class couples, none of whom had identified themselves as having serious relationship difficulties during pregnancy: (1) The *Planners*—50 percent of the couples—agreed about whether and when to have a baby. The other 50 percent were roughly evenly divided into three patterns: (2) The *Acceptance of fate couples*—15 percent—had unplanned conceptions but were pleased to learn that they were about to become parents; (3) The *Ambivalent couples—*

another 15 percent—continually went back and forth about their readiness to have a baby, even late in pregnancy; and (4) The *Yes-No couples*—the remaining 15 percent—claimed not to be having relationship difficulties but nonetheless had strong disagreements about whether to complete their unplanned pregnancy.

> Alice, thirty-four, became pregnant when she and Andy, twenty-seven, had been living together only four months. She was determined to have a child, regardless of whether Andy stayed in the picture. He did not feel ready to become a father, and though he dearly loved Alice, he was struggling to come to terms with the pregnancy. "It was the hardest thing I ever had to deal with," he said. "I had this idea that I wasn't even going to have to think about being a father until I was over thirty, but here it was, and I had to decide now. I was concerned about my soul. I didn't want, under any circumstances, to compromise myself, but I knew it would be very hard on Alice if I took action that would result in her being a single parent. It would've meant that I'm the kind of person who turns his back on someone I care about, and that would destroy me as well as her." And so he stayed.[24]

The *Planners* and *Acceptance of fate couples* experienced minimal decline in marital satisfaction, whereas the *Ambivalent couples* tended to have lower satisfaction to begin with and to decline even further between pregnancy and two years later. The greatest risk was for couples who had serious disagreement—more than ambivalence—about having a first baby. In these cases, one partner gave in to the other's wishes in order to remain in the relationship. The startling outcome provides a strong statement about the wisdom of this strategy: all of the *Yes-No couples* like Alice and Andy were divorced by the time their first child entered kindergarten, and the two *Yes-No couples* in which the wife was the reluctant partner reported severe marital distress at every postpartum assessment. This finding suggests that partners' unresolved conflict in making the decision to have a child is mirrored by their inability to cope with conflict to both partners' satisfaction once they become parents. Couples' styles of making this far-reaching decision seem to be a telling indicator of whether their overall relationship is at risk for instability, a finding that contradicts the folk wisdom that having a baby will mend serious marital rifts.

## Additional Risk Factors for Couples

Not surprisingly, when couples reported high levels of outside-the-family life stress during pregnancy, they are more likely to be unhappy in their marriages and stressed in their parenting roles during the early years of parenthood. When there are serious problems in the relationships between new parents and their own parents the couples are more likely to experience more postpartum distress.[25] Belsky and colleagues showed that new parents who recalled strained relationships with their own parents were more likely to experience more marital distress in the first year of parenthood.[26] In our study, parents who reported early childhoods clouded by their parents' problem drinking had a more stressful time on every indicator of adjustment in the first two years of parenthood—more conflict, less effective problem solving, less effective parenting styles, and greater parenting stress.[27] Although the transmission of maladaptive patterns across generations is not inevitable, these data suggest that without intervention, troubled relationships in the family of origin constitute a risk factor for relationships in the next generation.

Although it is never possible to make perfect predictions for purposes of creating family policies to help reduce the risks associated with family formation, we have been able to identify expectant parents at risk for later individual, marital, and parenting difficulties based on information they provided during pregnancy. Recall that the participants in the studies we are describing are the two-parent intact families portrayed as ideal in the family decline debate. The problems they face have little to do with their family values. The difficulties appear to stem from the fact that the visible fault lines in couple relationships leave their marriages more vulnerable to the shake-up of the transition-to-parenthood process.

## Risks for Children

We are concerned about the impact of the transition to parenthood not only because it increases the risk of distress in marriage but also because the parents' early distress can have far-reaching consequences for their children. Longitudinal studies make it clear that parents' early difficulties affect their children's later intellectual and social adjustment. For example, parents' well-being or distress as individuals and as couples during pregnancy predicts the quality of their relationships with their children in the preschool period.[28] In turn, the quality of both parent-child relationships in the preschool years is related to the child's academic and social competence during the early elementary school years.[29] Preschoolers whose mothers and fathers had more responsive, effective parenting styles had higher scores on academic achievement and fewer acting out, aggressive, or withdrawn behavior problems with peers in kindergarten and Grade 1.[30] When we receive teachers' reports, we see that overall, five-year-olds whose parents reported making the most positive adaptations to parenthood were the ones with the most successful adjustments to elementary school.

Alexander and Entwisle[31] suggested that in kindergarten and first grade, children are "launched into achievement trajectories that they follow the rest of their school years." Longitudinal studies of children's academic and social competence[32] support this hypothesis about the importance of students' early adaptation to school: children who are socially rejected by peers in the early elementary grades are more likely to have academic problems or drop out of school, to develop antisocial and delinquent behaviors, and to have difficulty in intimate relationships with partners in late adolescence and early adulthood. Without support or intervention early in a family's development, the children with early academic, emotional, and social problems are at greater risk for later, even more serious problems.

## Policy Implications

What social scientists have learned about families during the transition to parenthood is relevant to policy discussions about how families with young children can be strengthened.

We return briefly to the family values debate to examine the policy implications of promoting traditional family arrangements, of altering workplace policies, and of providing preventive interventions to strengthen families during the early childrearing years.

### The Potential Consequences of Promoting Traditional Family Arrangements

What are the implications of the argument that families and children would benefit by a return to traditional family arrangements? We are aware that existing data are not adequate to provide a full test of the family values argument, but we believe that some systematic information on this point is better than none. At first glance, it may seem as if studies support the arguments of those proposing that "the family" is in decline. We have documented the fact that a substantial number of new two-parent families are experiencing problems of adjustment—parents' depression, troubled marriages, intergenerational strain, and stress in juggling the demands of work and family. Nevertheless, there is little in the transition to parenthood research to support the idea that parents' distress is attributable to a decline in their family-oriented *values*. First, the populations studied here are two-parent, married, nonteenage, lower-middle- to upper-middle-class families, who do not represent the "variants" in family form that most writers associate with declining quality of family life.

Second, threaded throughout the writings on family decline is the erroneous assumption that because these changes in the family have been occurring at the same time as increases in negative outcomes for children, the changes are the *cause* of the problems. These claims are not buttressed by systematic data establishing the direction of causal influence. For example, it is well accepted (but still debated) that children's adaptation is poorer in the period after their parents' divorce.[33] Nevertheless, some studies suggest that it is the unresolved conflict between parents prior to and after the divorce, rather than the divorce itself, that accounts for most of the debilitating effects on the children.[34]

Third, we find the attack on family egalitarianism puzzling when the fact is that, despite the increase in egalitarian ideology, modern couples move toward more traditional family role arrangements as they become parents—despite their intention to do otherwise. Our key point here is that traditional family and work roles in families of the last three decades tend to be associated with *more* individual and marital distress for parents. Furthermore, we find that when fathers have little involvement in household and child care tasks, both parents are less responsive and less able to provide the structure necessary for their children to accomplish new and challenging tasks in our project playroom. Finally, when we ask teachers how all of the children in their classrooms are faring at school, it is the children of these parents who are less academically competent and more socially isolated. There is, then, a body of evidence suggesting that a return to strictly traditional family arrangements may not have the positive consequences that the proponents of "family values" claim they will.

## Family and Workplace Policy

Current discussions about policies for reducing the tensions experienced by parents of young children tend to be polarized around two alternatives: (1) Encourage more mothers to stay home and thereby reduce their stress in juggling family and work; (2) Make the workplace more flexible and "family friendly" for both parents through parental leave policies, flextime, and child care provided or subsidized by the workplace. There is no body of systematic empirical research that supports the conclusion that when mothers work outside the home, their children or husbands suffer negative consequences.[35] In fact, our own data and others' suggest that (1) children, especially girls, benefit from the model their working mothers provide as productive workers, and (2) mothers of young children who return to work are less depressed than mothers who stay home full time. Thus it is not at all clear that a policy designed to persuade contemporary mothers of young children to stay at home would have the desired effects, particularly given the potential for depression and the loss of one parent's wages in single paycheck families. Unless governments are prepared, as they are in Sweden and Germany, for example, to hold parents' jobs and provide *paid* leave to replace lost wages, a stay-at-home *policy* seems too costly for the family on both economic and psychological grounds.

We believe that the issue should not be framed in terms of policies to support single-worker *or* dual-worker families, but rather in terms of support for the well-being of all family members. This goal could entail financial support for families with very young children so that parents could choose to do full-time or substantial part-time child care themselves *or* to have support to return to work. (This idea is discussed further in Neil Gilbert's chapter.)

What about the alternative of increasing workplace flexibility? Studies of families making the transition to parenthood suggest that this alternative may be especially attractive and helpful when children are young, if it is accompanied by substantial increases in the availability of high-quality child care to reduce the stress of locating adequate care or making do with less than ideal caretakers. Adults and children tend to adapt well when both parents work *if both parents support that alternative.* Therefore, policies that support paid family leave along with flexible work arrangements could enable families to choose arrangements that make most sense for their particular situation.

### *Preventive Services to Address Family Risk Points*

According to our analysis of the risks associated with the formation of new families, many two-parent families are having difficulty coping on their own with the normal challenges of becoming a family. If a priority in our society is to strengthen new families, it seems reasonable to consider offering preventive programs to reduce risks and distress and enhance the potential for healthy and satisfying family relationships, which we know lead to more optimal levels of adjustment in children. What we are advocating is analogous to the concept of Lamaze and other forms of childbirth preparation, which are now commonly sought by many expectant parents. A logical context for these programs would be existing public and private health and mental health delivery systems in which services could be provided for families who wish assistance or are already in difficulty. We recognize that there is skepticism in a substantial segment of the population about psychological services in general, and about services provided for families by government in particular. Nonetheless, the fact is that many modern families are finding parenthood unexpectedly stressful and they typically have no access to assistance. Evidence from intervention trials suggests that when preventive programs help parents move their family relationships in more positive directions, their children have fewer academic, behavioral, and emotional problems in their first years of schooling.[36]

PARENT-FOCUSED INTERVENTIONS. Elsewhere, we reviewed the literature on interventions designed to improve parenting skills and parent-child relationship quality in families at different points on the spectrum from low-risk to high-distress.[37] For parents of children already identified as having serious problems, home visiting programs and preschool and early school interventions, some of which include a broader family focus, have demonstrated positive effects on parents' behavior and self-esteem and on children's academic and social competence, particularly when the intervention staff are health or mental health professionals. However, with the exception of occasional classes, books, or tapes for parents, there are few resources for parents who need to learn more about how to manage small problems before they spiral out of their control.

COUPLE-FOCUSED INTERVENTIONS. Our conceptual model of family transitions and results of studies of partners who become parents suggest that family-based interventions might go beyond enhancing parent-child relationships to strengthen the relationship *between* the parents. We have seen that the couple relationship is vulnerable in its own right around the decision to have a baby and increasingly after the birth of a child. We know of only one pilot program that provided couples an opportunity to explore mixed feelings about the "Baby-Maybe" decision.[38] Surely, services designed to help couples resolve their conflict about whether and when to become a family—especially "Yes-No" couples—might reduce the risks of later marital and family distress, just as genetic counseling helps couples make decisions when they are facing the risk of serious genetic problems.

In our own work, we have been systematically evaluating two preventive interventions for couples who have not been identified as being in a high-risk category. Both projects involved work with small groups of couples who met weekly over many months, in one case expectant couples, in the other, couples whose first child is about to make the transition to elementary school.[39] In both studies, staff couples who are mental health professionals worked with *both parents* in small groups of four or five couples. Ongoing discussion over the months of regular meetings addressed participants' individual, marital, parenting, and three-generational dilemmas and problems. In both cases we found promising results when we compared adjustment in families with and without the intervention.

By two years after the Becoming a Family project intervention, new parents had avoided the typical declines in role satisfaction and the increases in marital disenchantment reported in almost every longitudinal study of new parents. There were no separations or divorces in couples who participated in the intervention for the first three years of parenthood, whereas 15 percent of comparable couples with no intervention had already divorced. The positive impact of this intervention was still apparent five years after it had ended.

In the Schoolchildren and Their Families project intervention, professional staff engaged couples in group discussions of marital, parenting, and three-generational problems and dilemmas during their first child's transition to school. Two years after the intervention ended, fathers and mothers showed fewer symptoms of depression and less conflict in front of their child, and fathers were more effective in helping their children with difficult tasks than comparable parents with no intervention. These positive effects on the parents' lives and relationships had benefits for the children as well: children of parents who worked with the professionals in an ongoing couples group showed greater academic improvement and fewer emotional and behavior problems in the first five years of elementary school than children whose parents had no group intervention.[40]

These results suggest that preventive interventions in which clinically trained staff work with "low-risk" couples have the potential to buffer some of the parents' strain, slow down or stop the spillover of negative and unrewarding patterns from one relationship to another, enhance fathers' responsiveness to their children, and foster the children's ability both to concentrate on their school work and to develop more reward-ing relationships with their peers. The findings suggest that *without in-tervention*, there is increased risk of spillover from parents' distress to the quality of the parent-child relationships. This means that preventive ser-vices to help parents cope more effectively with their problems have the potential to enhance their responsiveness to their children *and* to their partners, which, in turn, optimizes their children's chances of making more successful adjustments to school. Such programs have the potential to reduce the long-term negative consequences of children's early school difficulties by setting them on more positive developmental trajectories as they face the challenges of middle childhood.

## Conclusion

The transition to parenthood has been made by men and women for centuries. In the past three decades, the notion that this transition poses risks for the well-being of adults and, thus, potentially for their chil-dren's development, has been greeted by some with surprise, disbelief, or skepticism. Our goal has been to bring recent social science findings about the processes involved in becoming a family to the attention of social scientists, family policymakers, and parents themselves. We have shown that this often-joyous time is normally accompanied by changes and stressors that increase risks of relationship difficulty and compro-mise the ability of men and women to create the kinds of families they dream of when they set out on their journey to parenthood. We con-clude that there is cause for concern about the health of "the family"—even those considered advantaged by virtue of their material and psy-chological resources.

Most chapters in this book focus on policies for families in more high-risk situations. We have argued that contemporary couples and their chil-dren in two-parent lower- to upper-middle-class families deserve the at-tention of policymakers as well. We view these couples as new pioneers, because, despite the fact that partners have been having babies for mil-lennia, contemporary parents are journeying into uncharted terrain, which appears to hold unexpected risks to their own and their children's devel-opment.

Like writers describing "family decline," we are concerned about the strength and hardiness of two-parent families. Unlike those who advocate that parents adopt more traditional family values, we recommend that policies to address family health and well-being allow for the creation of programs and services for families in diverse family arrangements, with the goal of enhancing the development and well-being of all children. We recognize that with economic resources already stretched very thin, this is not an auspicious time to recommend additional collective funding of family services. Yet research suggests that without intervention, there is a risk that the vulnerabilities and problems of the parents will spill over into the lives of their children, thus increasing the probability of the transmission of the kinds of intergenerational problems that erode the quality of family life and compromise children's chances of optimal development. This will be very costly in the long run.

We left Mark and Abby, and a number of other couples, in a state of animated suspension. Many of them were feeling somewhat irritable and disappointed, though not ready to give up on their dreams of creating nurturing families. These couples provide a challenge—that the information they have offered through their participation in scores of systematic family studies in many locales will be taken seriously, and that their voices will play a role in helping our society decide how to allocate limited economic and social resources for the families that need them.

## Notes

1. D. Blankenhorn, S. Bayme, and J. B. Elshtain (eds.), *Rebuilding the Nest: A New Commitment to the American Family* (Milwaukee, WI: Family Service America, 1990), 3–26; D. Popenoe, "American Family Decline, 1960–1990," *Journal of Marriage and the Family* 55:527–541, 1993.

2. S. B. Crockenberg, "Infant Irritability, Mother Responsiveness, and Social Support Influences on Security of Infant-Mother Attachment," *Child Development* 52:857–865, 1981; C. Cutrona, "Nonpsychotic Postpartum Depression: A Review of Recent Research," *Clinical Psychology Review* 2:487–503, 1982.

3. A. Hochschild, *The Second Shift: Working Parents and the Revolution at Home* (New York: Viking Penguin, 1989); J. H. Pleck, "Fathers and Infant Care Leave," in E. F. Zigler and M. Frank (eds.), *The Parental Leave Crisis: Toward a National Policy* (New Haven, CT: Yale University Press, 1988).

4. A. Skolnick, *Embattled Paradise: The American Family in an Age of Uncertainty* (New York: Basic Books, 1991).

5. D. Popenoe, *Disturbing the Nest: Family Change and Decline in Modern Societies* (New York: Aldine de Gruyter, 1988); Popenoe, "American Family Decline."

6. Popenoe, "American Family Decline." 41–42. Smaller two-parent families and larger one-parent families are both attributed to the same mechanism: parental self-focus and selfishness.

7. D. Blankenhorn, "American Family Dilemmas," in D. Blankenhorn, S. Bayme, and J. B. Elshtain (eds.), *Rebuilding the Nest: A New Commitment to the American Family* (Milwaukee, WI: Family Service America, 1990), 3–26.

8. Although the proportion of single-parent families is increasing, the concern about departure from the two-parent form may be overstated. Approximately 70 percent of American babies born in the 1990s come home to two parents who are married. If we include couples with long-term commitments who are not legally married, the proportion of modern families that *begins* with two parents is even higher. The prevalence of two-parent families has declined since 1956, when 94 percent of newborns had married parents, but, by far, the predominant family form in the nonteenage population continues to be two parents and a baby.

9. J. Belsky, M. Lang, and M. Rovine, "Stability and Change across the Transition to Parenthood: A Second Study," *Journal of Personality and Social Psy-*

*chology* 50:517–522, 1985; C. P. Cowan, P. A. Cowan, G. Heming, E. Garrett, W. S. Coysh, H. Curtis-Boles, and A. J. Boles, "Transitions to Parenthood: His, Hers, and Theirs," *Journal of Family Issues* 6:451–481, 1985; M. J. Cox, M. T. Owen, J. M. Lewis, and V. K. Henderson, "Marriage, Adult Adjustment, and Early Parenting," *Child Development* 60:1015–1024, 1989; F. Grossman, L. Eichler, and S. Winickoff, *Pregnancy, Birth, and Parenthood* (San Francico: Jossey-Bass, 1980); C. M. Heinicke, S. D. Diskin, D. M. Ramsay-Klee, and D. S. Oates, "Pre- and Postbirth Antecedents of 2-year-old Attention, Capacity for Relationships and Verbal Expressiveness," *Developmental Psychology* 22:777–787, 1986; R. Levy-Shiff, "Individual and Contextual Correlates of Marital Change Across the Transition to Parenthood," *Developmental Psychology* 30:591–601, 1994.

10. A. Engfer, "The Interrelatedness of Marriage and the Mother-Child Relationship," in R.A. Hinde and J. Stevenson-Hinde (eds.), *Relationships within Families: Mutual Influences* (Cambridge UK: Cambridge University Press, 1988), 104–118; K. A. Schneewind, "Konsequenzen der Erstelternschaft" [Consequences of the Transition to Parenthood: An Overview], *Psychologie in Erziehung und Unterricht* 30:161–172, 1983.

11. C. F. Clulow, *To Have and to Hold: Marriage, the First Baby and Preparing Couples for Parenthood* (Aberdeen, Scotland: Aberdeen University Press, 1982).

12. C. P. Cowan and P. A. Cowan, "Interventions to Ease the Transition to Parenthood: Why They Are Needed and What They Can Do," *Family Relations* 44:412–423, 1995.

13. A. F. Shapiro, J. M. Gottman, and S. Carrère, "The Baby and the Marriage. Identifying Factors that Buffer against Decline in Marital Satisfaction after the First Baby Arrives. *Journal of Family Psychology*, 14:59–70, 2000.

14. E. E. LeMasters, "Parenthood as Crisis," *Marriage and Family Living* 19:352–365, 1957.

15. S. B. Campbell, J. F. Cohn, C. Flanagan, S. Popper, and T. Myers, "Course and Correlates of Postpartum Depression during the Transition to Parenthood," *Development and Psychopathology* 4:29–48, 1992.

16. T. Benedek, "Parenthood during the Life Cycle," in E. J. Anthony and T. Benedek (eds.), *Parenthood: Its Psychology and Psychopathology* (Boston: Little, Brown, 1970); J. D. Osofsky and H. J. Osofsky, "Psychological and Developmental Perspectives on Expectant and New Parenthood," in R. D. Parke (ed.), *Review of Child Development Research 7: The Family* (Chicago: University of Chicago Press, 1984), 372–397.

17. A. Caspi and G. H. Elder, Jr. "Emergent Family Patterns: The Intergenerational Construction of Problem Behavior and Relationships," in R. A. Hinde and J. Stevenson-Hinde (eds.), *Relationships Within Families: Mutual Influences* (Oxford: Clarendon Press, 1988), 218–241; M. H. van Ijzendoorn, F. Juffer, M. G. Duyvesteyn, "Breaking the Intergenerational Cycle of Insecure Attachment: A Review of the Effects of Attachment-based Interventions on Maternal Sensitivity and Infant Security," *Journal of Child Psychology & Psychiatry & Allied Disciplines* 36:225–248, 1995.

18. D. A. Cohn, P. A. Cowan, C. P. Cowan, and J. Pearson, "Mothers' and Fathers' Working Models of Childhood Attachment Relationships, Parenting Styles, and Child Behavior," *Development and Psychopathology* 4:417–431, 1992.

19. Crockenberg, "Infant Irritability."

20. Hochschild, *The Second Shift.*

21. C. P. Cowan and P. A. Cowan, *When Partners Become Parents: The Big Life Change for Couples* (Mahwah, NJ: Lawrence Erlbaum, 2000).

22. M. S. Schulz, "Coping with Negative Emotional Arousal: The Daily Spillover of Work Stress into Marital Interactions," Unpublished doctoral dissertation. University of California, Berkeley, 1994; R. Repetti and J. Wood, "Effects of Daily Stress at Work on Mothers' Interactions with Preschoolers," *Journal of Family Psychology*, 11:90–108, 1997.

23. J. Belsky and M. Rovine, "Patterns of Marital Change across the Transition to Parenthood," *Journal of Marriage and the Family* 52:109–123, 1990.

24. We interviewed the couples in the mid-to-late stages of pregnancy. We were not, therefore, privy to the early phases of decision making of these couples, whether wives became pregnant on purpose, or whether husbands were coercive about the baby decision. What we saw in the Yes-No couples, in contrast with the Ambivalent couples, was that the decision to go ahead with the pregnancy, an accomplished fact, was still an unresolved emotional struggle.

25. M. Kline, P. A. Cowan, and C. P. Cowan, "The Origins of Parenting Stress during the Transition to Parenthood: A New Family Model," *Early Education and Development* 2:287–305, 1991.

26. J. Belsky and R. A. Isabella, "Marital and Parent-Child Relationships in Family of Origin and Marital Change Following the Birth of a Baby: A Retrospective Analysis," *Child Development* 56:342–349, 1985; C. P. Cowan, P. A. Cowan, and G. Heming, "Adult Children of Alcoholics: Adaptation during the Transition to Parenthood." Paper presented to the National Council on Family Relations, 1988.

27. Cowan, Cowan, and Heming, "Adult Children of Alcoholics."

28. Belsky, Lang, and Rovine, "Stability and Change across the Transition to Parenthood; Cowan and Cowan, *When Partners Become Parents*; Cox, Owen, Lewis, and Henderson, "Marriage, Adult Adjustment, and Early Parenting"; Heinicke, Diskin, Ramsay-Klee, and Oates, "Pre- and Postbirth Antecedents of 2-Year-Old Attention, Capacity for Relationships and Verbal Expressiveness."

29. D. Baumrind, "The Development of Instrumental Competence through Socialization," in A. D. Pick (ed.), *Minnesota Symposia on Child Psychology*, vol. 7, (Minneapolis: University of Minnesota Press, 1979); J. H. Block and J. Block, "The Role of Ego-Control and Ego-Resiliency in the Organization of Behavior," In W.A. Collins (ed.) *Minnesota Symposia on Child Psychology*, vol. 13 (Hillsdale, NJ: Erlbaum, 1980).

30. P. A. Cowan, C. P. Cowan, M. Schulz, and G. Heming, "Prebirth to Preschool Family Factors Predicting Children's Adaptation to Kindergarten," in R. Parke and S. Kellam (eds.), *Exploring Family Relationships with Other Social Contexts: Advances in Family Research*, vol. 4 (Hillsdale, NJ: Erlbaum, 1994). 75–114.

31. K. L. Alexander and D. Entwisle, "Achievement in the First 2 Years of School: Patterns and Processes," *Monographs of the Society for Research in Child Development* 53:2, Serial No. 218, 1988.

32. S. Asher and J. D. Coie, (eds.), *Peer Rejection in Childhood* (Cambridge: Cambridge University Press, 1990); S. G. Kellam, M. B. Simon, and M. E. Ensminger, "Antecedents in First Grade of Teenage Drug Use and Psychological Well-Being: A Ten-Year Community-wide Prospective Study," In D. Ricks and B. Dohrenwend (eds.), *Origins of Psychopathology: Research and Public Policy* (New York: Cambridge, 1982); N. Lambert, "Adolescent Outcomes for Hyperactive

Children: Perspectives on General and Specific Patterns of Childhood Risk for Adolescent Educational, Social, and Mental Health Problems," *American Psychologist* 43:786–799, 1988; E. A. Carlson, L. A. Sroufe et al. "Early Environment Support and Elementary School Adjustment as Predictors of School Adjustment in Middle Adolescence," *Journal of Adolescent Research* 14:72–94, 1999.

33. E. M. Hetherington and J. Kelly, *For Better of for Worse: Divorce Reconsidered* (New York: W. W. Norton, 2002). J. Wallerstein and J. Kelly, *Surviving the Breakup* (New York: Basic Books, 1980).

34. E. M. Cummings and P. T. Davies, *Children and Marital Conflict: The Impact of Family Dispute and Resolution* (New York: Guilford Press, 1994).

35. M. Moorehouse, "Work and Family Dynamics," in P. A. Cowan, D. Field, D. A. Hansen, A. Skolnick, and G. E. Swanson (eds.), *Family, Self, and Society: Toward a New Agenda for Family Research* (Hillsdale, NJ: Erlbaum, 1993).

36. P. A. Cowan and C. P. Cowan, "What an Intervention Design Reveals about How Parents Affect Their Children's Academic Achievement and Behavior Problems," in J. G. Borkowski, S. Ramey and M. Bristol-Power (eds.), *Parenting and the Child's World: Influences on Intellectual, Academic, and Social-Emotional Development* (Mahwah, NJ: Lawrence Erlbaum, 2002).

37. P. A. Cowan, D. Powell, and C. P. Cowan, "Parenting Interventions: A Family Systems View of Enhancing Children's Development," in I. E. Sigel and K. A. Renninger (eds.), *Handbook of Child Psychology*, 5th ed. vol. 4: *Child Psychology in Practice* (New York: Wiley, 1997).

38. L. Potts, "Considering Parenthood: Group Support for a Critical Life Decision," *American Journal of Orthopsychiatry* 50:629–638, 1980.

39. P. A. Cowan, C. P. Cowan, and T. Heming, T. "Two Variations of a Preventive Intervention for Couples: Effects on Parents and Children during the Transition to Elementary School," in P. A. Cowan, C. P. Cowan, J. Ablow, V. K. Johnson, and J. Measelle (eds.), *The Family Context of Parenting in Children's Adaptation to Elementary School* (Mahwah, NJ: Lawrence Erlbaum Associates, in press).

40. Ibid.

# 10

# Working Families: Hearth to Market

## Neil Gilbert

When the modern welfare state took shape after the Second World War, family life embodied the traditional division of labor—husband at work, wife at home caring for children—and hierarchical gender relations.[1] Much about family relations has changed since that time, generating new circumstances that are not adequately addressed by the legislative blueprints formulated half a century ago.

Characterized as a shift from traditional familism to individualism or child-centeredness to adult-centeredness, the conventions of postwar family life were reshaped by rising divorce rates, declining birth rates, and expanding labor force participation of women.[2] In 1950 there were more than four marriages for each divorce; by 1998 there were about two marriages for each divorce, at which rate almost half of all couples being joined in wedlock could expect their unions to dissolve. Over this period, the average family size declined from 3.54 to 3.18 members.

The trends toward fewer children and more liberal access to divorce have eased some of the customary restraints of family life.[3] At the same time, wives have gained a degree of liberation from the traditional division of labor through employment outside the home. Steadily on the rise, the labor force participation rate of married women with children under age eighteen climbed from 24 percent in 1950 to 40 percent in 1970 to 70 percent in 1999.[4] And these were not all women with older children. By 1999, close to 60 percent of all wives with children age three or younger were in the labor force.

Social policymakers have yet to formulate thoughtful and constructive responses to the profound change in family structure. In some cases, important policies, such as the dependent's benefit in Social Security pensions, remain based on the traditional family structure—two married parents with the men employed for pay and the women running the home and caring for the kids. In other cases, such as child care, a haphazard array of provisions has evolved without clear articulation of the policy choices being made and their implications. The need to reformulate social policies toward the family is clearly driven by social, demographic, and economic forces that have altered the traditional conventions of family life since the 1960s. In response to this need, various approaches may be taken to reform policies bringing them into sync with the social reality of family life at the dawn of the twenty-first century. In choosing among these policy options, one's preferences are influenced strongly, though not entirely, by values and beliefs about family life and where the changing structure of gender relations should be headed.

Using child care and Social Security as cases in point, this chapter analyzes alternative approaches to social policies that are responsive to the transformation of family life. The analysis begins by describing the values and beliefs underlying two models of family relations—functional equality and social partnership—that pose alternatives to the traditional division of labor in family life. This discussion is followed by two sections which examine the way functional equality, social partnership, and the traditional models of family relations inform preferences for the design of Social Security and child care policies. The concluding section analyzes the implications of policies designed to promote alternative models of family relations for economic independence, social choice, self-realization, and family stability.

## Functional Equality or Social Partnership?

Moving away from the traditional hierarchy of gender relations in which wives are financially dependent on their husbands, socially acquiescent, and legally constrained in family matters, the changing structure of family relations manifests the increasing value accorded to equality in family life. There are, however, different ideas about the calibration of equality in human affairs.[5] In the matter of gender equality, for example, feminists are not all of the same mind. Some believe that the goal should be simply to erase formal and informal discrimination; others would aim instead at "a thoroughly genderless world in which roughly as many fathers as mothers are in primary charge of children, and roughly as many women as men hold top military positions."[6] As the traditional guidelines for the division of labor dissolve, two schools of thought recommend alternative arrangements that delineate not only the meaning of gender equality in family life but also the appropriate design of social policies in support of these new conventions.

To liberate family life from the traditional hierarchy of male dominance, functional egalitarians recommend a model of gender relations
marked by a symmetrical division of labor and responsibility. This model
represents a system of belief organized around four tenets: negation of
gender roles, devaluation of traditional domestic activities, celebration of
paid employment, and recognition of the individual as the primary unit
of concern for policy.

The elimination of all gender distinctions is seen as a basic prerequisite for equality, a point on which functional egalitarians are explicit. As
Cynthia Fuchs Epstein explains, they call for "destruction of the traditional family in order to restructure society and abolish all gender roles."[7]
Expressing this view, for example, Susan Okin argues that in a just future
"one's sex would have no more relevance than one's eye color or the
length of one's toes. No assumptions would be made about 'male' or 'female' roles."[8] Since innate or natural differences between men and women
are viewed as trivial from this perspective, the fact that women tend to
be more involved than men in care giving and domestic activities is cred-
ited almost entirely to socialization.

Devaluating traditional domestic activities, advocates of functional
equality view care giving and household management as servile, tedious,
mind-numbing work of limited worth.[9] The low regard in which this work
is held, however, creates a curious dilemma. "If work in family wraps one
in a haze of domesticity and enrolls one in a cult of domesticity that blunts
all talents," Gordon inquires, "why would any man volunteer for this social lobotomy?"[10]

The liabilities attributed to domestic work contrast sharply with the
presumed benefits of wage labor. From this perspective, paid employment
imparts autonomy and self-respect as it liberates women from the repressive confinement of child care and household chores. The assumption is that women can achieve self-determination in the labor market but
not in the family.[11] Thus, equality between husbands and wives is only
possible if women participate in the paid labor force to the same extent
as men. Toward this end, several policy initiatives are typically advanced
to facilitate the shift of women's labor from the household to the market economy. First, an infrastructure of public family services is required
to provide social care and perform other traditionally female tasks. At the
same time that women are thus freed to compete in the labor market,
men must be encouraged to increase their involvement in domestic activities through, for example, parental leave policies such as in Norway
where several weeks of paid leave are reserved for fathers only.[12]

More generally, efforts to liberate women from the bridle of domesticity are guided by the principle that the individual rather than the family unit should be taken as the focal point for policy design. This principle has been advocated for some time. Suggesting that the United States
adopt the Swedish model, for example, almost twenty years ago Constantina Safilios-Rothschild wrote in favor of abolishing all social policy

distinctions based on family status, so that the law would always treat women and men as independent individuals.[13] It is a principle endorsed in recent years by the Organization for Economic Co-operation and Development (OECD). As the OECD Group of Experts on Women and Structural Change in the 1990s reports:

> In most OECD countries the tax system is now based on the individual as the unit of assessment. Applying the same rule to Social Security enhances consistency and promotes the principles of personal autonomy and economic independence.[14]

Beyond promoting autonomy and independence, the OECD officials see social policies that concentrate on individuals as a way to discourage role differentiation in family life "with regard to the division of time between paid employment, domestic duties, and leisure."[15] To achieve this state of affairs, they acknowledge the need to engage in the "social construction of gender," a process through which individual-oriented policies are reinforced by media messages that encourage men and women to adopt a functionally equal division of labor in family life.[16]

The ideal model of functional equality is characterized by a family in which: both spouses work, maintain separate accounts, pay separate taxes, and contribute more or less equivalent sums to their financial support; household tasks and caring functions which they are able to perform after work are divided equally between husbands and wives, with each contributing the same amount of time to the full range of domestic responsibilities (so that they do not fall back into the traditional division of labor in which men take out the garbage and protect the household, while women clean the floors and change the diapers); and the domestic tasks and caring functions to which they cannot attend are performed through arrangements with state-subsidized public or private service providers, for which any remaining charges are born equally by each parent. Extending into the realm of more intimate behavior, Safilios-Rothschild describes a model marriage contract which establishes that where sexual activity is concerned—"Half the time she uses a diaphragm, the other half he uses a condom."[17]

The model of family relations based on a social partnership offers an alternative to both functional equality in marital life and the traditionally conservative hierarchy of male dominance. Unlike functional egalitarians, for whom the family represents a voluntary union in which members' rights are derived from their status as individuals, those who favor a social partnership regard the family as a corporate entity that confers certain rights and duties upon its members;[18] marital relations are viewed as a partnership built on economic interdependence, mutual adjustment, and self-realization through a combination of domestic activity and paid employment. Couples decide how to divide their labor most effectively to satisfy personal needs and family responsibilities.[19] This approach rejects the egalitarian assumption that the particulars of a satisfying life are entirely the same for men and women, requiring that all duties be split evenly down the middle.[20]

Both the traditional hierarchy of marital relations and the tenets of functional equality subscribe to a more restrictive view of gender roles than the partnership model, which assumes a productive and fulfilling division of labor in family life can take many forms. In some families a wife or husband may want to stay home to manage child care and domestic affairs for an extended period of time; some families may find it convenient for one or the other partner to divide their labor between the household and part-time employment in the market; some may choose for both partners to work part time in paid employment and part time at home, and others may opt for both members to work full time and have hired help perform caring and domestic functions. Focusing on the family unit, the social partnership acknowledges that however members decide to allocate their labor, both are contributing to the management of a joint enterprise and deserve to share equally in the benefits that accrue over time, which has distinct implications for social policy.

## Social Security and Working Families

Indeed, each of these models of family relations—traditional hierarchy, functional equality, and social partnership—advances and is reinforced by different policy choices. The case of Social Security is instructive. The Social Security system in the United States, as in most industrialized democracies, is under immense fiscal pressure from demographic changes and the maturation of pension schemes. By 2040 the proportion of people over the age of sixty-five in the OECD countries is expected to average 22 percent of their populations (about half of those elderly will be over seventy-five years of age). This figure is more than twice the proportion of elderly people in the populations of these countries in 1960.[21] Projections for the United States show the number of people aged sixty-five or over climbing from 9 percent of the population in 1960 to 20 percent in 2040.

In the United States, not only is a higher proportion of the population surviving to age sixty-five, but those who reach this stage of life are living longer and retiring earlier than at the advent of the Social Security system. As Steuerle and Bakija point out, only 54 percent of the males and 61 percent of the females who were twenty-one years of age in 1896 lived to the age of sixty-five, which brought them to 1940, the first year that Social Security benefits were available.[22] In contrast, 72 percent of the men and 84 percent of the women who were twenty-one in 1946 lived to see age sixty-five in 1990. Among those who survived to age sixty-five in 1940, males could expect to live on the average another 12.7 years and females another 14.7 years. By 1999, average life expectancy at age sixty-five increased to 16 years for males and 19.1 years for females. During the same time that life expectancy was increasing, the average age of retirement declined by approximately five years (from 68.8 years for males and 68.1 years for females in 1940 to 63.7 years for males and 63.5 years for females in 1991).

These trends are pushing up the costs of Social Security to the point that the system's impending fiscal imbalance is again a serious issue in the United States. More than ten years ago, the Social Security Amendments of 1983 were designed to rectify the fiscal imbalance that was looming at that time. Although the 1983 amendments have created a temporary surplus, recent projections indicate that these reforms will be inadequate to finance the rising costs of benefit payments in the not-so-distant future. According to the Old Age, Survivors, and Disability Insurance (OASDI) Board of Trustees' best estimates (intermediate projections), the cost of benefit payments will begin to exceed OASDI tax revenues by 2013; the cumulated reserves and interest within the OASDI trust fund available will be exhausted by 2036 (or twenty years earlier than projected in 1983.[23] Examining these trends, Steuerle and Bakija conclude that to insure OASDI's fiscal integrity, government must eventually raise the tax rate, cut benefits, or do both, and the longer the delay in dealing with this problem, "the more dramatic will be the changes that must be achieved."[24]

The fiscal crisis in Social Security is complicated by the fact that in the United States and many other Western nations, old-age pension policies were introduced at a time when wives were not expected to have paid careers. When the Social Security Act of 1935 was first amended, in 1939, the insurance principle of "individual equity"—that retired workers receive benefits roughly equal to their contributions—was compromised by concerns that benefits should provide an adequate standard of living.[25] The extension of workers' benefits to dependents was a major revision enacted in 1939 to achieve adequacy.

Among married couples, a woman's right to old-age pension benefits is typically derived from her dependent status as a wife under social policies that support the traditional division of labor in family relations. The dependent's benefit remains a major feature of most public pensions schemes in modern welfare states.[26] Besides reinforcing the traditional view of the stay-at-home housewife dependent on her husband for financial support, this policy creates many inequities among married couples with different patterns of work and income.[27]

The dependent's supplement equals 50 percent of the worker's retirement benefit. If we compare the size of pension benefits working wives would receive based on their contribution records with the amount of the dependent's supplement they are entitled to based on their husband's earnings, it is often the case that they gain little or nothing from their own contributions beyond what they are eligible for simply as a dependent. As illustrated in Table 10–1, with average lifetime monthly earnings of less than one-sixth her husband's the employed wife in the Jones family is eligible for the same total monthly benefit as the unemployed wife in the Smith family, who received only the dependent's allowance.

*Table 10–1*　Alternative Models of Social Security

| | Averaged Monthly Earnings | Monthly Pension | Dependent's Allowance | Total Monthly Benefits Under Social Security Plans Based On: | | |
| --- | --- | --- | --- | --- | --- | --- |
| | | | | Pension plus Dependent's Allowance (Traditional Model) | Separate Pension Accounts (Functional Equality) | Shared Pension Accounts (Social Partnership) |
| **Jones Family:** | | | | | | |
| Husband | 1290 | 626 | — | 626 | 626 | 403 |
| Wife | 200 | 180 | 133 | 313 | 180 | 403 |
| Combined | 1490 | | | 939 | 806 | 806 |
| **Smith Family:** | | | | | | |
| Husband | 1290 | 626 | — | 626 | 626 | 313 |
| Wife | 0 | — | 313 | 313 | — | 313 |
| Combined | 1290 | | | 939 | 626 | 626 |
| **Green Family:** | | | | | | |
| Husband | 645 | 368 | — | 368 | 368 | 368 |
| Wife | 645 | 368 | — | 368 | 368 | 368 |
| Combined | 1290 | | | 736 | 736 | 736 |

*Source:* Social Security Administration calculations for monthly benefits and dependent's allowance, adapted from Ross and Upp (1988).

A wife's paycheck must amount to at least one-third of the couple's lifetime indexed income for the retirement benefit based on her earnings to be larger than the sum she is entitled to as a dependent.[28] According to Iams's calculations, the proportion of wives whose earnings are so low relative to their husbands that they would receive higher benefits as a dependent than as a retired worker has declined from approximately 66 percent of the women born in 1930 to 40 percent of those born in 1959.[29] Currently, about two-thirds of women aged sixty-two or older are receiving Social Security benefits based partly or totally on their husbands' contributions.[30]

However, even when the wife's earnings account for close to half the couple's joint income, the dependent's benefit may still discriminate against two-earner couples. Compare, for example, the total benefits received by the Smith and Green families in Table 10–1. Both couples have the same total income. But for the Greens it represents the combined equal earnings of the husband and wife, while for the Smith family it represents the total earnings of the husband. In this case, with the same family incomes, the one-earner couple's retirement benefit is higher than that of the two-earner couple.

Finally, inequities among married couples at different levels of income are magnified by the OASDI benefit structure. Although weighted in favor of the low-income worker, Social Security pension benefits rise with the wage level. Thus, by 1995 the nonworking wife whose husband earned a $60,600 income would be entitled to a dependent's benefit of $7470. This is about $1000 more than what an employed wife with an annual income of $11,400 would be entitled to on her own as a primary beneficiary (in a two-earner family with a husband earning $25,000 a year). And it is more than twice the dependent's benefit of $3245 which would be granted to a nonworking wife whose husband earned $11,400.[31] Even though the husband with the higher income paid more Social Security taxes over the years, the pension benefits for his family (as well as all other families) are partially subsidized by transfers from the next generation of contributors.[32] Here the circumstances that define the wives' entitlement are dependency status and economic class, with the dependent wife in the higher-income category receiving higher benefits than either dependent or employed wives in lower-income families. It is not clear why social policy should subsidize upper-income groups to maintain differential consumption patterns in old age.[33]

How are these inequities addressed by the alternative models of family relations? Viewing old-age pensions from the perspective of functional equality, wives are seen as independent individuals who should earn their own income and accumulate their own pension benefits in separate accounts. Egalitarians tend to reject spousal allowances because they may encourage dependency and reduce the incentive for women to become economically self-sufficient.[34] Support for separate pension accounts is expressed by an OECD report on the role of women, which recommends that taking the individual as the unit of assessment for pension benefits not only promotes personal autonomy and economic independence but "also helps to reject the notion that women's incomes are supplementary to and therefore dispensable portions of overall family income."[35] The main difficulty with this approach is that as things currently stand women earn considerably less income than men. The reasons for this are well recognized and, without going into great length, involve limited opportunities, employment bias, childbirth, and the fact that women continue to assume a disproportionate share of household duties and caring functions.

Although seeking to advance functional equality, the establishment of separate pension accounts would result in highly unequal levels of pension benefit for men and women. Thus, as the OECD Working Party on the Role of Women explains, the movement to secure equality through a system of individual pension rights for women "will have to go hand in hand with measures in other policy areas to improve women's position in the labor market."[36] These additional measures include market adjustments that eliminate wage and employment discrimination against women, the development of day care and other public services to reduce the burdens of family maintenance, and a greater effort by men to share responsibility for caring and domestic activities. It is evident from this list that in the drive toward functional equality, proposals for separate old-age pension accounts are tightly connected to a broader movement for institutional change.

Instead of discouraging role differentiation between men and women, policies that foster a social partnership enable husbands and wives to divide up the chores of running the family enterprise according to their preferences while they share equally in its benefits. With regard to retirement income, these family benefits would include all public and private pension assets and rights accumulated by both parties. Though not immediately liquid, pension entitlements represent major financial assets for most families. Thus, applied to old-age pensions, the principles of a social partnership translate into policies that dictate joint title to pensions and the sharing of benefits.

Uncommon, but not unheard of, pension schemes that involve credit-sharing between spouses are found in Canada and Germany.[37] Compared to the Canadian provisions, which entail splitting only entitlements to public pensions, the German scheme is broader in scope, encompassing all entitlements acquired in both public and private pensions. Although spouses have legal rights to an equal share of their combined pension credits, in both of these countries the tangible division of old-age pension entitlements occurs only in cases of divorce.[38]

Of course, the actual sharing of pensions need not be contingent upon divorce. One can imagine a credit-sharing arrangement based on a system of joint accounts that combine both partners' pension credits. In support of social partnerships, an exemplary policy for old-age pension reform would include the establishment of joint accounts that cover all public and private pension entitlements, and from which checks are issued in both parties' names on their retirement.

Among the issues sometimes raised about credit-sharing is the concern that it might dissuade people from marriage, because the scheme embodies an egalitarian approach to pension entitlements not fully accepted by society.[39] Yet there is no indication that marriage rates in Germany and Canada have suffered in comparison to those of other Western countries where pensions include dependents' allowances or separate accounts.

Although Germany and Canada are the only countries with credit-sharing arrangements for Social Security, the Netherlands and the United States have expressed serious interest in these arrangements. Supporting the basic tenet of social partnerships, the 1977 National Women's Conference called for federal and state legislatures to base laws relating to property, inheritance, and domestic relations "on the principle that marriage is a partnership in which the contribution of each spouse is of equal importance and value."[40] Embracing this principle, the 1979 Advisory Council on Social Security recommended consideration of credit-sharing arrangements.

The concept was generally attractive, but efforts to reform Social Security stalled for various reasons, including the fact that credit-sharing meant a reduction in benefits for the traditional one-earner family and divorced men. Substituting a credit-sharing scheme for the dependents' allowance would make Social Security benefits more equitable at the same time that it would diminish their adequacy for certain groups. This is a serious problem. If Social Security were redesigned along the lines of private insurance, with benefits directly related to contributions, one way to insure adequate support in old age would entail the increasing reliance on means-tested income maintenance schemes, such as the Supplementary Security Income program.[41] But many liberal interest groups and policy analysts oppose switching from universal benefits for the elderly, which are available to everyone regardless of income, to means-tested benefits, which are available only to those poor enough to qualify.[42] By the late 1980s these costs and conflicts seemed to have eliminated credit-sharing reforms from the political agenda.[43] Although a proposal to split Social Security entitlements resurfaced under Title IV of the Economic Equity Act introduced in Congress in 1992, the immediate prospects for this type of reform remain faint. Instead, the 2001 Presidential Commission on Social Security Reform, appointed by President Bush, is likely to recommend an individual-oriented measure that could allow workers to put part of their 12.4 percent payroll tax into private retirement accounts.

The choice of individual versus shared credits for retirement benefits could be finessed by providing universal or means-tested public pensions that are disconnected from employment records. Australia, New Zealand, and several other countries have such uniform payment systems, which extend benefits to all elderly citizens. But these uniform pensions provide only a minimum level of support, forming the first tier of systems that are then topped up by employment-based public schemes and occupational pensions, which still must contend with the issue of separate accounts versus split credits.

At one end of the life cycle, the need for dependents' benefits under Social Security has diminished because of the movement of wives and mothers into the labor force. At an earlier point in the life cycle, however, the increased labor force participation of women gives rise to new needs for child care services. And here, too, different models of family relations lead to alternative prescriptions for social policy.

## Family Relations and Child Care

Under the traditional division of labor in family relations, child care is regarded as a private family responsibility—a mother's job which requires no assistance from public authorities. As a basis for social policy in this area, the traditional model begets a formula for public inaction. Thus, when the legislative blueprints for the welfare state were drafted half a century ago, they included scant provisions for child care.

Since then, of course, the climbing labor force participation of mothers has created intense pressure on the traditional family-based arrangements for child care. As the median income of married-couple families (adjusted for inflation) remained almost constant since the early 1970s, in recent decades private capacity to finance alternative child care arrangements has not improved appreciably despite the rising number of two-earner families.[44] Fueled by mounting needs, public provisions for child care have expanded. In 1987, for example, Congress logged over seventy bills dealing with various aspects of child care assistance.[45] By 1994, the federal government was spending billions of dollars on a variety of child care initiatives including $668 million on AFDC and Transitional Child Care benefits, $352 million on child care for low-income families at risk of becoming AFDC recipients, $892 million on the Child Care and Development Block Grant program, about $450 million on child care under Title XX of the Social Security Act, $1.3 billion on the Child and Adult Care Food Program, and over $2.5 billion on the dependent care tax credit.[46] An exacting measure of the major funding streams indicates that spending on child care nearly doubled from $8.5 billion in 1994 to $15.9 billion in 1999 (both in 1999 dollars).[47]

Today the basic policy issue concerning child care is not a question of public action versus inaction, but a matter of what form public initiatives should take. Embodying the classic debate over cash versus in-kind benefits, it is a question of whether public aid should be devoted to the socialization of child care activities or socialization of costs through allowances and grants to families. Under the socialization of activities, the state may produce child care services, contract with private providers for these services, and offer tax incentives for business enterprises to supply child care services for employees. These measures are variants of the in-kind policy option, in each case public funds are allocated to service producers rather than to consumers.

Social policy literature abounds with arguments about the alternative benefits of public provisions being allocated either in cash or in-kind.[48] In regard to child care, the case for government producing or purchasing in-kind provisions rests, in part, on the grounds that this approach benefits from economies of scale and helps to create an adequate supply of services that meet public standards. Individual cash grants to parents, on the other hand, offer no guarantee that producers will emerge to meet the demand. In-kind assistance also allows greater control than cash grants over how tax dollars are being spent. If the objective is to insure that children are supervised in certain types of group settings outside the home, public funds can be designated to support this activity. Through income-testing measures, the allocation of both cash and in-kind child care provisions can be designed so that the poorest families receive the largest public subsidies. For services, this would require charging fees based on a sliding scale according to family income; cash benefits could be similarly targeted through, for example, refundable tax credits that decline as incomes rise.

Supporters of the functional equality model of family relations, for whom labor force participation of women is the main avenue to independence and autonomy, tend to favor policies that involve the socialization of child care activities. This is because furnishing child care assistance in the form of publicly sponsored services affords both a practical convenience and a work incentive for two-earner families. Public services available free of charge (or on a sliding scale) reduce the time and effort that working parents would need to invest in shopping around for day care, insure that services are available, and promise a basic standard of health and safety. As for an incentive to work, the day care system in Sweden illustrates the way provisions in-kind encourage the labor force participation of women. Functional equality is an explicit objective of Swedish family policy, which, according to a parliamentary committee, "must take as a basic principle that both parents have the same right and duty to assume breadwinning as well as practical responsibility for home and children."[49]

In Sweden, 83 percent of the married women with children under seven work, mainly because the average Swedish family cannot get by on the salary of one wage earner. It is not that the average production worker's wage is so low, but that in 1983 almost 62 percent of it went to pay direct and indirect taxes.[50] By 1990, taxes had declined, but at 57 percent of GDP Swedish taxes still consumed the highest proportion of the Gross Domestic Product of all the OECD countries.[51] These taxes finance a host of social welfare benefits distributed freely by the state, including an elaborate network of day care services. With trained staff, a supervisory ratio of two adults for every five children under three, and well-equipped facilities, day care services in Sweden are subsidized by as much as $11,900 per child.[52] But Swedish parents who might want to care for their children at home cannot choose between consuming this "free" day care service and, for example, receiving a tax rebate equal to the cost of this service. By investing labor in domestic child care activities they miss out on a huge public subsidy, while continuing to pay the taxes that support it. This arrangement creates a financial inducement to shift responsibility for the care of children from the family to the state.

At the same time that "free" child care services paid for by the taxpayer create a financial incentive to join the labor force, they also provide a source of state-sponsored employment. According to Esping-Andersen, employment in social welfare accounts for 75 percent of the net job creation in Sweden over the last twenty years, with virtually all of these jobs being filled by women.[53] These data suggest that for many women the emancipation from household work has mainly involved a shift from caring activities for children and aged performed voluntarily out of a personal commitment to family and friends, to performing social services for strangers for pay.

While state-supported child care services are popular in Sweden, there is some indication that many mothers would prefer more opportunity for other arrangements, particularly during the early years of childhood. When child care initiatives were being debated in the late 1980s, for example, a poll revealed that rather than increasing public investment in state-run day care centers, 60 percent of the Swedish women surveyed favored putting the resources toward a child care allowance that would assist parents who wanted to stay home with their children or to purchase care privately.[54] Efforts to develop a child care allowance for stay-at-home mothers in Sweden have been blocked by the Social Democrats claiming that it would help to preserve the traditional housewife system.[55]

When the state seeks to help families meet the costs of caring for children, aid in the form of a cash subsidy for child care is more consistent with the social partnership model of family relations than in-kind provisions in the form of services for out-of-home care. A policy of cash payments, whether through direct grants or refundable tax credits to all families with young children, socializes child care costs, but not the activity. This allows parents to decide together how each can best contribute to the welfare of the family enterprise. If the average cost for preschool child care were $5000, for example, parents with young children could choose to purchase day care services so that both might work or to keep all or part of the stipend to offset the loss of income from having one of the partners stay at home full time or part time to care for the children.[56] Along these lines, Finland is the only Western welfare state whose family policy offers parents a choice between subsidized day care for those who work and a cash benefit for those who wish to remain at home with their children during the early years.[57]

In the United States both parents work in most families with children. But they tend to divide their labor between child care and wage-earning activities in patterns of employment that are not always clearly reflected in the standard reporting of the Bureau of Labor Statistics (BLS) data on working mothers. Thus, in the mid-1980s 62 percent of mothers in the United States participated in the labor force, but only 41 percent were employed full time. Since "full time" is defined by the BLS as full time for any period during the calendar year, a breakdown of this category reveals that only 29 percent actually worked full time for an entire year. The mothers defined as part-time workers by the BLS represented employment situations that ranged from a few hours a week during holiday periods up to thirty-four hours a week for the year.[58]

Cash benefits offer an advantage over publicly subsidized services in that they permit parents to tailor arrangements for child care to varying patterns of employment without being penalized by the loss of subsidy. That is, benefits in cash can be used to pay for child care when both parents are employed or retained to compensate for the reduction in family income during periods when one or the other parent withdraws from the labor market in order to care for a child at home. What parents who stay home to care for children often do lose are the credits toward public pension retirement benefits that would accrue if they were otherwise employed during that period.

But the loss of pension credits need not accompany the choice to divide paid employment and care giving roles between marital partners. Several countries already provide pension credit for care giving. The amounts differ along with eligibility for men and women. In Austria, for example, women receive one year of credit for each child, while Sweden awards credit to either spouse for each year they care for a child under three. In Britain people who interrupt work careers to assume care-giving duties are compensated through the "Home Responsibility Protection" policy, which credits both men and women with a minimum level of contribution during the years they spend caring for children or the disabled.[59] Pensions benefits are increased by 10 percent for insured persons in France who have raised at least three children, and Hungary grants an increased benefit for three years of infant care.[60]

## Employment or Family Policy?

Vying to replace the traditional hierarchy of male dominance, functional equality and social partnership are models of family relations which form different templates for social policy. To judge the relative merits of these policy guidelines, let us examine their impact on social choice, economic independence, self-realization, and family stability.

On the issue of choice, the social partnership model has an apparent advantage in that it does not prescribe how families should organize their labor between household and market. Policies that encourage social partnerships allow couples who want a relation of complete functional equality to so organize their family life along those lines without any loss of

social benefits. In contrast, policies that support functional equality prescribe a shift of women's labor from the household to the market in order to benefit from, for example, separate Social Security accounts and
state subsidized child care services.

Under policies associated with social partnerships, all couples are
treated the same regardless of the division of labor within their family
units. However, some would say that this neutrality toward the division
of labor in family life merely serves to perpetuate the traditional hierarchy
of male dominance. That is, given "glass ceilings" and other sorts of employment discrimination, men's reluctance to share in household chores,
and the socialization of women into traditional caring roles, the so-called
choices promoted by social partnerships will inevitably result in traditional
arrangements that leave women economically dependent on men.[61] From
this viewpoint, the only way to safeguard against reinforcing the traditional division of labor is through social policies that encourage women
to join the labor force and seek to obliterate gender distinctions. As Susan Okin explains, "any just and fair solution to women's and children's
vulnerability must encourage and facilitate the equal sharing by men and
women of paid and unpaid work, of productive and reproductive labor."[62]
In her view, social policies should induce people to choose this mode of
life, under which "a just future would be one without gender."

That, of course, is a large order to fill. Okin's view raises a question
about the ultimate pliability of gender roles and the limits of resocializa-
tion. Rhona Rapoport and Peter Moss contend that if some men and
some women prefer "home activities more highly than employment activities, it is equitable as long as the choice is not involuntarily imposed."[63]
But to some extent biology imposes involuntary predispositions, particularly in regard to child rearing.[64] Thus Mary Ann Mason maintains that
"gender neutral laws work to the disadvantage of women in two ways:
they deny the biological and social reality of the importance of children
in women's lives, and they hold mothers to a male model of competition
when they are not in an equal position to compete."[65] On this issue, I
expect moderate feminists would agree with Elizabeth Fox-Genovese's
opinion that "sex is a difference that enlightened social policies cannot
be expected to wipe away entirely."[66]

Another reason that advocates of functional equality urge women to
enter the labor force full time involves Okin's claim that "in terms of the
quality of work, there are considerable disadvantages to the role of housewife."[67] Despite findings that full-time and part-time housewives work
fewer hours per week (on the average of 22 percent and 13 percent, re-
spectively) than their employed husbands, Okin believes that women
should prefer paid employment because much of household work is mo-
notonous and unpleasant. The fact that relatively few men choose to be
homemakers is offered as further evidence in support of this position.

Contrary to these claims, however, various polls indicate that large
proportions of married women would prefer not to work outside the home

or not to work in full-time careers outside the home. In response to a nationwide Gallup Organization survey in 1980, for example, 55 percent of the women who wanted to be married and have children did not wish to have a full-time job or career outside the home.[68] There is some indication that in recent years a growing proportion of American women are more inclined to stay home and care for their family than to join the labor force. The annual Virginia Slims survey of 3000 women in the United States, for example, reveals that the proportion of women who said that if free to choose they would prefer to have a job rather than stay home to take care of the family rose from 36 percent in 1974 to 52 percent in 1985, but then declined to 42 percent in 1989.[69] Data from the 1997 National Survey of America's Families show 49 percent of women agreeing with the statement "When children are young mothers should not work outside the home."[70]

A similar reluctance to full-time employment when children are young is expressed by Danish mothers, despite the fact that in Denmark public day care is provided from the age of six months and 90 percent of mothers of young children are employed an average of thirty-four hours per week. When asked to describe the ideal arrangement for a nuclear family with children of nursery school age, only 3 percent of the mothers preferred to have both parents working full time, 15 percent chose to have the mother home full time as a housewife, 42 percent favored part-time employment for the mother, and 40 percent preferred to have both parents working part time.[71] And in Austria, Badelt reports, "opinion polls make clear that women do not see paid work and family work as mutually exclusive alternatives but wish to combine both options in the long run."[72]

Whether these surveys reflect true preferences or choices shaped by existing social constraints that women encounter in the labor market is difficult to know. Critics of functional equality contend that respondents are expressing natural desires to spend time at home with their children.[73] Advocates of functional equality argue that the women's responses are influenced by social constraints.[74] Both of these claims may have some degree of validity. The extent to which many of the women surveyed are expressing an authentic preference for child care and domestic activities over the full range of paid work they are reasonably qualified to perform depends largely upon how much they gain in the way of self-realization and economic independence, which are often attributed to participation in the labor force.

Unpaid family work may be described as shaping unformed personalities, nurturing relatives, and household management or in more pedestrian terms as caring, cooking, and cleaning. However it is portrayed, the variability of this work is relatively narrow in comparison to the range of jobs in the paid labor force, which include, of course, cooking, cleaning, and caring. Participation in the labor force encompasses a vast array of activities from work that is low status, boring, physically demanding, poorly rewarded, and dangerous, to positions that are high status, exciting, physically easy, well rewarded, and safe. One might expect those laboring on the more favorable end of this continuum, for example, artists, writers, professors, lawyers, politicians, and media personalities, to choose full-time careers over household activities. On the other side, given the choice of employment, for instance, as coal miners, factory workers, taxi drivers, sales people, clerks, guards, service workers, and mail carriers, one might prefer to engage in a combination of family work and part-time paid employment or in a secondary career (or not to work at all in the labor force if one can afford it). The view of participation in the labor force as the thoroughfare to self-realization idealizes paid employment as much as it impugns family work. The sense of challenge, achievement, and personal satisfaction often attributed to the world of paid work is, in Deborah Fallows's experience, "indeed compatible with the major commitment of spending time at home raising children."[75]

With regard to economic independence, policies to achieve functional equality provide incentives for the development of two-wage-earner families, which reduces women's financial dependence on men. However, the immediate independence gained through employment and contracting out domestic work is in a larger sense paradoxical.[76] At the same time that a paycheck increases a wife's autonomy and economic independence within the family, it heightens her susceptibility to the vagaries of the marketplace and the interpersonal constraints on wage labor. There are, of course, exceptions, typically successful artists and writers, tenured professors, law partners, media personalities, and those at the top of the pyramid in their business firms. But for most men and women in the labor force, freedom from economic dependence on relatives has its own price. On the job they are subject daily to the authority of supervisors, the normal discipline of the work environment, and the demands of customers, all of which may be said to exercise their own form of oppression. In contracting out domestic work, the autonomy spouses may gain in relation to each other and the family unit they lose through increased social and economic dependence on the market economy for meeting many individual and family needs, which were previously satisfied through the division of family labor.

If a major objective of social policy is to stabilize family life, it can be argued that policies designed to facilitate the social partnership model of family relations will be more effective than those in support of functional equality. By prescribing an arrangement under which husbands and wives perform the same household tasks and divide their labor equally between housework and paid employment, functional equality strengthens the individual's ability to meet all of his or her social and economic needs independently. This reduces the degree of social and economic interdependence among family members, scraping away at some of the basic adhesion of the family unit. What remains are emotional attachments, which form a necessary but not always sufficient tie to hold the unit together over the rough patches of life. Many couples behave as an integral economic unit, pooling their resources for the common good, rather than as free agents joined for the advantageous exchange of goods and services.[77] While social and economic interdependence are not the most desirable reasons for family units to stay together, they thicken the glue. In any event, efforts to reinforce the stability of the family unit may involve sacrifices that do not always promote the individual happiness of its adult members.

How do the policy implications of alternative models of family relations apply to family units in which the partners are unmarried? The level of cohabitation in the United States has risen precipitously in recent times, with the number of unmarried-couple households multiplying from 500,000 in 1970 to three million in 1991.[78] This trend toward increasing cohabitation outside of marriage not only affects the legal edifice of traditional family life but challenges the basis of entitlements for family-oriented Social Security policies. Should men and women who enter into consensual unions be entitled to the same social rights as married couples?

The issue of whether cohabitation should confer entitlement to family benefits is largely bypassed by those who favor policies in support of functional equality. Since the individual is taken as the unit of concern, rights to benefits are perceived as appropriately organized in terms of separate accounts for everyone, as in the example of Social Security. From this perspective, marital status and living arrangements are irrelevant.

In contrast to the individualistic focus of functional equality, the nature of living arrangements and commitments that hold couples together are pertinent for defining benefit rights from the standpoint of social partnerships. Seeking a reasonable balance between rights and obligations, however, supporters of the partnership model would consider cohabitation per se an insufficient basis for entitlements to family benefits—commitments associated with the partnership of family life are more than a matter of two people sharing the same residence. This is not to say that social partnership maintains the traditional view of a marriage license as the only certification of a committed relationship.

However, to qualify for Social Security benefits as a family unit in the absence of a marriage license requires some formal expression of a social partnership—a mutual commitment to sharing the benefits and burdens of an enduring relationship. These benefits and burdens include social, emotional, legal, and economic dimensions of mutual care. Marriage is a formal covenant that embraces all of these dimensions of mutual care, whereas cohabitation often involves a relationship of similar commitments, secured only by informal agreement. For the same entitlement to family benefits as couples joined in wedlock, cohabiting couples should invest their relationship with an equivalent level of mutual obligation. Outside of marriage, this can be achieved through formal compacts centered on the most explicit and tangible dimension of mutual support, which involves financial interdependence. Such measures might include formal agreements by cohabiting couples to treat their assets as community property, to guarantee joint support of children, and to pool all their pension credits in a single account to be divided equally between the partners (as in the split-credit arrangements for Social Security described earlier).

Social partnerships that are founded on ties of affection reinforced by formal agreements to share the costs and gains of an ongoing relationship embody the interpersonal commitments and conventional obligations of family life. In which case, they should be entitled to social benefits designed for the family unit. And if social partnerships which behave like families deserve to be accorded the rights of families, there is no reason that these rights should not be extended to consensual unions of both heterosexual and homosexual couples that demonstrate an equivalent degree of commitment.

## Conclusion

However one assesses the merits of social partnership versus functional equality, it is clear that with the advancement in women's rights and the changing division of labor in family life, the traditional hierarchy of male dominance no longer serves as an adequate guide for family-oriented social policy. As guides to policy, there are essential differences between the alternative models of family relations. The functional equality model rewards the shift of women's labor from the household to the market economy, which increases the labor supply as well as consumer demand for goods and services that were previously produced at home. At one level, it is basically an employment strategy serving the needs of the marketplace. At another level, it constitutes a blueprint for structural change in society.

In contrast, the social partnership model emphasizes social choice more than structural change. This model favors policies that invite family members to make mutual decisions about how best to allocate their labor between housework and paid employment. Rather than a prescription for the wholesale transfer of household labor to the market, it enables varying patterns of paid and unpaid work to emerge in response to different family needs, life-cycle stages, and the partners' preferences. In this sense, the social partnership lends resiliency to family efforts to perform caretaking and domestic functions while regulating the movement of labor from the home to the market.

## Notes

1. This chapter is a revised and expanded version of material presented in Neil Gilbert, *Welfare Justice* (New Haven: Yale University Press, 1995).

2. Barbara Defoe Whitehead, "A New Familism?" *Family Affairs*, Summer, 1992; David Popenoe, *Disturbing the Nest: Family Change and Decline in Modern Societies* (New York: Aldine De Gruyter, 1988).

3. William Goode, *World Changes in Divorce Patterns* (New Haven: Yale University Press, 1993).

4. Andrew Cherlin (ed.), *The Changing American Family and Public Policy* (Washington, DC: Urban Institute Press, 1988; U.S. Bureau of the Census, *Statistical Abstract of the United States, 2000* (Washington, DC: Government Printing Office, 2000).

5. Social policy in race relations, for example, is sharply divided between measures favoring either equality of opportunity or equality of results (Nathan Glazer, *Affirmative Discrimination: Ethnic Inequality and Public Policy* [New York: Basic Books, 1975]). And the Aristotelian distinction between numerical and proportional equality poses the choice of distributive principles that treat everyone the same or grant similar treatment to people of similar merit (Gregory Vlastos, "Justice and Inequality," in Richard Brandt (ed.), *Social Justice* [Englewood Cliffs, NJ: Prentice Hall, 1962]).

6. Ronald Dworkin, "Feminism and Abortion," *The New York Review of Books* XI:11, June 1993.

7. Cynthia Fuchs Epstein, "Toward a Family Policy: Changes in Mothers' Lives," in Andrew Cherlin (ed.), *The Changing American Family and Public Policy* (Washington, DC: Urban Institute Press, 1988), 160.

8. Susan Okin, *Justice, Gender, and the Family* (New York: Basic Books, 1992), 180.

9. Wendy Kaminer, *A Fearful Freedom: Women's Flight from Equality* (New York: Addison-Wesley, 1990).

10. Suzanne Gordon, "Feminism and Caring," *The American Prospect*: Summer 1992, 127.

11. Louise Tilly and Joan Scott, *Women, Work, and Family* (London: Routledge, 1989).

12. Arnlaug Leira, "The Women-friendly Welfare State?" Paper presented at the Peder Sather Symposium on Gender Equality, Children and the Family: Evolving Scandinavian and American Social Policy, April 6–7, 1994, University of California, Berkeley.

13. Constantina Safilios-Rothschild, *Women and Social Policy* (Englewood Cliffs, NJ: Prentice Hall, 1974).

14. Organization for Economic Co-operation and Development (OECD), *Shaping Structural Change: The Role of Women*. Paris: OECD, 1991.

15. OECD, *The Integration of Women into the Economy* (Paris: OECD, 1985).

16. OECD, *Shaping Structural Change: The Role of Women*.

17. Safilios-Rothschild, *Women and Social Policy*, 118.

18. Elizabeth Fox-Genovese, "Feminist Rights, Individualist Wrongs," *Tikkun* 7:3, 29–34, 1992.

19. Katherine Kersten, "A Conservative Feminist Manifesto," *Policy Preview* 56:4–15, 1991.

20. Michael Levin, "Feminism Stage Three," *Commentary* 82:2, 27–31, 1986.

21. OECD, *Employment Outlook, 1988*. Paris: OECD, 1988.

22. Eugene Steuerle and Jon Bakija, *Retooling Social Security for the 21st Century* (Washington, DC: Urban Institute, 1994).

23. Board of Trustees, Federal Old-Age and Survivors Insurance and Disability Insurance Trust Fund, *1994 Annual Report of the Board of Trustees* (Washington, DC: Government Printing Office, 1994).

24. Steurle and Bakija, *Retooling Social Security for the 21st Century.*

25. Joseph Pechman, Henry Aaron, and Michael Taussig, *Social Security Perspectives for Reform* (Washington, DC: Brookings Institution, 1968).

26. Martin Tracy, "Credit-Splitting and Private Pension Awards in Divorce: A Case Study of British Columbia," *Research on Aging* 9:1, 148–159, 1987.

27. The dependent's benefit not only creates inequities among married couples with different patterns of work and income, it also provides the one-earner married couple a return on their Social Security contributions, which is 50 percent higher than that received by a single worker at the same income level.

28. Jane Ross and Melinda Upp, "The Treatment of Women in the United States Social Security System, 1970–1988," in *Equal Treatment in Social Security: Studies and Research No. 27* (Geneva: International Social Security Association, 1988).

29. Howard Iams, "Earning of Couples: A Cohort Analysis," *Social Security Bulletin* 56:3, 22–32, 1993.

30. Barbara Lingg, "Women Beneficiaries Aged 62 or Older, 1960–1988," *Social Security Bulletin* 53:7, 2–12, 1990.

31. U.S. House of Representatives, Committee on Ways and Means, *The Green Book: Overview of Entitlement Programs* (Washington, DC: Government Printing Office, 1992).

32. Ozawa estimates that a high-wage earner retiring at age sixty-five with a dependent spouse receives $828 per month in unpaid-for benefits compared to a monthly subsidy of only $482 for a low-wage earner in similar circumstances. Martha Ozawa, "Who Receives Subsidies Through Social Security and How Much?" *Social Work* 27:2, 129–136, 1982.

33. Burns (1956) points out that in a large geographical area such as the United States, wage and income levels vary substantially from one part of the country to another. Thus the case might be made that wage-related benefits help to insure pensions will be large enough to meet basic needs in terms of prevailing standards in those sections of the country where average earnings are high. However, the variance of incomes within states is also quite large. Wage-related benefits probably do less to compensate for regional variations in average income than to maintain the relative position among local income groups during retirement. Eveline Burns, *Social Security and Public Policy* (New York: McGraw Hill, 1956); Mancur Olson, "Social Security Survival: A Comment," *CATO Journal* 3:2, 355–359, 1983.

34. Martin Tracy, "Equal Treatment and Pension Systems: A Comparative Study," in *Equal Treatment in Social Security: Studies and Research, No. 27,* (Geneva: International Social Security Association, 1988).

35. OECD, *Shaping Structural Change: The Role of Women,* 28.

36. OECD, *The Integration of Women into the Economy,* 148.

37. In the Canadian scheme, evidence from British Columbia indicates that initially there was a very low take-up rate of under 5 percent among divorced couples, attributed in part to the lack of public awareness concerning the formal application procedures for voluntary credit-sharing. Tracy, "Credit-Splitting and Private Pension Awards in Divorce."

38. Hans-Joachim Reinhard, "The Splitting of Pension Credits in the Federal Republic of Germany and Canada—An Appropriate Way to Achieve Equality in Social Security Treatment for Men and Women?" in *Equal Treatment in Social Security: Studies and Research, No. 27.*

39. Anne-Marie Brocas, "Equal Treatment of Men and Women in Social Security: An Overview," in *Equal Treatment in Social Security: Studies and Research No. 27.*

40. Ross and Upp, "The Treatment of Women in the United States Social Security System, 1970–1988," 83.

41. Alicia Munnell, *The Future of Social Security* (Washington, DC: Brookings Institution, 1977).

42. Alvin Schorr, *Common Decency: Domestic Policies after Reagan* (New Haven: Yale University Press, 1986); Peter Townsend, "Does Selectivity Mean a Nation Divided?" in *Social Services for All?* (London: Fabian Society, 1968).

43. Ross and Upp, "The Treatment of Women in the United States Social Security System, 1970–1988."

44. U.S. Bureau of the Census, *Statistical Abstract of the United States, 1990* (Washington, DC: Government Printing Office, 1990).

45. Marcia Meyers, "The ABCs of Child Care in a Mixed Economy: A Comparison of Public and Private Sector Alternatives," *Social Service Review* 64:4, 1990.

46. U.S. House of Representatives, Committee on Ways and Means, *The Green Book: Overview of Entitlement Programs* (Washington, DC: Government Printing Office, 1994).

47. Douglas Besharov and Nazanin Samuri, "Child Care after Welfare Reform," American Enterprise Institute, Washington, DC, 2000.

48. Neil Gilbert, Harry Specht, and Paul Terrell, *Dimensions of Social Welfare Policy* (Englewood Cliffs, NJ: Prentice Hall, 1993).

49. David Popenoe, *Disturbing the Nest: Family Change and Decline in Modern Societies* (New York: Aldine De Gruyter, 1988), 149.

50. This tax rate is based on OECD Secretariat Estimates reported in the *Wall Street Journal* and includes payroll taxes, social insurance contributions, personal income taxes, and general consumption and excise taxes. According to the Swedish Institute an "80/85 percent rule" was established in the late 1970s to insure that the aggregate sum of national, local, and net worth taxes did not exceed 80 percent of the taxpayers' income or 85 percent for those with the highest earnings. "The Supply Side of OECD," *Wall Street Journal*, May 11, 1987; and Swedish Institute, *Taxes in Sweden* (Stockholm: Swedish Institute, 1978).

51. ECD, *Revenue Statistics of OECD Member Countries: 1965–1991.* Paris: OECD, 1992.

52. Swedish Institute, *Child Care in Sweden* (Stockholm: Swedish Institute, 1992).

53. Gosta Esping-Andersen, "The Welfare State in the Reorganization of Working Life," in Peter Sanders and Diana Encel (eds.), *Social Policy in Australia: Options for the 1990s,* vol. 1. (New South Wales: Social Policy Research Centre, University of New South Wales, 1991).

54. Sven Svensson, "Vardnadsbidrag fore dagis," *Dagens Nyheter*, April 12, 1987.

55. Popenoe, *Disturbing the Nest.*

56. The $5000 figure represents the average annual per pupil cost of public elementary and secondary education in 1990. According to an estimate by Gill and Gill, professionally approved quality day care for preschool children of full-time working parents would cost around $10,000 a year (which is close to what Sweden spends). Richard Gill and Grandon Gill, "A Parental Bill of Rights," *Family Affairs* 6:1/2, 1–6, 1994.

57. Sheila Kamerman and Alfred Kahn, "Mother Only Families in Western Europe: Social Change, Social Problem, and Societal Response." A report prepared for the German Marshall Fund of the United States, November 1987.

58. Douglas Besharov and Michelle Daly, "How Much Are Working Mothers Working?" *Public Opinion* 9:4, 48–51, 1986.

59. Nicholas Barr and Fiona Coulter, "Social Security: Solution or Problem?" in John Hills (ed.), *The State of Welfare: The Welfare State in Britain Since 1974* (Oxford: Claredon Press, 1990).

60. Martin Tracy and Patsy Tracy, "The Treatment of Women as Dependents Under Social Security: After 50 Years How Does the United States Compare to Other Countries," *Journal of Applied Social Sciences* 111, 5–16, 1987.

61. Hojat anticipates that radical feminists may challenge the United Nations Convention on the Rights of the Child, which affirms the "inalienable right of a child to be cared for by his or her parents in the home environment." Although this convention emphasizes the importance of child care by "parents" in the home environment, it is likely to create more pressure on women than men to assume traditional caring roles. Mohammadreza Hojat, "The World Declaration of the Rights of the Child: Anticipated Challenges," *Psychological Reports*, 72, 1011–1022, 1993.

62. Okin, *Justice, Gender, and the Family*, 171.

63. Rhona Rapoport and Peter Moss, *Men and Women as Equals at Work* (London: Thomas Coram Research Unit, 1990), 1.

64. David Popenoe, "Parental Androgyny," *Society* 30(6), 5–11, 1993.

65. Mary Ann Mason, "Motherhood vs. Equal Treatment," *Journal of Family Law* 29:1, 48, 1990.

66. Fox-Genovese, "Feminist Rights, Individualist Wrongs," 30.

67. Okin, *Justice, Gender, and the Family*, 150.

68. Gallup Organization, "American Families—1980." Report submitted to the White House Conference on Families, June 5, 1980, by the Gallup Organization, Princeton, NJ.

69. These findings are supported by other surveys. Whitehead and Blankenhorn cite the *Washington Post* Poll and a survey by Mark Baldassare and Associates, which reveal that a majority of working mothers sampled in Washington, D. C., and Los Angeles would prefer to stay at home with young children, if finances permitted. Barbara Defoe Whitehead and David Blankenhorn, "Man, Woman, and Public Policy: Difference and Dependency in the American Conversation." Working paper, Institute for American Values, New York, 1991; Norval Glenn, "What the Numbers Say," *Family Affairs* 5:1/2, 5–7, 1992.

70. These findings are reported in Richard Wertheimer, Melissa Long, Sharon Vandivere, "Welfare Recipient's Attitudes toward Welfare, Nonmarital Childbearing and Work: Implications for Reform." Series B, No. B-37, The Urban Institute, Washington DC, June 2001.

71. Ministry of Social Affairs, *Danish Strategies: Families with Children at Work and at Home* (Copenhagen: Danish Ministry of Social Affairs, 1992).

72. Christoph Badelt, "Austria: Family Work, Paid Employment and Family Policy," in Sheila Kamerman and Alfred Kahn (eds.), *Child Care, Parental Leave, and the Under 3s: Policy Innovation in Europe* (New York: Auburn House, 1992), 47.

73. Michael Levin, "Feminism Stage Three"; Elizabeth Fox-Genovese, "Feminist Rights, Individualist Wrongs"; Katherine Kersten, "A Conservative Feminist Manifesto."

74. Wendy Kaminer, *A Fearful Freedom: Women's Flight from Equality*; Susan Faludi, *Backlash: The Undeclared War Against Women* (New York: Crown Publishers, 1991).

75. Deborah Fallows, *A Mother's Work* (Boston: Houghton Mifflin, 1985), 234.

76. Neil Gilbert, *Capitalism and the Welfare State* (New Haven: Yale University Press, 1983).

77. Income pooling is prevalent in American families, among whom about two-thirds of married couples with bank accounts have joint accounts only. Couples are more likely to have separate accounts in families where either the husband or wife had a previous divorce or in which wives are employed outside the home. Judith Treas, "Money in the Bank: Transaction Costs and the Economic Organization of Marriage," *American Sociological Review* 58:5, 723–734, 1993.

78. U.S. Bureau of the Census, *Statistical Abstract of the United States, 1990.* (Washington, DC: Government Printing Office, 1990); U.S. Bureau of the Census, *Statistical Abstract of the United States, 1992* (Washington, DC: Government Printing Office, 1992).

# 11

# Immigrant Families

## Sylvia Guendelman

The idea of the self-made man is a myth of such enduring resonance that it not only fuels our cultural imagination but guides our immigration policy. Inspired by the idea that Americans should pull themselves up by their boot straps, U.S. immigration policy leaves the fate of immigrants up to their own ingenuity and focuses instead on the regulation of border flows. This numerical approach is at the expense of a more nuanced policy that would address the vulnerability of particular immigrant groups, especially low-income immigrant children. Alarming evidence shows that the longer these children remain living in vulnerable American communities, the *less* likely they are to succeed on some measurable criteria of success, particularly relating to health. Practical and moral imperatives demand that policymakers prevent at-risk immigrant children from falling through the cracks of ill-conceived policy.

Given current trends in immigration and the fertility rates of immigrant women, the children of immigrants will be key wage earners in the future economy. By addressing their needs, especially in education and health, our society will be more equipped to meet the challenges of supporting the aging baby-boom generation. Economic rationale aside, facilitating the adaptation of immigrant children is a social necessity. Although it is hard to say whether immigration policy itself perpetuates misconceptions about immigrants, damaging stereotypes of immigrants persist in America. Based on imagined identity, these stereotypes distort facts about both immigrants and nonimmigrants. Common stereotypes portray immigrants as unemployed welfare dependents and young single mothers whose values are incompatible with "American culture." In fact, when socioeconomic and demographic factors are taken into account, immigrant families are less likely to depend on cash assistance, and more likely to fulfill the traditional ideal of a two-parent household with an at-home mother and a wage-earning father than native families. Policy easing the adaptation of immigrant children within a multicultural framework would help break down notions of "us" and "them" and foster a more tolerant American society.

In this chapter, we demystify immigrant families. We begin by presenting some general characteristics of immigrant children and their families and juxtapose these with examples of the striking diversity among these families. We then consider the sociocultural and economic implications of immigrant diversity, with a particular focus on adaptation. Next, we examine current U.S. immigration policy, evaluating the logic behind it and weighing its positive and negative effects. Finally, we suggest some policy strategies that would ameliorate existing gaps by protecting immigrant children and promoting their integration as productive, healthy members of a multicultural American society.

## Who Are Immigrant Families?

In order to talk about immigrants precisely, we have to define who they are. This proposition is deceptively simple. In fact, there are several ways to define immigrants and their families, based on common, legal, and social conventions. The term "immigrant" is widely applied to individuals whose experiences entering and residing in the United States are markedly different. The International Encyclopedia of the Social Sciences defines migration as "the relatively permanent movement of persons over a significant distance."[1] This and other common definitions of international migration imply that "all individuals who have relocated across national boundaries, whether temporarily or permanently, whether voluntary or involuntary, whether repetitively or on a single occasion, and for whatever purpose, may be considered immigrants."[2]

Legal definitions of immigrants break this unwieldy group into three categories, based on their mode of admission to the United States.[3] The first group is composed of documented immigrants who legally enter the United States for personal or economic reasons. Within this group, the largest single mode of admission involves marriage to a U.S. citizen. Immigration and Naturalization Service (INS) data from 1994 showed that immigration via marriage to a U.S. citizen has been growing much more rapidly than immigration via a parent or child linked to a U.S. citizen.[4] A second group is granted legal permission to reside in the United States because of political turmoil, violation of human rights, or natural catastrophe in their home countries. This group of humanitarian admissions includes refugees who legally enter the country after submitting a petition to immigrate, and asylees who petition to remain in the United States, usually after entering illegally.[5] The third category of immigrants is composed of those who reside illegally in the United States. Illegal immigrants have crossed the border without documentation or, more commonly, have violated the terms of their visas.[6]

Whether or not they hold American citizenship further differentiates immigrants. Legal immigrants may become U.S. citizens through the process of naturalization.[7] But citizenship is not uniform among members of immigrant families. The generous and uniquely American policy that grants those born on U.S. soil automatic U.S. citizenship accounts for the fact that 75 percent of children in immigrant families are citizens.[8] Mixed-status families with one or more citizen children and one or two noncitizen parents are further differentiated based on the legal status of the noncitizen parent(s) and older siblings.[9] In all, one in ten families with children in the United States are of mixed status.[10]

Members of immigrant families are also distinguished based on the generation to which they belong in relation to their family's entry into the United States. Those born outside of the United States who have emigrated from their country of origin are referred to as first-generation immigrants. Children born in the United States to at least one immigrant parent are second-generation immigrants. Finally, the children of these American-born parents make up the third generation.[11] Studies relating immigrant education, health, and employment outcomes to duration of stay in the United States show that generational distinctions bear socioeconomic as well as cultural significance. In this chapter, we use the terms "immigrant children," "children in immigrant families," and "children of immigrants" interchangeably when referring to the large group composed of first- and second-generation children. In more specific cases, we refer to a particular generation or distinguish between "native" or "U.S.-born" and "foreign-born" children.

In addition to the diversity they represent in legal categories, immigrants vary by country of origin, as well as ethnicity, culture, education, and employment. Later in this chapter we see how legal status and generation interplay with various social factors to inform the process of adaptation.

## Demographics, Historical Change, and the Future

The number of immigrants who enter and remain in the United States has been steadily increasing each decade since the 1960s. Between 1990 and 2000, an average of one million individuals immigrated to the United States each year.[12] Although the absolute numbers today match those of the early 1900s, the dramatic growth in the country's population as a whole means that the proportion of immigrants in the current U.S. population is only two-thirds of what it was at that time.[13] Of the one million immigrants who enter the United States each year, 700,000 are legal permanent residents, 100,000 to 150,000 are humanitarian admissions, and the remaining 200,000–300,000 are undocumented immigrants.[14]

Compared with earlier immigration waves, the composition of the immigrant population has changed dramatically. One key difference is in region of origin. At the beginning of the twentieth century, most of the foreign-born population emigrated from Europe, particularly Eastern Europe and Italy.[15] Today, the vast majority of immigrants are from Asia (25.5%) and Latin America (51.0%)—with one-fifth of total legal admissions and one-half of illegal aliens coming from Mexico.[16] The increase in immigration from these two regions has led to the development of Hispanic and Asian enclaves in urban areas, especially in those states receiving the greatest number of immigrants (New York, California, Michigan). At the same time, immigrants are spreading throughout the United States more than ever before. The Urban Institute projects that immigration from Asia and Latin America (based on demographic assumptions consistent with the 1990 Immigration Act) will continue to increase until 2030, at which time the proportion of foreign-born individuals in the total population will equal that of the historic peak in the early 1900s, at around 14 percent.[17]

In addition to hailing from different world regions, today's immigrants represent more ethnic diversity and are more easily identified by skin color. Nevertheless, historian Nancy Foner notes that a century ago the difference between a "swarthy" Italian and a "white" German was every bit as visible as the difference today between an "Asian American" and a "European American."[18] Whether Hispanics and Asians become integrated into a white American mainstream as immigrants of Irish, Jewish, and Italian ancestry have, or whether U.S. society rises above color lines remains to be seen. What is sure is that ethnic labeling as it exists now in the United States forces a degree of self-consideration and the distinction of "otherness" along ethnic lines. Ethnic diversity also argues for the need to expand the dialogue on race issues beyond the "white" versus "black" dichotomy.

Contemporary immigrants are also distinguished from past immigrants by their educational and economic status. One hundred years ago, a booming industrial economy drew unskilled immigrants to the United States and provided them with paying jobs. Today, the postindustrial service economy demands skilled labor. More than ever before, educated immigrants are coming to the United States who fit this demand. About one in four immigrant children have a college-educated father, but at the other end of the spectrum, children in immigrant families are more likely than children in nonimmigrant families to have fathers who have very low levels of education.[19] And immigrants without professional skills face shrinking opportunities for employment and economic advancement. While the success of new immigrants depends largely on their level of education, female immigrants of all education levels fare better today than female immigrants at the turn of the century. Although working outside the home brings its own set of complications, the economic opportunities available to women arriving in the United States today provides a sharp contrast with the dearth of opportunities available to immigrant women in the past.[20] This is doubly important since females have comprised the majority (55%) of immigrants to the United States since 1941.[21]

The legal climate today also differs from that of the past. Until 1965, immigrants faced exclusionary laws based on racial quotas. These laws have since been replaced by laws based on the principle of family reunification. Today, three-fourths of legal immigrants to this country enter through family-based preference categories. Although in 1996 the law changed to require higher economic standing on the part of family sponsors of new immigrants, U.S. immigration policy remains extremely generous.[22] Family reunification and the provision of automatic citizenship for U.S.-born children provide an amount of legitimacy for the children of immigrants that is unmatched by any other country in the world.

Looking to the future, population growth in the United States will be fueled not only by immigration but also by the fertility of immigrants. Immigrants from Latin America and Asia tend to have larger families than natives or European immigrants.[23] Forty-two percent of households headed by an immigrant from Central America have at least five members, whereas less than 10 percent of European families are this large.[24] By 2030, immigrants and their families will account for 60 percent of the country's population growth.[25] With the majority of this growth occurring among ethnic minorities, 40 percent of the population in 2040 will consist of racial and ethnic minorities, including 18 percent Latinos and 10 percent Asians.[26] In some bellwether states, such as California, the rapid growth of Asian and Hispanic populations has already created a "majority minority state." According to the 2000 Census, the state's population, which grew 13.8 percent in the last decade, was 46.7 percent White nonminority, 32 percent Hispanic, 10.8 percent Asian, 6.4 percent African-American, and almost 4 percent other minority.

Increases in ethnic diversity will be most concentrated among children. Estimates project that by 2040, 75 percent of the elderly will be white, compared with 59 percent of working-age adults and 50 percent of children.[27] This change in the ethnic composition of the population has far-reaching implications. According to studies by the National Research Council of the Institute of Medicine, the aging baby-boom generation will depend increasingly for its economic support on the productivity, health, and civic participation of adults who grew up in minority immigrant families. Furthermore, the long-term consequences of contemporary immigration for the American economy and society will hinge more on the future prospects of children in immigrant families than on the fate of their parents.[28] For both ethical and economic reasons, we must ask whether immigrant children are being prepared to take on the social and financial responsibilities of adulthood, and whether current policies facilitate, deter, or ignore this process. To get at this question, we first assess whether immigrant families are attaining the building blocks of success: education, income, and health.

## General Characteristics: Education, Income, and Health

U.S. Census data indicate that on average, immigrants have lower levels of education than nonimmigrants and have lower incomes.[29] Often these incomes have to feed larger families. Given these indicators, it is not surprising that immigrants are more likely than natives to live in poverty. To make up for lower wages, immigrant-headed families often pool the incomes of several wage earners. For instance, a study of Mexican immigrants living in San Jose, California, found that in addition to pooling incomes of male workers, extended households depended on women's earnings from formal and informal jobs and the presence of single siblings and elderly parents and their wage and nonwage activities (e.g., taking care of the children, housework).[30] This helps to explain why income disparities between immigrant and nonimmigrant households are less pronounced than expected.

Overall, fathers in immigrant families with children have a rate of labor force participation equivalent to fathers in native families with children, although fathers in immigrant families have fewer chances of working full time year-round.[31] Whereas unemployment rates of native and foreign-born men are similar, foreign-born women tend to have higher unemployment rates than native women.[32] Because women in immigrant families are less likely to work outside of the home and because divorce among immigrant couples is less common, immigrant families are the most likely group to approximate the American traditional family—a two-parent household in which the father is the sole "breadwinner."[33] Overall, immigrants are more likely to work in a service occupation, while non-immigrants are better represented in managerial, professional, and clerical positions.[34] Since children's well-being depends largely on the attributes and living conditions of their parents, the socioeconomic and marital status of immigrant parents largely projects their children's futures.

The health status of immigrant children is harder to synopsize. On the one hand, immigrant children have difficulty accessing health care and use medical services less than their native-born counterparts. Findings from a national health survey showed that in 1997, foreign-born children were two and one-half times more likely than native-born children to be uninsured.[35] One explanation is that recently arrived immigrant parents are much less likely than natives to be employed in jobs that provide health insurance benefits to their families.[36] Furthermore, immigrant families are often reluctant to enroll in public insurance programs for fear of jeopardizing their green card or future citizenship status or that of other relatives.[37] Meeting the financial requirements for medical services is burdensome for the many immigrants in low-income occupations. Without insurance or the means to pay for health care, immigrants are less likely to seek care in a doctor's office.[38] The lack of English language proficiency compounds the access barriers for many families. Thus immigrants and their children often miss out on comprehensive, longitudinal, and preventative services including prenatal care, dental care, and immunizations.[39]

Moreover, immigrant children are at higher risk for certain health problems. Sending countries are often characterized by poor health conditions. Foreign-born children often have not received proper immunizations, and they may enter the United States carrying infectious diseases such as malaria, amebiasis, schistosomiasis, congenital syphilis, hepatitis A, hepatitis B, or tuberculosis.[40] Once in the United States, these conditions may persist if access to care is limited. Additionally, American doctors may be unfamiliar with such diseases and lack experience in their diagnosis and treatment.[41] Many refugee children are malnourished and may suffer long-term effects following deprivation of food or medical care in unstable political situations, including refugee camps.[42] Immigrant children also suffer from higher incidences of lead poisoning and pesticide exposure. Exposure to environmental toxins may have occurred in the country of origin or after immigration to the United States. Immigrant children often live in low-income housing that is more likely to harbor unhealthy levels of lead, and agricultural workers, many of whom are children and adolescents, are particularly vulnerable to pesticide exposure.[43] Finally, immigrant children tend to have poorer dental health and more vision problems.[44]

Immigrant children are also vulnerable to mental and behavioral problems. Researchers from the National Research Council of the Institute of Medicine note that "the immigration process is an event of extraordinary intensity and stress in which individuals are torn by conflicting social and cultural demands while trying to adapt to an unfamiliar and sometimes hostile environment, which may well be discriminatory."[45] Many immigrants, particularly refugees, have witnessed atrocities or experienced severe personal trauma in their country of origin. These individuals, many of them children, may suffer from post-traumatic stress disorder. As many as one-third of children exposed to political violence and trauma may have subsequent severe psychological problems.[46] Earlier trauma, especially when compounded with the psychological stress caused by moving, affects the mental health of immigrant families upon arrival and influences the ease with which these families settle into their new environment.

On the other hand, newly arrived immigrants originating from Latin America and Southeast Asia demonstrate surprisingly good health outcomes despite the negative exposures and increased socioeconomic risks and barriers to health care associated with immigrant status. Epidemiological studies reveal that immigrant mothers bear healthy babies, as indicated by low rates of low birthweight infants and low infant mortality rates.[47] For instance, despite risk factors such as delaying prenatal care, having large families with shorter birth spacing, and high rates of teen pregnancy, foreign-born Mexican mothers enjoy positive birth outcomes on a par with white Americans who are native-born.[48] Ths is partly explained by healthier habits among foreign-born Mexican women of reproductive age, including better nutrition and lower incidence of smoking and alcohol and drug use. The traditional orientation to motherhood among Mexican-born women and the respect for preganancy expressed by their partners may also positively impact birth outcomes.[49] Furthermore, with the exception of certain respiratory conditions, immigrant children have fewer acute and chronic health problems.[50] They are also less likely to suffer from unintentional injury—the primary cause of mortality and serious disability among American children and adolescents.[51] However, epidemiological research has also shown that these positive outcomes are not lasting. As individuals stay longer in the United States and from generation to generation, health outcomes among immigrant children and adolescents deteriorate.

## Recognizing Diversity

Although immigrant families share some general characteristics, they are distinguished more by diversity than homogeneity. In fact, among all ethnic groups in America today, native and foreign born, immigrants from different source countries account for both the highest and lowest rates of education, home ownership, poverty, and fertility.[52] Thus difference in region of origin not only contributes to cultural, linguistic, and ethnic diversity among immigrants, but also is an indicator of social and economic status.

Whereas nonimmigrants are more likely to have an intermediate level of education, immigrants are concentrated at opposite ends of the education spectrum. Educational attainment of immigrants is determined in part by the educational resources they bring from their home countries and by their legal status on arrival. Illegal immigrants, formerly illegal immigrants, and refugees tend to have lower levels of education than legal immigrants or natives.[53] Since illegal immigrants come predominantly from Mexico and Central America, and refugees are more likely to come from Southeast Asia and, increasingly, from Africa, we circle back to region of origin as a possible indicator of educational achievement.

As with education, the professional skills of immigrants are often predicted by nationality. Highly skilled immigrants dominate immigration flows from India, Korea, the Philippines, and China, whereas manual laborers and low-wage service workers are more likely to come from Mexico, El Salvador, and the Dominican Republic.[54]

Income and poverty levels also may vary by nationality, with the likelihood that low incomes and high poverty render Mexican and Central American immigrants, Haitian, Dominican and Southeast Asian immigrants the most vulnerable.[55] Altogether, children from twelve countries including those from the regions mentioned above, account for about half of all such children. Again, the legal status of these groups is significant. Many Mexican and Central American immigrants enter the United

States illegally and are therefore prohibited by law from working in industries that offer high-level positions. Immigrants from refugee source countries tend to have incomes that fall between those of Mexican and Central Americans, and native income levels. Immigrants from sending countries of primarily legal, nonrefugee immigrants have incomes comparable to those of natives.[56]

As with education, employment, and income, health status varies significantly by country of origin. This variation is not surprising, given that the environmental conditions and behavioral factors that impact health status are to some extent determined by regional context.

Birth outcomes, including low birth weight and infant mortality, is one area in which health differences by the country of origin of the mother have been studied. For instance, among Hispanic populations, Cuban-Americans have the best birth outcomes.[57] In contrast, Puerto Ricans have a higher percentage of unmarried and teen mothers, are more likely to smoke during pregnancy, and have the poorest birth outcomes.[58] Mexican-Americans are on a lower socioeconomic rung than Puerto Ricans but have better birth outcomes, showing that although socioeconomic status is a significant determinant of health, it is not conclusive.

Like the Hispanic population, Asian Pacific Islanders (A/PIs) are characterized by diversity. According to 1990 U.S. Census data, there are twenty-nine different Asian groups and twenty Pacific Islander groups that collectively speak more than 100 different languages.[59] Asian immigrants come from countries with very different socioeconomic and health profiles. Many Asian immigrants are refugees, especially those from Southeast Asian countries, including Cambodia, Vietnam, and Laos, while many others are well-educated "brain-drain" professionals from countries like India, Taiwan, and Korea. Asian Pacific Islanders are often construed as a "model minority."[60] As a group they have the lowest infant mortality rate and a relatively low rate of low birth weight infants compared with other U.S. ethnic minority groups.[61] These positive birth outcomes may be explained in part by the fact that A/PI mothers have low rates of inadequate prenatal care and high rates of insurance coverage.[62] Another explanation is that A/PI females, regardless of generation, generally refrain from risky behaviors, including smoking, drinking, and substance abuse.[63] Yet one notable exception to the overall positive birth outcomes for A/PIs is among Filipinas, who deliver a relatively high percentage of low birth weight babies when compared to nine other ethnic groups.[64]

In each decade since the turn of the century, African immigrants have been admitted to the United States in larger numbers. They have also represented a larger share of total immigrants admitted to the United States: while Africans represented 1.8 percent of legal immigrants in the 1970s, they represented 3.9 percent of total legal admissions from 1991 to 2000.[65] As these numbers increase, the profile of African immigrants is also changing. While in the past African immigrants were predominantly educated professionals, most recent African immigrants have migrated from rural areas and represent lower levels of educational attainment.[66] A study comparing infant mortality and low birth weight among foreign and U.S.-born women of ten ethnic groups including non-Latino African-Americans found that African immigrants have the highest rate of infant mortality and low birth weight in comparison to other immigrant groups in the United States.[67]

## Adaptation

Nationality, legal status, education, family income, and health mark immigrants on arrival and suggest their socioeconomic futures. According to a recent report by the National Academy of Sciences, children in immigrant families from about two dozen countries experience similar socioeconomic conditions as those in third-and-later-generations. At the other extreme are children with high poverty rates from twelve countries whose parents increase their level of education from the first to the second to the third generation, but most do not attain more than a high school education and they remain relatively poor.[68] In addition to individual and family attributes, contextual factors such as the size and nature of immigrant flows may predispose immigrants to challenges in adapting to U.S. society. Yet circumstances on arrival do not seal an immigrant family's fate. Immigrants' home-country identities are challenged the moment they set foot in the United States—and for the duration of their stay. The ways immigrants incorporate and resist American culture, as families and individuals, vary as much as their socioeconomic and health statuses. Although adaptation and prosperity are linked, *how* they are linked is a matter of debate in both scholarly and policy circles. Understanding the ramifications of this link is crucial because government policies that help or hinder immigrant children's adaptation will consequently impact their health and economic prospects. To envision policy that is more responsive to children's needs, we need to investigate how the adaptation process maps out future health and income.

Immigrant adaptation traditionally was construed as a linear process in which immigrants adopt, to good end, characteristics of a dominant American culture. In this model, immigrants give up their individual cultural identity as they blend into the great melting pot. With rates of ethnic intermarriage higher than ever, the melting pot seems alive and well.[69] Nevertheless, in the last twenty-five years, social scientists have come to regard assimilation as more of a two-way process of acculturation, in which successful adaptation depends upon the communities receiving immigrants as much as the immigrants trying to fit into (or rebuff) these communities. This paradigm shift has called into question the idea that native culture is a detriment to success in the United States, that American culture is monolithic, and that culture is the only element in the adaptation process.[70] Recent social theory responds to these issues by differentiating between patterns of adaptation. According to the theory of segmented assimilation, three basic trajectories are possible for immigrants adapting to American society: the first leads to growing acculturation and integration into the white middle class; the second ends in poverty and acculturation into the underclass; and the third combines economic advancement with the deliberate preservation of the immigrant community's values through solidarity.[71] Ultimately, the assimilation path an immigrant child takes depends on the social context into which the child is inserted—and the response of that receiving community. We use the segmented assimilation model to situate seemingly conflicting data, while reiterating the uniqueness of each immigrant family's experience.

Research shows that while immigrants are represented in academic fast tracks and prestigious high school contests, many others particularly children in low socioeconomic strata are vulnerable to school failure, gangs, and youth crime.[72] Accumulating evidence suggests that the educational achievement of children in immigrant families deteriorates over time in the United States.[73] Studies employing large national data sets,[74] ethnographic studies,[75] and a study focusing on cross-national students[76] consistently show lower educational achievement and educational aspiration among second- and third-generation adolescent students compared with their first generation peers.

Since educational attainment is the primary indicator of successful economic and cultural transition into American society,[77] it seems paradoxical that immigrant children lose motivation in school as they become increasingly acculturated. The fact that immigrant families often find themselves at the bottom of the social hierarchy, where high academic aspirations are uncommon among native and immigrant children alike, helps explain this phenomenon. Hispanic girls drop out of high school at twice the rate of African-American girls and more than three times the rate of white nonminority girls in the United States.[78] Explanations for the high dropout rate among Hispanic girls include teen pregnancy and its attendant cultural factors, a lack of identifiable role models who defy traditional expectations, and economic pressures in immigrant families, which push education down on the list of priorities. Immigrant children who live in inner-city ghettos are exposed to poor schools, violence, drugs, and a generally disruptive social environment, which reinforces messages "not to sell out" to middle-class values of achievement and competence.[79] Those children living in poor farm-working communities are no more likely to be exposed to middle-class values than their urban counterparts.

Whether their families settle in urban or rural areas, the majority of immigrant children, as ethnic minorities, face the added hardship of racial discrimination. These subjective experiences often reinforce oppositional attitudes and behaviors toward the mainstream culture and to parents. For children who have little hope of upward social mobility, focusing on school performance is not a useful coping mechanism. Without absorption by the middle class, and with a lack of meaningful role models, children in immigrant families who adapt to their new surroundings and peers are not likely to experience an improvement in their education or their educational aspiration and, consequently, their economic status. Given the stratification of American society, such vulnerable immigrants are just as likely, if not more likely, to find themselves adjusting to life on the bottom of the hierarchy rather than the ever-shrinking middle.[80] That is, they are subject to downward assimilation.

While first-generation immigrant children may find themselves in depressed environments, strong attachments to family and to ethnic community may protect them from the effects of unsupportive educational systems and peers. Zhou notes that recent research has shown that immigrant children from intact (especially two-natural-parent) families or from families associated with tightly knit social networks consistently show better psychological conditions, higher levels of academic achievement, and stronger educational aspirations than those in single-parent or socially isolated families.[81] First-generation immigrant families are much more likely to be intact than those of later generations, especially those living in poor areas.[82] In addition, immigrant parents who have struggled to migrate to the United States with the hope of upward mobility are more likely to emphasize the importance of education to their children. Close ties to family and culture, especially among Asian immigrants, may strengthen this motivation because of the value placed on education in Asian cultures.[83] According to Zhou, immigrant students who retain strong cultural and family identity tend to outpace others in school, including their native-born European-American peers, because their immigrant families reinforce the values of hard work and educational achievement. In situations where strong human capital prevails, immigrant children follow a hybrid assimilation model in which they are upwardly mobile (represented by their educational achievement) despite exposure to disenfranchised populations.

Family bonds and ties to native culture seem not only to protect immigrant children living in poor conditions, but also those who are fortunate enough to live in middle-class communities and are exposed to motivated children in affluent school districts. Thus the achievements of immigrant children benefiting from the safety of a middle-class environment and the added value of strong cultural identity increase their chances of upward mobility.

Cultural cohesion is not only a potential asset within the family, but in larger ethnic communities. Many immigrant families settle in enclaves established by their compatriots. More than physical neighborhoods represented by ghettos or barrios, cultural enclaves are networks of social and economic resources. The Cuban community in Miami is one of the most notable examples. Immigrant children who grow up in ethnic enclaves have the benefit of a social network that not only shelters them from racism and bolsters their psychosocial well-being, but increases their educational and employment opportunities.[84] As rates of interethnic marriages increase, cultural enclaves will perhaps be less important. It remains to be seen whether such marriages will facilitate or hinder immigrant adaptation.

However, not all immigrant families have the benefit of cultural enclaves, and not all are able to maintain family unity. Immigrant children
acculturate at a much faster pace than their parents. With increased duration of U.S. residence, children in immigrant families often come to
identify more with American youths. The resulting cultural conflict within
the home can have a destructive effect on family bonds. In addition, traditional family roles may break down as a result of delayed family reunification, or when both parents work outside the home. In these situations, children spend less time with their parents, particularly their
mothers, and the new economic status of the mother may challenge the
authority of the male household.[85] Furthermore, parental authority is
compromised when parents must depend on their children as interpreters.
When the pace of parent and child acculturation does not coincide, shame
and anger may set in. Zhou writes that immigrant children are likely to
rebel against parental educational expectations and to assimilate into an
adversarial academic orientation in response to discrimination, subcultural
pressures, and blocked mobility.[86]

Similar to educational achievement, research suggests that with increasing acculturation to U.S. society, immigrant health deteriorates. Data
from over 20,000 adolescents obtained from the National Longitudinal
Study of Adolescent Health, which consisted of a stratified probability
sample of high schools nationwide, found that second- and later-genera-
tion immigrant adolescents had worse physical and emotional health outcomes than first-generation immigrant adolescents, and they engaged in
more risk-taking behaviors.[87] Harris found that second-generation youth
were more likely than the first generation to report poor or fair health,
to have learning disabilities, asthma, and to experience obesity, to have
initiated sexual activity at a younger age, and to have engaged in delinquency, violence, and substance abuse. Even among first-generation immigrants, almost regardless of country of origin, health outcomes deteriorate and risk-taking behaviors increase with length of time in the United
States.[88] The link between increasing acculturation and the high-risk behaviors of urban youth, including smoking, drinking, and drug abuse,
sexual promiscuity, gang violence, and decline in nutritional status help
explain this phenomenon.[89] Harris writes that on virtually every measure
of health status, immigrants who have lived in the United States five years
or less are healthier than foreign-born persons who have lived in the
United States ten years or more.[90] As with education, deterioration in
health is most likely to occur in the absence of protective factors, which
include cultural cohesion and exposure to the American middle class.

## Immigration and Immigrant Policy: An Overview

Thus far, we have emphasized the social and economic significance of
immigrant children in American society and the diversity of this population. Defying negative stereotypes about them, many immigrant chil-

dren are healthy, academically successful, and well adapted to American life. Unfortunately, many others are overwhelmed by the risk factors and negative influences that attend immigrant status and consequently face poor prospects for the future. Whether immigrant children gain the tools for upward mobility or are trapped in a downward spiral depends on the social, economic, and health resources they bring from their home countries and the availability of these resources for them in the United States. Access to social and economic resources in the community of residence influences the adaptation process of immigrant children. Self-help efforts within the community are important sources of social capital, but they need to be supported and supplemented by donors. Federal, state, and local governments are positioned to ameliorate deficits in immigrant children's resources, as they do for disadvantaged members of the native-born population. However, the extent to which governing bodies are able and willing to provide necessary resources for immigrant children depends on political tradition, public opinion, the economy, and leadership.

There are two major policy avenues for dealing with immigrant issues in the United States. Immigration policy handles the question of which immigrants should be admitted to the United States and in what numbers; immigrant policy addresses the needs of immigrants who are already living in the United States. The United States allocates resources to both policy channels, but traditionally has emphasized immigration policy over immigrant policy. A 1999 report from the Urban Institute notes that while the United States has long had an immigration policy, the nation's immigrant policy has been implicit and de facto, made up of a variety of rules governing noncitizens' access to education, public benefits, and the like.[91] Immigration critics, led by the Federation for American Immigration Reform (FAIR), lobby for increased investment in border control and restrictive immigration legislation, and have a laissez-faire attitude toward policies that facilitate adaptation. FAIR posits that shaping the size and composition of immigrant flow is the key to maintaining social and economic balance in the United States. These immigration reform activists believe that by admitting too many unskilled workers from the developing world, current immigration law facilitates the creation of a burdensome class of immigrants, which threatens the livelihood of the native poor, compromises the environment, increases crime, and undermines the cultural integrity of American society.[92] In contrast, other reformers uphold the importance of immigration policy, but not as a substitute for nuanced immigrant policy. Members of this camp believe that the neglect of immigrant policy contributes to immigrant-related economic and social ills, as well as a lost opportunity to increase the future contributions of immigrant children to the United States. Since the September 11 terrorist attacks, politicians have concentrated most of their efforts on national security issues, proposing immigration laws that control who can come to the United States and how entry can best be monitored. Scant attention has been placed on immigrant policies that facilitate adaptation of newcomers.

In recent years, public opinion has swung dramatically on the question of immigration and immigrant policy. Resentment of immigrants seemed to be high when President Clinton signed the Personal Work and Work Opportunity Reconciliation act of 1996 (otherwise known as Welfare Reform) into law. This legislation represented the most sweeping changes to immigrant integration policy in sixty years, distinguishing for the first time between the rights of legal immigrants and those of citizens. Welfare Reform required individuals to prove that they were U.S. citizens, qualified immigrants, or refugees before receiving any federal benefits.[93] While certain federal programs were exempted, including vaccination programs and emergency Medicaid, many other crucial forms of support, such as Social Security Insurance (SSI), food stamps, and Temporary Assistance for Needy Families (TANF) were no longer available to many immigrants.

Overall, Welfare Reform has resulted in a chilling effect in the use of public benefits among immigrants, even those still legally eligible for such benefits.[94] Confusion about who was entitled to federal benefits and fear of the repercussions of using them resulted in a disproportionate drop in the use of public benefits from 1994 to 1997 among noncitizen and refugee households when compared to citizen households.[95] Immigrant children have been particularly impacted by Welfare Reform. Although benefits were restored to noncitizen children in 1998, three-quarters of immigrant children were already citizens. A larger source of strain results not from whether the children themselves receive benefits, but whether their parents do. Thus citizen children in mixed-status families receive fewer benefits now than they did before Welfare Reform.

Other policies have brought about the devolution of responsibility for fulfilling immigrant needs from the federal government to state and local government bodies. States, newly responsible for immigrant welfare, have responded with a "patchwork" of policies to fill gaps left by restricted federal programs.[96] A recent Urban Institute Study surveying and analyzing state policies noted several trends from state to state. With the exception of Texas, states with large immigrant populations (California, Illinois, New York) have made generous decisions to provide assistance to immigrants. Some states with smaller immigrant populations have also been generous, notably Nebraska and Maine. Those states that already have strong safety nets for their native-born population tend to reflect this largesse in their assistance programs for immigrants. Finally, states with higher per capita income are more likely to provide assistance than states with lower per capita income—meaning that states with the neediest populations provide the fewest benefits to immigrants.[97] In terms of assistance provided, states are generally more likely to provide health benefits than cash benefits (though some provide neither) and less likely to assist immigrants who entered the United States after August 22, 1996 (thereby drawing a line between pre- and post-Welfare Reform enactment immigrants). In all, new state policies have failed to fully fill the gap. Interestingly enough, while California has been known for anti-immigrant rhetoric, it provides more assistance to immigrants than almost every other state. Perhaps the economic and social reality of hosting the largest number of immigrants in the country has compelled the government of California to pass relatively progressive legislation. The wide discretion that states now have in granting benefits to immigrant families is likely to increase disparities among immigrant children.

Although legislation mitigating the effects of Welfare Reform has been instituted at both federal and state levels, whether these amendments have succeeded in reinstating safety nets for immigrants in health and welfare remains to be seen. Preliminary evidence suggests that state measures have not succeeded in replacing benefits extended to immigrants by the federal government before Welfare Reform. A 2000 study by Guendelman et al. found that disparities may be growing in health insurance coverage for immigrant children as a result of immigration and Welfare Reform. A critical question is whether access to existing benefits will remain limited because of lack of information about immigrants' rights and a general climate of fear.

Assistance programs are essential because they support basic needs, but they are not sufficient to ensure positive health and economic success. The evidence explored in this chapter suggests the need for policies that are oriented toward children's adaptation—immigrant policies that promise upward mobility rather than mere subsistence. Children everywhere have the same needs; however, the fact that many immigrant children are particularly vulnerable means that specially targeted resources may be required to meet their needs. We propose a range of policy approaches that, by fostering adaptation, would improve immigrant children's chances for healthy lives.

Positively affecting immigrant youth's adaptation experience requires changing the social and economic conditions that frame that experience. From the broadest perspective, the United States would do well to focus more on reducing the number of needy immigrants who come here in the first place. Trade agreements like NAFTA, immigration agreements, and foreign aid promote economic well-being beyond American borders and represent long-term steps to curtail immigration or improve the status of immigrants coming to the United States. On our own soil, reducing inequalities in income, education, and health care would maximize chances for upward mobility and eliminate much of the social tension caused by unbalanced resource distribution. Of course, effecting these kind of national and international changes is a long-term process requiring significant capital and political will. Focusing policies on the improvement of social and economic conditions from a community perspective would have more immediate impact.

Efforts should channel more support to grass-roots organizations that sustain communities by building social networks and providing self-help.

Faith-based organizations have an impressive track record of providing services and support. Bolstering grass-roots organizations would not only strengthen the delivery of services to immigrant families in need, but create a ripple effect by encouraging immigrants to act as role models for other immigrants and increasing the stake of local communities in their well-being. Paired with local capacity-building efforts, media campaigns promoting cultural identity within a multicultural framework of tolerance would create an atmosphere of inclusion and validation for immigrant children struggling to adapt to life in the United States. Similarly, information campaigns on the legal rights of immigrants could promote social harmony by increasing immigrant use of essential benefits and decreasing the climate of exclusion. Culturally appropriate health interventions are also needed to prevent the development of chronic disease among immigrant children and to increase the coping skills they need to resist risky behaviors.

Education is another universal need that is especially important for vulnerable immigrant children. Welfare Reform cut many immigrants out of programs such as Headstart, despite the fact that low-income immigrant children may be in greatest need of such programs. Policymakers should ensure the quality of basic education for all immigrants and reinstate supplementary education programs for them like Headstart. Given the significance of language acquisition in educational achievement and future employment, after-school programs that focus on English literacy improvement should be vigorously promoted. However, efforts to improve English language skills need to target immigrant children without overlooking the needs of immigrant parents. With a solid command of English and adequate job training, many immigrants would earn higher wages and be better equipped to improve the educational performance of their children.[98] Outreach efforts should encourage immigrant parents, regardless of their education level, to be involved in their children's education.

Currently, the political environment that can translate many of these recommendations into concrete policies is in a state of flux. In addition to sorting out the effects of domestic policies that were recently implemented such as the devolution of federal responsibilities in granting immigrant benefits to states, the country is grappling with the aftermath of September 11. This experience may profoundly influence immigration and immigrant policies in the future.

In sum, there are wide disparities in socioeconomic, educational and health conditions that characterize children in immigrant families from different countries of origin. These differences not withstanding, children from a dozen countries who account for about half of all children, now experience poverty rates that are comparable to those experienced by disadvantaged minority children in America. Obviously these children cannot pull themselves up by their own bootstraps. To prevent these children from becoming permanent members of an underclass, and to ensure that they can become productive adults who are able to contribute to support an increasingly aging population, long-term immigrant policies are required. They may even demand change at the deepest cultural levels. Although the United States has the most generous immigration laws of any country in the world, we need sustained change in educational, health and mental health policies that protect immigrant children's rights, reduce disparities and foster opportunities for their strong integration into society.

# Notes

1. Cited in S. Loue, "Defining the Immigrant," in S. Loue (ed.), *Handbook of Immigrant Health* (New York: Plenum Press, 1998), 19–36.

2. Ibid.

3. M. Fix and J. Passel, *Immigration and Immigrants: Setting the Record Straight* (Washington, DC: Urban Institute, 1994).

4. R. Rumbaut, "Ties That Bind: Immigration and Immigrant Families in the United States," in A. Booth, A. C. Crouter, and N. Landale (eds.), *Immigration and the Family: Research and Policy on U.S. Immigrants*. (Mahwah, NJ: Lawrence Erlbaum Associates, 1997), 3–46

5. Ibid.

6. Ibid.

7. E. Charney and D. Hernandez, *From Generation to Generation* (Washington, DC: National Academy Press, 1998).

8. M. Fix and W. Zimmerman, *All under One Roof: Mixed Status Families in an Era of Reform* (Washington, DC: Urban Institute, 1999).

9. Ibid.

10. Urban Institute calculations based on 1997 U.S. Census data.

11. Charney and Hernandez, *From Generation to Generation*.

12. D. Spain, "The Debate in the United States over Immigration," in *U.S. Society and Values* (Electronic Journal of the U.S. Information Agency) 4(2), 1999.

13. Ibid.

14. Fix and Passel, *Immigration and Immigrants*.

15. Ibid.

16. M. Zhou, "Growing Up American: The Challenge Confronting Immigrant Children and Children of Immigrants," *Annual Review of Sociology* 23:63–95, 1997.

17. Fix and Passel, *Immigration and Immigrants*.

18. N. Foner, *From Ellis Island to JFK: New York's Two Great Waves of Immigration* (New York: Russell Sage Foundation, 2000).

19. Charney and Hernandez, *From Generation to Generation*.

20. Foner, *From Ellis Island to JFK*.

21. Rumbaut, "Ties That Bind."

22. B. L. Lowell, "Immigrant Integration and Pending Legislation: Observations on Empirical Projections," in A. Booth, A. C. Crouter, and N. Landale (eds), *Immigration and the Family: Research and Policy on U.S. Immigrants* (Mahwah, NJ: Lawrence Erlbaum Associates, 1997), 271–280.

23. L. Lollock, "The Foreign-born Population in the United States: March 2000" (Washington, DC: U.S. Census Bureau, Department of Commerce, 2001).

24. Ibid.

25. Fix and Passel, *Immigration and Immigrants.*

26. Ibid.

27. Charney and Hernandez, *From Generation to Generation.*

28. Ibid.

29. Lollock, "Foreign-born Population in the United States."

30. C. Zlolniski, "Working but Poor: Mexican Immigrant Workers in a Low Income Barrio in San Jose," *CPS Brief* 8(9):7–16, 1996.

31. Charney and Hernandez, *From Generation to Generation.*

32. Ibid.

33. Ibid.

34. Lollock, "Foreign-born Population in the United States."

35. S. Guendelman et al.,"Unfriendly Shores: How Immigrant Children Fare in the U.S. Health System," *Health Affairs* 20(January/February):257–266, 2001.

36. F. LeClere et al., "Health Care Utilization, Family Context, and Adaptation among Immigrants to the United States," *Journal of Health and Social Behavior* 35(December):370–384, 1994.

37. Guendelman et al., "Unfriendly Shores."

38. Ibid.

39. American Academy of Pediatrics Committee on Community Health Services, "Health Care for Children of Immigrant Families," *Pediatrics* 100(July):153–156, 1997.

40. Ibid.

41. Ibid.

42. K. Olness, "Refugee Health," in Loue (ed.), *Handbook of Immigrant Health*, 227–242.

43. Charney and Hernandez, *From Generation to Generation.*

44. Ibid.

45. Board on Children and Families, Commission on Behavioral and Social Sciences and Education, National Research Council, and Institute of Medicine, "Immigrant Children and Their Families: Issues for Research and Policy," *The Future of Children* 5(2):72–89, 1995.

46. Olness, "Refugee Health."

47. S. Guendelman, "Effect of United States Residence on Birth Outcomes among Mexican Immigrants: An Exploratory Study, *American Journal of Epidemiology* 142(9):S30–S38, 1995.

48. S. Guendelman, "Health and Disease among Hispanics," in Loue (ed.), *Handbook of Immigrant Health*, 277–302.

49. S. Guendelman et al., "Orientations to Motherhood and Male Partner Support among Women in Mexico and Mexican-Origin Women in the United States," *Social Science and Medicine* 52:1805–1813, 2001.

50. Charney and Hernandez, *From Generation to Generation.*

51. Ibid.

52. R. Rumbaut, "Assimilation and Its Discontents: Between Rhetoric and Reality," *International Migration Review* 31(4,Winter):923–959, 1997.

53. Fix and Passel, *Immigration and Immigrants.*

54. Rumbaut, "Ties That Bind."

55. Lollock, "Foreign-born Population in the United States"; Charney and Hernandez, *From Generation to Generation.*

56. Fix and Passel, *Immigration and Immigrants.*

57. B. Cohen et al., "Ethnicity, Maternal Risk, and Birthweight among Hispanics in Massachusetts, 1987–89," *Public Health Report*. 108(3):363–371, 1993; S. J. Ventura, "Birth of Hispanic Parentage, 1985," Monthly Vital Statistics Reports, National Center for Health Statistics, Hyattsville, MD, 36(11)88–112, 1988.

58. Guendelman, "Health and Disease among Hispanics."

59. S. Loue et al., "HIV Prevention in U.S. Asian Pacific Islander Communities: An Innovative Approach." *Journal of Health Care for the Poor and Underserved* 7(4):364–376, 1996.

60. E. Takada et al., "Asian Pacific Islander Health," in Loue (ed.), *Handbook of Immigrant Health*, 303–328

61. N. Landale et al., "Immigration and Infant Health: Birth Outcomes of Immigrant and Native-Born Women," in D. Hernandez (ed.), *Children of Immigrants* (Washington, DC: National Academy Press, 1999).

62. L. Mayeno and S. M. Hirota, "Access to Health Care," in N. W. S. Zane et al. (eds.), *Confronting Critical Health Issues of Asian and Pacific Islander Americans* (Thousand Oaks, CA: Sage, 1994), 347–375.

63. Landale et al., "Immigration and Infant Health."

64. Ibid.

65. *2000 Statistical Yearbook of the Immigration and Naturalization Service* (United States Department of Justices, 2002).

66. B. R. McCaw and P. DeLay, "Demographics and Disease Prevalence of Two New Refugee Groups in San Francisco: The Ethiopian and Afghan Refugees," *Western Journal of Medicine* 143:271–275, 1985. M. Faust et al., "African Health," in Loue (ed.), *Handbook of Immigrant Health*, 329–347.

67. Landale et al., "Immigration and Infant Health."

68. Charney and Hernandez, *From Generation to Generation*.

69. Data on California, U.S. Census 2000.

70. A. Portes and M. Zhou, "Should Immigrants Assimilate?" *Public Interest* 116(18):18–34, 1994; Rumbaut, "Ties That Bind"; Zhou, "Growing Up American."

71. Portes and Zhou, "Should Immigrants Assimilate?"

72. Zhou, "Growing Up American."

73. Rumbaut, "Ties That Bind."

74. G. Kao and M. Tienda, "Optimism and Achievement: The Educational Performance of Immigrant Youth," *Social Science Quarterly* 76:1–19, 1995.

75. M. G. Matute-Bianchi, "Ethnic Identities and Patterns of School Success and Failure among Mexican-Descent and Japanese-American Students in a California High School," *American Journal of Education* 95:233–255, 1986.

76. C. Suarez-Orozco, *Transformations: Immigratio, Family Life, and Achievement Motivation among Latino Adolescents* (Stanford: Stanford University Press, 1995).

77. Zhou, "Growing Up American."

78. Government data cited in New York Times article by D. Canedy, "26% Hispanic Girls Drop Out/ 31% of Hispanic Boys-Highest in National Among all Teens", 3/25/2001.

79. Zhou, "Growing Up American."

80. Ibid.

81. Ibid.

82. Ibid.

83. Ibid.

84. Portes and Zhou, "Should Immigrants Assimilate?"

85. Zhou, "Growing Up American."

86. Ibid.

87. K. Harris, "The Health Status and Risk Behaviors of Adolescents in Immigrant Families," Hernandez (ed.), *Children of Immigrants.*

88. Rumbaut, "Ties That Bind."

89. Ibid.

90. Board on Children and Families, Commission on Behavioral and Social Sciences and Education, National Research Council, and Institute of Medicine, "Immigrant Children and Their Families: Issues for Research and Policy," *The Future of Children* 5(2):72–89, 1995.

91. W. Zimmerman and K. Tumlin, "Welfare Reform and the Devolution of Immigrant Policy," in *New Federalism: Issues and Options for States* (Washington, DC: Urban Institute, 1999).

92. FAIR, "Basic Questions and Answers about Immigration," in *Issue Brief,* April 2000. Available online at: www.fairus.org; L. Chavez, "What to Do about Immigration," *Commentary* 99(3):29–36, 1995.

93. K. Mautino, "Welfare Reform: An Update," *Journal of Immigrant Health* 2(1):1–3, 2000.

94. Ibid.; M. Fix and J. Passel, 1999.

95. Urban Institute, 1999.

96. Ibid.

97. W. Zimmerman and K. Tumlin, "Patchwork Policies: State Assistance for Immigrants under Welfare Reform" (Washington, DC: Urban Institute, 1999).

98. CA Policy Research Center Brief. 2000;12

# 12

# Abusive and Neglecting Parents and the Care of Their Children

Richard P. Barth

In 1999, nearly three million reports of child abuse or neglect were made to public child welfare service agencies because of concern about the health, safety, and developmental conditions of a child.[1] Although a report alone does not prove that abuse has occurred, this large number does show substantial national awareness of abuse and neglect and a willingness of the public to respond to those problems. Annual public opinion polls reveal that Americans are concerned about and report having done something about child abuse.[2]

Concerns about child abuse and neglect go back to at least 1735, when Massachusetts passed a statute intended to protect the developmental future of its children: "children whose parents were unable or neglected to provide for their support and education might be bound out by the overseers of the poor."[3] Most states, however, adopted child abuse and neglect laws in the late nineteenth century in response to the protective arguments of the burgeoning women's rights movement, religious institutions, and societies to protect animals.[4]

Although the most publicized form of child abuse may now be sexual abuse, it is far less commonly reported to public child welfare authorities than either physical abuse or neglect. Nearly three times as many children are reported for child neglect (including failure to supervise, parental abandonment, parental incapacity) as for sexual abuse, with the number of physical abuse reports falling in between. Reports of physical abuse and sexual abuse have recently declined.[5]

*Physical abuse* typically involves minor bruises or burns, but about 3 percent of the reports describe life-threatening assaults resulting in broken bones, fractured skulls, and serious burns.[6] *Physical neglect* includes inadequate provision of food, clothing, or personal hygiene also compounded by delay in or refusal to seek health care. Inadequate supervision—which has been called the "silent killer" because it results in a substantial number of deaths—is most typical of neglect.[7] Three-quarters of *sexual abuse* reports involve fondling or exposure, with genital contact and penetration claimed about one-quarter of the time.[8]

The way that reports are summarized by researchers often suggests that the child experienced only one form of harm. Yet many children who are exposed to one kind of abuse are also exposed to the others.[9]

Emily Hernandez, for example, was still only nine months old when she was raped and then fatally assaulted by her mother's boyfriend.[10] Before her death the state had substantiated three reports of child neglect in the family—one was for letting the children hang out of the window. Also it was reported that Emily's leg had been broken weeks before she was killed. A social worker had accepted the explanation that the injury was accidental. Emily, however, would have been reported as having only one type of abuse in most research studies and administrative databases on child abuse.

Child abuse and neglect are so prevalent in part because the risk of child abuse is inherent to all parenting. Parental responsibilities are complex and changing, but at some point inevitably involve coercing children into giving up their momentary personal desires to better accommodate the expectations of others. As such, the commonly proclaimed, if overstated, notion that child abuse occurs in all parts of society follows from the fundamentally conflictual nature of parent-child relationships. So, too, basic risk of child sexual abuse arises from the myriad of physical exchanges between parent and child. The parenting role may, at times, include deep sensory experiences involving the sharing of touch and closeness between parent and child which may cross over into sexual feelings.

Of course, these basic aspects of parenting do not make all parents equally likely to engage in physical abuse or sexual abuse nor do they excuse abusive parental behavior. The likelihood of abuse is precipitated by many factors including the psychological makeup of the parent (including the strength of internal inhibitions), community sanctions against abuse, the child's resistance (where possible), and, perhaps as important, the available support for parenting.[11] Parents who are alone, poor, involved with drugs and alcohol, have a large family, and are parenting one or more children with difficult characteristics are at the greatest risk of child abuse or neglect and reabuse.[12]

Poverty is the setting in which it is most likely to find children living in conditions below the standard of the minimum sufficient level of care.[13] Especially because of their relatively more frequent contact with public health and welfare officials, it is not surprising that poor children are far more likely to be reported for abuse and to enter foster care than other children. But more than public scrutiny is involved, as confidential household surveys and data from child abuse deaths show that severe and very severe violence are far more likely to occur in households with annual incomes below the poverty line.[14] For example, one study found that among children under six the rate of very severe violence was about 5 percent for children below the poverty level and 2 percent for children living above poverty. Plausible explanations for this relationship between poverty and problems in parenting include greater parental stress, isolation, more drug abuse, and more chaotic circumstances. On the other hand, most poor parents do not abuse their children and few poor parents will ever have their children removed from them.

## Effects of Child Abuse

The physical consequences of abuse and neglect can be substantial, persistent, and permanent. Battered and shaken babies are often permanently handicapped. Some, like Emily Hernandez, die from the abuse or die later on because they continue to live in high-risk situations. A thirteen-year follow-up study of abused children in Washington State found that they were three times as likely to die during the study period than the general population and almost twenty times more likely than the general population to die from homicide.[15] In Illinois, very young children are the most at-risk group to suffer child abuse fatalities, with 50 percent of deaths to infants under one year old and over 90 percent to children ages five and younger attributable to child abuse.[16] Although child death as a result of abuse is a very dramatic and, often, public event, injuries are far more common.[17] Children age six and under are most at risk of very severe violence (i.e., being kicked, bit, hit with a fist, beaten up, burned or scalded, threatened with or injured by a gun or knife).[18] Very young children are also less able to protect themselves and more vulnerable to the absence of food, clothing, or support.

Although attention has been given for some time to the observable physical effects of maltreatment, contemporary researchers are also examining broader consequences of abuse and neglect.[19] For example, abused and neglected children have more social and emotional problems and fare worse in school (factoring out the impact of poverty alone).[20]

Moreover, in one study specific types of maltreatment tended to be related to particular behavior problems. Physically abused children tended to be impulsive, unable to organize their behavior effectively, and to function less well on cognitive tasks. Many lacked the skills necessary for kindergarten, so that almost half had been referred for either special intervention or retention by the end of their kindergarten year. Neglected children had even more problems at kindergarten age. Their ratings on cognitive assessments were low; they were anxious, inattentive, lacked initiative, and had trouble understanding their work. Socially, they were both aggressive and withdrawn. They were uncooperative, insensitive, and rarely had a sense of humor. Nearly two-thirds of the neglected group had been referred for either intervention or retention by the end of kindergarten.

Social development is also hindered by child abuse. Maltreated children depend more on outer controls than on inner controls to shape their behavior.[21] Physically abused children are at a higher risk of growing up to commit criminal offenses, and children subjected to greater violence are more likely to commit more violent offenses as adults.[22] Again, although the link that exists between child neglect and delinquency is partially related to the strong association between neglect and poverty, child neglect also has an independent, significant effect on delinquency.[23] In sum, while the connections between childhood maltreatment and later outcomes are certainly the result of multiple interactive factors, there is generally a direct negative relationship between child abuse and neglect and poorer adult outcomes. For this reason, a lifetime developmental perspective is needed to understand and ameliorate the effects of abuse.

## Services to Abused and Neglected Children and Families

Although adverse early experiences can have a profound impact on later relationships, this is not inevitable. Interventions may be successful at almost any point, although earlier interventions have the greater chance of success.[24] Even though about one-third of fatal victims of abuse or neglect were currently being served or had been served by the child welfare services system prior to the child's death, the usual consequence of early adversities is vulnerability and not necessarily a lasting incapacity. Even children who experience severe and prolonged childhood maltreatment can usually benefit from equally intense and lasting services or environmental changes.

Consider the case of Harley Sapp. Born prematurely, he had heart disease and needed surgery to mend his diaphragm. When he finally left the UC Davis Medical Center, he was not under the care of his thirty-three-year-old mother, Dawna Eastep. Instead, he was under the protection of Sacramento County Department of Social Services (DSS) because the mother had been reported to DSS by hospital personnel. An investigation was conducted which led child protection officials to place him with foster parents because his mother was unable to stay sober. "The only time I wasn't drinking is when I was passed out," reported Eastep.

It took months before Dawna Eastep showed up for a 10 A.M. appointment with a social worker. She was fortified with a couple of drinks and four months pregnant with her second child when she met her infant son Harley's worker, Lucy Tosti. "She confronted me, (saying) 'You and your baby have been drinking this morning'," Eastep recalled. Eastep denied it. Tosti offered her a drug test down the hall. Eastep finally admitted her use and said she was ready, then and there, to go into treatment. Tosti got her into residential treatment and visited her in the center. By the time her son Korie was born, Eastep had reformed enough so that Tosti allowed the baby to go home with her. A year later (nearly two years since his birth), Harley was also returned home. Eastep went on to take college math and science classes, earned a 3.4 grade point average, and hopes to become a nurse practitioner.[25]

Help for abused and neglected children, if provided at all, typically follows upon a child abuse report and a face-to-face assessment by a child welfare worker of the Child Welfare Services branch of the local Department of Social Services. In 1999, about half of child abuse reports were on white children, about 25 percent on African-American children, and about 22 percent on Latino children, with the remainder being on children of other backgrounds.[26] There is no disagreement that these figures are sharply different from the national census data on the races of American children, yet there is little agreement on the causes of these differences. African-American children have a much higher rate of child poverty, large families, and involvement with the law—all risk factors for abuse and neglect. Yet some critics suggest that similarly situated African-American families are more likely to be investigated for child abuse than other families. Other yet unmeasured characteristics may be at work.[27]

Generally, child abuse reports are quite unlikely to proceed to a juvenile court review and then to a foster care placement. On the contrary, most children reported for abuse receive no ongoing child welfare services. Investigations were conducted into just over half (56 percent) of the 2.9 million alleged abuse or neglect reports filed in 1999. About 30 percent of investigations resulted in a finding of *substantiated* or *indicated as true* for a total of about 500,000 cases. About a quarter of a million were referred for court action—the gateway to the vast majority of foster care placements.[28]

## In-Home Services

When services other than foster care are provided they are usually minimal. Most families who are reported for suspected child abuse do not receive any ongoing services at all. There are simply not enough staff to provide services to all children at risk. Moreover, in home services appear to be declining. Nationally, less than half of the estimated one million abused and neglected children on the rolls in 1994 received some child welfare services in their own home. By contrast, in 1977 nearly 72 percent of the 1.8 million children receiving child welfare services received them at home.[29]

Despite this general paucity of in-home services, certain types of *intensive* in-home services (i.e., home visits from a social worker and some practical services to repair dangerous aspects of the home situation) are increasingly available for some children. Many last only a month and are intended, primarily, to resolve only the most recent crisis in a family's life.

Evaluations of such intensive family preservation services have been mixed, although the preponderance of evidence from the largest, most rigorous study indicates that these services do not reduce the eventual placement of children into foster care, or the time that children spend in foster care, nor do they reduce the likelihood that children who remain at home will be reabused.[30] Yet the same study shows that such programs are well received by parents, prized by the child welfare workers who provide the services, and yield a greater sense of control by the parents served.

Moreover, leaving children in abusive environments while those environments are rehabilitated is a bit like keeping a school open while earthquake damage is repaired—the risk of subsequent harm may not be neutralized despite careful planning, shoring up, and routine surveillance. Although many children can be safely protected at home, every year scores and perhaps hundreds of children die while receiving in-home child welfare services in response to a child abuse report. Unfortunately, predicting which families will succeed, which will fail (and their children subsequently placed into foster care), and which will fail tragically (and their children maimed or killed) is very difficult for child welfare service providers. It has been said of child welfare work that "it is not rocket science, it is much more complicated."

This raises the question of whether it is wiser not to risk a catastrophic end by taking into foster care every child whose abuse or neglect is substantiated or indicated. There are three reasons why this approach cannot for long be implemented. The first is that in some cases the child's plight is not considered to be the parent's fault—for example, although being homeless with children was once a reason for removal of children, such removals are no longer considered appropriate as long as homelessness is the only justification for concern. Nowadays the dominant social services philosophy is that these parents should somehow be assisted to find shelter and keep their children. A second reason is that the cost of providing foster care placement is dramatically higher than the cost of providing in-home services. In California, the average monthly cost of out-of-home care payments exceeds $1000 a month—not including social worker time. A third reason is that even if cost were not a concern, the supply of foster care placements is finite, and finding foster families to care for children who have experienced (and have often now developed) substantial problems is made more difficult every day with the growing participation in the labor force of able adults.

Notwithstanding the implausibility of an enormous increase in the use of foster care, there is a growing sentiment across the American landscape to reassert a fundamental understanding of child welfare services— that protecting the child is its highest goal and that preserving the family comes second. States, and there have been many, whose policies have been ambiguous about the balancing of the dual roles of child welfare services are finding good cause to clarify their programmatic priorities to emphasize child protection. Although it is too soon to tell exactly where this movement will lead, its power grows every time a child who was identified as at risk is maimed or killed when left home or returned home to its family.

## Foster Care

Although placement of a child in foster care occurs following fewer than half of substantiated child abuse reports, nearly a quarter of a million children entered foster care in the United States in 1994. While this means that about 3 in 1000 children enter foster care each year, among some population subgroups (like African-American infants) the incidence rate approaches 4 percent per year. Although the length of children's stays in foster care have remained relatively constant in the last half decade, they are almost certainly shorter than they were prior to 1980.[31] Median stays vary dramatically across states, however (from nine months in Texas to thirty-four months in Illinois), with eighteen to twenty months serving as a reasonable national estimate. More than half of all children who enter foster care will eventually return home.

The trend toward shorter median foster care stays, especially for children not living with relatives, has been partially offset by a growth in placement of foster children with relatives for typically longer stays. Foster care is considerably shorter in large urban regions than it is elsewhere. Infants have the longest spells. African-American children have median durations that are 40 percent greater than those for other children, and because they also enter foster care at high rates, the proportion of African-American children in foster care at any time is as much as five times the rate for the general population.

About 30 percent of the children who entered foster care in 1983 and had later been reunified with their parents, had reentered foster care by the end of 1993.[32] The percentage of children who went home and then reentered foster care was consistently greater across the states for children who had been in foster care a short time (e.g., less than three months), as compared with those children who have longer stays and are then reunified.[33]

Empirical data on the long-term outcomes for those children who are placed in foster care are sparse. Still, the limited American and European studies consistently indicate that children who had been in family foster care function better than those similarly situated children who remain at home; that is, foster care per se is not responsible for the later problems of foster children and, generally, does provide some benefit.[34] Indeed, if a child is placed in foster care, longer stays in foster care are associated with a higher degree of life satisfaction and better measures of adult functioning, especially when the long-term placement is in a normal, stable, foster family setting and when the child maintains contact with the fos-

ter family and receives support in adulthood.[35] When children are in foster care, close relationships with foster parents may help overcome abusive early relationships. Children who feel more secure with their foster
parents, who experience more emotional ties with them, and who receive
physical affection are better adjusted and have fewer achievement problems in school.[36]

By contrast, although study results are not unanimous, it is safe to
say that multiple foster care placements are more often associated with
poorer outcomes than most other variables.[37] One must be cautious in
interpreting the data, because children who are difficult to care for tend
to have more placements. Nevertheless, multiple placements also occur
for very young children who do not have such problems.[38] Moreover,
children who remain in foster care a long time and are not living with
relatives move on an average of more than once every two years.[39] On
balance, it seems that residential and school mobility among abused and
neglected children can have substantial negative effects on school achievement above and beyond the negative effects of abuse.[40] More broadly,
just as children who change schools frequently are likely to have lower
grades, placement moves also take their toll on children, setting off a negative chain reaction requiring children to expend substantial effort to adjust to new adults, siblings, teachers, and surroundings.

## The Policy Response

The twentieth century has witnessed growing consensus that the "public
ought to protect all citizens, including children, from cruelty and im-
proper care."[41] In the last two decades, intricate federal and state laws
have grown to codify the public interest in preventing child abuse, protecting abused children, and, when necessary, providing proper (and time-
limited) out-of-home care for children.

### *Adoption Assistance and Child Welfare Act*

The basic federal structure for child welfare services has been guided by
the Adoption Assistance and Child Welfare Act (AACWA) (1980–1997)
which required that every *reasonable effort* be made to prevent the placement of abused and neglected children in foster care, and when placement occurred to reunify them with their parents within two years, and
if that is not going to occur, to place them promptly for adoption. To
help facilitate adoption, the AACWA provided for non-means-tested
adoption subsidies to insure that foster parents who adopt children with
special needs would not be financially penalized. This law was based on
a concept known as "permanency planning," which emphasized the need
for children to have a single legal and permanent relationship to a family
(preferably the family of origin, but if not, an adoptive family or a
guardian) at an early and feasible point.

## Adoption and Safe Families Act

The Adoption and Safe Families Act (ASFA) of 1997 (PL 105–89) represents a substantial retooling of the first federal child welfare law—the Adoption and Child Welfare Act (AACWA) of 1980. Some of the fundamental provisions of ASFA that communicate a value shift from AACWA include: (1) provisions allowing agencies to forego reasonable placement prevention and reunification efforts for some children; (2) permission to use concurrent planning—that is, engaging in reunification and adoption planning at the same time for children who are unlikely to go home—as a legitimate tool and not as an infringement of reasonable efforts provisions of PL 96–272; (3) acknowledging that children are entitled to "reasonable efforts" to an adoptive home if they cannot go home; (4) provisions that agencies must be willing to allow their children to participate in the interstate compact—that is, that if a child can be adopted into another county or state more expeditiously than in their local jurisdiction, cooperation is required; and (5) stricter time limits for children in foster care so that decisions about whether to stop reunification efforts and to terminate parental rights and responsibilities have to be routinely made after a child has been in foster care for 12 months (rather than 18 months). The balance of the law has clearly moved against the presumption that every child must be reunified no matter how treacherous the child's home environment and no matter how long it takes to complete the job. The emphasis is on more quickly freeing children, who are not safe to go home, for adoption.

## Chafee Foster Care Independence Program (CFCIP)

Recognizing the difficulties faced by young people upon their emancipation from foster care, the federal government first became involved in supporting state independent living servics in 1996. The John Chafee Foster Care Independence Program (CFCIP), created when the Foster Care Independence Act of 1999 (PL 106–109) amended Title IV–E of the Social Security Act, provided states with increased funding and greater flexibility in meeting the needs of children aging out of foster care. It more than doubled the appropriation to $140 million per year, while expanding both the eligible population and the range of services covered. States must now pay a match to obtain the funds and are now *required* to serve, without regard to IV–E eligibility, those up to age twenty-one who have aged out, or are likely to age out, of foster care at age eighteen. Services provided under the program can include educational, vocational, and employment training; substance abuse prevention; pregnancy prevention; preventive health services; and connections to supportive adults. States may use up to 30 percent of funds for living expenses (allowing the more willing foster children to stay in foster care longer) and have the option of extending Medicaid coverage to youths aged eighteen to twenty-one who were in foster care on their eighteenth birthday. The legislation also mandates evaluations of these efforts, although the federal government and the states have been unable to agree upon evaluation procedures and standards.

## Family Preservation and Family Support Services

From 1998 to 1999, a total of approximately $250 million a year was allocated to states "for the purpose of encouraging and enabling each State to develop and establish, or expand, and to operate a program of family preservation services and community-based family support services." The intent of the law was to help to redress the imbalance in spending that had developed over the years of the AACWA, under which out-of-home care after placement was funded as an entitlement but in-home services were not. The result was that out-of-home care was funded at a rate sixteen times higher than the funding of in-home services designed to prevent placement.[42] This new measure was initially intended to generate a wide array of low-cost, in-home services for low-risk parents as well as an expansion of intensive in-home services. Yet, the vast majority of resources went to "family support" programs that often failed to reach families that were likely to become involved in child welfare services. Other resources were directed to preventing placements, but the evaluations were not showing success.[43] Especially given the lack of evidence on the efficacy of these services, there is a growing feeling (noted earlier) that children at high risk of reabuse should not be unduly trusted to modest services of brief duration.

## MEPA and the Interethnic Adoption Provisions

To address perceived discrimination in adoptive and foster placement that was keeping African-American children from being adopted at a rate that was equal to other children and that was unfair to Caucasian families wanting to adopt children of color, the Multi-Ethnic Placement Act (MEPA) was passed in 1994. MEPA prohibited federally funded agencies and entities from, on the one hand, denying anyone the opportunity to become a foster or adoptive *parent* due to the race of either the parent or the child, and, on the other hand, denying a *child* the opportunity to be placed due to the race of either the parent or child. In addition, the legislation required states to develop plans for the diligent recruitment of potential foster and adoptive families that reflect the diversity of children in need of placement. MEPA did not prohibit *all* consideration of race, however; it merely prohibited "*categoriacally*" denying placement "*solely*" on this basis. The race of the child, and the capacity of propsective adoptive or foster parents to meet the needs of a child of this background, could be considered along with other factors in determining the child's best interest.

Primarily to address the concerns of civil rights advocates that race was not an appropriate tool for policy making unless there was clear evidence of discrimination against minority groups, MEPA was revised two years later by the Interethnic Adoption Provisions (IAP), which limited further the extent to which race could be considered in adoptive and foster placements. The new law did this by deleting just a few words from the language in MEPA. Now the prohibition is on federally funded agencies and entities denying placement "on the basis of race . . ." rather than "*solely* on the basis of race. . . ." In addition, agencies may not "deny to any person the opportunity to become an adoptive or foster parent," whereas under MEPA, they could not "*categorically*" deny such an opportunity. MEPA's requirements regarding the recruitment of foster and adoptive families remained unchanged.

Precisely how MEPA and the IAP will affect placement practices is unclear, but the general rule favoring inracial placement is no longer legal. Now a decision to place a child inracially must be specifically justified with regard to the needs of the particular child and the parents' capacity to meet the child's needs. Thus, in each individual case, the child welfare worker must begin with no presumptions. The most immediate impact of the new laws, then, is likely to be on the *process* of making and implementing a decision. Whether the number of transracial adoptions has increased has not been studied.

## From Legal Permanence to Psychological Permanence: A Questionable Paradigm Shift

Although formal public policies matter, individual beliefs and actions by those inside the system may have more impact on the operation of child welfare services. The astounding complexity of abused and neglected lives leaves great discretion for child welfare workers and judges. They often look beyond the law for meaning. Thus, although permanency remains the single most central idea in child welfare, it has at least two meanings. The first is a legal definition which refers to the time frames, reasonable efforts requirements, and administrative procedures that were established as a result of the AACWA and that are now in place, albeit rather loosely, in every jurisdiction in America. This use of permanency planning refers only to the *process*, not to the underlying ideas that shape the actual decisions of social workers, attorneys, and judges. The goal of the process is to create a secure permanent legal status for children; although this implies that foster care stays should be brief, it reflects no less preference for reunification or adoption.

In practice, however, a second profoundly psychological meaning of permanence has become more central in making child welfare decisions. The underlying idea has early roots in the pre-AACWA child welfare reform movement and refers to the child's psychological sense of permanence. That psychological meaning has been emphasized because it was seen to be associated with better behavior in foster care.[44] Although it is hard to argue against the importance of a child's feeling of permanence as a positive experience, it is at least as likely that causality is in the other direction; that is, it may well be that the better behavior comes first, so that well-behaved foster children end up feeling as if they are loved and can stay where they are. There is simply not enough evidence to justify the claim that a child's psychological sense of permanence is a necessary or sufficient cause of a child's's well-being.

Yet because of this common misinterpretation, permanency began to be interpreted primarily as psychological in nature and as the most important contributor to a child's development.[45] Once this transformation of the concept was accepted, it was but a small step to see the preferred substantive outcome as keeping a child with kin or other long-term foster parents—because they maintain the child's preexisting psychological ties, even if they will not adopt the child.

The upshot is that the phrase *family continuity* has now emerged as the expression of psychological permanency and has been proposed by many as a new paradigm for child welfare services. The term is used to "depict the way in which family-based practice had moved permanency planning conceptually to a more holistic framework which includes preventive services for families and refocuses onto the network of extended family and community relationships in which children are embedded across the course of their lives."[46]

The underlying psychological concept is that "the individual's sense of identity and continuity is formed not only by the significant attachments in one's intimate environment but also is deeply rooted in the biological family—in the genetic link that reaches back into the past and ahead to the future."[47] There can be little question here that the most important value in family continuity is on maintaining biological family relationships, but there is also much support for keeping children in long-term foster care rather than disrupting a child's continuity with an adoptive placement.

In addition to an overvaluing of the finding about the connection between psychological permanence and well-being, three other forces can be identified as helping to propel "family continuity" to the fore. The first draws on the fact that the human service professions have become increasingly devoted to the concept of social support. Despite difficulties in conceptualization and measurement, the idea of social support draws on the general tendency of social workers to value personal relationships. The basic way that the social support message is operationalized by social workers is that "people need people and the more people and, especially, the more kin you are involved with the better it is." There is an assumed longing for connectedness and, in the adoption literature, discussion about "genealogical bewilderment" during which children who grew up adopted are pulled, as if in a genetically induced force field, to search for information about their genetic heritage. (In fact, while some adoptees do search for their biological parents, more do not.)

The countervailing influences of ASFA are unclear, although there has been a growth in adoptions of foster children and a shortening of lengths of stay in foster case since the time of ASFA. New federal performance measures and incentives are also encouraging more disciplined adherence to the legal requirements of law and less room for practices based merely on psychosocial conjecture.

Second, multiculturalism has also captured the imagination of the human services community. Basically, this view holds that children are most successful when they are connected to a racial or ethnic culture that is defined by their birth.[48] Detachment from this racial or ethnic culture can lead to a negative or weak racial identity and, subsequently, low self-worth and, ultimately, individual failure. It is almost universally accepted (whether true or not) within the child welfare community that children of color (whether biracial or not) who are not connected to their minority ethnic origins are more vulnerable to the harms of racism than children who are connected. From this perspective, then, multiculturalism calls for connectedness to community (since our communities are often racially segregated), to family, and to people of the same ethnic or racial background.

Third, and perhaps the most profound influence on child welfare practice in the last decade, has been the development and institutionalization of the concepts of attachment and bonding. They are put together here because so many child welfare professionals do so, although the concepts are really quite different. Bonding is, almost certainly "a scientific fiction" for human beings.[49] Attachment research has a little more weight behind it, yet it is overused to justify keeping young children with foster parents who refuse to adopt them and preventing children from being adopted by willing foster parents because they lived with their biological parent for as little as three months and are judged to be "attached" or "bonded." In some states, like California, judges can (and often do) waive the requirement for pursuing adoption for children who cannot go home on the grounds that they have bonded to a foster parent. (Given the fact that many of these children will move to other homes despite this "attachment," advocates for legal permanence for children have recently proposed that this "attachment or bonding" waiver be limited to children older than six years old.) This, of course, turns on its head the original idea of permanency contained in the AACWA. In short, family continuity supporters reject the AACWA's assumption that an equally valuable form of permanency may be achieved through legal adoption, especially by those who do not intend that the children have ongoing contact with their biological family.

Unfortunately, family continuity practice may deny children the benefits of adoption, including a secure legal status in their primary relationships, by so strongly affirming the importance of maintaining psychological connections to biological parents, kinfolk, and foster parents. As part of his testimony on the need for the strict time limits and rules of the Adoption and Safe Families Act, Peter Digre, former director of the nation's largest child welfare services agency, has challenged the dominance of psychological permanency, a recommitment to achieving legal lifetime permanency for children.[50] He argues that legal permanency (i.e., reunification to the home of the parent or adoption by other parents) is an essential component of developmental, psychological, and economic well-being for children. No child can ever feel truly safe and secure when he or she can be taken from a placement at any time with little warning. Further, legal permanence insures that no parent should be able to divest him- or herself of responsibility to the child at will. Unlike long-term kin foster care, legal permanency implies both an intent on the part of parents to make a lifetime commitment to the child, and the family's autonomy from interference from outside governmental agencies.

## A Lifetime Developmental Perspective

Because of its overemphasis on psychological connections, the family continuity movement relies too much on long-term kin foster care and too often returns children to unsafe homes. Yet pursuing adoption above all is also too simplistic. What should be kept foremost in mind is that children have needs for high-quality developmental experiences in the home, at school, and in the community—both now and later when they become adults.

Hence what is needed is a lifetime developmental perspective—one that calls for safely returning children to their birth families or providing alternative lifetime living arrangements for children that offer a sufficient commitment of financial, social, and interpersonal resources to help them achieve and grow into productive adults.[51] A lifetime developmental perspective combines attention to the growth of a child's affective, cognitive, and physical capacity toward self-sufficient and successful functioning as an adult. A developmental perspective requires some understanding of what, given the educational and vocational requirements of society, will, ultimately, add to the well-being of a child across an entire lifetime. Developmental considerations are unlikely to be incorporated into practice and policy without some understanding of the research findings about what promotes long-term success.

Robert Haveman and Barbara Wolfe have reviewed hundreds of studies by economists, sociologists, and developmental psychologists, and in *Succeeding Generations* they conduct elegant analyses of longitudinal data to identify the most important determinants of children's social success as measured by children's ultimate education, earnings, and avoidance of destructive behaviors.[52] Although other criteria (e.g., psychological maturity) could have been chosen, surely the reviewers indicators are highly relevant to public policy goals. Although successful participation in our social institutions may at first seem like a societal objective, rather than an objective for each individual, it is very clearly related to the positive health and mental health of individuals.[53]

According to Haveman and Wolfe's review the most important determinant of children's future success is their parents' education—especially the mother's. Regarding education, more is certainly better. More siblings in the family is not better, though, and has a negative effect on children's success, perhaps because family economic and time resources too often become stretched too thin. Children whose parents divorce or choose nonmarital childbearing tend to do worse. Changes in family structure have persistently negative effects on young children. Further, disrupted families and single parents are less likely to provide necessary ongoing educational support during young adulthood. Children whose immediate family members have had serious scrapes with the law also do worse. Of course, none of these challenges to positive outcomes for children is damning—each simply decreases the odds of growing up to be happy and well.

Economic circumstances have a persistent linkage to children's success, although this relationship in Haveman and Wolfe's analysis is not quantitatively large. The quality of the neighborhood and the characteristics of peers also appear to affect children's attainment, apart from economic factors. School characteristics—especially teacher skills, parental involvement levels, class sizes, and the socioeconomic composition of the student body—have effects. Opportunities in the community for recreation and employment influence attainment as well.

Child welfare services should try to promote experiences that bolster the odds of success. Admittedly, child welfare services are neither designed for nor are capable of providing *optimal* developmental opportunities for every child reported for child abuse or neglect. Moreover, if parents can use the services that the state provides to create a minimally sufficient level of care, they should be able to maintain control over their children. Otherwise, too many families would be under public supervision and resources would be spread too thin. Moreover, parental autonomy has several desirable outcomes. It limits disruption for children, who typically love their parents and families even under the most hazardous conditions. And maintaining children at home provides substantial insurance that children will have the lifetime relationships that they may need to call on in times of personal or family crisis. This does not mean that no services should be offered to minimally competent parents. For example, a new program model is emerging that encourages abusive families to leave their home and live together in a foster home so that family preservation can be given a reasonable chance without compromising child protection.[54]

Practitioners, program developers, and policy makers often do not know or do not agree on what they want from the child welfare system. In the past we have relied on mechanistic standards based primarily on psychologically-oriented principles, for example: children should not be moved from a foster family and placed in another if they are "attached" to the foster family; every child must be placed in a same-race placement; siblings must remain together whenever possible; children should be cared for in their own communities; children should all have ongoing contact with biological family members; whenever kin are available to take care of a child the child must be placed with kin. A more systematic approach to decision making needs to replace these absolute standards that have no self-evident link to promoting a child's lifetime welfare.

Children who are dependents of the court too often remain in families that do not offer the best available chance of helping them to become productive adults. Every day, social workers make choices about permanently placing children in homes that have few or no characteristics that bolster the child's chance of succeeding. They too often place children with single older foster parents; without a high school education; living in poor health; in neighborhoods with ill-equipped schools; with many children in the home; and, even commingled with nieces, nephews, and siblings with serious problems of substance abuse and the law.[55] At times, but certainly not always, homes with a far more positive developmental profile are available but are ruled out because of concerns about maintaining psychological, cultural, racial, or community continuity.

Applying a lifetime developmental framework to placement of children with their relatives in long-term foster care is an admittedly special challenge. Typically, that relative is a grandmother who knows and loves her grandchild, and in about 60 percent of the cases, the child returns to live with his or her mother (the grandmother's daughter) within four years after placement into foster care. This leaves another 40 percent of children who then tend to remain in long-term foster care with grandparents. This is a sizable number of children who are growing up with older relatives who are unlikely to provide substantial assistance during young adulthood and, perhaps more troubling, may not even be able to maintain the vigilance and support needed to guide children safely through adolescence. Some of these relatives have the even greater burden of raising children in environments that have already claimed the lives of their own children, nieces, and nephews. In deciding between long-term kin foster care and adoption by "strangers" the guiding principle should be that children should have the opportunity to reside with families who are most likely to promote their best lifetime developmental opportunities for success and self-sufficiency. This is likely to lead to more interracial adoption and more adoptions by middle-class parents living further away from the biological parents.

This is not to deny that extended family, psychological, cultural, racial, and community continuity may contribute to the well-being of a child. If such continuity can be achieved without compromising child protection and lifetime developmental opportunities, kin care may well be the best choice. Moreover, kinship support centers, devised to help kinship foster parents meet the parenting needs of their children despite their own struggles with illiteracy, poor health, and parental fatigue may have a useful role to play. But where kin foster care remains unpromising, continuity on child welfare decision making should be reduced. Moreover, open adoption arrangements are now common and generally allow children to maintain some connection to parents who care about them but who cannot care for them. In addition, there are children who cannot return home and for whom no permanent legal home is available. Decisions about the best placement for these children should also employ the standard of providing the best lifetime developmental opportunities for a child. This may, at times, mean residing in an enriched group care environment or in treatment instead of with a conventional foster family.

Children who are taken from dangerous biological families and then placed and left in foster care risk failure to achieve their goals or society's goals for them. This is no less true if those children are viewed as psychologically "attached" to their foster parents. The foster parents may care for those children until they retire or a child becomes too recalcitrant and angry. Then the child may be moved to a family or group home that is willing to tolerate him or her. We can expect those children to emancipate to independent living at age eighteen without a reasonable shot at self-sufficiency. When children who have left foster care are subsequently asked by researchers to indicate the ways that they can depend on their former foster parents when they have a major problem they may well answer "I don't know, we never talked about it."[56]

In conclusion, first, recognizing that predictions of future abuse are difficult to make, we nonetheless need to be more aggressive in removing from and keeping from their parents those children who are seriously at risk of grave physical danger (as ASFA now allows). Second, we need to be more aggressive in establishing legally permanent arrangements for children who have been victims of abuse and neglect, and those arrangements should more rigorously take into account the child's long-term developmental interests (rather than giving excessive weight to transitory psychological ties the claims of community and extended kin as too frequently happens now). When protection, legal permanence, and developmental opportunities can all be assured for a child in several possible placements, then other more psychological concerns can be decisive.

# Notes

1. U.S. Department of Health and Human Services, Administration on Children, Youth, and Families, *Ten Years of Reporting: Child Maltreatment 1999* (Washington, DC: GPO, 2000).

2. National Committee for the Prevention of Child Abuse, *Public Opinion and Behaviors among Child Abuse Prevention: The Results of NCPCAs 1995 Public Opinion Poll* (Chicago: 1995).

3. Homer Folks, *The Care of Destitute, Neglected, and Delinquent Children* (New York: Macmillan, 1902), 10.

4. L. Gordon, *Heroes of Their Own Lives: The Politics and History of Family Violence* (New York: Viking, 1988).

5. J. Jones and D. Finkelor, "The Decline in Child Sexual Abuse Cases," *Juvenile Justice Bulletin* (January 2001), 1–11.

6. A. J. Sedlak, *National Incidence and Prevalence of Child Abuse and Neglect: 1988* (Rockville, MD: Westat, 1991).

7. P. Pecora, J. K. Whittaker, A. N. Maluccio, and R. P. Barth (eds.), *The Child Welfare Challenge: Policy Practice and Research* (2nd Ed.) (New York: Aldine De Gruyter, 2000), 196.

8. A. J. Sedlak, *Supplementary Analyses of Data on the National Incidence of Child Abuse and Neglect* (Rockville, MD: Westat, 1991).

9. R. P. Barth, M. Courtney, J. D. Berrick, and V. Albert, *From Child Abuse to Permanency Planning: Child Welfare Services Pathways and Placements* (New York: Aldine De Gruyter, 1993).

10. K. J. McLarin, "Slaying of Connecticut Infant," *New York Times*, July 30, 1995.

11. D. Finkelor, *Child Sexual Abuse: New Theory and Research* (New York: Free Press, 1984).

12. D. J. English and J. P. Pecora, "Risk Assessment as a Practice Method in Child Protective Services," *Child Welfare* 73: 451–474, 1994.

13. C. J. Coulton, J. E. Korbin, M. Su, and J. Chow, "Community Level Factors and Child Maltreatment Rates," *Child Development* 66:1262–1276, 1995.

14. R. J. Gelles, "Poverty and Violence toward Children," *American Behavioral Scientist* 35(3):258–274, 1992.

15. E. E. Sabotta and R. L. Davis, "Fatality after Report to a Child Abuse Registry in Washington State, 1973–1986," *Child and Neglect* 16:627–635, 1992.

16. L. Martinez and P. Sommer, *Illinois Child Abuse and Neglect Fatalities: Characteristics and Profiles* (Springfield, IL: Department of Children and Family Services, 1988).

17. S. Gallagher, K. Finison, B. Guyer, and S. Goodenough, "The Incidence of Injuries among 87,000 Massachusetts Children and Adolescents: Results of the 1980–1981 Statewide Childhood Injury Prevention Program Surveillance System," *American Journal of Public Health* 74:1340–1347, 1984.

18. Gelles, "Poverty and Violence toward Children," 258–274.

19. For a discussion of the historical context, see C. H. Kempe, F. N. Silverman, B. F. Steele, W. Droegmuller, and H. K. Silver, "The Battered Child Syndrome," *Journal of the American Medical Association* 18:17–24, 1962.

20. M. F. Erickson, B. Egeland, and R. Pianto, "The Effects of Maltreatment on the Development of Young Children," in D. Cicchetti and V. Carlson (eds.), *Child Maltreatment: Theory and Research on the Causes and Consequences of Child Abuse and Neglect* (New York: Cambridge University Press, 1989), 647–684.

21. J. Aber, J. Allen, V. Carlson, and D. Cicchetti, "The Effects of Maltreatment on Development during Early Childhood: Recent Studies and Their Theoretical, Clinical, and Policy Implications." in Cicchetti and Carlson (eds.), *Child Maltreatment: Theory and Research on the Causes and Consequences of Child Abuse and Neglect*, 579–619.

22. B. Rivera and C. S. Widom, "Childhood Victimization and Violent Offending," *Violence and Victims* 5(1):19–34, 1990; R. H. Starr, D. J. MacLean, and D. P. Keating, "Life-span Developmental Outcomes of Child Maltreatment," in R. H. Starr, Jr., and D. A. Wolfe (eds.), *The Effects of Child Abuse and Neglect* (London: Guilford, 1991), 1–32.

23. M. Zingraff, J. Leiter, K. Myers, and M. Johnsen, "Child Maltreatment and Youthful Problem Behavior," *Criminology* 31(2):173–202, 1993.

24. M. Rutter, "Family and School Influences on Cognitive Development," *Journal of Child Psychology and Psychiatry* 26(5):683–704, 1985.

25. C. Alcala, "Addiction, Abuse Go Hand in Hand." *Sacramento Bee*, February 14, 1996, 41, A6.

26. U.S. DHHS, *Child Maltreatment 1999.*

27. For a discussion of African-American families' likelihood to be investigated for child abuse, see R. Hampton, "Race, Class, and Child Maltreatment," *Journal of Comparative Family Studies* 18(1):113–126, 1987. For a broader discussion of research on the role of race in child welfare, see M. E. Courtney, R. P. Barth, J. D. Berrick, D. Brooks, B. Needell, and L. Park, "Race and Child Welfare Services," *Child Welfare* 75:99–137, 1996.

28. U.S. DHHS, *Child Maltreatment 1999.*

29. Westat and James Bell Associates, *National Study of Preventive, Protective, and Reunification Services Delivered to Children and Their Families: Preliminary Findings* (Washington, DC: 1995).

30. J. R. Schuerman, T. L. Rzepnicki, and J. H. Litell, *Putting Families First* (New York: Aldine De Gruyter, 1994).

31. K. Brunner, R. M. George, F. H. Wulczyn, and A. Harden, *A Report from the Multistate Data Archive: Foster Care Dynamics (1983–1998)* (Chicago: Chapin Hall Center for Children, 2000).

32. Ibid.

33. F. Wulczyn, "Caseload Dynamics and Foster Care Reentry," *Social Service Review* 65:133–156, 1991; J. D. Berrick, B. Needell, R. P. Barth, and M. Jonson-Reid, *The Tender Years: Toward Developmentally Sensitive Child Welfare Services* (New York: Oxford University Press, 1997), 252–271.

34. For a review of American and European studies on foster care, see R. B. Barth and M. Berry, "Implications of Research on the Welfare of Children under Permanency Planning," in R. B. Barth, J. D. Berrick, and N. Gilbert, *Child Welfare Research Review* (New York: Columbia University Press, 1994), 323–368.

35. T. McDonald, R. Allen, A. Westerfelt, and I. Piliavain, *Assessing the Long-Term Effects of Foster Care: A Research Synthesis* (Madison, WI: Institute for Research on Poverty, 1993).

36. R. F. Marcus, "The Attachments of Children in Foster Care," *Genetic, Social and General Psychology Monographs* 365–394, 1991.

37. McDonald et al., *Assessing the Long-Term Effects of Foster Care: A Research Synthesis.*

38. Berrick et al., *The Tender Years: Toward Developmentally-Sensitive Child Welfare Services.*

39. Ibid.

40. J. Eckenrode, R. Rowe, M. Laird, and J. Brathwaite, "Mobility as a Mediator of the Effects of Child Maltreatment on Academic Performance," *Child Development* 66:1130–1142, 1995.

41. W. J. Schultz, "The Humane Movement in the United States, 1910–1922." *Columbia University Studies in History, Economics, and Public Law,* CXIII (1):223, 1924.

42. U.S. General Accounting Office, *Foster Care Services to Prevent Out-of-Home Placements Are Limited by Funding Barriers* (Washington, D. C.:, GAO/HRD 93-76, June 29, 1993).

43. U.S. Department of Health and Human Services, Assistant Secretary for Planning and Evaluation, *Evaluation of Family Preservation and Reunification Programs: Interim Report.* Washington, DC, January 2001. Available online at http://aspe.os.dhhs.gov/hsp/fampres94/index.htm#top.

44. A. Emlen, J. Lahti, G. Downs, A. McKay, and S. Downs, *Overcoming Barriers to Planning for Children in Foster Care* (Portland, OR: Regional Research Institute, 1978).

45. A. N. Maluccio, E. Fein, and K. A. Olmstead, *Permanency Planning for Children: Concepts and Methods* (New York: Routledge, Chapman, and Hall, 1986), 5.

46. E. J. McFadden, "Practice in Permanency Planning for Family Continuity," *Contemporary Group Care Practice, Research and Evaluation* 5:13–21, 1995.

47. J. Laird, "An Ecological Approach to Child Welfare: Issues of Family Identity and Continuity," in C. Germain (ed.), *Social Work Practice: People and Environments* (New York: Columbia, 1979).

48. A. Hacker, *Two Nations: Black and White, Separate, Hostile, Unequal* (New York: Ballantine, 1992).

49. D. E. Eyer, *Mother-Infant Bonding: A Scientific Fiction* (New Haven: Yale University Press, 1992).

50. D. Digre, *Our First Priority Is Safety and Our Primary Mission Is Legal Permanency* (Los Angeles, April 23, 1996).

51. Berrick et al., *The Tender Years: Toward Developmentally-Sensitive Child Welfare Services.*

52. R. Haveman and B. Wolfe, *Succeeding Generations: On the Effects of Investments in Children* (New York: Russell Sage Foundation, 1994).

53. K. E. Bolger, C. J. Patterson, and W. W. Thompson, "Psychosocial Adjustment among Children Experiencing Persistent and Intermittent Family Economic Hardship," *Child Development* 66:1107–1129, 1995; R. A. Hahn, E. Eaker, N. D. Barker, S. M. Teutsch, W. Sosniak, and N. Krieger, "Poverty and Death in the United States—1973 and 1991," *Epidemiology* 6(5):490–497, 1995.

54. R. P. Barth, "Shared Family Care: Child Protection and Family Preservation," *Social Work* 39:515–534, 1994; R. P. Barth and A. Price, "Shared Family Care: Providing Services to Parents and Children Placed Together in Out-of-home Care," *Child Welfare* 78:88–107, 1999.

55. R. P. Barth, "Policy Implications of Foster Family Characteristics," *Family Relations* 50:16–19, 2001.

56. R. P. Barth, "On Their Own: The Experiences of Youth after Foster Care," *Child and Adolescent Social Work* 1:419–446, 1990.

# 13

# Solomon's Children: The New Biologism, Psychological Parenthood, Attachment Theory, and the Best Interests Standard

## Arlene Skolnick

At the beginning of Steven Spielberg's film *AI* (*Articial Intelligence*), set in the distant future, scientists succeed in creating a child robot named David who not only looks human, but is capable of love. David is "adopted" by a couple who becomes attached to him, but because of a series of misunderstandings, they eventually abandon him in the woods. The rest of the film tells of David's desperate search for a way to go home again and win back his mother's love.

Some critics wondered whether this dark fairy tale would be too painful for children, arousing their deepest fears of loss and abandonment. For those adults who saw it, the film is a visceral reminder of what can be emotionally at stake for children involved in the loss or disruption of an existing parent-child relationship. In the 1990s, Americans witnessed disturbing real-life scenes involving such disruption.

On August 2, 1993, the American television public looked on as a screaming toddler was taken from her mother's arms to be sent to another family in another state. The Iowa Supreme Court had ruled that Jan and Roberta DeBoer had no right to keep Baby Jessica, the child they had raised since shortly after birth. Cara Clausen, the birth mother, and the man she had named as the father had signed the adoption papers. Three weeks later, she changed her mind and said she had named the wrong man. She told her ex-boyfriend, Dan Schmidt, that he was the father and the couple married. He established his parternity, pursued custody, and won.

A similar drama played out as Baby Richard was removed from his adoptive parents at the age of four. At around the same time, Gregory K., an eleven-year-old boy, made headlines around the world when he sued to "divorce" the biological mother who had abandoned him and be adopted by his foster family. Other cases recently in the news include a mother who lost custody because she had placed her child in day care while going to college, and a professional woman who lost custody because the judge thought she spent too much time at the office.

This chapter takes stock of the research evidence concerning children's emotional attachments to their caretakers, and its implications for efforts to resolve custody disputes. It also raises questions about the uses and limits of psychological research in dealing with the tangled emotional webs of family life.

Although few cases attract the kind of media attention Jessica's and Richard's did, custody battles have become everyday events in the nation's courtrooms. In the wake of the dramatic transformations in family life since the 1970s, the courts have been called upon to make increasing numbers of Solomon-like judgments about where and with whom children shall live. According to one estimate, about 50 percent of children born in 1990 are likely to come under court jurisdiction in a custody case.[1] Most of these cases arise out of parental divorce, not contested adoptions. But state intervention in children's living arrangements has also grown, owing to rising numbers of child abuse and neglect cases. Further, new reproductive technologies have led to custody struggles that raise questions about the very definition of biological parenthood.

At a time when the family has become an explosive political issue, custody disputes have aroused passionate public debates as well as complex and troubling questions for the legal system. How should a family be defined? What qualifies one parent—or one set of parents—to be chosen over the other to retain custody? Should the courts focus on the rights of the adults, or the best interests of the child? What in fact are the child's best interests?

To the vast majority of Americans, as poll after poll revealed, the decision in the Baby Jessica case was heartless and baffling. How could judges take a child away from the only parents she had known? The decision revealed to a public not familiar with family law that, while children may be the central characters in the courtroom dramas that determine their fate, their roles are actually very small. As one family court judge put it, "The single biggest failing in our system today is that the voice of the child is not heard. That goes for adoption cases and custody."[2]

Even when courts do try to focus on the child's well-being, the efforts can seem misguided, as in the case where the mother lost custody because she put her child in day care. More than two decades ago, the concept of "psychological parenthood" was introduced to the legal community to designate the person to whom the child has the closest emotional ties, whether or not that person is biologically related to the child. The authors of the concept argued that the child's emotional well-being and future development are critically dependent on maintaining the relationship with the psychological parent. Since then, the concept has been enormously influential, part of the everyday vocabulary used in juvenile and family courts around the country. Yet it has also provoked a great deal of debate.

One major criticism deals with the lack of evidence presented by the authors of the psychological parenthood concept in support of their argument. Indeed, "psychological parenthood" is not a psychological term—it is not used by psychologists except in the context of child custody and placement decisions.

Disputes over the custody of children arise in many contexts. Cases like those of Baby Jessica and Baby Richard, where a biological mother or father seeks to undo an adoption and get the child back, are not rare, but they are plainly not the most common kind of situation that comes before a family court judge. As already noted, custody battles most often arise when the child is living with two parents and they divorce. But the two adults could also be a biological parent and a stepparent, two biological parents who are unmarried, or two partners of the same sex raising a child. As one example, Martha, a woman with two children of her own, married a man with a deaf daughter. She learned sign language to communicate with the child, something the child's father had not done. Martha and her children, who also learned to sign, became emotionally close to the girl. When Martha and her husband divorced, she sued for custody of the deaf child. As another example, Jane and Jill are a lesbian couple who decided to have children together. Jane became pregnant through artificial insemination, and gave birth to a son. The women defined themselves as the child's two mothers, and shared in his care. When the boy was four, however, Jane and Jill separated. Jane, as the biological mother, had legal custody and, on that basis, refused to allow Jill to visit the child.

In another kind of situation, the child is being cared for by someone who is not the biological parent, and another person seeks custody of the child. For example, a child may have been raised by his mother and her second husband. When the mother dies, this leads to a contest between the child's biological father, the stepfather, and the mother's parents.

In recent years, an increasing number of disputes have been between foster parents and state agencies having legal custody of the child who want to remove the child to the biological parent or parents, another foster home, or relatives or others who want to adopt the child. In one case, for example, Mary, a drug addict, abandoned her infant. The child was placed in a foster home. Three years later, Mary cleaned up her act, found a job, and was ready to reclaim the child. The foster parents, however, had come to love the child and wanted to adopt her.

There are cases where the child has been in the care of what might be called informal foster parents—grandparents, a friend of the family, a boarding school teacher—who seek to prevent the return of the child to the biological parents. As one illustration, Maria and Eduard were political refugees who had to flee their country, leaving their eighteen-month-old baby behind with a neighbor family. Ten years later they returned, and claimed the child. But neither the child nor the family was willing to make the change.

Finally, in addition to custody disputes, there are cases in which relatives or other third parties claim the right to visit with a child. Gary and Jenifer Troxel had sued and won in a Washington State court for the right to have overnight visits with their two granddaughters, even though their son, the girls' father, was dead. The mother did not oppose some visits, but she argued that the court's ruling infringed on her constitutional rights to raise her children without state interference. In a 2001 decision, the U.S. Supreme Court agreed with her.

## Thicker than Water

Traditionally, there has been a presumption in favor of biological parents in disputes with other people. The media spotlight on Jessica, Richard, Gregory, and other children revealed to the public that the focus of the courts was clearly on the legal rights and wrongs of the adults involved, rather than the child's perceptions and emotional needs. However, different jurisdictions and judges place different weights on the rights of parents and the interests of the child. Thus custody decisions are marked by a great deal of uncertainty and inconsistency.

In some states today, unless a parent is found to be unfit or to have abandoned the child, the rights of biological parents are all but inviolate. Thus the courts who decided the fate of Baby Jessica acted without consideration of her "best interests" or the circumstances of her life—the only issue the court considered was whether the parental rights of the biological father had been correctly terminated.

It was this aspect of the case that provoked the most public outrage—that a child could be plucked from her family by a man who happened to have impregnated the birth mother, at a time when she was engaged to another man. Some commentators see this biological preference as a legacy from the era when children were considered property. A dissenting justice in Jessica's case complained that his colleagues were treating Jessica like "a carload of hay" and trying to decide who had the better legal title.[3] (Because Jessica's father was unmarried to her mother at the time of Jessica's birth, legal recognition of his biology-based claims is actually a rather recent development.) A judge in the Baby Richard case compared the outcome of the case to the infamous Dred Scott decision—in which the Supreme Court ruled that an escaped slave should be returned to his "rightful" owner.

Many commentators, however, believe that the child's best interests are in fact served by growing up with biological parents, and that parents not only have a right to their children but that "natural bonds of affection" lead parents to care for their children in a way that no "stranger" could.

This biological slant of the legal system also reflects widespread, but usually unarticulated assumptions about ties based on blood and genes in American culture. Because they are so taken for granted, there is a danger that unless they are made explicit, these assumptions may well guide decision making and discussion of the issues in an unreflective way. The belief that family bonds are the natural and essential product of biological ties is deeply rooted in American kinship beliefs. The saying "blood is thicker than water" tells us that ties not based in biological kinship cannot be as strong as those that are. This belief is enshrined in a host of tales in which children discover their real parents and live happily ever after.

Yet such terms as "natural" and "real" have traditionally raised suspicions among philosophers and cultural anthropologists. Philosophers ask how do you get from "is" to "ought"—from the brute facts of biological reproduction to moral claims of a right to rear. Anthropologists point to the enormous variation around the world in kinship systems as well as concepts of what is "real." Thus anthropologist David Schneider argues that American beliefs in blood kinship are no more rooted in the facts of biology than supernatural beliefs in ghosts are based in the real nature of such beings.[4] Both kinship and religion, he argues, are cultural constructs. To be sure, there are biological facts, but kinship systems make use of these facts in various symbolic ways.

One of the most striking features of the way Americans think about the family, Schneider observes, is the emphasis on the family as natural. The nuclear family—mother and father and child—is a cultural icon; the man and woman are united in physical love—"one flesh"—and a child is imagined to be the "flesh and blood" of both parents. The cultural symbolism of family is very different in other cultures. For example, the traditional Chinese family is understood to be a long line of fathers and sons, including remote ancestors and unborn descendants. Women constitute the links in the male chain of descent, but they are not included in anyone's genealogy.[5]

Schneider distinguishes among three aspects of family: "the family" as a cultural symbol, the kinship norms of different ethnic and class groups, and everyday life in families and households. For example, even in cultures in which the three-generation household is the ideal norm, most households may in fact be nuclear, because most people do not live long enough to overlap the lives their grandchildren. In the United States, Schneider writes, the cultural symbolism of the "natural" family coexists with a wide variety of actual family patterns. In a number of ethnic groups and regions of the country, for example, much of daily life and child socialization are embedded in social networks, often including extended kin like grandparents, aunts, uncles, and cousins. So-called fictional kin—nonrelatives who are considered "part of the family"—are also common in these networks and are found in many cultures around the world. In many Latin cultures, godparents are a well-institutionalized aspect of child rearing. The exchange of children, or a child going to live for a time with a relative living near or far, is a common custom in American subcultures and around the world.

In recent years, the traditional biological concept of family in American culture and law has been joined by what might be called a new biologism, a growing sense that the true essence of a person is rooted in the primordial differences of gender, race, ethnicity, genes. It's true that the recent advances in genetic research have made biological information about one's family background an important part of a person's medical history. But the new biologism is a much broader cultural phenomenon that encompasses identity politics and the emphasis on ethnic roots, the search movement among adoptees, and the antiadoption movement which has emerged in recent years.

The fact that adopted children or those of surrogate parents may seek out their "natural" parents, however, is not in itself evidence that knowledge about one's genetic heritage is essential to one's sense of identity. Instead of some basic truth about human nature, the search for biological roots may reflect the cultural importance of genes, and the stigma and sense of difference a person feels when growing up in a culture that increasingly defines identity and belongingness in biological terms. As one observer notes, in these postmodern times, the parent-child bond has taken on new and urgent meanings; as the relationship between the sexes becomes more fragile, it has become "the source of the last remaining, irrevocable, unexchangable primary relationship."[6]

Some legal scholars argue that Jessica's case and the others like it were correctly decided. They advance a number of arguments justifying the legal system's emphasis on biological parents. Most fundamental, perhaps biology provides a clear standard, a "bright line" for making legal judgments. However unfortunate the outcome of any particular case, according to this view, the absence of a presumption in favor of biological parents would open up a Pandora's box of troublesome and unjustified claims.

In 1993, for example, the Kansas Supreme Court rejected the claim by a day care provider that the court should recognize the visitation rights of those who had been close to a child. The court granted that "the realities of modern life mean that individuals . . . may end up caring for a child for weeks, months, or even years, and then have the natural parents . . . abruptly end a relationship that is important to the child. It could be the only stable relationship the child has known." However, the court refused to recognize a visitation right on grounds that would likely lead to more lawsuits, more court intrusion into families, and misuse of the right by anyone who had taken care of or had a relationship with a child for some period—a nanny, a housekeeper, a teacher, even a parent's former lover.

A more fundamental concern, however, is the issue of justice for the parent as well as for the child. In 1982, the U.S. Supreme Court held that the right of a fit biological parent to the custody of a minor child is a fundamental liberty interest.[7] Historically, poor and minority families have been vulnerable to state intervention and the removal of children. The lack of family rights on the part of slaves was one of the most painful and resented features of that infamous system. The Fourteenth Amendment, which insured the rights of former slaves, was "conceived by people who regarded slavery's denial of family rights as a uniquely deplorable usurpation of fundamental human entitlements."[8]

Ironically, the Iowa court that ruled in favor of Jessica's biological father aroused public outrage in a 1966 case for the opposite reason—ignoring the interests of a father. Harold Painter was a San Francisco man whose wife and daughter were killed in a car accident. At one point when he had trouble arranging for child care, he placed his young son Mark temporarily in the care of his wife's parents in Iowa. When Painter later claimed the child, the grandparents sued for custody and won. The Iowa Supreme Court ruled that while Painter was not an unfit father, Mark's churchgoing, midwestern grandparents provided a better home for him than the more artistic, bohemian setting of his father's home in California. In justifying the decision, the court contrasted many aspects of the father's and the grandparents' lifestyles, including the decor of the Painter house, the state of the paint job on its exterior, and the wild oats growing on the hillside behind it.

In an outraged reaction to this decision, legislatures all over the country wrote laws clarifying and reinforcing the rights of biological parents. The new Iowa law declared that the "best interests of the child" standard could only be invoked if the child had been abandoned or the parent declared unfit.

For a variety of reasons, then, the facts of biological parenthood carry more legal weight than in the past. Courts have shown a strong preference for awarding custody to what they call "natural parents" whether or not a parent-child relationship exists. Large numbers of adults who have actually nurtured and raised children—relatives, stepparents, and foster parents—have no legal standing. As Mason points out: "An unwed father who has never lived with a child will probably receive custodial preference over a stepfather who raised the child. Surrogate mothers who give birth to a child are deemed incapable of contracting away their biological rights to that child. Foster parents who raise a child have little hope of adopting the child, except under unusual circumstances."[9]

## Dilemmas of Divorce

In the past, the rules for deciding the custody arrangements for a child after divorce were clear-cut. Before the nineteenth century, following the tradition of English common law, fathers enjoyed paramount rights to custody and control of their children. The interests of the particular child were not a legal concern. In the course of the nineteenth century, family law in general, as well as the law of custody, was transformed. Courts across the country became increasingly concerned with the well-being of children and the importance of a mother's love and nurturance. The "Tender Years Doctrine" described this new presumption in favor of awarding the custody of infants and young children to their mothers. By the 1920s, the maternal preference in custody decisions was as firmly settled in law and practice as the earlier paternal preference had been.[10]

It remained unchallenged until the family upheavals of the 1960s and 1970s. In the wake of rising divorce rates, challenges to women's traditional roles, and men's claims of sex discrimination in custody awards, most states abandoned the maternal presumption in favor of a more gender-neutral "best interests" standard. Despite the new standard, most awards of physical custody are still granted to women, reflecting the greater involvement of women in the care of children before divorce.

But the shift in rules has added uncertainty to the divorce process. A variety of custody arrangements exists—shared physical custody, joint legal custody, divided custody, etc.[11] Also, fathers are more likely to win custody disputes than in the past. But the largest source of uncertainty arises out of the difficulties of defining the meaning of the "child's best interests" standard.

## Is the Best Interests Standard the Best Standard?

Over the years the best interests standard has been subjected to severe criticism by an array of distinguished legal scholars. The basic complaint is that it is dangerously vague, allowing the free play of judicial bias, and apt to result in very different outcomes in similar cases. Critics point to a lack of consensus among lawyers, judges, mental health authorities, and the general public about what a child's best interests are in custody disputes. Should the court choose the parent who has more money, the one who will spend the most time with the child, the one who is more conventional or religious, the one with the largest extended family, the one who lives in the suburbs rather than the city?

Aside from these kinds of lifestyle considerations, critics point to the common bias against parents whose sexual behavior or orientation departs from conventional norms. In 1993, a Virginia court removed a two-year-old boy from his mother and awarded custody to his grandmother on the sole grounds that the mother was a lesbian who lived with her lover.

Judgments about the child's interests can also reflect ethnic and class biases. There is a long and painful history of poor and minority families being broken up by social workers incapable of distinguishing between truly unfit parents and adequate parents who depart in one way or another from conventional middle-class norms of cleanliness, neatness, child-rearing practices, or mental health. *The Autobiography of Malcolm X* provides an especially vivid and bitter account of the misguided destruction of a family opened to state scrutiny because it was on welfare.

Some commentators on the Baby Jessica case perceived class bias in the outpouring of public support for the adoptive parents; the DeBoers seemed more prosperous and better educated than the Schmidts. To its critics, the best interest standard threatens to lead down a slippery slope at the bottom of which lurks the possibility that any child could be removed from its parents by anyone who offered a "worthier home" or a more advantaged life.

## Psychological Parenthood and Attachment Theory

The danger of rejecting the best interests standard is that it reinforces the traditional emphasis on the adults' rights and behaviors rather than the perspective of the child. It also reinforces a traditional tendency to underestimate the psychological competence of young children as well as their capacity to sustain emotional attachments and suffer at their loss.

Although cultural images of children and childhood have changed over time, older images linger on. William James once described the infant's mind as a "buzzing, blooming confusion." Psychoanalytic writers have traditionally believed that infants are virtually autistic, incapable of distinguishing between themselves and their mothers. Developmental researchers have traditionally assumed that preschool children were locked into their own egocentric perspective, unable to understand another person's point of view.

Recent research, however, has found that infants and young children are far more cognitively competent than previously believed. Infants have been found to be able to discriminate most of the speech sounds in human language, form concepts and categories, and distinguish among numbers of things. Further, children as early as two can understand a variety of social rules, such as those dealing with ownership and responsibility.[12] Similarly, until recently it was thought that very young children lacked the wherewithal for profound emotional experience, such as depression. Now the study of emotional adjustment extends down to infants in the first year of life.

Traditional assumptions about young children's lack of understanding have made it possible for court decisions to be made with little regard for the child's emotional attachments. The comments of an English judge in a 1926 case are remarkably similar to current thinking in many American courts:

> It is said that the little girl will be greatly distressed and upset at parting from Mr. and Mrs. Jones. . . . it may be so, but at her tender age, one knows from experience how mercifully transient are the effects of partings and other sorrows, and how soon the novelty of fresh surroundings and new associations effaces the recollection of former days. . . . I cannot attach much weight to this aspect of the case.[13]

The most forceful and influential challenge to this way of thinking was presented to the legal world and the public in 1973, in a book entitled *Beyond the Best Interests of the Child*. The first volume of a trilogy, the book was a collaboration between Joseph Goldstein, a law professor, Anna Freud, a child analyst, and Albert Solnit, a child psychiatrist. These authors offered a solution to the problem of the best interests standard: custody decisions should focus on children's psychological and developmental needs.

Goldstein and his colleagues introduced the term "psychological parent" to designate the adult who "filled the child's psychological needs for a parent" through day-to-day "interaction, companionship, interplay and mutuality."[14] The psychological parent could be the biological parent or a person who had raised the child for some time, but without a traditionally recognized legal claim to the child. In either case, the authors urge that custody decisions preserve this psychological bond, since the child's normal development depends on continuity and stability in relationships and surroundings.

Instead of seeking the best interests of the child—which encourages unrealistic hopes of finding some ideal solution for the dilemma before them—they argue for a "least detrimental standard." They stress that a child in a custody battle is in a psychological emergency—harm has already been done, the child is still at risk, and the best that courts can do is to avoid more harm, not find some optimal solution. Above all, the child's sense of time, and his or her need for steady caretaking and continuity in relationships, should govern decision making rather than biological bonds or the rights of parents.

Thus, in the Baby Jessica case and others like it, the judges would leave the child in the custody of the adoptive parents, the only parents the child has ever known. On the other hand, when the biological parent is the psychological parent, the same principles would demand that a court maintain that relationship under all but the most extreme circumstances. The only exceptions might be for a child of Holocaust survivors, who had been raised by another family. Worst of all, a child ought not to be left to languish in the uncertainties of the foster care system.

The most controversial aspect of the book concerned the focus on a single psychological parent; thus the authors recommended that in a typical divorce, the task of the court is to identify which spouse is the psychological parent, and then to give that person sole custody of the child, along with the authority to control or even eliminate visits of the other parent. This recommendation is grounded in the belief that children are unable to maintain healthy emotional bonds with individuals who are at odds with one another. Critics, however, faulted the authors for neglecting to back up their claims with empirical evidence, other than clinical experience and psychoanalytic expertise.

In the decades since *Beyond the Best Interests*, there have been major developments in the study of parent-child relationships in infancy and later on. As noted earlier, "psychological parenthood" is a legal term, not a psychological one. Similar to the way "insanity" is a legal term that maps onto the psychiatric concept of psychosis, psychological parenthood corresponds to the psychological concept of attachment. In both instances, however, the fit between terms is not exact.

John Bowlby's attachment theory has become a major theoretical framework in developmental psychology, and research on attachment has become a leading growth industry in the field. Although it springs from the same psychoanalytic roots as the psychological parenthood concept, and, indeed, Goldstein et al. acknowledge Bowlby's influence, there are important differences between the two approaches.[15] Most significantly, attachment research relies on a large body of systematically gathered empirical evidence, including the direct observation of parent-child interaction, rather than on accounts by patients of what may or may not have happened in their childhood. Further, by studying normal, or at least non-clinical parents and children, it avoids the theoretical pitfalls of basing a theory of normal development on clinical cases.

Bowlby began to develop his theory over forty years ago, and revised his ideas over time, often leading to misunderstanding about what his claims actually are. Bowlby first became famous in the years after World War II for his studies of "maternal deprivation." His work was part of a wave of psychoanalytically oriented investigations of the mental health of children who had been separated from their families during the war and raised in orphanages and nurseries.

His major contribution to the understanding of human development, however, was attachment theory, as presented in his monumental three-volume work, *Attachment and Loss*. In recent years, work in attachment theory has been carried on by a younger generation of researchers. It has come to be a major topic of academic research and has come to be identified with particular experimental procedures.

Bowlby's early work on maternal deprivation overlapped the writings of a number of other psychoanalytic observers of orphaned and institutionalized children. He and the others postulated that a lack of maternal care in infancy and early childhood leads to lasting physical, intellectual, and emotional damage. Mother love, he contended, is as necessary to healthy psychological development as vitamins and proteins are to physical health.

In his later, more popular writing, Bowlby generalized his warnings about maternal deprivation from children who had experienced almost a complete lack of maternal care to children in general. Bowlby implied that if prolonged maternal absence is dangerous to a child's development, any separation from the child in the first five years could also pose a threat to the child's mental health. Further, he warned that even a child in a seemingly normal family could suffer maternal deprivation through lack of sufficient love and attention.

Although many of the assumptions underlying Bowlby's early work live on in pop psychology, the simple medical model of deprivation, with mother love compared to vitamins and proteins, and brief separation equated with complete deprivation of maternal care, has not been supported by the evidence. Bowlby's early pronouncements met with strong criticism by other researchers, and Bowlby himself later repudiated the more extreme implications of his early work.

Researchers pointed out that many different social and psychological factors had been lumped together under the heading "maternal deprivation."[16] Children in the institutions that had been studied by Bowlby were deprived not only of their mothers but of human attention, stimulation, and consistent care. These extreme conditions do indeed lead to terrible effects, as can be seen in today's Romanian orphanages. But short of this extreme, the loss or separation from a mother or psychological parent may not be a direct cause of later disturbances. Rather, it may act more like a vulnerability factor, a psychological weak spot, which may make the person more susceptible to later losses.

Attachment theory is far broader in scope than Bowlby's early work. Although still focused mainly on children and their relationships to the mother, Bowlby saw attachment as one of the fundamental experiences of humans across the life span—the development of enduring emotional bonds between one person and another. "What for convenience I am terming attachment theory," he wrote, "is a way of conceptualizing the propensity of human beings to make strong affectional bonds to particular others and of explaining the many forms of emotional distress and personality disturbance, including anger, anxiety, depression, and emotional detachment, to which unwilling separation and loss give rise."[17]

Ultimately, Bowlby intended attachment theory to be an alternative to classical Freudian theory as an account of normal development and an explanation of the origins of adult psychological disorders. According to attachment theorists, early attachment relationships become transformed into mental blueprints or "working models" of the self and others which persist across the life span; secure attachment leads to confidence that the self is lovable and that other people are trustworthy. Early insecurity can lead to a lifelong sense of unworthiness and difficulty in relationships across the life-course, especially with one's own children.

In evaluating the claims of the theory, it is important to keep in mind the distinction between attachment as an observable phenomenon, and the theoretical edifice that has been built up to interpret those observations. One of the early demonstrations of attachment, for example, was a famous film by James Robertson called *A Two Year Old Goes to Hospital*. The film, which revolutionized hospital visiting practices, showed the intense distress of a small child separated from her mother, her apparent return to normality in the hospital, and her intense clinging to her mother after her return home. Similar observations were made of many other children in many settings, some seemed to reject the mother after being reunited with her.

In the 1950s another associate, Mary Ainsworth, applied Bowlby's ideas in an observational study of infants in Uganda. She identified three key features that reveal an attachment relationship in a young child; the first is seeking to be near the preferred person. Every parent has experienced the sometimes unsettling tendency of a toddler to follow the parent wherever he or she goes. The same behavior can be seen in any culture around the world, and in animals. This tendency to cling to and follow the attachment figure is especially strong when the child feels tired, frightened, or sick.

The second feature is the secure base phenomenon—the child's tendency to explore and roam away from the attachment figure. Thus, paradoxically, a child with a secure attachment may appear more independent of the parent, by playing at some distance from the parent, periodically returning or checking on the parent's whereabouts. Meanwhile, a less securely attached child may be observed clinging to the mother's knees.

The third sign of an attachment bond is separation protest—a baby crying when the mother leaves the room, for example, or an older child kicking and screaming or clinging to the parent as the parent tries to go out. The response to separation is considered the best test of the presence of an attachment bond.

Some of the most interesting observations by attachment researchers deal with the question of what it is that leads children to become attached to an adult. It seems as if simply feeding and taking care of a child is not sufficient to create an attachment bond. For example, in Israel, Kibbutz children traditionally have been raised in communal nurseries, and see their parents for an hour or two each day, and all day on the Sabbath. Yet all observers of Kibbutz children agree that they ordinarily become deeply attached to their parents, not their nurses. The emotional quality of the interaction, not the quantity, is critical. Parents are more affectionate, responsive, and attentive to the child than the nurses. However, children can and do form attachments to nurses who are particularly responsive to them.

Although in most families a child's primary attachment is usually to the mother—because in our country and around the world, mothers do most of the child care—children of all ages are capable of forming multiple attachments. Usually they are also attached to their fathers. Most researchers believe, however, that even in cultural settings where the child is cared for by several people, there is usually a hierarchy of preference—a particular person that the child most strongly wants to be there when in distress, or whose departure is most likely to be protested. This primary attachment figure need not be the biological mother, but a father, a grandmother, an older sister or brother, or nanny.

Since the late 1970s, research on infant-parent attachment has moved into the laboratory and come to be based on an assessment technique called the Strange Situation procedure. The procedure consists of a twenty-one-minute series of separations from and reunions with the mother in the presence or absence of a stranger. Attachment researchers assume that the infant's behavior in the laboratory reflects the child's expectations of parental support, which in turn are believed to reflect the parent's typical interaction with the child in everyday life. Children are classified as either "secure"—the optimal category, or in one of two "insecure" categories, depending on the child's reactions to separation and reunion.

The Strange Situation has become the gold standard of attachment research—the virtual definition of the concept of attachment. In recent years, however, some researchers have raised serious questions about what exactly is being measured in the Strange Situation. Some researchers have found that the child's response to the Strange Situation may reflect other qualities in the child—especially the child's temperamental tendency to become upset when encountering new people and circumstances. Further, children's responses may be affected by many other aspects of their lives than the mother—including the role of the father and siblings, the number of strangers they typically encounter, the wider social network of the family, economic strains and other stresses, as well as cultural norms of child rearing. As a result, the use of the procedure in custody disputes—in order to infer the kind of caretaking a child may have received, or to make assessments of children's future adjustment—is highly questionable.

Bowlby's work ushered in a new era in the understanding of child development, but attachment theory as it currently stands may be only a provisional structure. Attachment theory articulated a broad view of emotional and social development, but now research is advancing on a number of fronts—including the study of emotions, self-concepts, social cognition, and the ecologies in which children and their families live.

Perhaps the most controversial aspect of attachment theory concerns the impact of early relationships on later development. Like Freud, Bowlby and his followers believe that the infant's first attachment becomes the "prototype" for all future relationships with peers, romantic partners, and future children. Some researchers have found links between early attachment patterns and later functioning; for example, secure infants have been found to be more sociable in the preschool and grade school years. However, such findings may reflect not the effects of infant experience so much as consistency in the child's temperament, and the ongoing parent-child relationship.

Psychological development is coming to be understood as not so much a direct outcome of early events as a complex, transactional process, involving a changing child, a changing environment, and an ongoing series of life events and transitions. As a result, we need to think of development as a set of pathways through childhood and beyond. Starting out from a set of similar circumstances, two children can end up very differently. And there are different routes to similar outcomes. Some children manage to overcome adversity and loss, others do poorly later in life after promising beginnings. These more recent views are more optimistic than the older assumption that children who experience early insecurity are doomed to later difficulties. In the future, development research will focus on the question of the conditions under which positive change occurs and the interventions that can make it more likely.

## Implications for Custody Decisions

Given what is currently known about the limitations of attachment theory and the psychological parenthood concept, what can these models of parent-child relations contribute to resolving custody disputes? The fact that much still remains to be learned about emotional development should not lead judges, lawyers, and other legal experts to dismiss the substance of what we do know. The research evidence does not contain formulas for resolving specific disputes, but it does suggest some general guidelines to inform legal decision making. These include:

1. The early loss of a parent, whether through death or separation, increases the risk of emotional and social dysfunction in later life. This loss does not mean that the child is doomed to irreparable psychological damage. We cannot make that sort of long-term prediction. But we do know that the disruption of a parental relationship can be a risk factor for later difficulties.[18] Much depends on how the child responds to the pain of loss, the kind of care he or she receives later on, and the losses and other misfortunes encountered over the course of childhood and adult life.

Thus, Goldstein and his colleagues were justified in advocating that custody decisions should focus on the child's point of view and the urgent emotional salience of a continuing relationship with the person or persons who have provided ongoing, loving care. Conversely, judges and lawyers should be aware of the harm of sudden removal of a child from the home, or sudden separation from a primary attachment figure.

2. Children at all ages can develop attachment to more than one person. Children being raised in two-parent families can be assumed to be attached to both mother and father. At the same time, not all attachments are equal. For young children in particular, the distinction between a primary and secondary caretaker may be an important one. But in most circumstances the child will benefit from maintaining ties with a noncustodial parent, even if this inconveniences the custodial parent. Further, the child is likely to benefit from some kind of contact with anyone with whom he or she has established an emotional bond, whether through visits, letters, or other means.

3. Children's needs change with development. The very young child's emotional needs are urgent, and only psychological, not biological ties have meaning. But the needs of a one- or two-year-old child are not the same as those of a six-year-old, and the needs of a fourteen-year-old are different from those of younger children. While the young child's cus-

tody arrangements should accommodate an immature sense of time and the anxieties of separation, arrangements should be made more flexible as the child changes. After the ages of five to seven, children's increasing cognitive and emotional maturity mean that they are able to comprehend more of the complexities of parent-child relationships.

4. Caretaking is not necessarily parenting; quality matters more than quantity. In divorce cases, when a "primary caretaker" standard is used by the court, caretaking is often evaluated by counting the number of hours spent in the home with the child, or the number of routine tasks undertaken by each parent—preparing meals, bathing, and dressing. The assumption is that these activities are likely to indicate which parent is closer to the child. A parent, particularly a mother, who works full time, and uses a nanny or day care, may be judged an inadequate caretaker by these standards.

For example, in a case mentioned earlier, Jennifer Ireland, an unmarried mother who won a scholarship to the University of Michigan, lost custody of her three-year-old daughter to the child's father because she had placed the child in day care on campus while she attended classes. A part-time maintenance worker, the father lived with his parents and planned to have his mother, a full-time homemaker, look after the child. The judge stated that day care was the deciding factor; he was concerned about the impact on the child of being cared for by "strangers." (The ruling was later overturned.) In the case of the high-powered mother also mentioned earlier, Sharon Prost, a counsel to Senator Orrin Hatch, lost custody of her two sons on grounds that her long hours on the job made her a "workaholic" rather than a concerned, involved mother.[19] Men's careers are less likely to disqualify them as parents in custody cases.

But we know from the research literature that it is the emotional quality of the interaction that has significance for the child, not the quantity of time. It is the give and take reciprocity of interaction, attention to what the child is feeling or trying to communicate, and being in touch with the child's interests and concerns, that create a strong adult-child bond.

5. Lack of apparent distress on the part of child may be misleading. Child development experts who testified in the Baby Jessica case predicted devastating psychological damage would result from her removal from her adoptive parents—she would lose her toilet training, regress to earlier stages of development, and suffer from anxiety and nightmares.

Some months after Baby Jessica had been removed to the home of her biological parents—where she was renamed Anna Schmidt—a television program presented an interview with the Schmidts and the child. If a viewer looked at the program without knowing the background, he or she would assume this was a normal happy child in a normal happy family. The rest of the media picked up the story and set forth a new conventional wisdom—children can thrive despite what appears from the outside to be a wrenching change in custodial arrangements.

Could Jessica-Anna have escaped unscathed from her abrupt separation and loss? The answer is, we don't know. It's possible that the first three years of her life made her a resilient child who could bounce back from trauma, or that the removal of a child from one set of loving parents to another is not as upsetting as the other kinds of separations that have been observed. On the other hand, we know from studies of hospitalized children that a child may appear to return to normal after the stress of separation, only to reveal hidden distress later on. Emotional numbing and denial are common responses to death and separation at all ages. Children who have been exposed to traumatic events, such as the murder of a parent or wartime brutality, may also seem to be "normal," only to show the effects of trauma years afterward.

## The Best Interests Standard Revisited

It is clear that strict adherence to the parental rights standard can lead to painful outcomes like those in the cases of Baby Jessica and Baby Richard, or to children languishing for years in foster care. On the other hand, the Painter case stands as a warning against the dangers of allowing judges unlimited discretion in deciding what they assume to be the best interests of the child.

Some legal scholars have suggested a compromise solution to the dilemma, a system that allows the court to determine the best interests of the child, but with guidelines to steer the judging process. Thus there would be guidelines regarding which factors to consider, how to weight them, how to attend to the child's developing needs over time. For example, rules could be written that would heavily weigh the child's psychological well-being, including the existing love and emotional ties between the child and the contending adults, and the child's need for continuity and stability in caretaking. There would also be negative rules, directing the court not to take into account the kind of lifestyle judgments made in the Painter case, or to consider conduct on the part of the parent that does not directly impair his or her relationship with the child.

An advantage of this kind of modified best interest standard is that it may better reflect evolving societal values and understandings. Carl Schneider points to several principles of conventional custody law that probably reflect the consensus of social opinion—namely, that children should generally be in the custody of their biological parents, that children should have close contact with both parents, that stability and continuity with parents or parent figures are important, that a parent who is loving and attentive to a child is likely to be a better parent that one who is not, to name some of these.[20]

The public reaction to the cases of Baby Jessica and Baby Richard suggests that additional principles are now part of the social consensus; that the child's well-being should be the paramount consideration in custody decisions, no matter whether the case involves divorce or disputes

between biological parents versus third parties, that the emotional attachments between child and parent should be defined as the central component of well-being, that the rights and interests of biological parents
should be seriously considered, but separate and apart from the issue of
the child's well-being.

This set of understandings is already guiding decisions in Canada,
where courts and legislatures have been extending the definition of family to one that is more functional and pluralistic.[21] Among other changes,
the Canadian legal system has been according increasing recognition of
the child's emotional bonds with adults other than their biological parents, especially with stepparents, but also with adoptive or foster parents.

A 1985 decision by the Supreme Court of Canada made the child's
welfare the paramount consideration in disputes between biological parents and third parties. In the case of *King* v. *Low*, the court stated that
although the claims of the biological parents were also to receive serious
consideration, they must give way to the best interests of their child when
the child has developed close psychological ties with another individual:
"it is the parental tie as a meaningful and positive force in the life of the
child and not in the life of the parent that court has to be concerned
about."[22] The principles spelled out in *King* v. *Low* are now an established part of Canadian law.

Despite the traditional and newer forms of biological preference in
the United States, American family law seems to be evolving in the same
direction as Canadian. As Schneider observes, there is a general move
away from rules to discretion in defining what a family is. The tendency
is to accept "functional equivalents" of family as family. For example, in
the much publicized *Marvin* v. *Marvin* "palimony" case some years ago,
the breakup of a long-term cohabiting relationship was recognized to entail some of the obligations of a divorce. In a 1977 case, the U.S. Supreme
Court ruled that a grandmother living with her son, his child, and a grandchild from another son, were a "family," and therefore could not be
evicted from her house in a neighborhood that was zoned for family
homes.[23] In another decision the Court also recognized that the existence of a family does not necessarily depend on biological ties, but also
arises out of "the emotional attachments that derive from the intimacy of
daily association."[24] Some individual judges have begun to give greater
consideration to the child's needs rather than the rights of biological parents.[25] A Denver judge told *Time* magazine, "In my courtroom, they stay
where they've been nurtured. You have to consider who the child feels
is the psychological parent. If you have a good bond in that home, I'm
not about to break it."[26]

## Conclusion

The American public has been moving toward a more functional definition of family. By large majorities, American men and women define

family values as being about loving, caring relationships, rather than the traditional two-parent family and its biological children.[27] If, as most scholars of the family believe, the family transformations of the past three decades are unlikely to be reversed, then the judicial system will continue to have the burden of making fateful decisions about child custody.

A more pluralistic, child-centered approach to custody decisions makes it extremely important that lawyers and judges be educated to be competent consumers of developmental psychology. Far too often, judges and lawyers may ignore social science evidence, accept it uncritically, or apply it selectively. On the other hand, researchers may offer recommendations based on their research, without being aware of the complexities and concerns of the legal process, or of the full impact their suggestions may have on the lives of children and parents who come under the jurisdiction of a court.

Another problem with the use of social science evidence is its possible misapplication by "experts" who offer their services to the court. For example, behavioral research typically focuses on group trends, rather than individual cases. Thus, while researchers can describe average tendencies, the same measures cannot reliably be used to predict a particular child's individual outcomes. Yet the Strange Situation is sometimes being used in such inappropriate ways in child custody cases. (On the other hand, assuming this "test" is not to be used to determine the outcome of a dispute, many cases, at least for now, will admittedly come down to a "battle of experts" who will try to apply other psychological generalities to the children involved.)

For all these reasons, there is a need for ongoing collaboration among the legal community, developmental researchers, other social scientists, and those in allied fields such as public health. Perhaps such a collaboration would ultimately lead to a change in the discourse surrounding custody decisions. Instead of winner-take-all battles of rights and derogatory facts, perhaps custody conflicts could be recognized as the tragic human situations they are. Perhaps the goal could be negotiation rather than confrontation, partial, rather than total, victory for one side over the other, and the child's welfare the central consideration.

In the end, however, the legal system has broader concerns than those of social science. Beyond the pragmatic issue of what is the likely effect on a child of a particular judicial decision, the courts are concerned with basic societal values and constitutional mandates. The current preference for biological parents is rooted not merely in the ancient tradition of viewing children as property but also in a concern with a fundamental human right.

Based on an evolving scientific understanding of children's development, the concepts of psychological parenthood, attachment or any newer term may not in themselves be strong enough to stand up against legal arguments favoring the rights of biological parents. Perhaps we need an additional perspective. In his philosophical analysis of children's rights, David Archard draws a distinction between biological and moral parenthood.[28] A moral parent is committed to providing care and concern, but beyond that, feels "a self-sacrificial affection" for the child. The mother in the Solomon story qualifies as a moral parent.

The public outrage at the decision in the Baby Jessica case, beyond reflecting worry over Jessica's psychological health, may reflect this moral concern as well. In short, perhaps the Schmidts should have refrained from claiming their baby back, whatever their legal rights in the matter. The concept of moral parenthood (or its absence) may also explain why it does not seem right, despite possible evidence of attachment to the contrary, to award custody to someone who has kidnapped a child, or to deny it to Holocaust parents and others who have been separated from children through no fault of their own. Finally, the concept of moral parenthood is incompatible with notions of the child as property. It does not insist on a specific style of nurturance or form of family. Nor does it necessarily decide difficult cases. But it does demand a view of children as persons in their own right.

## Notes

1. M. Mason, *From Father's Property to Children's Rights* (New York: Columbia University Press, 1994).

2. Mimi Hall, "Chaos in Adoption Law Hurts Kids," *USA Today* Sept. 6, 1994.

3. Cited in B. Weaver-Catalana, 22, "The Battle for Baby Jessica: A Conflict of Best Interests," *Buffalo Law Review* 43:1995.

4. D. M. Schneider, *American Kinship: A Cultural Account* (Englewood Cliffs, NJ: Prentice-Hall, 1968).

5. M. Wolf, *Women and the Family in Rural Taiwan* (Stanford, CA: Stanford University Press, 1972).

6. C. Jenks, "The Post-Modern Child," in J. Brannon and M. O'Brien, (eds.), *Children in Families* (London: Falmer Press, 1996).

7. Santosky v. Kramer, 455 U.S. 745 (1982).

8. P. Davis, "Law Science and History: Reflections on the Best Interests of the Child," *Michigan Law Review* 86:1988.

9. Mason, *From Father's Property to Children's Rights*, p. 191.

10. Ibid.

11. J. Kelly, "The Determination of Child Custody," *The Future of Children* 4:1, 121–142, 1994.

12. J. Dunn, *The Beginnings of Social Understanding* (Cambridge: Harvard University Press, 1988).

13. Quotation cited in E. E. Wynne, 20. "Children's Rights and the Biological Bias," *Connecticut Journal of International Law*: 397:1996.

14. J. Goldstein, A. Freud, and A. Solnit, *Beyond the Best Interests of the Child* (New York: Free Press, 1973).

15. E. Waters and D.M. Noyes, "Psychological Parenting vs. Attachment Theory," *NYU Review of Law and Social Change* 12:505–513, 1983–4.

16. M. Rutter, *Maternal Deprivation Reassessed* (London: Penguin, 1981).

17. J. Bowlby, *The Making and Breaking of Affectional Bonds* (London: Tavistock Publications, 1979).

18. G. Brown and T. Harris, *The Social Origins of Depression* (London: Tavistock, 1982).

19. Ibid.

20. Carl Schneider, "Discretion, Rules and Law: Child Custody and the UMDA's Best Interest Standard," *Michigan Law Review* 89:2215–2298, 1991.

21. N. Bala, "The Evolving Canadian Definition of the Family: Towards a Pluralistic and Functional Approach," *International Journal of Law and the Family* 8:293–318, 1994.

22. King v. Low 1 S.C.R. 87 (1985); E. E. Wynne, "Children's Rights and the Biological Bias: A Comparison between the United States and Canada in Biological Parent versus Third-Party Disputes," *Connecticut Journal of International Law* 11:367, 1996.

23. Moore v. City of East Cleveland, Ohio, 431 U.S. 494 (1977).

24. Smith v. Organization of Foster Families, 1977, cited in B. Warzynski, "Termination of Parental Rights: The Psychological Parent Standard," *Villanova Law Review* 39:1994.

25. Wynne, "Children's Rights and the Biological Bias."

26. N. Gibbs, "In Whose Best Interest?" *Time Magazine* July 19, 1993, 44.

27. Families and Work Institute, "*Women: The New Providers,*" 1995.

28. D. Archard, *Children, Rights and Childhood* (New York: Routledge, 1993).

# Index